TACTICS FOR THE TOEFL iBT® TEST

A strategic new approach
to achieving TOEFL success

Christien Lee

OXFORD
UNIVERSITY PRESS

OXFORD
UNIVERSITY PRESS

Oxford University Press is a department of the University of Oxford.
It furthers the University's objective of excellence in research, scholarship,
and education by publishing worldwide. Oxford is a registered trade mark
of Oxford University Press in the UK and in certain other countries.

Published in Canada by
Oxford University Press
8 Sampson Mews, Suite 204,
Don Mills, Ontario M3C 0H5 Canada

www.oupcanada.com

Library and Archives Canada Cataloguing in Publication
Lee, Christien, 1970–, author
Tactics for the TOEFL iBT test / Christien Lee.

ISBN 978-0-19-902017-1 (student book).—ISBN 978-0-19-902018-8 (test pack)

1. Test of English as a Foreign Language—Study guides. 2. English
language—Study and teaching as a second language. 3. English language—
Examinations—Study guides. I. Title.

PE1128.L43 2015   428.0076   C2014-907050-0

1 2 3 4 — 18 17 16 15

Introduction

Achieving a successful score in the TOEFL test can be a challenge, but it's one that millions of students every year must undertake. *Tactics for the TOEFL iBT® Test* is intended as a new kind of coursebook for TOEFL test takers. Each unit in the book focuses on one type of reading, listening, speaking, or writing question that students will see in the TOEFL test. Through a unique combination of detailed explanations, strategic practice, step-by-step guidance, focused vocabulary coverage, and practical test preparation advice and tips, each unit explains what students need to do to achieve success in the TOEFL test and why they need to do it. This approach is based on teaching methods that the author has developed during his 20 years of classroom experience as a TOEFL instructor.

Acknowledgements

Every book involves a team effort; this one more than most.

My grateful thanks to everyone at Oxford University Press who has worked on the book: I truly appreciate your hard work, dedication, encouragement, advice, patience, and passion. Thanks especially to Antoinette and Jennifer for shaping the early manuscript, and to Jason, Nadine, and everyone else at OUP Canada for believing in the book and for turning it into a finished product.

My grateful thanks also to the thousands of students who have trusted me to help them raise their TOEFL scores and whose questions and ideas have helped me develop and hone the strategies and tactics in this book.

Finally, thanks to my family for their support and good advice. Above all, my thanks to Miki for putting up with all of the changed plans, lost weekends, and to Kenzo for the snuggles and for understanding that sometimes Papa was too busy to play trains. I love you both.

—Christien Lee

Oxford University Press would like to acknowledge the advice of teachers from all over the world who participated in online reviews, focus groups, and editorial reviews. We relied heavily on teacher input throughout the extensive development process of the *Tactics for the TOEFL iBT® Test*, and many of the features in the book came directly from feedback we gathered from teachers in the classroom. We are grateful to all who helped. The following reviewers shared their valuable insights with the author and the editorial department:

Patricia Blackstone-Evans, EC Brighton, UK; **Caron Broadbent**, EC Brighton, UK; **Sam Buchan**, EC London, UK; **Beatrice Calixo**, Rennert New York, US; **Judy Chao**, LSI New York, US; **Ray Ming Chao**, Cheng Kung University, Taiwan; **Lori Chinitz**, University of Pennsylvania, US; **Joanna Chung**, CYJ English Academy, Korea; **Cameron Dean**, EC London, UK; **Vern Eaton**, St. Giles International, Canada; **Melody Elliott**, Tokai University, Japan; **Sonia Fantauzzi**, ILSC, Canada; **Dan Genereaux**, Korea University, Korea; **Susan Gilfert**, Kwansei Gakuin University, Japan; **Ted Gray**, Hongik University, Korea; **Sven Greve**, Hansa Language Centre, Canada; **Steve Herder**, Doshisha Women's College, Japan; **Frits Holst**, EC London, UK; **Tsuyoshi Iida**, Doshisha Women's College, Japan; **Greg Jeong**, Live Lecture, Korea; **Yu-Jung Kang**, Ewha University, Korea; **Sotiria Koui**, Harcum College, US; **Shawn Krause**, ILSC, Canada; **Noga Laor**, Rennert New York, US; **Kerry Linder**, LSI New York, US; **Joanna Lockspeiser**, Rennert, US; **Mark Lucas**, Kansai University, Japan; **David McCoy**, Gakushuin University, Japan; **Brian McManus**, University of Pennsylvania, US; **Jesse Miller**, English School of Canada, Canada; **Jo Osborne**, EC Brighton, UK; **Joo-Young Park**, Sungshin Women's University, Korea; **Ben Parkin**, EC Brighton, UK; **Briana Raissi**, GEOS New York, US; **Rosie Roumiana Luczay**, ILSC Toronto, Canada; **Daniel Schulstad**, Embassy CES, US; **Karen Stanley**, Central Piedmont Community College, US; **Claudio Sung**, High Five, Taiwan; **Christos Theodoropulos**, University of Pennsylvania, US; **Ksenia Torutanova-Ducey**, Embassy English, US; **Yvonne Tseng**, Chang Jung University, Taiwan; **Gerald Williams**, Kansai University, Japan; **James Winward-Stuart**, GABA, Japan

About the Author

Christien Lee has been involved in English language teaching and training since 1992. He has specialized in English proficiency tests like TOEFL, IELTS, TOEIC, MELAB, and CELPIP—as an instructor, teacher trainer, and writer. He founded a specialist test preparation academy in Toronto, Canada, in 2004 and ran the school for nine years. During that time, he developed a unique, strategic teaching system that helped thousands of students achieve test success in TOEFL, IELTS, and TOEIC. He regularly speaks about effective ways to teach test preparation classes at conferences for English language teaching professionals. He has also worked with ETS Canada to facilitate teacher training workshops for TOEFL instructors. In addition to writing *Tactics for the TOEFL iBT® Test*, he has written TOEFL practice tests (available at www.oxfordenglishtesting.com) and is a question writer for the Oxford Online Placement Test. He can be contacted via his personal website: www.christienlee.com.

Contents

Reading Tactics   6

Listening Tactics   92

Speaking Tactics   168

TACTICS FOR THE TOEFL iBT TEST WALKTHROUGH

Tactics for the TOEFL iBT® Test offers a new approach to achieving success in the TOEFL test. It offers a unique combination of innovative tasks that build key skills, authentic test practice, focused test preparation strategies, and high-frequency academic language related to the subjects and topics that most commonly appear in the test.

Reference Sections Provide Detailed Information about Key Aspects of the TOEFL Test

A **general Reference Section** gives students essential information about TOEFL, including how to register, what to expect on the day of the test, and when they will receive their test score.

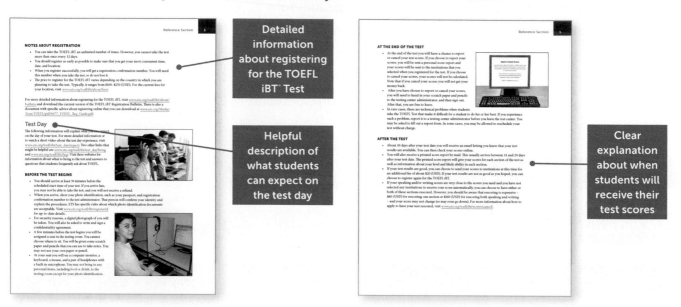

Detailed information about registering for the TOEFL iBT® Test

Helpful description of what students can expect on the test day

Clear explanation about when students will receive their test scores

Individual reference sections for reading, listening, speaking, and writing give students an in-depth understanding of those sections. Students will receive clear instructions for how to answer the different types of questions in each section and detailed information about scoring. They will also see computer screenshots that simulate what they will see in the actual test.

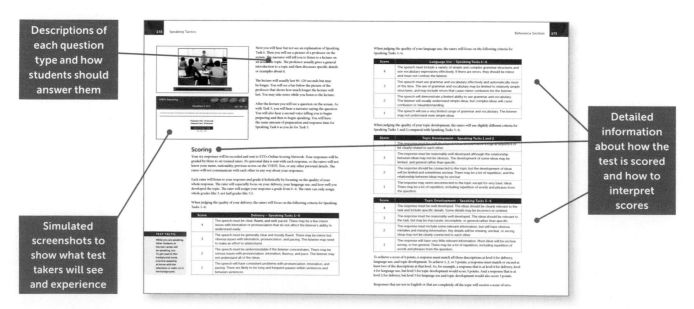

Descriptions of each question type and how students should answer them

Simulated screenshots to show what test takers will see and experience

Detailed information about how the test is scored and how to interpret scores

Diagnostic and Review Tests Provide Authentic Test Practice to Help Students Recognize Areas of Need and Assess Improvement

Each section of *Tactics for the TOEFL iBT® Test* includes both a **diagnostic test** and a **review test** that can be completed in less than one hour. Students can choose how and when to take these tests, but the recommended approach is to take the diagnostic test before starting on a section and the review test after going through the units.

The diagnostic and review tests have a realistic balance of question types that are at the same level as the actual TOEFL test. A score conversion chart at the end of each test lets students get an accurate sense of their likely score on the real TOEFL test.

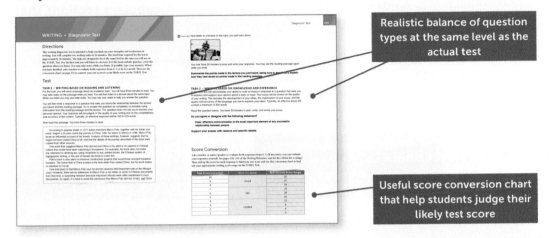

Realistic balance of question types at the same level as the actual test

Useful score conversion chart that help students judge their likely test score

Two Complete Tests Help Students Practice and Assess Readiness

Tactics for the TOEFL iBT® Test also includes **two full practice tests at the back of the book** that accurately reflect the balance and difficulty of questions in the real TOEFL test. For added authenticity and convenience, **students can take these tests online** using a sophisticated digital testing platform developed by Oxford University Press.

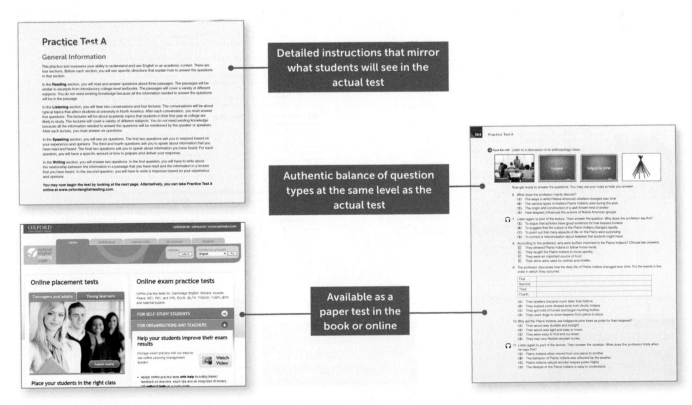

Detailed instructions that mirror what students will see in the actual test

Authentic balance of question types at the same level as the actual test

Available as a paper test in the book or online

Content Units Focus on Individual Question Types in TOEFL plus Useful Vocabulary

Tactics for the TOEFL iBT® Test includes 26 content units that **cover every TOEFL question type** from the reading, listening, speaking, and writing sections of the TOEFL test. In addition, each unit focuses on **one academic subject that often appears in the TOEFL test** as well as **key vocabulary** for achieving test success, including words related to specific academic disciplines and student life at university in North America.

Each content unit begins with a **Warm-up section** designed to get students to think about the focus of that unit, and activate and share their existing knowledge of that subject. Many Warm-up tasks practice key skills for the test like listening, speaking, or writing. Each unit also has one or two **Vocabulary sections that introduce essential words for the TOEFL test** related to the academic subject of the unit.

Each unit contains one or two sections that **analyze and describe a question type from the TOEFL test** in detail. The analysis includes examples of the question type, strategies for how to answer that question and how to recognize and avoid mistakes, plus a realistic practice activity.

> In-depth focus on one or two of the official question types that appear in the TOEFL test

> Each unit focuses on one academic subject; these subjects were chosen based on analysis of TOEFL questions published by ETS

> Detailed analysis of specific question types to help students build knowledge and confidence

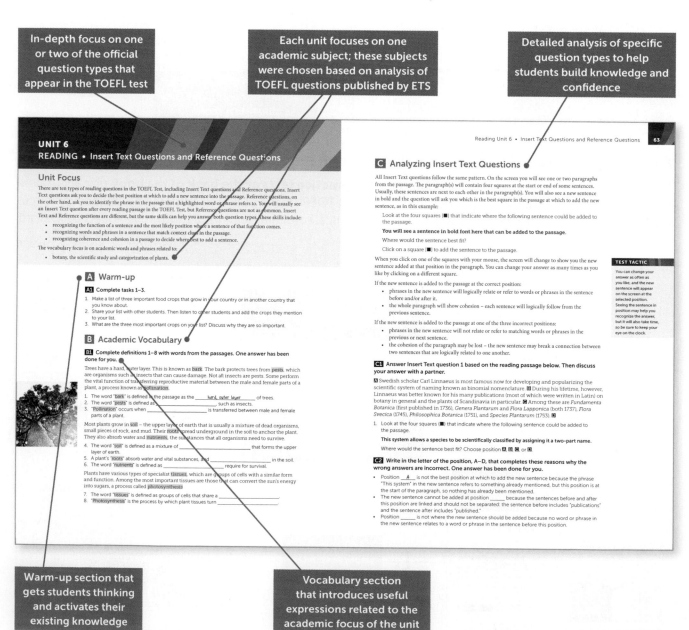

> Warm-up section that gets students thinking and activates their existing knowledge

> Vocabulary section that introduces useful expressions related to the academic focus of the unit

Content Units Introduce and Practice Key Skills and Strategies for TOEFL

Every content unit includes several sections that include multiple tasks designed to help students master **key skills for answering specific question types** accurately and effectively. These sections have a range of activity types.

Some **activities help students build key skills** that will help them answer specific question types. Other activities help students think in the right way or give step-by-step instructions or explanations to achieve improved results. Additional activities provide realistic test questions so that students can practice the key skills and ways of thinking that they have learned.

Tactics for the TOEFL iBT® Test also includes **more than 120 test tactics** that give practical and proven suggestions to raise students' test scores. Some tactics offer a solution to a common problem students have when taking the TOEFL test. Others describe a useful way of thinking or a helpful action that students can take.

Multiple sections that break down key skills into manageable chunks and guide students towards mastery

Each unit has test tactics with practical, proven suggestions and strategies

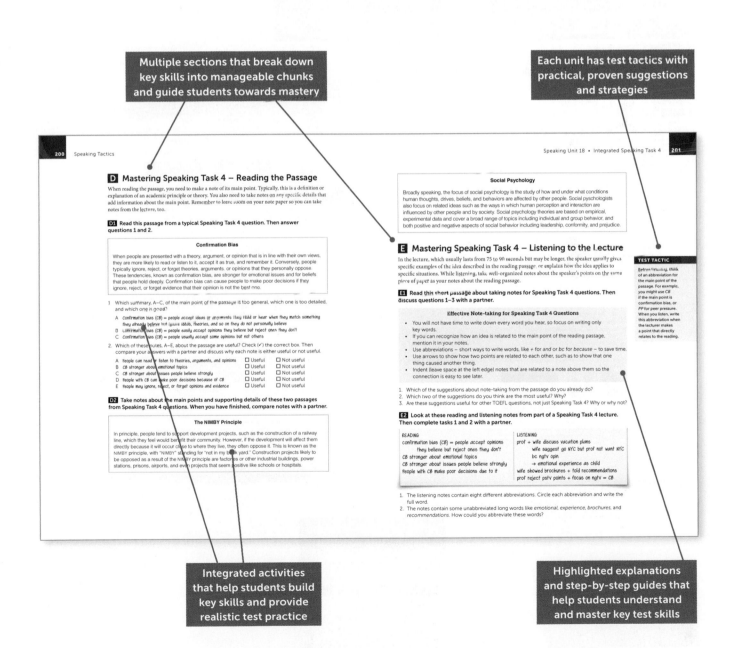

Integrated activities that help students build key skills and provide realistic test practice

Highlighted explanations and step-by-step guides that help students understand and master key test skills

Content Units Provide Authentic Test Practice and Practical Suggestions for Further Study

Every content unit ends with a **Test Challenge** section that provides **realistic test practice** so that students can practice the skills and strategies they have learned. The reading and listening sources in the Test Challenge section were carefully written to include many of the words and phrases that students learned earlier in the unit. They also use many expressions from the **academic word list**.

After the Test Challenge, students will see a **Next Steps** section that offers practical and effective step-by-step activities students can do on their own. These ideas help students build key skills to become better at answering specific question types. The ideas are also designed to help students continue to improve their knowledge of an important academic subject as well as useful vocabulary related to that subject.

Test Challenge section that provides realistic test practice for the question types covered in each unit

Broad coverage of authentic topics and natural academic language in the test questions

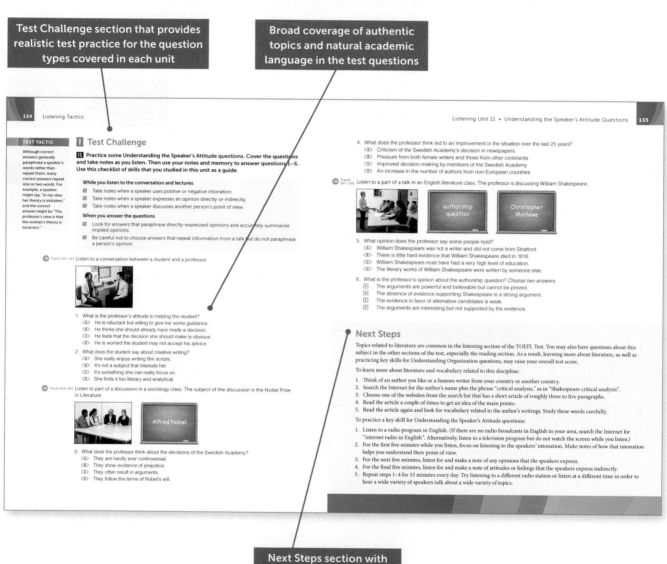

Next Steps section with step-by-step activities to help students build further understanding and confidence

Unique Vocabulary Index Helps Students Learn and Use Key Expressions for TOEFL

Tactics for the TOEFL iBT® Test also has a **unique Vocabulary Index** of all the useful words used in the book. The index is color-coded to show the category to which a word belongs—an academic discipline, campus vocabulary, or academic word list—and includes each word's part of speech to help students understand how to use it.

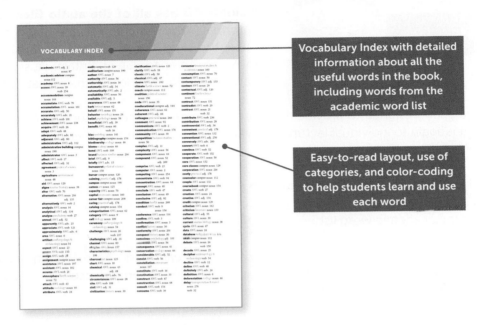

Vocabulary Index with detailed information about all the useful words in the book, including words from the academic word list

Easy-to-read layout, use of categories, and color-coding to help students learn and use each word

Online Practice Site Provides Additional Lessons to Help Students Achieve Success in the TOEFL Test Quickly and Effectively

Students will also have access to a practice website offering more than 150 online lessons designed to complement the material in the student book. In total, the lessons will provide an estimated 100 hours of additional practice.

The website will have three types of lessons. **Language focus lessons** will expand students' knowledge and understanding of useful vocabulary and expressions. **Skills focus lessons** will help students to build key skills to answer specific question types that appear in the TOEFL test. And **Test focus lessons** will provide additional authentic test practice.

The online lessons will include plenty of new material, but will also recycle content from the student book in innovative ways. The vocabulary and subject focus of the online lessons will match the focus of the content units in the student book.

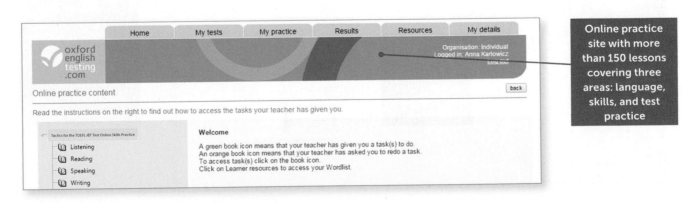

Online practice site with more than 150 lessons covering three areas: language, skills, and test practice

Full Pack Version Includes Answer Key, Audio Scripts, and All Audio Material

The Pack version of *Tactics for the TOEFL iBT® Test* includes all the student book material as well as the Audio Script and Answer Key Booklet, and the Audio on CD.

The **single CD has all of the audio files** in convenient MP3 format. When listening to the audio files, students will hear the same range of accents—including speakers from North America, Great Britain, Australia, and New Zealand—that they will hear in the actual TOEFL test.

The audio files have been designed to provide the most flexible experience for students and teachers. This makes it easy to listen again to individual lectures or even individual questions. There are even audio tracks for the speaking and writing responses.

Students will also be able to read the **complete Audio Scripts** in order to gain maximum understanding of what the speakers say. The audio scripts include plenty of examples of key vocabulary from each unit as well as expressions from the academic word list.

An **Answer Key** provides quick access to the right answers for each task. An extended answer key that provides explanations for why each answer is right or wrong as well as sample responses for speaking and writing questions is available on the companion website.

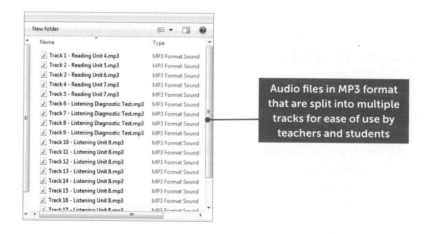

Audio files in MP3 format that are split into multiple tracks for ease of use by teachers and students

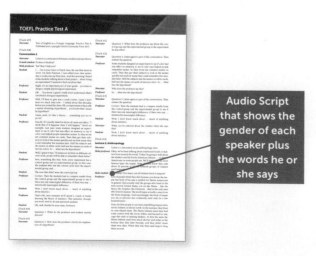

Audio Script that shows the gender of each speaker plus the words he or she says

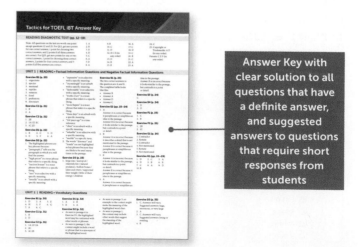

Answer Key with clear solution to all questions that have a definite answer, and suggested answers to questions that require short responses from students

Companion Website Offers Comprehensive Support for Teachers, Students Working Independently, and Tutors

Users who purchase the Pack version for *Tactics for the TOEFL iBT® Test* will also have **access to a companion website** designed for teachers and students studying independently. The website will offer detailed teaching notes and self-study suggestions that include ideas for extending individual activities in the book. The website will also include an extended answer key that provides explanations for why each answer is right or wrong as well as sample responses for speaking and writing questions.

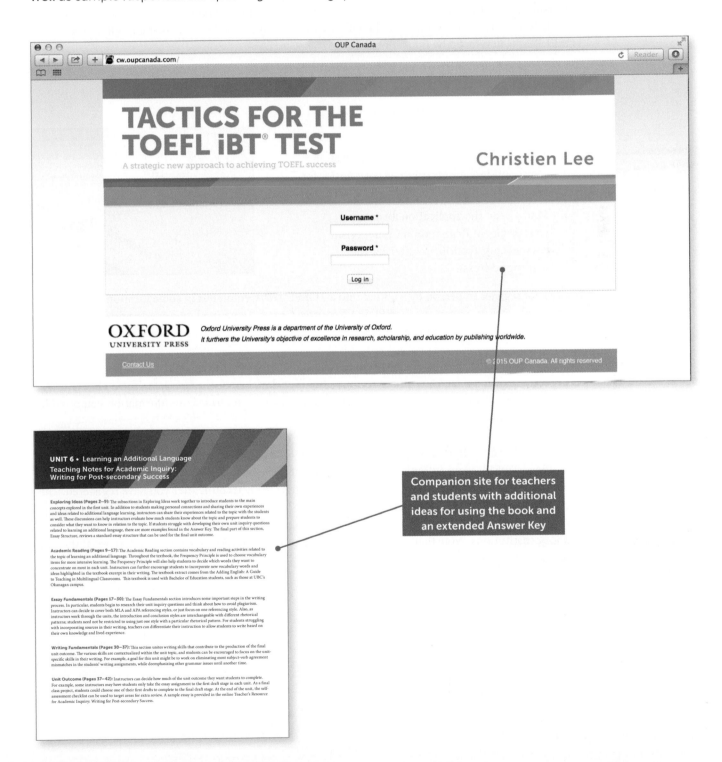

Companion site for teachers and students with additional ideas for using the book and an extended Answer Key

About the Test

The TOEFL Test measures your ability to read, listen to, speak, and write English in an academic setting. It is a computer-based test that is delivered via the Internet. The name TOEFL stands for Test of English as a Foreign Language, and iBT stands for Internet-based Test. More than 9,000 universities, colleges, governments, and employers around the world request that people take the TOEFL Test in order to demonstrate their ability to communicate effectively using English. The TOEFL Test is developed by Educational Testing Service (ETS).

How to Register for the Test

There are three ways you can register for the TOEFL iBT:

- Online – visit www.ets.org/toefl/ibt/register.

- Telephone – call your Regional Registration Center (visit www.ets.org/toefl/ibt/register for the telephone number).

- Mail – send the application form to your Regional Registration Center (visit www.ets.org/toefl/ibt/register for the mailing address).

You cannot register in person by walking into a TOEFL Test Center, but in some locations you might be able to register in person at a TOEFL iBT Resource Center. In general, however, registering online is the easiest and most convenient option.

If you choose to register online or by telephone, you can register for tests eight days before the test date. For an additional fee you can register for a test four days before the test date. If you choose to register by mail, you will be assigned a test date, time, and location based on information you provide on your application.

When you take the TOEFL Test, you can choose up to four universities or other institutions to receive your official TOEFL score automatically. You can select these institutions for free when you register. Alternatively, you can select them by logging in to your TOEFL account after you have registered. The deadline for selecting the institutions is one day before your test. After that time, you will have to pay a fee of about $20 (USD) to select each institution. You can also pay this fee if you wish to select more than four institutions. Note that you cannot select institutions to receive your TOEFL score at the test center on your test day.

NOTES ABOUT REGISTRATION

- You can take the TOEFL iBT an unlimited number of times. However, you cannot take the test more than once every 12 days.
- You should register as early as possible to make sure that you get your most convenient time, date, and location.
- When you register successfully, you will get a registration confirmation number. You will need this number when you take the test, so do not lose it.
- The price to register for the TOEFL iBT varies depending on the country in which you are planning to take the test. Typically, it ranges from $160–$250 (USD). For the current fees for your location, visit www.ets.org/toefl/ibt/about/fees/.

For more detailed information about registering for the TOEFL iBT, visit www.ets.org/toefl/ibt/about/bulletin and download the current version of the TOEFL iBT Registration Bulletin. There is also a document with specific advice about registering online that you can download at www.ets.org/Media/Tests/TOEFL/pdf/4677_TOEFL_Reg_Guide.pdf.

Test Day

The following information will explain what you can expect on the day of your test. For more detailed information or to watch a short video about the test day experience, visit www.ets.org/toefl/ibt/test_day/expect/. Two other links that might be helpful are www.ets.org/toefl/ibt/test_day/bring and www.ets.org/toefl/ibt/faq/. Visit these websites for information about what to bring to the test and answers to questions that students frequently ask about TOEFL.

BEFORE THE TEST BEGINS

- You should arrive at least 30 minutes before the scheduled start time of your test. If you arrive late, you may not be able to take the test, and you will not receive a refund.
- When you arrive, show your photo identification, such as your passport, and registration confirmation number to the test administrator. That person will confirm your identity and explain the procedures. ETS has specific rules about which photo identification documents are acceptable. Visit www.ets.org/toefl/ibt/register/id for up-to-date details.
- For security reasons, a digital photograph of you will be taken. You will also be asked to write and sign a confidentiality agreement.
- A few minutes before the test begins you will be assigned a seat in the testing room. You cannot choose where to sit. You will be given some scratch paper and pencils that you can use to take notes. You may not use your own paper or pencil.
- At your seat you will see a computer monitor, a keyboard, a mouse, and a pair of headphones with a built-in microphone. You may not bring in any personal items, including food or drink, to the testing room except for your photo identification.

DURING THE TEST

- You will first see your photograph and personal information on the screen. For security reasons, you will need to confirm that the picture is you and the information is correct.

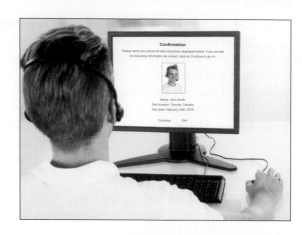

- You will then see several screens that give you general information about the TOEFL Test including regulations about taking the test. You will also see a confidentiality agreement on the screen that you must accept.
- Next the test will begin. The test has four sections. Each section has special

directions that you will see and/or hear. Each section lasts a different amount of time:

Section	Notes
Reading Section	About 62 or 82 minutes (including directions and time to read and answer the questions)
Listening Section	About 62 or 92 minutes (including directions and time to listen and answer the questions)
10 minute break	
Speaking Section	About 20 minutes (including directions and time to prepare for and respond to the questions)
Writing Section	About 60 minutes (including directions and time to prepare for and respond to the questions)

The length of the reading and listening sections depends on how many passages you see in the reading section. If you see three reading passages, the reading section will take about 62 minutes and the listening section will take about 92 minutes. If you see four reading passages, the reading section will take about 82 minutes and the listening section will take about 62 minutes.

- If you have a problem at any time during the test, raise your hand and a testing center administrator will help you. Note that the administrator can only help you with problems related to the test, such as a problem with your computer; he or she cannot help you by answering or explaining any of the questions on the test.

- Also raise your hand if you need new scratch paper on which to take notes. A testing center administrator will take back your used scratch paper and replace it with new scratch paper.
- Every student taking the TOEFL Test at the same test center as you will start at a slightly different time and may answer the questions more quickly or more slowly than you. This means that you are likely to hear background noise while you are taking the test from other people listening to lectures or responding to speaking tasks. You will need to learn to ignore this noise.
- If you need to use the bathroom at any time, you will need to raise your hand and alert a testing center administrator. Note that the clock will not stop while you are out of the room.

AT THE END OF THE TEST

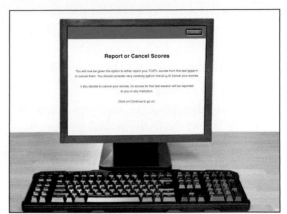

- At the end of the test you will have a chance to report or cancel your test scores. If you choose to report your scores, you will be sent a personal score report and your scores will be sent to the institutions that you selected when you registered for the test. If you choose to cancel your scores, your scores will not be calculated. Note that if you cancel your scores you will not get your money back.
- After you have chosen to report or cancel your scores, you will need to hand in your scratch paper and pencils to the testing center administrator, and then sign out. After that, you are free to leave.
- In rare cases, there are technical problems when students take the TOEFL Test that make it difficult for a student to do his or her best. If you experience such a problem, report it to a testing center administrator before you leave the test center. You may be asked to fill out a report form. In some cases, you may be allowed to reschedule your test without charge.

AFTER THE TEST

- About 10 days after your test date you will receive an email letting you know that your test results are available. You can then check your scores online.
- You will also receive a printed score report by mail. This usually arrives between 14 and 20 days after your test date. The printed score report will give your scores for each section of the test as well as information about your level and likely ability in each section.
- If your test results are good and you have not selected any institutions to receive your score automatically, you can choose to send your scores to institutions at this time for an additional fee of about $20 (USD). If your test results are not as good as you hoped, you can choose to register again for the TOEFL iBT.
- If your speaking and/or writing scores are very close to the scores you need and you have not selected any institutions to receive your score automatically, you can choose to have either or both of these sections rescored. However, you should be aware that rescoring is expensive – $80 (USD) for rescoring one section or $160 (USD) for rescoring both speaking and writing – and your score may not change (or may even go down). For more information about how to apply to have your test rescored, visit www.ets.org/toefl/ibt/scores/cancel/.

Overview

The reading section measures your ability to understand university-level academic texts. You will see:

- Directions for the reading section — about 2 minutes
- Three or four reading passages, each approximately 700 words long, with 12–14 questions after each passage (36–42 questions in total for three passages or 48–56 questions for four passages) — 60 or 80 minutes

Your answers will be scored by a computer and your raw score will be converted to a scaled score from 0–30.

NOTES

- The reading passages on the TOEFL Test come from university-level textbooks and often introduce a subject or topic. You will not need any previous knowledge about these subjects: all the information you need to answer the questions is mentioned in the passage.
- You may see three different types of passages: expositions, which explain a single topic; arguments, which express and support a point of view; and historical or biographical narratives, which describe a past event or somebody's life. Expository passages are the most common type.
- Some passages contain difficult words or phrases. These expressions are underlined in the passage, and clicking on them will bring up a definition of the word in the lower left part of the screen.
- You may see up to ten different types of questions in the reading section, divided into three categories: basic information questions, inferencing questions, and reading to learn questions.
- If you see four passages, the questions about one of the passages may NOT count towards your raw score. However, there is no way to know which of the passages will not count, so you should answer all questions as well as you can.

Detailed Guide

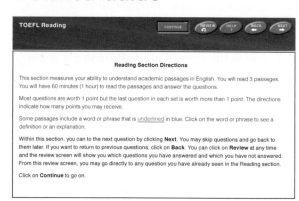

When you begin the reading section of the TOEFL Test, the first screen you see will be the directions for the reading section.

When you are ready, click the button labeled **Continue** in the top right of the screen to begin the reading section.

TEST TACTIC

If you find it hard to answer all the questions in 20 minutes, save time by scrolling to the end of the passage without reading it. You can read the relevant parts of the passage later when you answer each question.

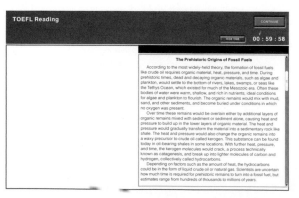

Next you will see a reading passage on the right side of the screen and a blank area on the left side of the screen. The timer will begin counting down.

The passage will be too long to fit on the screen. To see the final paragraphs of the passage you will need to scroll to the bottom using the scrollbar to the right of the passage. After you scroll to the bottom of the passage you will be able to click the **Continue** button to see the questions.

After you click **Continue**, you will see the first question. You will also see a toolbar with various buttons at the top right of the screen. Each button has a different function.

When you click the **Review** button, you will see a screen that shows the status of all the questions about the current passage. Questions you have looked at will be marked "Answered" or "Not Answered." Questions you have not looked at yet will be marked "Not Seen."

You can use the Review screen to jump to any question you have already answered. This is a useful tool to save time and make sure you have answered all of the questions. Note that the timer will continue to count down while you look at the Review screen.

Clicking the **Help** button gives you helpful information about how to answer the questions and use the onscreen buttons. Note that the timer will continue to count down while you look at the Help screen. Also note that the Help screen will NOT give you specific advice about the correct answer for a question, only general advice about how to answer the questions.

Clicking the **Back** button will take you back to previous questions. You can review and change your answer to any question that you have already answered. You can also answer any questions that you skipped. If you are currently looking at the first question about a passage, clicking **Back** will take you to the last question about the previous passage, if there is one.

In most cases, clicking the **Next** button will show you the next question about the current passage. If the current question is the last question about the current passage, clicking **Next** will take you to the next passage. If the current question is the last question about the last passage, clicking **Next** will show a message on the screen.

The message will explain that while there is time remaining, you can answer any questions that you skipped, or change your answers to any of the questions. If you choose to continue on to the Listening section, you will not be able to return to the Reading section.

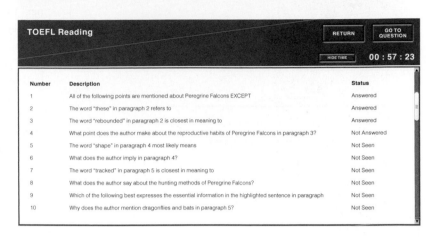

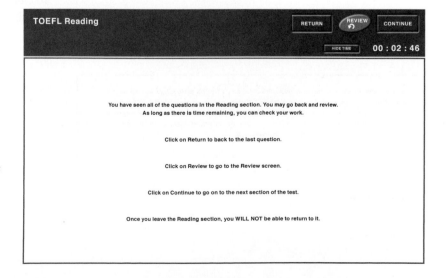

Most questions in the reading section ask you to choose one answer from four choices.

To choose your answer, click on the answer or on the oval next to it. To change your answer, click on a different answer choice.

After you have chosen your answer, click on the **Next** button to go on to the next question.

---

1. According to paragraph 3, what method has been used to try to control mountain pine beetles?

    ⬭ other insects

    ⬭ predators

    ⬭ viruses

    ⬬ pesticides

Paragraph 3 is marked with an arrow ➤.

Rarely, you might see a question that requires you to choose more than one answer. These questions have special directions.

To choose your answers, click on the squares next to them. To change an answer, click on the square next to a different answer choice and the most recently selected answer will be canceled.

You need to click on the required number of answers to get credit for these questions. If you select too many answers, you will see a warning message.

Select the TWO answer choices that describe cities in which René Descartes lived in the early 1630s.

To receive credit, you must select TWO answers.

☐ Amsterdam
☒ Leiden
☒ Utrecht
☐ Santpoort

Some questions – called Insert Text questions – require you to add a sentence to the passage at one of four locations marked by black squares. These questions have special directions in a gray box.

In the passage you will see four black squares (■). To choose your answer, click on the black square at the position where you think the new sentence should be added. The square will disappear and the sentence will be added at that position in **bold text**.

To change your answer, click on a different square. You can change your answer as often as you need.

Look at the four squares [■] that indicate where the following sentence can be added to the passage.

Published in 1882, these were very popular and Abbey's career flourished.

Where would the sentence best fit?

Click on a square [■] to add the sentence to the passage.

American painter Edwin Austin Abbey was born in Philadelphia, Pennsylvania. ■ He first gained a reputation as an illustrator while working in the art department of Harper & Brothers publishing in New York. ■ In 1878 he moved to the UK and produced illustrations for the poems of Robert Herrick. ■ He later became closely identified with the art life of England, and received various awards, including election to the prestigious Royal Academy. ■

American painter Edwin Austin Abbey was born in Philadelphia, Pennsylvania. ■ He first gained a reputation as an illustrator while working in the art department of Harper & Brothers publishing in New York. ■ In 1878 he moved to the UK and produced illustrations for the poems of Robert Herrick. **Published in 1882, these were very popular and Abbey's career flourished.** He later became closely identified with the art life of England, and received various awards, including election to the prestigious Royal Academy. ■

Some questions – called Prose Summary questions – require you to choose three answers from six choices and add them to a summary of the passage. These questions have special directions in a gray box.

To choose an answer, click on it with your mouse. Keep the mouse button held down and drag the answer to an empty space in the answer box. The answer will be added to the box. Do this twice more to choose all three answers. It does not matter in which order you add the three answers.

You can change your answers as often as you wish. To change an answer, click on it or drag it outside of the answer box. The answer will return to its original position among the six answer choices.

Prose Summary questions take up the whole screen, so you will not be able to see the reading passage at the same time. To view the passage, click on the **View Text** button at the top right of the screen. The text on the button will change to **View Question**, and you will see the passage. When you want to see the question again, click on **View Question**.

Some questions – called Fill in a Table questions – require you to choose five answers from six or more choices. You will see two or three categories, each with space for one, two, or three answers. No answer matches more than one category, and at least one answer does not match any category. These questions have special directions in a gray box.

You can choose and change your answers for Fill in a Table questions in the same way as for Prose Summary questions.

Fill in a Table questions take up the whole screen in the same way as Prose Summary questions, so you must click the **View Text** button if you want to see the passage to help you decide on your answers.

Directions: An introductory sentence for a brief summary of the passage is provided below. Complete the summary by selecting the THREE answer choices that express the most important ideas in the passage. Some sentences do not belong in the summary because they express ideas that are not presented in the passage or are minor ideas in the passage. **This question is worth 2 points.**

Drag your answer choices to the spaces where they belong.
To remove an answer choice, click on it. To review the passage, click **VIEW TEXT**.

When first discovered, antibiotics represented a significant advance in healthcare.

-
- Over-prescription of antibiotics has led to the a rise in bacteria resistant to multiple drugs.
-

Answer Choices

Drug resistant bacteria are the cause of widespread environmental problems.

Superbugs such as MRSA cause thousands of people to fall sick each year.

Research conducted in the US has shown that veterinarians like prescribing antibiotics.

Scientists are studying various ways to combat the threat of antibiotic resistance.

Patients who have surgical procedures need antibiotics to avoid getting infections.

TOEFL Reading

VIEW TEXT   REVIEW   HELP ?   BACK   NEXT

Question 14 of 42   HIDE TIME   00 : 42 : 31

Directions: Select the answers that correctly describe the treasure found as part of each hoard. One of the answers will NOT be used. **This question is worth 3 points.**

Drag your answer choices to the spaces where they belong.
To remove an answer choice, click on it. To review the passage, click **VIEW TEXT**.

Answer Choices

Silver tableware

Pepper pots

Gold coins and jewelry

Dishes with pedestals

Inscribed rings

Mildenhall Treasure
-
-

Hoxne Hoard
-
- A broken handle in the shape of a tiger
-

TEST TACTIC

If a question is taking a long time to answer, select your best idea, make a note of the question number on your scratch paper, and go on to the next question. If you have time remaining at the end, click the **Review** button to go back to these questions.

Scoring

Your answers for the reading section will be scored by computer. For most questions, you will get 1 point for a correct answer. For Prose Summary questions (see Reading Unit 7), you can get 1 or 2 points depending on how many answers you get right. For Fill in a Table questions (also Reading Unit 7), you can get 1–3 points depending on how many answers you get right.

The computer will add up all of your correct answers to get your raw score. The maximum raw score depends on how many passages you had and on the types of questions you saw. In general, though, for three passages, the maximum raw score is roughly 45 points. For four passages, the maximum raw score is around 60 points.

After your raw score has been calculated, the computer will convert it to a scaled score from 0–30. ETS does not give specific information about how your raw score is converted. However, it is likely that your raw score is calculated as a percentage of the maximum raw score, and your scaled score is then calculated as the same percentage of 30 (the maximum scaled score). So, for example, if your raw score is 36 points out of a maximum of 45 points, your percentage of correct answers is 80%. This would give you a scaled score of 80% of 30, or 24 points.

This chart shows an estimate of how many answers you need to get right in order to get a scaled score of 15–30.

Percentage Correct	Raw Score (three passages)	Raw Score (four passages)	Scaled Score
99–100%	39	52	30
95–98%	37–38	49–51	29
92–94%	36–37	48–49	28
89–91%	35	46–47	27
85–88%	33–34	44–46	26
82–84%	32–33	43–44	25
79–81%	31–32	41–42	24
75–78%	29–30	39–41	23
72–74%	28–29	37–38	22
69–71%	27–28	36–37	21
65–68%	25–27	34–35	20
62–64%	24–25	32–33	19
59–61%	23–24	31–32	18
55–58%	21–23	28–30	17
52–54%	20–21	27–28	16
49–51%	19–20	25–27	15

TEST TACTIC

Most questions are worth one point, but Prose Summary and Fill in a Table questions are worth two or three points. Be sure to leave enough time to answer these questions because they can have a big effect on your score.

When you receive your score from the TOEFL Test, you will get a score report. The report will give your scaled score in reading from 0–30, your reading level (High, Intermediate, or Low), plus a short description of the typical performance of students at that level.

Here are the levels and descriptions for reading:

Level (Scaled Score)	Your Performance
High (22–30)	Test takers who receive a score at the HIGH level, as you did, typically understand academic texts in English that require a wide range of reading abilities regardless of the difficulty of the texts. Test takers who score at the HIGH level, typically: • have a very good command of academic vocabulary and grammatical structure; • can understand and connect information, make appropriate inferences, and synthesize ideas, even when the text is conceptually dense and the language is complex; • can recognize the expository organization of a text and the role that specific information serves within the larger text, even when the text is conceptually dense; and • can abstract major ideas from a text, even when the text is conceptually dense and contains complex language.
Intermediate (15–21)	Test takers who receive a score at the INTERMEDIATE level, as you did, typically understand academic texts in English that require a wide range of reading abilities, although their understanding of certain parts of the texts is limited. Test takers who receive a score at the INTERMEDIATE level typically: • have a good command of common academic vocabulary, but still have some difficulty with high-level vocabulary; • have a very good understanding of grammatical structure; • can understand and connect information, make appropriate inferences, and synthesize information in a range of texts, but have more difficulty when the vocabulary is high level and the text is conceptually dense; • can recognize the expository organization of a text and the role that specific information serves within a larger text, but have some difficulty when these are not explicit or easy to infer from the text; and • can abstract major ideas from a text, but have more difficulty doing so when the text is conceptually dense.
Low (0–14)	Test takers who receive a score at the LOW level, as you did, typically understand some of the information presented in academic texts in English that require a wide range of reading abilities, but their understanding is limited. Test takers who receive a score at the LOW level typically: • have a command of basic academic vocabulary, but their understanding of less common vocabulary is inconsistent; • have limited ability to understand and connect information, have difficulty recognizing paraphrases of text information, and often rely on particular words and phrases rather than a complete understanding of the text; • have difficulty identifying the author's purpose, except when that purpose is explicitly stated in the text or easy to infer from the text; and • can sometimes recognize major ideas from a text when the information is clearly presented, memorable, or illustrated by examples, but have difficulty doing so when the text is more demanding.

Source: www.ets.org/Media/Tests/TOEFL/pdf/TOEFL_Perf_Feedback.pdf

Directions

This reading diagnostic test is intended to help you find out your strengths and weaknesses in reading. You will have 40 minutes to read two passages and answer 25 questions (worth 28 points). The passages and questions are designed to be at the same level as the ones you will see on the TOEFL Test. When you have finished, check your answers with your instructor or against the Answer Key. Then use the conversion chart on page 19 to convert your raw score to your likely score on the TOEFL Test.

Test

Read the two passages and answer questions 1–25. You have 40 minutes.

Peregrine Falcons

Peregrine Falcons, which are commonly known as Duck Hawks in North America, are medium-sized birds of prey with dark blue or slate-gray feathers on their backs and wings, often with darker bands. Their underparts are pale with dark bars. They have a dark head and cheeks with a pale neck and throat. Peregrines range in size from 35–50 centimeters (14–20 inches) with a wingspan of 100–110 centimeters (39–43 inches) and a body weight between 500 and 1,600 grams (roughly 18–56 ounces), which makes them among the largest of the falcons. Like other falcons they are members of the family *Falconidae* and exhibit sexual dimorphism in that males are smaller than females.

Peregrines live in an extremely broad range of habitats, including in many cities, and are found on all continents with the exception of Antarctica. They are not just the most widespread raptor, or bird of prey, but also the bird with the broadest range of natural habitats. During the 1960s and 1970s Peregrine populations declined sharply as a result of the use of pesticides for farming and other purposes. Since the employment of these was reduced, numbers have rebounded strongly, and Peregrines are now considered in no danger of extinction.

Peregrine Falcons typically mate for the first time when they are two or three years old. The nesting pair then mate for life and even return to the same nesting location each year. The nest is usually a hollow on a cliff edge protected by an overhang; in cities, Peregrines regularly make nesting sites on bridges or skyscrapers. In most cases, a female will lay between one and five eggs a year, with three to four being average. Chicks hatch after about one month, and leave the nest after a further six to seven weeks. Peregrine eggs and chicks are regularly predated by eagles and other large raptors.

Peregrines typically prey on other birds and bats while they are in flight. Occasionally they will also hunt small but abundant terrestrial mammals such as rats, mice, voles, and shrews. When hunting, they usually fly high and then look down for potential prey. When they see a target, Peregrines launch into a steep and extremely fast dive to catch their prey. When diving, they regularly reach speeds of 320 kilometers per hour (200 miles per hour), but have been measured traveling as fast as 389 km/h (242 mph), which makes them the fastest animals in the world. They strike their prey in mid-flight with a foot, either killing it outright or stunning it, and then catch it before it falls to the ground. Peregrines exhibit a number of physical adaptations that allow them to reach such speeds. They have nictitating membranes – sometimes called third eyelids – to protect their eyes while still allowing them to see. They also have bony projections on their nostrils that shape the flow of air around them in such a way that pressure from the air does not damage their lungs.

Until recently, scientists were uncertain how Peregrines tracked prey species when hunting. An innovative study that involved outfitting the birds with miniature video cameras, however, has shed interesting light on their methods. Scholars had theorized that Peregrines might use one of two methods, either diving straight towards their prey or following a flight path that kept the prey at a 45-degree angle in the Peregrine's vision – the angle at which Peregrines can see most sharply. The video evidence showed that Peregrines actually used a strategy called *motion camouflage* that scholars first identified when analyzing the hunting methods of bats and dragonflies. A hunting Peregrine predicts the point at which it will meet its target and dives towards that spot making sure it keeps its prey at a constant angle in its field of view. The advantage of this approach is that the prey species may be fooled into thinking the raptor is not a threat – until it is too late – because it does not seem to be coming closer. The disadvantage, and it is a significant one, is that if the target changes direction, the Peregrine's real position will be obvious and the target can easily take evasive measures.

1. All of the following points are mentioned about Peregrine Falcons EXCEPT:
   - (A) They are medium-sized falcons.
   - (B) They have both dark and light feathers.
   - (C) Female birds are larger than male ones.
   - (D) They are able to live in most environments.

2. The word "these" in paragraph 2 refers to
   - (A) purposes
   - (B) pesticides
   - (C) populations
   - (D) habitats

3. The word "rebounded" in paragraph 2 is closest in meaning to
   - (A) turned out
   - (B) come back
   - (C) fallen off
   - (D) opened up

4. What point does the author make about Peregrine Falcons in paragraph 3?
   - (A) Most Peregrines are physically able to mate every six to seven weeks.
   - (B) Peregrines prefer not to protect their young from other birds of prey.
   - (C) Peregrines prefer artificial nesting sites like bridges to natural cliffs.
   - (D) The same male and female birds mate with each other each year.

5. The word "shape" in paragraph 4 most likely means
   - (A) shelter
   - (B) prevent
   - (C) influence
   - (D) pattern

6. What does the author imply in paragraph 4?
   - (A) Peregrines would not be able to fly so fast if they did not have bony nostril projections or nictitating membranes.
   - (B) Peregrines rarely fly as fast as 389 km/h because the flow of air at that speed can cause damage to their lungs.
   - (C) Peregrines need to be able to fly very fast because most of their prey species are also capable of extreme speed.
   - (D) Peregrines are able to catch stunned targets before they reach the ground because they can fly and dive so quickly.

7. The word "tracked" in paragraph 5 is closest in meaning to
   - (A) modified
   - (B) copied
   - (C) selected
   - (D) followed

8. What does the author say about the hunting methods of Peregrine Falcons?
   - (A) They use a technique that allows them to trick potential targets into believing there is no immediate danger.
   - (B) They adopt several methods to help them easily catch targets that are attempting to take evasive measures.
   - (C) They tend to dive directly towards a target and then maintain a flight path at a sharp but constant angle.
   - (D) They are more effective at hunting when it is light because they can more easily identify specific targets.

9. Which of the following best expresses the essential information in the highlighted sentence in paragraph 5? Incorrect choices change the meaning in important ways or leave out essential information.
   - (A) The two most popular theories of how Peregrine Falcons dive towards their prey were found to be incorrect after the angle of most dives was measured at 45 degrees.
   - (B) Scientists expected that Peregrines would dive towards prey in a way that either allowed them to see it best or reach it most directly.
   - (C) Scholars found that most Peregrines dive straight towards their prey at an angle that allows them to see as many other birds as possible.
   - (D) Peregrines that follow a flight path when diving typically use two different methods and diving angles to catch prey depending on how sharp their vision is.

10. Why does the author mention dragonflies and bats in paragraph 5?
   - (A) To point out that the results of analysis of hunting methods are hard to predict
   - (B) To explain that scientists who study Peregrines often study other animals, too
   - (C) To imply that other animals that hunt while in flight use motion camouflage
   - (D) To give an example of some common animals that Peregrine Falcons prey upon

11. Look at the four squares (■) that indicate where the following sentence could be added to the passage.

In fact, the video footage shows that close to three-fourths of all Peregrine hunting dives end in failure.

Where would the sentence best fit? Choose position **A**, **B**, **C**, or **D**.

The video evidence showed that Peregrines actually used a strategy called motion camouflage that scholars first identified when analyzing the hunting methods of bats and dragonflies. **A** A hunting Peregrine predicts the point at which it will meet its target and dives towards that spot making sure it keeps its prey at a constant angle in its field of view. **B** The advantage of this approach is that the prey species may be fooled into thinking the raptor is not a threat because it does not seem to be coming closer. **C** The disadvantage, and it is a significant one, is that if the target changes direction, the Peregrine's real position will be obvious and the target can easily take evasive measures. **D**

12. **Directions:** An introductory sentence for a brief summary of the passage is provided below. Complete the summary by selecting the THREE answer choices that express the most important ideas in the passage. Some sentences do not belong in the summary because they express ideas that are not presented in the passage or are minor ideas in the passage. **This question is worth 2 points.**

> **Peregrine Falcons are medium-sized raptors with a broad geographical range.**
>
> •
>
> •
>
> •

- Ⓐ Peregrines rarely hunt mammals like rats or mice because these animals are difficult to catch.
- Ⓑ Mating pairs of Peregrines typically have three or four offspring yearly, not all of which survive.
- Ⓒ Peregrines mainly hunt and catch prey in flight using a fast dive as their main hunting method.
- Ⓓ Physical adaptations allow Peregrines to live and reproduce in a wide range of different habitats.
- Ⓔ Peregrines were briefly threatened during the 1960s and 1970s, but are no longer in danger.
- Ⓕ A photographic study of Peregrines helped scientists understand the hunting methods of birds.

Intellectual Property Protection

Intellectual property refers to any kind of work that is the result of human creativity and intelligence. These works include inventions, processes, designs, names, symbols, manuscripts, and musical works, among others. The owner or creator of the property has the exclusive legal right to use it for business purposes. To prevent others from infringing on their exclusive rights, businesses that operate in the United States have three broad options for protecting their intellectual property depending on the type of property it is: copyright, trademarks, and patents.

Copyright is a form of intellectual property protection that is granted to the creator of an original work of authorship, which typically includes written, musical, artistic, and theatrical or cinematic works. Copyright gives a property owner the exclusive right to benefit financially from a work through its use, reproduction, or distribution. In most nations the default period of copyright protection is the life of the named author plus an additional 50 or 70 years. For works published under no name or a fake name, the default period is usually 50 or 70 years from the date of publication. In cases where different countries grant different periods of copyright protection, nations may follow the rule of the shorter term. Under this rule, the maximum length of copyright for a work is the maximum term in the country of origin if that term is shorter.

It is important to note that copyright protects the form of expression, not the subject matter of a work. If, say, a photograph of the Grand Canyon is copyrighted, the creator of that photograph is the only entity with the right to sell, distribute, or benefit from it in any way. However, there is nothing to stop a different entity from taking a photograph of the same scene and selling or distributing that, provided the second work is distinguishable from the first. And copyright protection does allow users of a copyrighted work to make "fair use" of it. Generally this means users may copy at least part of a copyrighted work for personal use, though the precise definition of what constitutes fair use is rarely given.

A trademark is a word, name, symbol, or design that companies use to indicate the source of goods or services. When used for the latter, the term *servicemark* is sometimes used in place of the more general term. Unlike copyrights or patents, trademarks can last indefinitely if the owner continues to use the mark commercially, although in most countries the mark must be renewed periodically. Trademarks grant businesses the exclusive right to sell or distribute a particular product or service under a particular name or brand. Other businesses can sell or distribute similar products and services under a trademark that is clearly different, or can sell or distribute different products and services under a similar mark. To illustrate, a private business offering educational services using the name Yale might violate the trademark of Yale University, a car wash business would safely be able to use the name Yale, however, because the service being offered is in no way similar to the services offered by a university.

A patent works differently from copyright and trademarks. Whereas the latter two give the owner of an intellectual property exclusive rights to that property, a patent grants the owner the right to prevent others from making, using, or selling an invention, idea, or design. A patent's term is typically 20 years from the date when the application is filed. In some cases this can be extended.

In the United States, inventors may file for three types of patents. Utility patents cover new or useful improvements to processes, machines, or manufacturing methods. Design patents cover original new designs for manufactured products. And plant patents cover inventions or discoveries of new or distinct types of plants. A common element to all types of patents is that the invention must exhibit novelty. Patents for inventions that have already been described or are known to exist in the world are usually not granted. Patents for inventions that are new but obvious are rarely granted either. For instance, a patent would not be given for an invention that is merely a larger or smaller version of an existing product.

13. What feature do the three different kinds of intellectual property protection have in common?
- Ⓐ They give the owner of an intellectual property an advantage in business.
- Ⓑ They prevent non-owners of an intellectual property from using it in any way.
- Ⓒ They allow owners of one or more creative works to sell those works to others.
- Ⓓ They give certain exclusive rights to the owner of a work of the human mind.

14. The word "infringing" in paragraph 1 is closest in meaning to
- Ⓐ unloading
- Ⓑ disregarding
- Ⓒ excavating
- Ⓓ defending

15. The author makes all of the following points in paragraph 2 EXCEPT:
- Ⓐ Works by named authors get longer copyright protection than works by unnamed authors.
- Ⓑ Property owners can apply to extend the default copyright period for between 50 and 70 additional years.
- Ⓒ Countries may apply a shorter period of copyright protection for works originating in another country.
- Ⓓ Only the owner of a copyrighted intellectual property should get a monetary advantage from that work.

16. What does the author imply in paragraph 3?
- Ⓐ "Fair use" would not apply to commercial uses of copyrighted works.
- Ⓑ Photographs of natural scenes like the Grand Canyon are often copyrighted.
- Ⓒ Copyright laws provide ineffective protection for owners of copyrighted works.
- Ⓓ The subject matter of copyrighted works affects how people can use them.

17. The word "precise" in paragraph 3 is closest in meaning to
- Ⓐ prolific
- Ⓑ useful
- Ⓒ specific
- Ⓓ conscious

18. The word "periodically" in paragraph 4 most likely means
- Ⓐ in the short term
- Ⓑ with great care
- Ⓒ after due process
- Ⓓ from time to time

19. Which of the following best expresses the essential information in the highlighted sentence in paragraph 4? Incorrect choices change the meaning in important ways or leave out essential information.
- Ⓐ Businesses operate under different trademarks so they can sell and distribute different products from their competitors.
- Ⓑ Companies with similar names can do business provided they offer dissimilar products or services from each other.
- Ⓒ Other companies can operate a different business using a similar name or a similar business using a different name.
- Ⓓ Businesses with a trademark similar to one owned by another company must provide a variety of different services.

20. Why does the author mention Yale University in paragraph 4?
   - (A) To give an example of a specific case of trademark violation
   - (B) To clarify the way in which trademark protection works
   - (C) To argue that trademarks offer little intellectual property protection
   - (D) To demonstrate how companies can use trademarks safely

21. The word "this" in paragraph 5 refers to
   - (A) application
   - (B) date
   - (C) term
   - (D) design

22. The word "novelty" in paragraph 6 is closest in meaning to
   - (A) originality
   - (B) navigation
   - (C) popularity
   - (D) sentiment

23. What does the author say about patent applications?
   - (A) In some cases a patent may be granted for something that a person discovered rather than invented.
   - (B) Design and utility patents are only granted when they are for new and useful manufacturing methods.
   - (C) There are three times more applications for patents in the United States than in other countries.
   - (D) The term of protection that a patent provides is 20 years from the date the application is approved.

24. Look at the four squares (■) that indicate where the following sentence could be added to the passage.

   The duration of copyright protection is generally limited.

   Where would the sentence best fit? Choose position **A**, **B**, **C**, or **D**.

   A Copyright is a form of intellectual property protection that is granted to the creator of an original work of authorship, which typically includes written, musical, artistic, and cinematic works. **B** Copyright gives a property owner the exclusive right to benefit financially from a work through its use, reproduction, or distribution. **C** In most nations the default period of copyright protection is the life of the named author plus an additional 50 or 70 years. **D** For works published under no name or a fake name, the default period is usually 50 or 70 years from the date of publication. In cases where different countries grant different periods of copyright protection, nations may follow the rule of the shorter term. Under this rule, the maximum length of copyright for a work is the term in the country of origin if that term is shorter.

25. **Directions:** Select the phrases that correctly describe each type of intellectual property protection. One of the phrases will NOT be used. **This question is worth 3 points.**

Copyright or Trademarks

-
-

Patents

-
-
-

Ⓐ   Protection may continue after the owner's death.
Ⓑ   Protection lasts no more than 50 years unless renewed.
Ⓒ   Protection is only available for non-obvious inventions.
Ⓓ   Protection applies to works of art and literature or product names.
Ⓔ   Protection can be applied for in one of several categories.
Ⓕ   Protection allows owners to stop others from using a product.

Score Conversion

Check your answers to questions 1–25. Then use this conversion chart to find out your approximate reading score range on the TOEFL Test.

Raw Score (out of 28)	Probable Level	Approximate Score Range
26–28		28–30
23–25	High	25–27
20–22		22–24
18–20	Intermediate	19–21
14–17		15–18
10–13		11–14
6–9	Low	7–10
3–6		3–6
0–2		0–2

Unit Focus

There are ten types of reading questions in the TOEFL Test, including two similar question types called Factual Information and Negative Factual Information questions. Factual Information questions ask about specific information mentioned in part of the reading passage. They are one of the most common questions in the test; you can expect three to six Factual Information questions after every passage. Negative Factual Information questions ask about details NOT mentioned in the passage. They are less common than Factual Information questions; you can expect zero to two such questions after each passage. The skills you need to answer both of these question types are the same. These skills include:

- recognizing key phrases in the question and answer choices.
- recognizing whether answer choices paraphrase or contradict part of a reading passage.
- recognizing whether answer choices are mentioned or not mentioned in a reading passage.

The vocabulary focus is on academic words and phrases related to:

- paleontology, the study of plants and animals that lived on Earth a long time ago, but are now all dead.

A Warm-up

A1 Which of the three fields of paleontology that are mentioned in this passage would you most like to study? Why? Share your reasons with other students.

The science of paleontology involves the study of prehistoric life. It first began as an academic discipline in the eighteenth century and over the years it has developed as human knowledge and technological ability have increased. There are now several fields within the discipline including paleobotany, the study of ancient plants, paleoclimatology, the study of changes in the Earth's climate, and paleoecology, the study of interactions among ancient animals and plants.

B Academic Vocabulary

B1 Use the letter clues to help you choose the best answer to complete missing words 1–8 in this passage. Then use a dictionary to check your answers. One answer has been done for you.

Living things such as plants, animals, or even bacteria are known as 1. ___organisms___. Scientists use the term 2. s_____ to describe organisms that look similar to each other and have essentially the same DNA. The word 3. _____l is used to describe species, such as dogs, that have warm blood and give birth to live babies, while species like snakes that have cold blood and lay eggs are known as 4. r_____. When a mammal, reptile, or other organism dies, the dead body is called its 5. r_____. If the remains of an organism are buried and then turned to stone as a result of heat and pressure over a long period of time, the remains are known as a 6. _____l. Scientists have discovered many fossils of species that are now extinct, which means they have all died out, including fossils of extinct reptiles from 7. _____t_____ times before humans were alive. These reptiles, which were often very large, are known as 8. _____s. You can see specimens, or examples, of prehistoric fossils in certain museums.

dinosaurs	mammal	prehistoric	reptiles
fossil	organisms	remains	species

C Analyzing Factual Information Questions

All Factual Information questions ask you about specific points that are mentioned in part of the reading passage. Factual Information questions may be written in one of several ways, as in these examples:

According to paragraph 3, which of the following is true about _____?

What does the author say about _____ in paragraph 4?

What event caused _____?

The author explains that _____ led to

According to paragraph 6, _____ most likely happened because

For many Factual Information questions, the paragraph number in which the answer can be found is mentioned in the question. This paragraph will be indicated on the computer screen by an arrow.

The correct answer to Factual Information questions:

- restates information that is mentioned in the passage.
- may include information from two different parts of the relevant section or paragraph.

In contrast, incorrect answers:

- often restate or repeat information from the passage, but do not answer the question.
- may use words from the passage to express an idea that is not actually mentioned in the passage.
- sometimes change a detail from the passage or contradict information mentioned in the passage.

C1 Answer Factual Information questions 1 and 2. Then discuss your answers with a partner.

One of the most effective ways of dating fossils is through the use of so-called index, or guide, fossils. These are fossils of organisms that lived during a specific period of time, but which are easily recognizable and commonly found over a wide area. These three characteristics allow scientists to date other fossils found in the same sedimentary layer. For example, if a fossil to be dated is found in the same rock layer as some index fossils, it can be assumed that the undated fossil and the index fossils all lived at roughly the same time. Among the most useful index fossils are certain species of corals, trilobites, and ammonites. Tiny microfossils, such as radiolarians and foraminifera, are more numerous but harder to identify, even for experts. They are useful for providing more precise dates than larger index fossils.

1. According to the author, which of these is a characteristic of index fossils?
   A They are found in at least two different rock layers.
   B They typically have a broad geographical distribution.
   C They are usually tiny microfossils, such as ammonites.
   D They are formed from organisms that lived in rock layers.

2. What point does the author make about microfossils?
   A They are more abundant than larger fossils.
   B They include fossil trilobites, ammonites, and corals.
   C Radiolarians are more abundant than foraminifera.
   D They are rarely difficult for experts to recognize.

> **TEST TACTIC**
>
> Factual Information questions are one of the two most common types of reading question in the TOEFL Test. As a result, becoming better at answering these questions accurately and quickly is likely to have a positive effect on your reading score.

C2 Match the wrong answers from exercise C1 to the correct description. Work with a partner. One answer has been done for you.

1. This answer is mentioned in the passage, but does not answer the question.	2B
2. These answers describe something that is not mentioned in the passage.	
3. These answers contradict or change information in the passage.	

D Mastering Factual Information Questions – Recognizing Key Phrases

An important skill for answering Factual Information questions is recognizing key phrases in the questions and answers. Noting these key phrases can help you find the right part of the passage as well as recognize the right answer more easily.

D1 **Complete this explanation about key phrases by choosing the best phrase from A–F to fill blanks 1–6. One answer has been done for you.**

Key phrases in the question and answer choices can help you identify where in the passage you will find the answer. For example:

- If a question includes the key phrase *paragraph 2*, you can be sure the answer will only be found in that paragraph.
- If a question contains the key phrase 1. ___after the bones were discovered___, you can be sure the answer will be found in the part of the passage that focuses on events that happened after the discovery.

Other key phrases in the question or answer choices will help you identify the correct answer. For example:

- If a key phrase is a name or specific term like 2. _____ or *go extinct*, a number like *100*, or a time reference like 3. _____, you should be able to identify a name or specific term, number, or time reference in the passage that has the same meaning.
- If a key phrase is an adjective like *many* or *fewer*, an adverb like *still* or 4. _____, or a noun phrase that refers to a specific thing, person, or place, such as 5. _____ or *paleontologists*, you should look for an adjective, adverb, or noun phrase with the same meaning.

Paying close attention to these key phrases can help you choose the right answer or to eliminate wrong ones. If a particular phrase is omitted or changed, it will make an answer choice incorrect.

Of course, not every phrase in the question and answer choices is a key phrase. For example, phrases like 6. _____ or *what does the writer say* are not likely to be helpful. Similarly, if a reading passage is about fossils, the word *fossils* is not likely to be a useful key phrase because it will appear in the passage so often.

A according to the author	D several million years
B after the bones were discovered	E these days
C Carboniferous period	F prehistoric North America

D2 **Use information from D1 to complete tasks 1 and 2 about the Factual Information question below. Work with a partner.**

1. Discuss why the highlighted phrases in the Factual Information question below are key phrases.
2. Discuss why the words "dinosaur" and "fossils" are NOT highlighted as key phrases.

According to paragraph 2, why do many dinosaur fossils sell for high prices at auction houses?
- A Rare items such as dinosaur fossils are usually expensive.
- B Fossils are becoming increasingly fashionable as works of art.
- C There are more buyers for fossils these days than 100 years ago.
- D Dinosaur fossils are often found in valuable rocks like marble.

D3 Work with a partner to highlight the key phrases in this example Factual Information question and answer choices. One key phrase has been highlighted for you.

1. What is one factor that probably led to the large size of sauropod dinosaurs?
   A They had relatively few natural predators.
   B Like other dinosaurs, they had hollow bones.
   C They lived in lakes and rivers that supported their weight.
   D They spent little of their energy raising their children.

E Mastering Factual Information Questions – Recognizing Right and Wrong Answers

Another important skill for answering Factual Information questions is recognizing right and wrong answers. Most right or wrong answers follow certain patterns. Knowing these patterns will help you to choose the right answer and avoid errors.

E1 Read the passage and answer the Factual Information question. Then complete the table. One answer in the table has been done for you.

Probably the most famous hoax in paleontology is that of the Piltdown Man. In 1912, fragments of what appeared to be a prehistoric human skull were apparently dug out of the ground near Piltdown in England. The bones initially caused great excitement because of what they suggested about the development of modern humans. After 40 years, however, scientists realized that the bone fragments came from two separate species: part of a human skull and an orangutan jawbone. Both bone fragments were relatively modern, but had been stained to look much older.

What does the author say about the Piltdown Man? *Choose two answers.*

A A prehistoric human skull found in England turned out to be fake.
B The Piltdown bones seemed to explain aspects of human development.
C The Piltdown bone fragments included an orangutan jawbone and skull.
D Relatively modern bones can be stained to look older than they are.

This answer paraphrases or simplifies an idea mentioned in the passage.	Right	
This answer paraphrases information from two parts of the passage.	Right	Answer A
This answer paraphrases part of the passage, but does not answer the question.	Wrong	
This answer looks similar to the passage, but contradicts a point or detail.	Wrong	

E2 Choose the statement, A or B, that answers Factual Detail questions 1–4. Then work with a partner to decide why each statement is right or wrong.

The woolly mammoth died out around the time of the last glacial retreat about 10,000 years ago. The reasons for its extinction are unclear. Climate change has been suggested, but several previous climate changes had not had an effect. Another hypothesis is that hunting by bands of humans put the mammoth population under severe pressure.

1. According to the author, woolly mammoths might have gone extinct because of
   A the actions of groups of humans.
   B several periods of climate change.

One of the most ambitious works of modern scholarship is the *Treatise on Invertebrate Paleontology*. When originally conceived in the 1950s, the assumption was that it would require three volumes totaling perhaps 3,000 pages. In fact, even though it is still a work-in-progress, the treatise currently comprises 50 volumes containing hundreds of thousands of words.

2. Which of the following statements about the *Treatise on Invertebrate Paleontology* is true?
   A It was originally thought scholars would finish it in the 1950s.
   B It contains many more words than people originally expected.

TEST TACTIC

Most wrong answers to Factual Information questions are not completely wrong. It is common for a wrong answer to include some words that match the passage and only a few words – sometimes just one word – that make the answer wrong. Keep this point in mind when you are analyzing the answer choices.

Scientists have various techniques for dating rocks and materials. These include several different radiometric dating methods. The basic principle of all radiometric dating methods is the same, but they differ in terms of their accuracy and time frame. Radiocarbon dating, for example, can be used to date materials up to 60,000 years old, whereas uranium-lead dating can be used for objects between 1 million and 4.5 billion years old.

3. What does the author say about radiometric dating?
    A The only two reliable methods are radiocarbon dating and uranium-lead dating.
    B Some methods are more useful than others for dating younger rocks and materials.

The term *fossils* generally refers to the petrified remains of parts of an organism's body, but paleontologists also study *trace fossils*, such as fossilized footprints or droppings, to learn about the behavior of prehistoric creatures.

4. What does the author say about trace fossils?
    A They can help paleontologists understand how ancient organisms acted.
    B They are the petrified remains of organisms studied by paleontologists.

E3 Which of these statements does NOT correctly describe at least one of the wrong answers in exercise E2?

A Wrong answers typically repeat a few of the words and phrases that are used in the passage.
B Wrong answers sometimes include a word that refers to an idea not mentioned in the passage.
C Wrong answers generally describe something that is unrealistic or unlikely to be true in real life.
D Wrong answers may include a different form of a word from the passage, such as move instead of movement.

E4 Use the techniques you just learned to answer the Factual Information questions below.

Studies of prehistoric climate data show that until approximately 2.5 billion years ago, Earth's atmosphere held almost no oxygen. After that time, levels of atmospheric oxygen began to rise as a by-product of photosynthesis by cyanobacteria. This event, known as the Great Oxidation, or sometimes the Great Oxygenation Event, was arguably the most significant climate event in history. Oxygen was poisonous to most species of bacteria living at the time, and the Great Oxidation was thus responsible for a mass extinction. But oxygen in the atmosphere also gave rise to the development of multi-cellular organisms, which use oxygen to power biological processes. In that sense, the Great Oxidation was a prerequisite for all modern life forms. The Great Oxidation also led to climate change. Free oxygen in the atmosphere reacted with and reduced levels of atmospheric methane. As methane is a greenhouse gas that helps maintain warm surface temperatures, reduced levels led to lower surface temperatures that eventually resulted in a prolonged ice age known as the Huronian Glaciation. One final change attributed to the Great Oxidation is a dramatic increase in the diversity of minerals found on Earth. Research has suggested that hundreds of new minerals were formed when existing minerals were oxidized, a process that, as its name suggests, requires oxygen.

1. What effect did the Great Oxygenation Event have?
    A An increase in the number and diversity of cyanobacteria
    B The creation of several new mineral-forming processes
    C A rise in the level of methane in the atmosphere
    D The poisoning of many existing species of bacteria

2. What does the author say about the Huronian Glaciation?
    A It reduced surface temperatures exactly 2.5 billion years ago.
    B It caused levels of several atmospheric greenhouse gases to fall.
    C It lasted for a short time until surface temperatures warmed.
    D It resulted from increased levels of free atmospheric oxygen.

F Analyzing Negative Factual Information Questions

Negative Factual Information questions ask you to decide which point is not mentioned in the reading passage. They are easy to recognize because they include the word NOT or EXCEPT in capital letters, as these examples show:

According to paragraph 3, which of the following is NOT true about _____?

In paragraph 6, the author makes all of the following points EXCEPT

What point does the author NOT make about _____?

The correct answer to Negative Factual Information questions:

- may contradict or change information that is mentioned in the passage.
- may express an idea that is not mentioned anywhere in the passage (although it may seem likely to be true).
- can usually be found by reading just one paragraph, but may require looking at two or more paragraphs.

In contrast, incorrect answers:

- restate, summarize, or simplify information that is stated in the passage.

Remember that Negative Factual Information questions are the opposite of Factual Information questions in that the right answer is the one that you cannot find in the passage and the wrong answers are the ones that you can find.

F1 Answer Negative Factual Information questions 1 and 2. Then discuss your answers with a partner.

A popular story type in fantasy literature involves the idea of prehistoric animals surviving to the present-day in remote or underground areas. The earliest story of this type, Jules Verne's *Journey to the Center of the Earth*, was published in 1864. In this tale, some travelers descend into a volcano and find an underground world filled with prehistoric plants and animals, including a herd of mastodons, a type of elephant that in the real world went extinct roughly 12,000 years ago. Almost five decades after Verne, Sir Arthur Conan Doyle, most famous now for his series of tales about the fictional detective Sherlock Holmes, wrote a novel titled *The Lost World*. In the story, some scientists discover a remote plateau in the South American rainforest. Upon reaching the top of the plateau, they are attacked by pterosaurs and dinosaurs. They also encounter various reptiles and prehistoric mammals that are now extinct before escaping from the plateau and reaching safety.

> **TEST TACTIC**
>
> Reading passages in the TOEFL Test may include unfamiliar vocabulary. Many students waste time trying to understand every unknown word, but usually this is unnecessary. You can often answer questions just by focusing on the words you know.

1. The author mentions all of the following about Jules Verne's *Journey to the Center of the Earth* EXCEPT:
   A The story is set in a world that exists under the Earth's surface.
   B It was the first story to be published of a popular type of genre.
   C The events of the story take place more than 10,000 years ago.
   D The characters in the story encounter prehistoric creatures.

2. What does the author NOT say about *The Lost World* by Sir Arthur Conan Doyle?
   A Its author is mostly known as a writer of detective stories.
   B It was published shortly after the story by Jules Verne was written.
   C The characters in the story are attacked by various creatures.
   D The story is set in a distant part of the jungle in South America.

F2 Work with a partner to answer questions 1 and 2.

1. Which right answer in exercise **F1** contradicts or changes information in the passage?
2. Which right answer in **F1** expresses an idea that might be true but is not mentioned anywhere in the passage?

G Mastering Negative Factual Information Questions – Analyzing the Answer Choices

The skills for answering Factual Information questions also work for Negative Factual Information questions, especially recognizing incorrect answer choices that either contradict the passage or introduce an idea that is not mentioned in the passage.

G1 Decide if statements 1–6 Restate the passage, Contradict the passage, or are Not mentioned in the passage. One answer has been done for you.

Tyrannosaurus rex is arguably the best known dinosaur among the general population, in part due to its reputation as a fearsome predator. But was *T. rex* actually so deadly? Among paleontologists there has been a long-running, and sometimes heated, debate about how tyrannosaurs acquired food. Some have argued that their relatively slow speed of movement and tiny, weak forearms mean they weren't efficient killers, but rather they must have acted as scavengers, feeding off dinosaurs that had died from natural causes or been killed by other predators. Others have claimed they were active hunters that would attack other species including hadrosaurs such as *Edmontosaurus*, and possibly even huge sauropods like *Diplodocus*. The recent discovery of a fossil *Edmontosaurus* with part of a *T. rex* tooth completely embedded in its bone sheds new light on the issue. The only explanation is that the tooth became stuck in the bone, which then healed around the tooth. And the only scenario that accounts for this is the *Edmontosaurus* being attacked by a *Tyrannosaurus* while alive and, crucially, not just surviving the attack, but living long enough afterwards for its bones to heal. This evidence strongly supports the idea that tyrannosaurs were active hunters because the *Edmontosaurus* was alive when attacked and scavengers do not typically attack live prey. However, this evidence neither shows how often *T. rex* attacked live prey nor proves that it never acted as a scavenger.

1. It is not clear why *Tyrannosaurus rex* is so well known.
   ☐ Restate   ☑ Contradict   ☐ Not mentioned
2. Some scientists believe *T. rex* ate already dead dinosaurs.
   ☐ Restate   ☐ Contradict   ☐ Not mentioned
3. Others paleontologists claim *T. rex* hunted sauropods but not hadrosaurs.
   ☐ Restate   ☐ Contradict   ☐ Not mentioned
4. *Diplodocus* moved more slowly than *T. rex* because of its huge size.
   ☐ Restate   ☐ Contradict   ☐ Not mentioned
5. The evidence of the tooth supports the idea that *T. rex* hunted live prey.
   ☐ Restate   ☐ Contradict   ☐ Not mentioned
6. Additional evidence is likely to prove whether *T. rex* ever scavenged food.
   ☐ Restate   ☐ Contradict   ☐ Not mentioned

H Test Challenge

H1 Answer Factual Information and Negative Factual Information questions 1–10 on the next page. Try to answer all of the questions in 15 minutes or less in order to get realistic practice for the test. The following checklist of skills that you learned in this unit may help you.

☑ Look for key phrases in the answer choices that are paraphrased in the passage.

☑ Eliminate answer choices that contradict the passage or are not mentioned in it.

Lazarus Species and Living Fossils

Paleontologists analyze fossils to determine when a particular species went extinct. When fossils of a species no longer appear in the fossil record after a particular geological period, it is generally safe to assume the species died out during that period. In rare cases, however, fossils of a species are sometimes found in the fossil record after a long absence. Such species are called Lazarus species. If living specimens of the Lazarus species are found that are barely changed from fossil specimens, the species may also be called a living fossil. An example of a species that meets the criteria for both names is the Wollemi Pine. The first fossils of this species appear in the fossil record dating from the middle of the Mesozoic era roughly 200 million years ago, but no fossils have been found younger than two million years old. Scientists therefore believed that the species had gone extinct at around this time. However, living Wollemi Pines were found in 1994 in a remote area of Wollemi National Park in southeastern Australia.

1. According to the author, a living fossil is
   - Ⓐ an organism that is only known from its fossil record
   - Ⓑ a species that does not have any gaps in its fossil record
   - Ⓒ a species that has existed for more than 200 million years
   - Ⓓ a living species that looks almost the same as its fossils

2. The author mentions all of the following about the Wollemi Pine EXCEPT:
   - Ⓐ Scientists thought it had died out two million years ago.
   - Ⓑ It is both a living fossil and a Lazarus species.
   - Ⓒ It last appeared in the fossil record in the Mesozoic era.
   - Ⓓ It was discovered in an isolated part of Australia.

Dinosaur Sounds

Modern technology has helped scientists learn an increasing amount of information from fossils. In a fascinating study, scientists at the New Mexico Museum of Natural History and Sandia National Laboratories simulated the sound of a living dinosaur. They first used a medical scanner to view the interior of a well-preserved skull of a *Parasaurolophus*, a dinosaur that lived about 75 million years ago. They then used powerful computers to analyze the scanner data and create a software model of the air passages inside a long, bony crest on the skull. This model let the scientists establish the frequency of the sound waves the dinosaur could produce. The software also simulated blowing air through the skull to produce sounds. The noise produced was a loud, low-frequency rumble that could change in pitch. *Parasaurolophus* roamed in huge herds grazing the land, and paleontologists speculate that the dinosaurs may have used the sound to warn other members of the herd of danger or as a means of socializing.

3. Which of these steps did scientists NOT follow when simulating the sound made by *Parasaurolophus*?
   - Ⓐ Using medical technology to preserve the skull well
   - Ⓑ Scanning and analyzing the interior of the skull
   - Ⓒ Creating a model of air passages within the skull
   - Ⓓ Simulating the movement of air through the skull

4. Why do scientists think that *Parasaurolophus* made sounds?
   - Ⓐ To locate other herds of large dinosaurs
   - Ⓑ To recognize nearby sources of nutrition
   - Ⓒ To have social interactions with other species
   - Ⓓ To advise herd members of potential hazards

The Prehistoric Origins of Fossil Fuels

According to the most widely-held theory, the formation of fossil fuels like crude oil requires organic material, heat, pressure, and time. During prehistoric times, dead and decaying organic materials, such as algae and plankton, would settle to the bottom of rivers, lakes, swamps, or seas like the Tethys Ocean, which existed for much of the Mesozoic era. Often these bodies of water were warm, shallow, and rich in nutrients; ideal conditions for algae and plankton to flourish. The organic remains would mix with mud, sand, and other sediments, and become buried under conditions in which no oxygen was present.

Over time these remains would be overlain either by additional layers of organic remains mixed with sediment or sediment alone, causing heat and pressure to build up in the lower layers of organic material. The heat and pressure would gradually transform the material into a sedimentary rock like shale. The heat and pressure would also change the organic remains into a waxy precursor to crude oil called kerogen. This substance can be found today in oil-bearing shales in some locations. With further heat, pressure, and time, the kerogen molecules would crack, a process technically known as catagenesis, and break up into lighter molecules of carbon and hydrogen, collectively called hydrocarbons. Depending on factors such as the amount of heat, the hydrocarbons could be in the form of liquid crude oil or natural gas. Scientists are uncertain how much time is required for prehistoric remains to turn into a fossil fuel, but estimates range from hundreds of thousands to millions of years.

5. All of the following are required for the formation of fossil fuels EXCEPT
   - (A) sand or mud
   - (B) available oxygen
   - (C) heat and pressure
   - (D) organic remains

6. According to paragraph 2, what is kerogen?
   - (A) A mixture of mud, sand, and dead organic material
   - (B) A wax-like material that can turn into crude oil
   - (C) Lighter hydrocarbon molecules like natural gas
   - (D) Organic remains fossilized in sedimentary rock

7. According to the passage, what is one factor that influences whether catagenesis leads to oil or gas?
   - (A) The amount of pressure
   - (B) The location of the kerogen
   - (C) The temperature
   - (D) The amount of time

Baron Georges Cuvier

The French scientist Georges Cuvier was one of the fathers of modern paleontology. He is most famous now for his work on vertebrate paleontology and for establishing the fundamental principles of biostratigraphy, which involves using fossils to assign relative ages to strata, or layers of rock, in Earth's crust. During his lifetime, he was even more famous than he is now, and accrued many academic and professional honors. He was made a French peer in 1819 for his contributions to science, after which he was known by his title Baron Cuvier.

Cuvier was born in eastern France, close to the border with Switzerland, in 1769. He was a gifted child who excelled at school, but after graduation his family circumstances initially made it hard for him to get an academic position. By the age of 27, however, he was working as a lecturer in Paris. In 1796 he delivered an important paper that analyzed bones from African and Indian elephants as well as fossilized bones from mammoths and another elephant-like species.

In his paper he proved not only that African and Indian elephants were distinct species, but also that the fossilized bones were from two other different species. As these other species no longer existed, Cuvier argued that the animals must have gone extinct. This was an important argument because many scientists at that time did not believe that species could die out. Cuvier's paper, along with another paper he delivered later the same year in which he identified and named the species *Megatherium*, an extinct prehistoric sloth, effectively ended the debate and forced other scientists to accept the reality of species extinction.

8. Which of these events did NOT occur during the life of Georges Cuvier?
   - (A) He accepted the idea of extinction as a result of work by other scientists.
   - (B) He delivered a paper discussing several different species of elephant.
   - (C) He produced work that led to the development of biostratigraphy.
   - (D) He received numerous professional awards, as well as being given a title.

9. According to paragraph 2, what is true of Cuvier's childhood?
   - (A) His family moved from Switzerland to Paris.
   - (B) He did not enjoy school and failed to graduate.
   - (C) He delivered several important academic papers.
   - (D) His intelligence made him an excellent student.

10. What point does the author make in paragraph 3?
   - (A) Cuvier's work proved the existence of fossils of *Megatherium*.
   - (B) Some scholars did not accept that species could become extinct.
   - (C) Cuvier had a debate with other scientists about *Megatherium*.
   - (D) Cuvier's academic theories made it hard for him to find work.

> **TEST TACTIC**
>
> Every time you get a Factual Information or Negative Factual Information question wrong, learn from your mistake. First, understand why the right answer is right and your answer is wrong. Next, understand why you chose the wrong answer. Finally, think about how to avoid making similar mistakes in the future.

Next Steps

Topics related to paleontology are common in the reading section of the TOEFL Test. You may also have topics about this subject in the other sections of the test. As a result, learning more about paleontology, as well as practicing key skills for Factual Information and Negative Factual Information questions, may raise your overall test score.

To learn more about paleontology and vocabulary related to this discipline:

1. Read an article in your language about one aspect of paleontology to get some background knowledge about this topic.
2. Read an English article about the same topic to understand the main ideas, but do not try to understand every word.
3. Read the English article again. When you see an unfamiliar word, try to understand the word from its context and write a definition. Then check your dictionary. If your definition was wrong, study the context again to understand your error. After checking your dictionary, decide if the word is useful; if it is, study the word carefully and find other examples of it.

To practice key skills for Factual Information and Negative Factual Information questions:

Factual Information questions, which are also called detail questions or comprehension questions, are probably the most common type of reading comprehension question for all types of reading materials. As a result, you can find thousands of such questions in books or online. You can practice these questions to build useful skills for the TOEFL Test.

1. Find a source of a large number of reading questions that you think are too easy for you.
2. Keep answering exercises from this source until you have answered 20 questions in a row perfectly.
3. When you have completed 20 questions in a row perfectly, find a new source with harder exercises and repeat step 2.

Many students make careless mistakes when they answer reading questions. You can train yourself to avoid making careless mistakes by trying to answer more difficult questions *only* after you have answered 20 easier questions in a row perfectly.

Unit Focus

There are ten types of reading questions in the TOEFL Test, including Vocabulary questions. These questions test if you can understand the meaning of a word or phrase as it is used in a specific part of the passage. Vocabulary questions usually ask about words that are common in general or academic English, not words related to a specific academic subject. They are one of the most common questions in the reading section, and you will usually have from three to five Vocabulary questions after every passage. Several key skills can help you answer Vocabulary questions effectively, including:

- recognizing context clues in the passage that help you understand the meaning of a word.
- recognizing clues to the meaning of a word in the word itself.

The vocabulary focus is on academic words and phrases related to two similar academic subjects:

- history and ancient history, the study of events, situations, and people from earlier times to the recent past.

A Warm-up

A1 **Read these sayings about history. Then work with a partner to complete tasks 1–3.**

> "Study history if you want to know the future."
> "If you don't know history, you are certain to repeat it."
> "History is a set of lies that people have agreed on."

1. Do you think each saying about history is true? Why or why not?
2. Use the sayings as a guide to make up your own saying about history.
3. Share your saying from task 2 with others and vote on the best three sayings in the class.

B Academic Vocabulary

B1 **Choose the best definition, A–H, for each word to complete this table of useful words related to history and ancient history. One answer has been done for you.**

Word	Definition	Synonym
civilization (noun)	1.	society
conflict (noun)	2. a disagreement between groups that leads to fighting	war
conquest (noun)	3.	invasion
found (verb)	4.	establish
monarch (noun)	5.	sovereign
reign (verb)	6.	rule
settlement (noun)	7.	community
territory (noun)	8.	kingdom

A a disagreement between groups that leads to fighting
B a place where people live, such as a village or town
C a region that is governed and controlled by a ruler
D a society with a high level of culture and organization
E an attack on a region that leads to control of that region
F the person who rules over a kingdom or empire
G to be the head of a territory or nation for a period of time
H to start something, especially a settlement or colony

C Analyzing Vocabulary Questions

Vocabulary questions ask you about the meaning of a word or phrase as it is used in the passage. The key word or phrase will be highlighted in both the question and the passage:

The word "＿＿＿＿＿＿" in paragraph 3 is closest in meaning to

The phrase "＿＿＿＿＿＿" in the passage most likely means

In stating that "＿＿＿＿＿＿" the author means that

Remember that Vocabulary questions only ask about the meaning of the highlighted word or phrase *as it used in the passage*. If the highlighted word has several meanings, be careful. Make sure that the answer you choose matches the meaning used in the passage, not another meaning of that word. For example, the most common meaning of the word "company" is "business," but in the phrase "a company of soldiers," the meaning of "company" is "group" not "business."

The correct answer to Vocabulary questions:

- will have the same meaning as the highlighted expression as it is used in the passage.
- can replace the highlighted expression in the passage without changing the meaning of the passage.

In contrast, incorrect answers:

- never have the same meaning as the highlighted expression as it is used in the passage. However, if the highlighted expression has several meanings, an incorrect answer may match one of the other meanings.
- sometimes mean the opposite of the highlighted expression as it is used in the passage.
- may look similar to the highlighted expression, such as by having similar spelling or the same beginning or ending.

TEST TACTIC

Every answer choice for Vocabulary questions is grammatically possible. You only need to decide whether each choice has the same meaning as the highlighted word, not whether it is grammatically correct.

C1 Answer Vocabulary questions 1 and 2. Then compare answers with a partner.

Despite its being an extraordinarily complex issue, many believe that President Abraham Lincoln handled the emancipation question in a comparatively successful fashion.

1. The word "fashion" in the passage is closest in meaning to
   A trend
   B manner
   C faction
   D design

The rise of Octavian, later known as Augustus Caesar, to the leadership of the Roman state ended years of civil war and brought order to Roman politics for the first time in decades.

2. The word "order" in the passage is closest in meaning to

   A demand
   B ordeal
   C turmoil
   D stability

C2 Match the wrong answers from exercise C1 to the correct description, 1, 2, or 3. Use a dictionary if necessary. Then compare answers with a partner. One answer has been done for you.

1. Wrong answers that have the same meaning as a different meaning of the highlighted word	1A
2. Wrong answers that have the opposite meaning of the highlighted word	
3. Wrong answers that look similar in some way to the highlighted word	

D Mastering Vocabulary Questions – Using Context Clues from the Passage

The context – the sentence in which the highlighted word is used as well as nearby sentences – often contains information that can help you understand the meaning of the highlighted word. For instance, in the phrase "the event was deferred until later instead of being canceled", "until later" and "canceled" are context clues which suggest that "deferred" probably means "delayed."

D1 **Use the underlined context clues in these passages to help you answer questions 1–4.**

A major epidemic popularly called the Black Death occurred in the mid-fourteenth century. It caused the deaths of up to 60% of the population of affected areas as doctors were able to provide almost no help to those who became sick.

1. The word "epidemic" most likely means
   A outbreak of disease
   B natural disaster

The Bayeux Tapestry, which despite its name is actually an embroidered cloth, was completed around 1077 A.D. and depicts the events that led to the Norman conquest of England. It also shows the people involved in those events.

2. The word "depicts" is closest in meaning to
   A explains
   B illustrates

During the Heian period of Japanese history, there was an emphasis on art and works of fiction. Indeed, during this time the first Japanese novels and poems were published, such as The Tale of Genji, which is widely considered a masterpiece.

3. The phrase "works of fiction" means
   A imagination
   B literature

Unlike the League of Nations, which endured for just 27 years and never had more than 58 members, the United Nations has existed since 1945 and has seen a steady increase in membership from 51 initially to nearly 200 today.

4. The word "endured" probably means
   A continued
   B suffered

D2 **Fill in the blanks with the correct answer. When you have finished, compare your answers with a partner. One answer has been done for you.**

Clues that you can find in the passage are called context clues. These clues can help you understand the meaning of highlighted expressions in the TOEFL Test. You may see four common types of context clues:

- As seen in passage __4__ in exercise **D1**, the highlighted word may be contrasted with other words or phrases.

- As seen in passage _____, the context might include a word or phrase that is a synonym of the highlighted word.

- As seen in passage _____, an example in the context might make the meaning of the highlighted word clear.

- As seen in passage _____, the context may include other words that suggest the meaning of the highlighted word.

D3 Work with a partner to answer questions 1–4. If neither answer is correct, write your own.

One of the defining acts of Thomas Jefferson's presidency was the Louisiana Purchase, in which the United States of America acquired a vast area from France for $15 million. The purchase effectively doubled the size of the United States, making it by far the largest territorial gain in US history. There was broad domestic opposition before the Purchase was completed because it was felt the Constitution did not allow for the acquistion of land. However, a vote by members of the House of Representatives narrowly approved the sale by a count of 59 in favor to 57 against.

1. The word "vast" in the passage probably means
   A useful   B valuable   C _your answer_

2. The word "domestic" in the passage is closest in meaning to
   A national   B commercial   C _your answer_

There are several myths about the founding of Rome. In the most well-known story, twin brothers Romulus, after whom the city was named, and Remus established the city in 753 B.C. on the Palatine Hill. In reality, archaeological data suggests that humans began dwelling in the area thousands of years before the traditional founding date and that the city developed from crude settlements on the Palatine and Quirinal hills. Not every scholar accepts this interpretation of the evidence, however.

3. The word "dwelling" in the passage most likely means
   A dating   B traveling   C _your answer_

4. The word "interpretation" in the passage is closest in meaning to
   A occupation   B viewpoint   C _your answer_

D4 Choose the best word from A–L to complete blanks 1–10 in these sentences. Two of the words do NOT match any of the blanks. One answer has been done for you.

Prehistoric humans used 1. _____fire_____ for many purposes, including providing heat, keeping away dangerous 2. _____, cooking food, and making tools.

Scholars estimate that the various 3. _____ and towns that formed the Indus Valley Civilization, one of the world's earliest and largest urban cultures, might have had a maximum 4. _____ of almost 5 million people.

Less is known about the Dark Ages, which spanned the sixth to thirteenth centuries A.D., than either earlier or later times because relatively few written 5. _____ have survived from this 6. _____.

During the Second Barons' War, the first major 7. _____ at Lewes in southern England was fought between an army of 8. _____ led by Baron Simon de Montfort and another led by King Henry III.

In the 1930s, the Netherlands, like many other 9. _____ around the world, experienced a severe economic crisis known as the Great Depression, though the 10. _____ happened later there than in many places.

A battle   E documents   I period
B cities   F experience   J population
C creatures   G fire   K soldiers
D decline   H nations   L strengths

D5 Underline the words and phrases in exercises D3 and D4 that helped you choose each answer. Work with a partner.

E Mastering Vocabulary Questions – Using Clues from the Highlighted Word

In addition to context clues from the passage, clues from the highlighted word itself such as its prefix (beginning) or word root (main part) may help you understand its meaning. For example, the word *submarine* has the prefix *sub*, which means "under," and the word root *mar*, which means "sea." These clues suggest that *submarine* means "under (the) sea."

E1 Choose the best answers to complete blanks 1–10 in these tables of common prefixes and word roots. One answer has been done for you.

Common Prefix	Meaning	Example Word
auto–	self	**auto**matic (adj.)
bi–	1. two/twice	**bi**lingual (adj.)
co– (also col–, com–, con–, cor–)	2.	**com**municate (verb)
contra– (also contr–)	3.	**contr**ast (noun/verb)
inter–	between	**inter**national (adj.)
mis–	wrong/bad	**mis**take (noun/verb)
post–	after	**post**pone (verb)
pre–	4.	**pre**paration (noun)
re–	5.	**re**peat (noun/verb)
trans–	across	**trans**late (verb)

again/back

before

opposite/against

together/with

two/twice

Common Word Root	Meaning	Example Word
cede (also ceed, cess)	go	pre**cede** (verb)
dict	speak	contra**dict** (verb)
labor	6.	colla**bor**ate (verb)
memor (also mem)	7.	misre**mem**ber (verb)
nect	8.	intercon**nect** (verb)
nomy	law	auto**nomy** (noun)
nov	9.	re**nov**ate (verb)
port	10.	trans**port** (noun/verb)
script	write	post**script** (noun)
sect	cut/divide	bi**sect** (verb)

carry

join/bind

new

remember

work

E2 Work with a partner to write a definition of each example word listed in the table of word roots. Use the example below as a guide. When you finish, check your definitions in a dictionary and correct any mistakes.

Example   *"Precede" probably has a meaning similar to "go before."*

E3 Choose the best example words from the tables in exercise E1 to complete sentences 1–5. Compare answers with a partner when you finish. One answer has been done for you.

1. Sir Arthur Evans is justly famous for discovering the remains of Bronze Age palaces on the island of Crete, though his decision to _____renovate_____ the ruined buildings has been criticized by many scholars.

2. The roots of the American War of Independence lay in the desire of Americans to create laws themselves rather than be ruled by Great Britain; to have _____, in other words.

3. In 1648, representatives from Spain and the Dutch Republic signed a series of treaties that not only formally ended both the Thirty Years' War and the Eighty Years' War but also provided a foundation for modern _____ relations.

4. During the Bronze Age in Ancient Greece, battles were fought in the heroic style described in Homer's epic poems the *Iliad* and *Odyssey*. Ritual insults and duels between individual warriors would often _____ the general battle.

5. In 1990, scientists from multiple countries, including the US, the UK, Japan, and France, began to _____ on a joint venture called the Human Genome Project. It was expected that this project would take 15 years to finish, but in fact it was completed ahead of schedule in 2003.

E4 **Complete tasks 1–3 with a partner. When you have finished, share your lists with the rest of the class.**

1. The prefix *bi–* means "two or twice." Make a list of other number prefixes, such as *tri–*. Include examples of each prefix.

2. The prefix *mis–* has a negative meaning. Make a list of other negative prefixes that you know. Include examples.

3. Make a list of additional examples for every prefix and word root in the two tables in exercise **E1**.

E5 **Answer questions 1–5. Underline any word clues or context clues from the passage that help you.**

Marco Polo spent 24 years traveling from Europe to Asia and back. When he returned to Venice in 1295 A.D., he was imprisoned for four years. He used the time productively, though, by dictating his memoirs to another prisoner.

1. The word "memoirs" in the passage most likely means

   A reason for a journey   B story of a person's life   C trouble with the law

In December, 1901, the Italian inventor Guglielmo Marconi claimed to have sent a broadcast by radio across the Atlantic Ocean from southwest England to Newfoundland, Canada, a distance of approximately 3,500 kilometers.

2. The word "broadcast" in the passage is closest in meaning to

   A passage   B transmission   C signature

The 1383–1385 Crisis is the name given to the period when Portugal had no ruling monarch. It began when King Ferdinand I died without a son and ended after much civil unrest with the crowning of King John I after the Battle of Aljubarrota.

3. The word "period" in the passage is closest in meaning to

   A perquisite   B governance   C interval

The first threshing machine was invented by Andrew Meikle in 1784 and allowed farmers to separate grain from stalks and husks easily and cost-effectively. Until its invention, this laborious task could only be done by hand.

4. The word "laborious" in the passage is closest in meaning to

   A studious   B mistimed   C challenging

The Code of Ur-Nammu from the Sumerian city-state of Ur is the oldest known surviving law code. It predates the better-known Code of Hammurabi from Babylon by at least 300 years. Scholars know that the full version of the Code includes 57 separate offenses. However, the Code is written on stone tablets that are more than 4,000 years old and only 40 of the laws have been reconstructed. Each offense is listed with the punishment that a guilty person should receive after the verdict was handed down.

5. The word "predates" in the passage is closest in meaning to

   A maintained for   B lasted until   C existed before

TEST TACTIC

To avoid being distracted by the highlighted word, imagine that the question and passage have a blank instead of a highlighted word. Then think "Which of these answers is the best choice to fill in the blank?"

TEST TACTIC

Saving time is important in the reading section. So if you know the meaning of the highlighted word and all three answer choices, and if you are 100% sure which answer is right, quickly choose that answer and move on to the next question.

F Test Challenge

F1 **Answer Vocabulary questions 1–8. Try to finish in 12 minutes or less so as to get realistic practice for the test. Use the checklist of skills that you learned in this unit as a guide.**

- ☑ Look for context clues in the passage that help you understand the meaning of the highlighted expression
- ☑ Look for clues within the highlighted word itself such as its prefix or its word root

---

The Delian League

The Delian League, founded in 478 B.C., was an alliance of 150 to 170 city-states under the leadership of Athens, which had the most powerful navy. The aim of the League was to offer its members mutual protection against the Persian Empire, which had made a number of attacks on Greek city-states. The League's name derives from the island of Delos where the treasury was housed and where meetings of the member states took place. Within a few years of the League's founding, Athens began taking advantage of its strength and forced the other member states to continue making financial contributions even after fighting with Persia had ended. As members were not allowed to secede from the League, this resulted in some city-states becoming poorer and weaker. This behavior led to conflict between Athens and the less influential members of the League, and in due course prompted the outbreak of the Peloponnesian War in 431 B.C.

---

1. The word "derives" in the passage most likely means
   - Ⓐ delivers
   - Ⓑ occurs
   - Ⓒ comes
   - Ⓓ causes

2. The phrase "secede from" in the passage is closest in meaning to
   - Ⓐ repay
   - Ⓑ leave
   - Ⓒ impede
   - Ⓓ support

3. The word "influential" in the passage is closest in meaning to
   - Ⓐ affluent
   - Ⓑ controversial
   - Ⓒ automatic
   - Ⓓ powerful

4. The phrase "in due course" in the passage is closest in meaning to
   - Ⓐ pragmatically
   - Ⓑ eventually
   - Ⓒ occasionally
   - Ⓓ optionally

King George III

George III was the monarch of Great Britain and Ireland from 1760 until his death in 1820. Numerous conflicts occurred during his reign, including the Seven Years' War, the American Revolutionary War, and campaigns against Napoleon. During his rule, George III suffered from episodes of mental illness. These occurred more frequently and became more severe in the later years of his reign, and by 1810 it was felt that he was no longer able to perform his duties as monarch, so his son, George IV, was made regent. At the time, the cause of and best way to cure his problem baffled doctors, but a recent review of medical reports from the time and analysis of samples of preserved hair from George III suggest that he was possibly suffering from arsenic-induced porphyria, a disease of the blood that can cause neurological symptoms.

5. The word "episodes" in the passage most likely means
   - (A) stories
   - (B) epics
   - (C) periods
   - (D) doubts

6. The word "severe" in the passage is closest in meaning to
   - (A) fallible
   - (B) serious
   - (C) austere
   - (D) periodic

7. The word "regent" in the passage is closest in meaning to
   - (A) ruler
   - (B) advisor
   - (C) creator
   - (D) caregiver

8. The word "baffled" in the passage most likely means
   - (A) interested
   - (B) puzzled
   - (C) treated
   - (D) dominated

Next Steps

Topics related to history and ancient history are common in the reading section of the TOEFL Test. You may also have topics about these subjects in other sections of the test. As a result, learning more about these subjects, as well as practicing key skills for Vocabulary questions, may raise your overall test score.

To learn more about history and ancient history, and vocabulary related to these disciplines:

1. Read an article in your language about one aspect of history to get some background knowledge about this topic.
2. Read an English article about the same topic to understand the main ideas, but do not try to understand every word.
3. Read the English article again. When you see an unfamiliar word, check its meaning in your dictionary. If the word has a useful prefix or word root, make a note of it and think of or find three other words with the same prefix or root. (You can find useful lists of word roots and prefixes online. Try searching for "learn word roots" or "useful academic prefixes".)

To practice key skills for Vocabulary questions:

1. If you see an unfamiliar word or phrase when you are reading, try to understand its meaning from the context.
2. Write one word or phrase that you think has the same meaning and another word or phrase that means the opposite.
3. Check your ideas in a dictionary and, if they are not a good synonym or antonym for the word, look again at the context.
4. Using a dictionary, thesaurus, or the Internet, learn one more synonym and one more antonym for each word.

Unit Focus

There are ten types of reading questions in the TOEFL Test, including Rhetorical Purpose questions. These questions test how well you can understand why the author mentions specific information in one paragraph or in the whole passage. Typically, you will get between zero and two Rhetorical Purpose questions after each passage. To answer these questions accurately, you need to practice and use several key skills that you will learn in this unit, including:

- comparing infinitives used in the answer choices with the function of the passage.
- recognizing answers that contradict information in the passage.
- recognizing answers that describe information not mentioned in the passage.

The vocabulary focus is on academic words and phrases related to:

- marine biology, the scientific study of plants and animals that live in the ocean.

A Warm-up

A1 Write short paragraphs to complete statements 1–3. Write about only one of the two options in each statement. Include a reason and example in each response. When you have finished, exchange answers with a partner and give each other feedback.

1. I would be interested / not be interested in studying marine biology because ...
2. One type of seafood that I like / dislike is ... because ...
3. My favorite / least favorite type of sea creature is ... because ...

B Academic Vocabulary

B1 Choose a highlighted word from the passage to complete each definition, 1–8. One answer has been done for you.

Marine biology is the study of organisms that live in the oceans, including fish, mammals, reptiles, birds, and plants and algae. Some marine biologists study organisms that live in shallow waters near the shore or in coastal environments that, depending on the level of the tide, are sometimes under water and sometimes above water. Others study submarine creatures found in deep water zones or even on the seabed at the bottom of the ocean. Marine biologists also study how environmental factors such as ocean currents, water temperature, and levels of pollution affect marine organisms.

1. Stable movements of water in one direction _____ currents _____
2. Organisms that are similar to plants _____
3. Related to the oceans _____
4. The area where the land meets the sea _____
5. The bottom of the ocean _____
6. The daily change in the level of the ocean _____
7. The opposite of deep _____
8. Under the water _____

C Analyzing Rhetorical Purpose Questions

Rhetorical Purpose questions focus on the reason why the author mentions something. These questions often include a phrase like "in order to," "function," or "purpose," as in the examples below. Some Rhetorical Purpose questions ask about a specific detail within a paragraph. If a word or phrase is highlighted in the question, it will also be highlighted in the passage.

The author discusses _____ in order to

Why does the author mention "_____" in paragraph 2?

You may also see Rhetorical Purpose questions that ask about the purpose of a whole paragraph, as in these examples:

What is the main function of paragraph 3?

What purpose does paragraph 4 serve in the passage as a whole?

The correct answer to Rhetorical Purpose questions:

- will not be directly stated in the passage, so you will have to use indirect evidence to recognize the author's purpose.
- will describe the most likely reason why the author mentions a specific detail or the most likely purpose of a paragraph.
- typically paraphrases words and phrases from the passage rather than repeating them.

In contrast, incorrect answers often paraphrase, summarize, or repeat information from the passage, <u>but</u>:

- may describe a purpose that paraphrases some words from the passage, but does not match the passage.
- may describe a purpose that matches a different part of the passage than the question asks about.
- may describe a purpose that is contradicted by other information in the relevant part of the passage.

TEST TACTIC

Sometimes, the position of a sentence within the paragraph can give you an idea of its function. For example, definitions often come near the start of a paragraph, but examples are more often found in the middle of a paragraph.

C1 Answer Rhetorical Purpose questions 1 and 2. Then discuss your answers with a partner.

Brightly-colored clownfish live in warm, shallow areas of the Pacific and Indian oceans where they form symbiotic relationships with a few species of sea anemone. When predators are nearby, clownfish gain protection by swimming among the anemone's tentacles, which are poisonous to other species. The tentacles also provide a safe nesting site. It is believed that clownfish are immune to the toxin because of a slimy coating on their skin. Clownfish will also eat both bits of food left over from the anemone's meal and individual tentacles that have died. In return, the waste products of clownfish are of value to sea anemones because they provide nutrients like nitrogen that are believed to promote tissue growth and regeneration. Clownfish also defend anemones from predators, keep them clean by consuming the remains of meals, and their bright colors may even lure small fish that anemones eat.

1. What is the main function of this paragraph?
   A To compare the feeding habits of clownfish with those of sea anemones
   B To discuss the ways in which clownfish benefit from being brightly colored
   C To describe the mutually beneficial relationship of sea anemones and clownfish
   D To disprove a theory about why clownfish are immune to sea anemone poison

2. The author mentions "waste products" in order to
   A suggest that clownfish get both benefits and disadvantages from sea anemones
   B argue that the only benefit sea anemones get from clownfish is access to food
   C explain how sea anemones and clownfish protect each other from predatory attacks
   D introduce an example of an advantage that clownfish bring to sea anemones

C2 Work with a partner to explain why each wrong answer to exercise **C1** is wrong. One example has been done for you.

Example   Answer 1A paraphrases some information from the passage but it is wrong because it describes a function that does not match the passage.

D Mastering Rhetorical Purpose Questions – Analyzing Infinitives in the Answer Choices

The answer choices to Rhetorical Purpose questions often begin with a full infinitive (such as *to argue*) or a bare infinitive (*argue*). Focusing on these words can help you eliminate choices that do not describe the function of the author's words.

D1 Complete this table by choosing the best infinitive from answers A–F. One answer has been done for you.

Common functions	Common infinitives in Rhetorical Purpose questions		Example phrase
make a point directly	1. *argue*	state	*
make a point indirectly	suggest	imply	*
introduce an example	2.	give an example	such as ...
say how two things differ	compare	4.	compared with ...
discuss a point in detail	explain	describe	in addition, ...
stress an important idea	3.	point out	most important ...
show that an idea is right	demonstrate	prove	this shows that ...
argue against an idea	contradict	5.	however, ...
describe a (new) concept	define	6.	known as ...

* These two functions are common, but there are no specific example phrases that can help you recognize them.

A contrast   C emphasize   E introduce
B disprove   D illustrate   F argue

D2 Choose one of the common functions from exercise **D1** to describe the function of passages 1–5. Work with a partner. One answer has been done for you.

Large areas of the ocean that have a high density of anchored kelp are known as kelp forests. Such areas form ecosystems that are both extremely productive and dynamic.

1. The function of this passage is to _____ describe a (new) concept _____ .

Some intertidal zones, such as those found on Pacific islands with a narrow tidal range, form just a thin strip of land.

2. The function of this passage is to _____
_____ .

Scientists had long considered the coelacanth to be extinct. The discovery and identification of a specimen of the fish off the coast of South Africa in 1938, however showed that, although it was rare, the species did in fact still exist.

3. The function of this passage is to _____
_____ .

Dolphins and porpoises are both cetaceans, but they differ in several ways. Compared with dolphins, porpoises tend to be smaller and stouter. They also have blunt jaws with square teeth instead of beak-like jaws with conical teeth.

4. The function of this passage is to _____
_____ .

D3 Underline the words and phrases in each passage that helped you answer exercise **D2**. When you have finished, compare your ideas with a partner.

D4 Choose the best infinitive from answers A–F to complete statements 1–5. One of the answers does NOT match any of the statements. One answer has been done for you.

Herman Melville's *Moby-Dick* tells the story of an attempt to hunt down and kill a giant sperm whale of the same name. When first published in 1851 it was criticized strongly and, as a consequence, had poor sales. It was not until the early decades of the twentieth century that critics began to recognize the power of Melville's writing. Indeed, many critics now rank the work with books like Mark Twain's *Adventures of Huckleberry Finn* as a great American novel.

1. The purpose of this paragraph is to _____contrast_____ critical opinions about Herman Melville's novel *Moby-Dick*.
2. The author mentions *Adventures of Huckleberry Finn* to _____ another well-regarded American novel.

Marine snow is the name given to the remains of dead or dying animals or plants and other organic matter that continuously descends from the upper layers of the ocean to its depths. Deep-sea organisms live at depths where sunlight cannot penetrate, so they cannot directly rely on the sun for energy. Because the composition of marine snow is largely organic, it forms the basis of an important source of energy and nutrients for such organisms.

3. The purpose of this paragraph is to _____ the concept of marine snow.
4. The author mentions "the sun" in order to _____ some oceanic organisms rely on it for energy.
5. The author mentions the "composition of marine snow" to _____ its value for some organisms.

A give an example of
B introduce
C contrast
D emphasize
E suggest
F explain

D5 Answer questions 1 and 2. Compare answers with a partner when you have finished.

Algal blooms occur when there is a rapid increase in the number of algae in a body of water, most likely as a result of increased levels of nutrients in the water. Changes in the level of nutrients may be a natural phenomenon caused by the movement of ocean currents, or may be the result of human activities like farming or industry that cause chemicals to enter the water. Algal blooms have often been noted in areas with declining populations of oysters and other shellfish that feed by filtering nutrients from the water, which implies another possible contributing factor.

Some blooms are harmful to marine organisms like dolphins and sea turtles. Such blooms are popularly known as red tides because of the characteristic reddish-brown color of the algae that cause them, although they are not tidal and do not always color the water red. In fact, blooms may change the color of the water to various hues of green, red, or brown, depending on the species of algae causing the bloom.

1. Why does the author mention "oysters and other shellfish" in paragraph 1?
   A To suggest a point indirectly
   B To contrast one point with another
   C To define a new concept

2. The author mentions "sea turtles" in paragraph 2 in order to
   A argue against an idea
   B introduce an example
   C discuss a point in detail

TEST TACTIC

When two or three answer choices have the same infinitive (or different infinitives with the same meaning), one of those answers is often correct. As a result, you should focus on those answer choices first.

E Mastering Rhetorical Purpose Questions – Analyzing the Answer Choices

Some Rhetorical Purpose questions have answers that do not include infinitives, or have several answers with infinitives that have the same meaning. For these questions, an important skill is analyzing an answer choice to recognize if it paraphrases (restates) the passage, contradicts the passage, or makes a point that is not mentioned in the passage.

E1 **Match statements A–H to the correct category. One answer has been done for you.**

Until 1960, many scientists believed that the conditions found in the deepest parts of the ocean – extreme cold and pressure more than 1,000 times the pressure at sea level – were too harsh for life. In that year, however, during a submarine voyage to the bottom of the Mariana Trench – the deepest point on Earth – living organisms were seen.

A   Challenging conditions exist at the deepest point of the oceans.
B   Scientists expected to find life at the bottom of the Mariana Trench.

King crabs are a high-value fishery. Red king crabs have the most-prized meat, followed by blue king crabs. However, populations of both these species have remained low for decades, so many fishermen focus on golden king crabs. Scarlet king crabs also have delicious meat, but are not fished commercially owing to their small size and rarity.

C   Populations of red and blue king crabs have been increasing for decades.
D   Golden king crabs are easier to catch than red or blue king crabs.

Seaweeds, like plants, derive energy from the sun through the process of photosynthesis. Despite this, biologists classify them as algae, not plants since, among other things, they have no need for tissues with specialist functions such as roots, leaves, or a vascular system for transporting nutrients, water, and other resources.

E   Unlike seaweeds, plants have tissues that have specialist functions.
F   Seaweeds grow in warm waters to obtain more energy from the sun.

Swordfish are named for the characteristic sword-shaped bill that extends a meter or more beyond their body, and which they use to kill prey such as squid, fish, and crustaceans. Like other billfish, swordfish are large, predatory fish – up to 4 meters in length or more – and exhibit sexual dimorphism in that females grow bigger than males. They are found in all of the world's oceans at depths above 500 meters or so, which is another trait shared by other billfish.

G   Swordfish resemble other kinds of billfish.
H   Female swordfish are not as large as males.

Answers that paraphrase the passage
• _Challenging conditions for life exist at the deepest points of the oceans._
•
•

Answers that contradict the passage
•
•
•

Answers that are not mentioned in the passage
•
•

E2 Rewrite the answers to exercise **E1** that contradict the passage so that they paraphrase the passage. Compare your rewritten answers with a partner when you have finished.

E3 Answer questions 1–5. If neither answer A nor B is correct, write your own answer.

Pinnipeds, the scientific name for seals, sea lions and fur seals, and walruses, are classified as a superfamily of marine mammals. They are semi-aquatic, meaning they spend time both on land and in the water. Like other mammals that sleep in water, only one hemisphere of the brain of a pinniped sleeps at a time. This allows them to maintain a sufficient level of consciousness to breathe and detect and avoid predators. Recent analyses of the brains of sleeping seals have suggested that a specific neurotransmitter, a chemical that affects the brain, may be responsible for the different level of consciousness of each hemisphere. As the neurotransmitter in question, acetylcholine, is found in many organisms, there is a possibility that this finding will enable better understanding of sleep mechanisms in other species, including humans.

1. What is the main function of this passage?
   A To explain the lifestyle of pinnipeds
   B To explain the way that pinnipeds sleep
   C _____ *your answer* _____

2. Why does the author mention "acetylcholine"?
   A To identify a substance that may explain pinniped sleep patterns
   B To identify a cause of consciousness in pinnipeds and other species
   C _____ *your answer* _____

Reefs form in shallow, coastal waters when individual coral polyps become attached to a submarine rock or the seabed. When the polyps die, their exoskeleton of calcium carbonate – the same material as limestone – remains. Over time, additional polyps attach themselves to these skeletal remains and the reef grows. The health and growth of coral reefs require specific water conditions. The water must be clean, warm but not too warm (roughly 20–29 degrees Celsius, which is 68–84 degrees Fahrenheit), and clear enough for sunlight to reach the coral. If any of these conditions are not met, corals either grow slowly or become damaged and eventually die, as is happening now in many places.

It has been estimated that about 10% of coral reefs are already dead with at least 60% more at risk. Several general factors are thought to be the cause, including warmer waters caused by a rise in global temperatures. Climate change has also caused a rise in sea levels, which is another factor. Higher levels of CO_2 in the atmosphere mean more CO_2 is taken up by the oceans, leading to more acidic water that can dissolve the calcium carbonate of the coral polyps' skeletons.

3. Why does the author mention "limestone" in paragraph 1?
   A To clarify the meaning of a scientific expression
   B To clarify the type of rock coral polyps attach to
   C _____ *your answer* _____

4. The author mentions water temperatures in paragraph 1 in order to
   A give an example of a condition that can kill coral polyps
   B give an example of how sunlight warms the oceans
   C _____ *your answer* _____

5. What purpose does paragraph 2 serve in the passage as a whole?
   A To describe conditions that cause coral reefs to grow slowly
   B To describe the factors that are affecting climate change
   C _____ *your answer* _____

E4 Which words in the passages, questions, and answers helped you complete exercise **E3**? Discuss with a partner.

> **TEST TACTIC**
>
> When a question asks about the function of a specific highlighted phrase, the information that gives you the answer is often found either in the sentence that contains the specific phrase, or in the sentence just before or after it.

F Test Challenge

F1 Answer Rhetorical Purpose questions 1–6. Try to finish in 9 minutes or less so as to get realistic practice for the test. Use the checklist of skills you learned in this unit as a guide.

☑ Analyze infinitives in the answer to eliminate answers that do not match the function of the passage

☑ Eliminate answer choices that contradict the passage or include details not mentioned in the passage

---

Octopus Defenses

Octopuses can employ a number of defensive behaviors when threatened. They have a hard beak with which to bite predators, and many, if not all, species of octopus are venomous, so this bite can be fatal. However, octopuses usually prefer to avoid confrontations and when threatened they usually either hide or try to escape. When they need to move quickly, octopuses can suck in and then expel water in the form of a jet. It is a seldom-used, energy-intensive method of movement, but it allows them to move fast and with great acceleration when threatened.

Probably the most well-known defensive strategy of the octopus is to expel ink. The ink contains mucus and melanin, a natural color-forming pigment found in most organisms. If an octopus expels a lot of ink, it spreads out in the water and forms a dark cloud that hides the octopus from its attacker. In other cases, an octopus might expel a smaller quantity of ink that contains a higher concentration of mucus, allowing the ink to hold its form for longer and make a cloud that can be similar in shape to the octopus itself. This can confuse a predator into attacking the ink, not the octopus.

---

1. The primary purpose of paragraph 1 is to
   - Ⓐ explain why the bite of octopuses is venomous
   - Ⓑ describe how octopuses try to avoid being attacked
   - Ⓒ describe where octopuses usually hide from danger
   - Ⓓ illustrate different methods of octopus locomotion

2. Why does the author mention "melanin" in paragraph 2?
   - Ⓐ To suggest that many organisms can produce ink
   - Ⓑ To emphasize that octopus ink is very colorful
   - Ⓒ To imply that melanin is the main component of ink
   - Ⓓ To explain the reason why octopus ink is colored

3. Why does the author discuss the concentration of mucus in octopus ink in paragraph 2?
   - Ⓐ To explain why predators prefer attacking ink clouds instead of octopuses
   - Ⓑ To clarify why some expelled ink clouds retain their structure for longer
   - Ⓒ To argue that predators are confused when the ink contains little melanin
   - Ⓓ To explain why the ability of octopuses to expel ink is so well-known

---

Scientific Nomenclature

In biology, all life is classified according to shared physical characteristics, with international scientific authorities recognizing seven main ranks. The ranks are hierarchical in that top level ranks are more general and contain fewer members than each successive lower level. The first rank is the kingdom, which describes whether an organism is an animal, a plant, a fungus, and so on. The two ranks below kingdom are phylum (in zoology) or division (in botany) and then class. Below class are order, family, and then genus and species, the two most basic ranks. The binomial, or two-part, scientific name of a species is a combination of its genus name and its species name.

The way this system works can be seen by looking at the classification of two marine organisms. The blue whale is a member of the class Mammalia, or mammals, the order Cetacea, or whales, dolphins, and porpoises, and the family Balaenopteridae, or baleen whales. Its genus and species are *Balaenoptera* and *Balaenoptera musculus* respectively. The blue shark, on the other hand, is classified as belonging to the class Chondrichthyes, meaning cartilaginous fish, the order Carcharhiniformes, and the family Carcharhinidae, which includes 51 other species of requiem sharks as they are informally, but commonly, known in English. The genus name is *Prionace* and the species name is *Prionace glauca*.

4. What is the main function of paragraph 1?
   - (A) To compare different kinds of organisms
   - (B) To define a method for ranking kingdoms
   - (C) To describe a scientific classification system
   - (D) To illustrate the benefits of classifying organisms

5. The author mentions zoology and botany in order to
   - (A) emphasize how these subjects differ from one another
   - (B) demonstrate how the number of scientific ranks can differ
   - (C) explain the usage of two different but equivalent rank names
   - (D) imply that botanists and zoologists rarely talk to each other

6. In paragraph 2, the author's primary purpose is to
   - (A) give specific examples of the biological classification of organisms
   - (B) contrast the scientific names of whales, dolphins, porpoises, and sharks
   - (C) explain why the color of an animal is not reflected in its scientific name
   - (D) give a general overview of the ways in which whales and sharks differ

Next Steps

Topics related to marine biology are common in the reading section of the TOEFL Test. You may also have topics about this subject in the other sections of the test. As a result, learning more about this subject, as well as practicing key skills for Rhetorical Purpose questions, may raise your overall test score.

To learn more about marine biology and vocabulary related to this discipline:

1. Read widely about marine biology in your language. This will give you useful background knowledge of the subject.
2. Read an English article about a topic related to marine biology several times until you understand the main concepts.
3. Read the English article again and make a list of unfamiliar words related to marine biology. Then do an Internet search for each word on your list and note the number of times it can be found on the Internet. (Most search engines list the number of results at the top of the page.) Then study and learn the ten most common words.

To practice key skills for Rhetorical Purpose questions:

1. Find a short article about marine biology (or another subject) online and choose one paragraph from the article.
2. Write a short, simple description of the purpose of every sentence in the article. For example, you might describe a sentence in an article by writing "This sentence defines bioluminescence." or "This sentence compares crabs and lobsters."
3. Next, use your descriptions of the function of each sentence to write a simple description of the function of the whole paragraph. For example, you might write "This paragraph describes how marine creatures use bioluminescence," or "This paragraph discusses the economic importance of crab and lobster fishing."
4. If possible, compare your sentence and paragraph descriptions with those written by a study partner and discuss any differences of opinion.

UNIT 4
READING • Inference Questions

Unit Focus

There are ten types of reading questions in the TOEFL Test, including Inference questions. These questions test how well you can recognize ideas and points that are suggested by the author, but not directly stated in the passage. Typically, you will see one or two Inference questions after each reading passage. To answer Inference questions accurately, you need to be able to "read between the lines," which involves using several key skills that you will learn in this unit, including:

- recognizing key phrases in the question that will help you find the right information in the passage.
- distinguishing between ideas that are stated directly in the passage and ideas that are mentioned indirectly.

The vocabulary focus is on academic words and phrases related to:

- ecology, the scientific study of the connections among plants, animals, people, and the environment.

A Warm-up

A1 Work with a partner. Deliver a short speech in response to topics 1 and 2. Organize your answers well and speak for up to 45 seconds. After each speech, give your partner feedback.

1. Some people think that humans are the biggest threat (danger) to the environment. Do you agree or disagree with this idea? Why? Support your opinion with details and examples.
2. What is one thing that you think everybody in your country could do to protect the environment? Support your position with details and examples.

B Academic Vocabulary

B1 Choose the word from answers A–H that best completes the definitions of the highlighted words in sentences 1–8. One answer has been done for you.

1. Biodiversity, or biological diversity, is the term used to describe the _____variety_____ of all forms of life found in a certain habitat.
2. A large, naturally-occurring ecological _____ of plants and animals in a particular habitat is known as a biome.
3. Conservation is the act of providing _____ to endangered species so that they survive. Preservation is a synonym.
4. Deforestation occurs when many of the trees in a heavily-wooded _____ are cut down but not replanted.
5. Scientists define an ecosystem as a group of organisms that interact with one another and with their _____.
6. In ecology, the word habitat has the specific meaning of the natural conditions and environment in which _____ live.
7. A predator, such as a wolf or lion, is a(n) _____ that actively hunts and kills other organisms in order to survive.
8. A prey species is one that is eaten by a(n) _____ species. Typically, prey species are more numerous than predators.

A community	C organism	E protection	G species
B environment	D predator	F region	H variety

C Analyzing Inference Questions

Inference questions ask about ideas that are indirectly mentioned in the passage. They typically include words like "infer," "imply," "conclude," or "suggest," as these examples show. Most inference questions either state the paragraph in which the answer can be found, or include a specific reference that allows you to find the paragraph(s) easily:

What can be inferred from paragraph 2 about _____ _____?

What does the author imply about _____ described in paragraph 3?

What can be concluded from paragraph 4 about the recent actions of _____?

What does the author suggest might happen to _____ if _____ were to occur?

The correct answer to Inference questions:
- must be suggested in the passage rather than directly stated.
- is generally related to the main idea of the passage and/or the main topic of the relevant paragraph.

In contrast, incorrect answers:
- may seem to restate an idea from the passage, but actually contradict information in the passage.
- may seem like a reasonable answer to the question, but are neither mentioned nor implied in the passage.

TEST TACTIC

If two of the answer choices for an Inference question have opposite or very different meanings, there is a chance that one of those two answers is correct. If you focus on those two choices first, you might be able to save time.

C1 **Answer Inference questions 1 and 2. When you have finished, discuss your answers with a partner.**

The modern discipline of ecology began in the latter part of the nineteenth century with the publication of works first by German biologist Ernst Haeckel and then by Danish botanist Eugen Warming. Haeckel gave the discipline its name in a work written in 1866, while Warming was the first to write a textbook and teach a university course on the subject. This is not to say that the concepts and principles of ecology were unknown before Haeckel and Warming. Many previous scholars, including Aristotle and Theophrastus in classical times, van Leeuwenhoek and Bradley in the early part of the 1700s, and then Lamarck, von Humboldt, and Darwin, developed and wrote about various concepts – including soil nutrient, cycles, food chains, and population regulation – that are now considered aspects of ecology.

1. Which of these statements can be inferred from the passage?
   A Warming's textbook on ecology was published in 1866, the same year as Haeckel's work.
   B Haeckel's work in 1866 described several concepts that are now considered aspects of ecology.
   C Warming's first university course on the discipline of ecology was popular among students.
   D Scientists studied ecological ideas before 1866, but did not describe their subject as ecology.

2. What can be concluded from the passage?
   A Darwin and von Humboldt worked together to develop their concepts.
   B Lamarck's work came after that of van Leeuwenhoek and Bradley.
   C Darwin's ideas about ecology were based on work by von Humboldt.
   D Aristotle and Theophrastus knew of each other's work on ecology.

C2 **Match the wrong answers from C1 to description 1 or 2. Work with a partner. One answer has been done for you.**

1. The answer choice seems to restate the passage, but contradicts, adds, or omits a key detail.	1A
2. The answer choice seems like a reasonable answer, but is not mentioned or implied in the passage.	

D Mastering Inference Questions – Analyzing the Question

An important skill for answering Inference questions is recognizing key phrases in the question. Recognizing these key phrases can help you more easily find the sentences in the passage where the answer will be implied.

D1 Match the underlined phrases in this example Inference question to the correct description. One answer has been done for you.

What can be <u>inferred</u>^A from <u>paragraph 4</u> about the <u>effects of wildfires</u>?

A   This word or phrase tells you that this is an Inference question.
B   This phrase tells you in which paragraph of the passage you should look for the answer.
C   This phrase tells you to look for sentences in the passage that are related to this specific topic.

D2 Work with a partner to explain why the underlined phrases in example Inference questions 1–4 are key phrases. Use the descriptions from exercise **D1** as a guide.

1.   What can be <u>inferred</u> from <u>paragraph 2</u> about <u>food webs</u>?
2.   In <u>paragraph 3</u>, what does the author <u>imply</u> about the <u>keystone species model</u>?
3.   What can be <u>concluded</u> from <u>paragraph 4</u> about the <u>recent actions of conservationists</u>?
4.   What does the author <u>suggest</u> might happen to <u>European oak trees</u> if <u>moderate climate change</u> were to occur?

D3 Underline the key phrases in example Inference questions 1–4. Be prepared to say why you think each phrase is a key phrase.

1.   What does the author imply about biodiversity in paragraph 1?
2.   What does the author suggest about the role of earthworms in maintaining soil fertility?
3.   What can be understood about the difference between biotic and abiotic environments?
4.   What can be inferred from paragraph 3 about the importance of honeybees to agriculture?

D4 Identify the key phrases in questions 1–4. Then underline the sentence(s) in the passage that give information about the key phrases. When you have finished, compare your underlined sentences with a partner.

Although they were once considered to be purely destructive events to be prevented if possible, modern ecologists view wildfires as a natural disturbance that shapes habitats much like floods, storms, or landslides do. Indeed, several ecosystems rely on regular wildfires to ensure their ongoing vitality just as other species depend on other natural events. Within these ecosystems, species may be fire dependent, meaning they rely on fires to change the local environment in beneficial ways. Other species are fire adapted, meaning they have traits that allow them to survive fires, such as fire-resistant bark, the ability to grow rapidly after a fire, or seeds that need intense heat to germinate.

1.   What does the author suggest about the effects of natural disturbances like wildfires?
2.   What can be concluded about how fire-dependent and fire-adapted organisms differ?

Two books were published in 1962 – *Our Synthetic Environment* by Murray Bookchin using the pen-name Lewis Herber, and *Silent Spring* by Rachel Carson – that are generally considered to have begun the modern movement to protect the environment. At first, the movement focused on limiting the use of chemical pesticides, but over time other issues have become more important, including nuclear power, acid rain, and now climate change. The widespread use of expressions with *eco-* as a prefix, including eco-friendly, eco-awareness, and eco-tourism, show how mainstream the movement has become.

3.   What can be inferred about the author of the book *Our Synthetic Environment*?
4.   What is implied about how the environmental protection movement has changed?

TEST TACTIC

In general, the correct answer can be found in or close to the sentence(s) that match key phrases in the question. If you think the correct answer is implied in a sentence that is not close to the relevant sentence(s), you might have made a mistake.

D5 Use the three steps to help you answer questions 1–4. Then compare answers with a partner.

Step 1	Identify the key phrases in question 1. Then scan the passage to find sentence(s) that include these key phrases.
Step 2	Read the sentence(s) in the passage that you found in task 1. Then answer question 1.
Step 3	Repeat steps 1 and 2 for questions 2, 3, and 4.

Estimates vary, but it is likely several billion Passenger Pigeons lived in North America at the start of the nineteenth century. Yet several factors caused them to go extinct in just over 100 years. The birds depended on hardwood forests for food as well as for nesting and roosting sites. Massive deforestation meant the birds not only had fewer places to nest and roost but also had to turn to farmers' fields for food, which led to farmers shooting the birds to protect their crops. Professionals also began killing the birds on an industrial scale as a source of cheap, easy-to-hunt meat. The flocks were so enormous that bands of hunters were frequently able to kill 50,000 or more birds a day for months at a time. Eventually, the twin pressures of habitat destruction and hunting reduced the number of survivors significantly. At this point, the bird's behavior became a factor in its own decline. Passenger Pigeons were a communal species, meaning they were only able to breed when part of a large flock. As the population continued to fall, flocks became too small for optimum breeding, and fewer and fewer young hatched each year until, by the 1890s, the bird had almost completely died out. The final Passenger Pigeon is believed to have died in the Cincinnati Zoo in 1914.

1. What does the author imply about Passenger Pigeons at the start of the nineteenth century?
   A The number of birds had declined since the eighteenth century.
   B There were so many birds it was impossible to count them accurately.

2. What can be concluded about the feeding habits of Passenger Pigeons?
   A They found food in the same place they nested and slept.
   B They preferred agricultural crops to other food sources.

3. What does the author suggest about the hunting of Passenger Pigeons?
   A There were only a few professional hunters.
   B Hunting the birds was not a difficult task.

4. What can be inferred from this paragraph about the extinction of Passenger Pigeons?
   A The last pigeon was not killed as a direct result of hunting or habitat loss.
   B The species went extinct because the surviving birds could no longer breed.

E Mastering Inference Questions – Recognizing Implied Information

Another key skill for Inference questions is distinguishing between information that is stated directly in the passage and information that is implied. It is also useful to recognize answers that express an idea that is not mentioned in the passage.

Track 1 **E1** Listen to part of a TOEFL class. The teacher and students are talking about Inference questions. Complete this summary of the ideas they discuss by adding the correct example, A or B, to 1 and 2.

Information that is directly stated in the passage can help you make a conclusion. For example, 1. _____. Another technique is to imagine some words are missing from the passage. If those words are added, the indirect meaning becomes direct. For example, 2. _____

A if a writer says "there was no rain and many animals died," it is possible to imagine adding the explanation "because they had no water" to make the writer's idea direct.

B if a passage says a book was published in 1962, we can conclude that the author of that book was born before 1962.

E2 Practice recognizing inferences by reading these passages and then answering questions 1–4.

A very simple example of the often complex feeding relationships among different species can be seen with foxes and rabbits. The former feed on rabbits, which in turn eat grasses and other plants, which ultimately derive energy from the sun. This kind of linear sequence in which one species depends for food on another species is called a food chain, or, when all the interlinked food chains in an ecological community are considered together, a food web.

1. Which answer can be inferred from the passage?
   A   Food chains usually include only three species.
   B   Food webs are more complex than food chains.

2. Which highlighted phrase in the passage helps you answer question 1?
   A   grasses and other plants, which ultimately derive energy from the sun
   B   the interlinked food chains in an ecological community are considered together, a food web

The keystone species model lends itself to computer simulation. In simple terms, a keystone species is one that plays an essential role in maintaining an ecological community even though it is not very abundant. The classic example of a keystone species can be seen in simulations like "fox and rabbit" in which a small population of foxes controls the number of rabbits in a simplified ecosystem. By varying the conditions of the simulation, such as the size of the initial population of foxes or rabbits, or the availability of food plants, different outcomes can be observed. If the initial conditions of the simulation lead to a decline in the number of ■ the keystone species, the number of rabbits may keep rising until all their food plants have been eaten, which in turn leads to a crash in their population.

3. What can be concluded from the passage?
   A   Foxes are sometimes considered a keystone species.
   B   Simulations of the keystone species model are accurate.

4. Which phrase could be added to the passage at the square (■) so that the answer to question 3 is stated directly?
   A   foxes, which are
   B   simulations of

E3 Read these passages. Then check (✓) the box to indicate if each statement is Stated directly, Implied, or Not mentioned. Compare your answers with a partner when you have finished. One answer has been done for you.

In the natural world, all organisms interact with other organisms. Two male deer of the same species fighting each other during breeding season, for instance, is an example of intraspecific competition. Other kinds of intraspecific interaction include cooperation and antagonism. Interspecific interactions, in contrast, occur when two different species interact in some way, such as when a bee pollinates a flower.

1. Intraspecific interactions occur among individuals of the same species.
   ☐ Stated directly   ☑ Implied   ☐ Not mentioned
2. An interspecific interaction occurs between two species.
   ☐ Stated directly   ☐ Implied   ☐ Not mentioned

Amensalism is the name given to a type of biological interaction in which the behavior or a product of one organism has no effect on that organism but a detrimental effect on other organisms. The classic example is the black walnut tree which secretes a chemical called juglone into the soil that harms most other species of plants living nearby and can also affect humans who come into contact with it. Commensalism is the opposite of amensalism.

3. Black walnut trees are unaffected by juglone.
   ☐ Stated directly   ☐ Implied   ☐ Not mentioned
4. Animals living near black walnut trees are harmed by juglone.
   ☐ Stated directly   ☐ Implied   ☐ Not mentioned

E4 Use the skills you have learned to answer questions 1 and 2.

Mutualism occurs when two organisms interact in a way that benefits both individuals. Cooperation differs from mutualism in that it occurs between two individuals of the same species. Mutualism can be classified according to the nature of the relationship. In resource-resource interactions, the most common type, each individual provides a resource, such as nutrients, that benefits the other. In a service-resource interaction, one species provides a service to the other and in return gets access to a resource. The Oxpecker, for example, is a bird that eats disease-causing ticks and other parasites that live on the skin of some species of large mammals. Service-service interactions are the final, and rarest, type of mutualism. In such interactions, both species give and receive a beneficial service, such as protection from predators. Most service-service relationships also have a service-resource or even a resource-resource aspect.

1. What can be inferred about mutualistic relationships? *Choose two answers.*
   A They are the most common interaction between species.
   B They occur between individuals of different species.
   C Relatively few species practice such relationships.
   D They involve a mutually advantageous exchange.

2. What is implied about service-resource interactions? *Choose two answers.*
   A They are rarer than resource-resource relationships.
   B They benefit some species more than others.
   C They commonly involve an exchange of nutrients.
   D One species may protect the other from illness.

TEST TACTIC

If an Inference question is hard, try thinking about it as a Rhetorical Purpose question. For example, change the question "What is implied about prey species" into "Why does the author mention prey species?" This might help you recognize the implication more easily.

F Test Challenge

F1 Answer Inference questions 1–8. Try to finish in 12 minutes or less so as to get realistic practice for the test. Use the checklist of skills you learned in this unit as a guide.

☑ Read the question carefully and note key words that will help you choose the right answer.

☑ Find the key sentence(s) in the passage that include the key words. Read these sentences carefully.

☑ Compare the answer choices with the key sentence(s) and select the answer that implies the same idea.

Conservation of California Condors

California Condors first received protection in 1967 under the US Endangered Species Preservation Act and were then formally identified and protected as part of the US Endangered Species Act of 1972. The California Condor Recovery Plan was passed in 1975 with the aim of increasing the number of birds by preserving their natural habitat. The Plan was revised in 1979 with a continued focus on habitat preservation, plus a project to breed Condors in captivity for release into the wild. A further revision in 1984 recognized that the continued decline in Condor numbers made more intensive and urgent action necessary, especially efforts to increase the low reproductive rates of the birds. By 1986 the Condor was on the brink of extinction, with just 22 birds still alive, only three of which were in the wild. A decision was made that the only hope for the species was to capture the last remaining wild birds and focus on captive breeding.

Initial efforts to breed the birds in captivity met with limited success, but by 1992 researchers felt confident enough to try reintroducing the species into the wild; there were problems, however, and a decision was made in 1994 to recapture the released birds. Another attempt at releasing captive birds into the wild was made in 1995, again in southern California, but this time with more success. In 1996 the California Condor Recovery Plan was revised again with a continued emphasis on captive breeding and a new aim of reintroducing the species into the wild. Further release sites in Arizona, central California, and northwestern Mexico were chosen in 1996, 1997, and 2002 respectively. The results of these conservation efforts and plans have been very successful.

The International Union for the Conservation of Nature (IUCN) lists the California Condor as critically endangered still, a status reserved for those species most at risk of extinction, but the number of birds alive now is estimated at more than 400, with more than 200 of those living in the wild. Despite this success, a review of the California Condor Recovery Plan in 2008 argued that without sustained investment and human intervention, the species might again become extinct in the wild. As the total cost of the conservation efforts to date is roughly $40 million, and ongoing costs are likely to run to several million dollars per year, continued investment and intervention cannot be assured.

1. What does the author suggest about efforts to preserve the habitat of California Condors?
   - Ⓐ   They began in 1972 when the US Endangered Species Act passed.
   - Ⓑ   Optimum habitat conditions for California Condors are hard to find.
   - Ⓒ   They were not successful at increasing the number of Condors.
   - Ⓓ   They were effective after the California Condor Recovery Plan was revised.

2. The author implies that the first release of captive Condors into the wild
   - Ⓐ   took place in the southern part of California
   - Ⓑ   was more successful than people had expected
   - Ⓒ   occurred after the successful release of other species
   - Ⓓ   led to the creation of a new conservation plan

3. What can be concluded about the IUCN?
   - Ⓐ   It lists the conservation status of numerous bird species.
   - Ⓑ   It has out of date information about the number of Condors.
   - Ⓒ   It played an important role in the conservation of Condors.
   - Ⓓ   It only records how many of a given bird species live in the wild.

4. What can be inferred about future of the California Condor?
   - Ⓐ   It is highly unlikely that the bird will become extinct in the wild.
   - Ⓑ   It will cost approximately $40 million to preserve the species.
   - Ⓒ   Condors are no longer in danger because of past conservation work.
   - Ⓓ   The cost of continued conservation efforts might be too high.

Tropical Rainforests

Tropical rainforests are found in equatorial regions. They are characterized by high average temperatures of 24 degrees Celsius or more, annual rainfall in excess of 8,000 millimeters, and relatively little seasonal change in weather. Examples of this type of biome can be found in southeast Asia, Africa, and Central and South America. Another defining characteristic is their incredible biodiversity. To take one example, a typical temperate forest may have just a handful of species of trees in total; a tropical rainforest may have close to 500 species of trees in just 10,000 square meters. Tropical rainforests are the most biologically diverse ecosystems on the planet, containing perhaps 50% of all species of animals and plants, many of which have still not been given a scientific classification.

The products of these biomes are essential to modern society. More than 3,000 commonly eaten foods are originally from tropical rainforests, including avocados, citrus fruits, bananas, tomatoes, corn, potatoes, rice, chocolate, ginger, coffee, and some nuts. In addition, tropical rainforests are a valuable source of medicines. Up to a quarter of modern pharmaceuticals derive from tropical rainforests. Just a fraction of tropical rainforest plants have been surveyed for their medicinal value, and scientists working for universities, governments, and drug companies are convinced that additional compounds of medical value will be found among such species. Sadly, industries like cattle ranching and logging are causing considerable deforestation resulting in the extinction of an estimated 100-plus species daily.

5. What can be concluded about temperate forests from paragraph 1?
  - (A) They receive about as much rain as tropical rainforests.
  - (B) They are usually smaller than tropical rainforests.
  - (C) They have less biodiversity than tropical rainforests.
  - (D) They are found in the same regions as tropical rainforests.

6. Which of the following can be inferred from paragraph 1?
  - (A) A total of about 500 species of trees can be found in tropical rainforests.
  - (B) Species found in tropical rainforests look very different from one another.
  - (C) A number of species in tropical rainforests have not been identified.
  - (D) About half of all species in tropical rainforests are animals or plants.

7. Which of these ideas does the author suggest about drugs in paragraph 2?
  - (A) Medically-useful compounds may be found in unsurveyed plant species.
  - (B) Most species that provide medically useful drugs have already been surveyed.
  - (C) Tropical rainforests are a less useful source of drugs than other ecosystems.
  - (D) Common food items may contain drugs that could become valuable medicines.

8. What does the author imply about deforestation? *Choose two answers.*
  - [A] It does not yet affect medically-useful species.
  - [B] It is caused by human activities.
  - [C] It may cause the loss of valuable species.
  - [D] It is sad, but necessary for modern society.

Next Steps

Topics related to ecology are common in all four sections of the TOEFL Test. As a result, learning more about this subject, as well as practicing key skills for Inference questions, may raise your overall test score.

To learn more about ecology and vocabulary related to this discipline:

1. Read an article in your language about one aspect of ecology to get some background knowledge about this topic.
2. Read again and make a list of useful words for ecology. Use a dictionary to find the English translation for these words.
3. Read an English article about the same topic. First, understand the main ideas. Then read again in order to identify which of the words you studied in step 2 are used in the English article.

To practice a key skill for Inference questions:

Find an article in English about ecology (or another subject you find interesting). Read the article and find an opinion, idea, or point that the writer states directly. Decide how to change this section of the article so that the opinion, idea, or point is implied not stated. For example, you might have to cut some words or phrases from the original article, or rewrite some phrases using less direct language. By learning how to change direct statements into indirect ones, you will improve your ability to recognize and understand implied ideas in both the reading and listening sections of the TOEFL Test.

Unit Focus

There are ten types of reading questions in the TOEFL Test, including Sentence Simplification questions. These questions ask you to look at a highlighted sentence in the passage and choose the answer that paraphrases the major ideas in that sentence. Typically, you will get one Sentence Simplification question after each passage, but some passages may not have this type of question. To answer Sentence Simplification questions accurately, you need to learn and practice several key skills, including:

- recognizing answer choices that either restate or simplify a sentence from the passage.
- recognizing the function of sentences from the passage and the answer choices to the question.
- recognizing answer choices that leave out or change essential information.

The vocabulary focus is on academic words and phrases related to two academic disciplines:

- anthropology, the study of human cultures, and archaeology, the study of human history by analyzing found objects.

A Warm-up

A1 Which of the books described below would you NOT like to read? Give a speech explaining your opinion and reason.

A number of classic but controversial works of anthropology were published in the twentieth century, including *Coming of Age in Samoa* (1928), by Margaret Mead, a book about the lives of teenagers on the Pacific island of Ta'u; *The Chrysanthemum and the Sword* (1946), by Ruth Benedict, which discusses Japanese culture; and *Yanomamö: the Fierce People* (1968), by Napoleon Chagnon, which is about a group living in the Amazon rainforest.

B Academic Vocabulary

B1 Complete this table with one of the definitions, A–H. Check your answers with a partner when you have finished. One answer has been done for you.

Word	Part of speech	Prefix, suffix, or word root		Definition
1. artifact	noun	fac	*make / do*	F
2. ceremony	noun	—		
3. decipher	verb	cipher	*a code / mystery*	
4. descend	verb	de	*down / from*	
5. excavation	noun	ex	*out of / away* from	
6. indigenous	adjective	gen	*race / kind*	
7. inherit	verb	—		
8. kinship	noun	ship	*relation between*	

A to come from a particular ancestor (a relative who lived in the past)
B to receive something when a person, usually a relative, dies
C a formal ritual event, such as a marriage or funeral
D a relationship, either by birth or marriage, to other people
E describing people who come from a particular place
F a historically important object made by humans
G to make sense of an unknown code or writing system
H the act of digging something out from the ground

C Analyzing Sentence Simplification Questions

Sentence Simplification questions test how well you can recognize answers that restate or simplify a highlighted sentence in the passage. These questions always have the same directions:

> Which of the following best expresses the essential information in the highlighted sentence in paragraph 2? Incorrect choices change the meaning in important ways or leave out essential information.

Note that Sentence Simplification questions focus on one highlighted sentence only. To answer them, you do not need to spend any time reading the other, non-highlighted sentences in the passage.

The correct answer to Sentence Simplification questions:

- almost always paraphrases the ideas from the highlighted sentence rather than using the same words.
- may simplify the highlighted sentence, but will not omit any of the major ideas in that sentence.
- usually has the same function as the highlighted sentence, such as contrasting two ideas or giving the cause of a particular situation.

In contrast, incorrect answers usually include some words from the highlighted sentence, but may:

- change key information from the highlighted sentence or include an idea not in that sentence.
- summarize only part of the highlighted sentence and leave out an essential idea or detail.
- change the function of the highlighted sentence by, for example, describing the effect of a situation, not its cause.

TEST TACTIC

Sometimes the highlighted sentence includes a word or phrase like "it" or "this project" that refers to an idea in the previous sentence. In these cases, you should read the previous sentence quickly to understand the reference.

C1 Answer the following Sentence Simplification question. When you have finished, discuss with a partner.

The aim of participant observation, a traditional data-collection technique used by anthropologists, is to gain a deep, first-hand understanding of a group of people by spending time with them in their cultural environment. Several levels of participant observation have been identified: passive, moderate, and active. In passive participation, the researcher closely watches, but does not engage with, the group being studied. Moderate participation includes more involvement with the group, but the researcher still preserves some distance from it to remain emotionally detached and objective. Active participation requires the researcher to accept and adopt completely the customs and behaviors of the group to gain the most complete understanding possible.

1. Which of the following best expresses the essential information in the first highlighted sentence? Incorrect choices change the meaning in important ways or leave out essential information.
   A Anthropologists seek to observe an environment in which a group of people spend time.
   B Collecting data about various groups of people allows anthropologists to understand those people's traditions.
   C An established way for anthropologists to understand a group is to spend time in its environment.
   D By observing a group for a period of time, anthropologists aim to become part of its cultural environment.

2. Which of the following best expresses the essential information in the second highlighted sentence? Incorrect choices change the meaning in important ways or leave out essential information.

   A Moderate participation requires the researcher both to participate with the group and to retain objectivity.
   B The researcher must stay emotionally separate from the group when engaging in moderate participation.
   C The objective of moderate participation is to allow the group being studied to become involved in the research.
   D An increased level of engagement with the group by the researcher is a feature of moderate participation.

C2 Match the wrong answers from **C1** to description 1 or 2. Work with a partner. One answer has been done for you.

1. The answer choice changes some essential information from the highlighted sentence.	1A
2. The answer choice leaves out some essential information from the highlighted sentence.	

D Mastering Sentence Simplification Questions – Recognizing Restated and Simplified Answers

A key skill for answering Sentence Simplification questions accurately is recognizing the answer choice that either restates or simplifies the essential ideas from the highlighted sentence.

D1 Which answer, A or B, restates the essential information in the highlighted sentence in these short passages? The incorrect choice changes the meaning in important ways.

In one model of human social development used by anthropologists, societies are organized in one of four ways. In order of increasing complexity and size, these are called bands, tribes, chiefdoms, and states. In the modern world, most societies are states; in earlier times, however, bands, tribes, and chiefdoms were more common.

1A. Bands, tribes, chiefdoms, and states are all large and increasingly complex types of organized human society.

1B. When ranked from simplest to most complex and smallest to largest, societies can be bands, tribes, chiefdoms, or states.

Bands, the simplest form of human society, are typically made up of a group of related individuals, usually numbering no more than 100. They are often egalitarian, with decisions being shaped by informal leaders and agreed upon by consensus. Every band that has been studied has practiced hunting and gathering.

2A. Bands usually do not have formal chiefs and each member has the same amount of authority to make decisions.

2B. Members of a band often act informally and rarely make decisions unless they agree that the decision makes sense.

Tribes are more difficult to define, but in general terms, tribal societies are formed from bands that are politically integrated under a formal leader or council of elders. Each member of the tribe usually shares the same language, culture, and ideology. The term ethnic group is now often used in preference to tribe.

3A. Although it is hard to define the term, tribes are usually composed of bands under the political control of a leader.

3B. Tribes are formally defined as a band that is led by a group of politically-integrated elders or chiefs.

Chiefdoms typically consist of a number of communities under the permanent control of a chief or group of leaders. Usually the community in which the chief lives is the dominant community; smaller subsidiary communities, each with their own leader who is subservient to the overall chief, often form part of the chiefdom, too.

4A. The leaders of each community in a chiefdom usually move to the dominant community from subsidiary communities.

4B. Chiefdoms often have one main community in which the chief resides, plus other smaller, less important communities.

States, which control a society composed of numerous communities located within a territory, are highly organized. States are politically autonomous with a centralized government that can collect taxes, enact and enforce laws, and attack or enter into treaties with other states. Unlike other forms of society, states are not based on kin relationships.

5A. States with a central government collect taxes and perform other functions automatically.

5B. The central government of a state can use its political power in several ways.

TEST TACTIC

When the correct answer to a Sentence Simplification question simplifies the highlighted sentence, the answer is often more general than the original. For example, if the original sentence includes the words "an artifact worth thousands of dollars," the simplified correct answer might just say "a valuable object."

D2 Read these two passages. Then work with a partner to complete tasks 1 and 2.

In 1836 the Danish scholar Christian Jürgensen Thomsen proposed that early human history could be divided into three ages: the Stone Age, Bronze Age, and Iron Age. Other scholars had previously suggested systems for classifying history based on the materials used to make tools and weapons, but their systems did not allow for these objects to be dated. Thomsen's system not only allowed for the relative dating of objects, but also led to a greater understanding of human cultural development, and became one of the foundations of modern archaeology.

1. Choose three answers from A–D to complete this restatement of the first passage. One of the answers does NOT match any of the blanks. One answer has been done for you.

Christian Jürgensen Thomsen proposed dividing 1. ____human prehistory____ into the Stone Age, Bronze Age, and Iron Age. He was not the first scholar to suggest a 2. _____, but all previous such systems had flaws. Modern archaeology is based on Thomsen's system, which let scholars date objects and better comprehend 3. _____.

A classification system
B cultural development
C human prehistory
D tools and weapons

Ground-penetrating radar (GPR) allows archaeologists to see below the earth without the need to excavate, and thus destroy, surface features of the site. High frequency radio waves from a GPR device are sent into the earth and any subsurface features, spaces, materials, or artifacts will reflect the waves back to the device. Typically, GPR is useful at depths of up to 10 meters and is often used to find artificial and natural features like buried objects, buildings, roads, or rivers.

2. Choose three answers from E–H to complete this restatement of the second passage. One of the answers does NOT match any of the blanks.

GPR gives archaeologists the opportunity to see what lies beneath the earth without destroying 4. _____. The device works by emitting radio waves into the ground that bounce back off features or 5. _____. Commonly used to locate both natural and manmade features, GPR devices work best above a 6. _____.

E certain depth
F excavation work
G objects of interest
H surface structures

D3 Put five sentences from A–F in order to form a paragraph that restates this passage. One of the sentences does NOT belong in the restated paragraph.

A key principle of archaeology is the importance of context in fully understanding an excavated object. Context can be defined as the specific locale – even down to the soil layer – in which an artifact is found. Context also includes the other objects or materials found with, nearby, or in the same soil layer as the artifact. Context allows scholars to better understand the purpose of an object and the culture of the people who made it. For example, a sword might be understood as having either a military or ceremonial purpose depending on the context in which it was found.

A Another aspect of context is the other items found in the same location as the object.
B Without a clear sense of an object's context, less information can be known about it.
C Context includes the precise location where a buried object was discovered.
D An important idea in archaeology is how context helps scholars understand an artifact.
E Whether a sword was used for war or another purpose might be unclear without knowledge of its context.
F When archaeologists know an artifact's context, they can better understand it and the culture that made it.

E Mastering Sentence Simplification Questions – Recognizing the Function of a Sentence

Another valuable skill for Sentence Simplification questions is recognizing the function of both the highlighted sentence and the answer choices. Incorrect answers sometimes have a different function than the highlighted sentence.

Track 2 **E1** **Listen to an experienced teacher discuss some common functions in Sentence Simplification questions. Put the functions in the order that the teacher mentions them. One answer has been done for you.**

1. Compare or contrast two ideas
2.
3.
4.
5.

A Describe all or part of a process
B Explain a cause, reason, or result
C Compare or contrast two ideas
D Summarize some information or an idea
E Describe a problem with something

E2 **Which sentence, 1–5, is an example of the common functions described in E1? Discuss your ideas with a partner.**

1. Although Heinrich Schliemann made several astonishing discoveries, he is widely criticized by modern archaeologists for his destructive methods and his fanciful interpretations of his finds.
2. After identifying a potential site, archaeologists survey the area to learn as much as possible before starting to excavate.
3. Archaeology is regarded as a branch of anthropology in the US, whereas in Europe it is considered a separate academic discipline.
4. Many of the burial sites of Egyptian pharaohs were looted by thieves before they were discovered and excavated by archaeologists, meaning little of value remained.
5. The law of superposition, which states that, in general, older material is found below younger material, is a key axiom in archaeology and some other sciences.

E3 **Use information from these passages to answer questions 1 and 2.**

Ethnography is the study of a recent or existing culture. Its principal focus is on how people from that culture think and act as determined through direct observation and interviews with living individuals. Social systems are often studied, including marriage customs, political and economic organization, religious beliefs, and art and music. Ethnography should not be confused with ethnology, which entails a comparative study of more than one culture.

1. Which answer, A or B, has both the same meaning and the same function as the highlighted sentence?
   A Studying ethnology can be confusing because it requires comparing a number of diverse cultures.
   B Ethnology involves looking at how several cultures are similar and dissimilar, and as such it differs from ethnography.

Ethnocentrism, that is the judging of another culture by the standards of one's own culture, is considered a natural part of human psychology. Notwithstanding this, anthropologists working in the first part of the twentieth century including Franz Boas and Bronisław Malinowski saw ethnocentrism as a barrier to understanding. Boas developed the principle of cultural relativism – exemplified by the idea that all cultures are relative and ideas that hold true for one culture may not be true for other cultures – as a way to overcome ethnocentric viewpoints.

2. Which answer, A or B, has both the same meaning and the same function as the highlighted sentence?
   A The principle of cultural relativism was developed as a way to counter ethnocentricity.
   B The idea of cultural relativism differs markedly from commonly-held ethnocentric opinions.

F Mastering Sentence Simplification Questions – Recognizing Distractors

A further skill for Sentence Simplification questions is recognizing and avoiding distractors – that is, answer choices that may look similar to the highlighted sentence, and may even paraphrase one part of that sentence, but which are incorrect.

F1 **Compare each pair of sentences, 1–4. In each case, sentence B does NOT correctly restate sentence A. Put a check (✓) in the correct column to indicate the problem with sentence B. One answer has been done for you.**

1A. The Yanomamö are a group of roughly 20,000 people living in villages of up to 400 people in the Amazon rainforest in the border region between Brazil and Venezuela.

1B. The Amazon rainforest between Brazil and Venezuela is home to around 20,000 small villages of Yanomamö people.

2A. Although non-invasive techniques exist for learning about an archaeological site, in most cases, excavation remains the primary method for acquiring data.

2B. Archaeologists acquire the majority of information about archaeological sites through excavating them.

3A. Numerous ancient writing systems have been discovered by archaeologists, including Linear B, which has been deciphered, and Linear A, which has not.

3B. Archaeologists have discovered and deciphered a number of ancient writing systems, including Linear A and Linear B.

4A. The Kula ring is a complex ceremonial exchange system that occurs among communities living on islands northeast of Papua New Guinea.

4B. People that live on islands to the north and east of Papua New Guinea exchange complex items with communities on that island.

	1B	2B	3B	4B
Sentence B changes the function of Sentence A.				
Sentence B changes essential information in Sentence A.	✓			
Sentence B leaves out essential information from Sentence A.				

TEST TACTIC

Some distractors paraphrase the highlighted sentence but leave out an essential detail. These can be difficult to recognize because they correctly restate part of the highlighted sentence. To avoid choosing these wrong answers, make sure you look at all four answer choices before selecting your final answer.

G Test Challenge

G1 **Answer Sentence Simplification questions 1–6. Try to finish in 9 minutes or less so as to get realistic practice for the test. Use the checklist of skills that you learned in this unit as a guide.**

☑ Eliminate answers that change essential details from the highlighted sentence

☑ Eliminate answers that leave out essential information from the highlighted sentence

☑ Eliminate answers that change the function of the highlighted sentence

Kinship and Descent

Because it is a key organizing principle of many traditional societies, kinship is an important and often-studied concept in anthropology. In broad terms, kinship can be understood as one's relationships with family members either by blood – known as consanguinity – or marriage – known as affinity. This definition of kinship does not account for adoptive kin or fictive kin, but has the benefit of being both simple and applicable to most cultures and situations.

The kinship ties that an individual can claim depend on the system of descent employed by his or her society. This system is important because in many cultures an individual's duties, eligibility to join certain groups, and rights of inheritance and residence may all follow kinship lines. Anthropologists have identified several descent systems.

The most common system is unilineal kinship, in which descent is either patrilineal (through the father) or matrilineal (mother). Double descent, also called double unilineal or bilineal, describes kinship in which patrilineal ties are considered in some contexts and matrilineal ties in others. Bilateral descent describes cultures in which an individual is considered to descend equally from both the patrilineal and matrilineal sides of the family. Ambilineal descent, which like bilateral descent is a form of cognatic descent, gives individuals the chance to choose whether to trace descent from their mother or father, or, in some cultures, from their mother-in-law or father-in-law.

TEST TACTIC

If time is running out, count the number of ideas in the highlighted sentence. In general, the correct answer will either have the same number of ideas as the highlighted sentence or one idea less. Incorrect answers, however, may include more ideas or two ideas less.

1. Which of the following best expresses the essential information in the highlighted sentence in paragraph 1? Incorrect choices change the meaning in important ways or leave out essential information.

   (A) Adoptive kin and fictive kin have advantages in some cultures and situations that the definition does not include.

   (B) Most cultures prefer to use a simple and widely applicable definition of kinship that does not account for all kin types.

   (C) Although is easy to understand and relevant to most situations, the definition does not include every form of kinship.

   (D) Some types of kin cannot be included in a simple definition of kinship because they do not exist in most cultures.

2. Which of the following best expresses the essential information in the highlighted sentence in paragraph 2? Incorrect choices change the meaning in important ways or leave out essential information.

   (A) An important system of descent is one that adopts the kinship lines that a culture follows with relation to eligibility.

   (B) The system of kinship descent that a culture adopts affects an individual's status and rights within that culture.

   (C) Many societies limit the duties, eligibility, and rights of individuals according to the system of descent he or she follows.

   (D) Certain cultures may limit what an individual is allowed to do based on where that individual chooses to reside.

3. Which of the following best expresses the essential information in the highlighted sentence in paragraph 3? Incorrect choices change the meaning in important ways or leave out essential information.

   (A) Ambilineal descent allows individuals to select the relative from whom they descend.

   (B) Cognatic forms of descent are flexible systems because individuals have more choice.

   (C) The system known as ambilineal descent is traced from an individual's parents and in-laws.

   (D) Under ambilineal descent, the choice of kinship connection depends on the culture.

Underwater Archaeology

A common misconception is that underwater archaeology, which, as its name implies, deals with the excavation, analysis, and interpretation of sites or objects of historical interest found at the bottom of a body of water, always involves the exploration of shipwrecks. In fact, any human settlement, artifact, or structure that was once on land but is now submerged may be the object of study, including sites from prehistorical, classical, historical, and industrial times.

Underwater archaeology shares the same principles, methodologies, and even many of the same techniques as dry-land archaeology, but is inevitably more complex, dangerous, and costly owing to the challenging environment in which it occurs. Many sites can only be reached by diving, which requires specialist equipment and training and limits how much time divers can spend at the site. Furthermore, study of some locations can be affected by currents, tides, and severe weather.

One of the most ambitious underwater archaeology projects was the excavation of the *Mary Rose*, a British warship dating from the time of King Henry VIII. The ship sank during a battle in 1545, but was rediscovered in 1971 at which time a plan to salvage the wreck was proposed. From 1979 to 1982, divers spent more than 20,000 hours exploring the site. In 1982 archaeologists and project leaders were able to overcome some major technical obstacles and raise the ship from the bottom of the sea for preservation and exhibition in a museum.

4. Which of the following best expresses the essential information in the highlighted sentence in paragraph 1? Incorrect choices change the meaning in important ways or leave out essential information.
   - (A) As the name underwater archaeology implies, it is common for shipwrecks to be excavated.
   - (B) Sites and objects of historical interest such as shipwrecks can even be found under water.
   - (C) People misinterpret shipwrecks because the concept of underwater archaeology is unclear.
   - (D) Many do not realize that underwater archaeology may encompass studying any submarine site or artifact.

5. Which of the following best expresses the essential information in the highlighted sentence in paragraph 2? Incorrect choices change the meaning in important ways or leave out essential information.
   - (A) It uses the same methods as land archaeology, so the cost, danger, and challenge of underwater archaeology are high.
   - (B) The difficulties and techniques of underwater archaeology are effectively the same as those of dry-land archaeology.
   - (C) The challenge that underwater archaeology provides is balanced by its use of the same techniques and ideas as other branches of archaeology.
   - (D) Despite the challenging environment in which underwater archaeology takes place, it is similar in many ways to dry-land archaeology.

6. Which of the following best expresses the essential information in the highlighted sentence in paragraph 3? Incorrect choices change the meaning in important ways or leave out essential information.
   - (A) Archaeologists and leaders overcame obstacles in 1982 when the *Mary Rose* project ended.
   - (B) After the *Mary Rose* was raised from the sea bed, archaeologists preserved it in a museum.
   - (C) Despite challenges, the *Mary Rose* was successfully raised for conservation and viewing.
   - (D) A 1982 exhibition highlighted the difficulties archaeologists faced in raising the *Mary Rose*.

Next Steps

Topics related to anthropology and archaeology may appear in any section of the TOEFL Test. As a result, learning more about these subjects and practicing key skills for Sentence Simplification questions may raise your overall test score.

To learn more about anthropology, archaeology, and vocabulary related to these disciplines:

1. Read an article in your language about one aspect of anthropology or archaeology to get some background knowledge.
2. Read an English article about the same topic several times until you understand all of the main ideas. When you see an unfamiliar word, try to understand the word from its context and write a definition. Check your definition in a dictionary and correct any mistakes. Then decide if the word is useful for anthropology or archaeology; if it is, study it in more detail.

To practice a key skill for Sentence Simplification questions:

1. Find two news articles about the same story and read each article once. (Stories about academic discoveries are ideal.)
2. Look for sentences in the second article that accurately paraphrase sentences in the first article.
3. Look for sentences in the second article that paraphrase sentences in the first article, but leave out or change a detail.

Unit Focus

There are ten types of reading questions in the TOEFL Test, including Insert Text questions and Reference questions. Insert Text questions ask you to decide the best position at which to add a new sentence into the passage. Reference questions, on the other hand, ask you to identify the phrase in the passage that a highlighted word or phrase refers to. You will usually see an Insert Text question after every reading passage in the TOEFL Test, but Reference questions are not as common. Insert Text and Reference questions are different, but the same skills can help you answer both question types. These skills include:

- recognizing the function of a sentence and the most likely position where a sentence of that function comes.
- recognizing words and phrases in a sentence that match context clues in the passage.
- recognizing coherence and cohesion in a passage to decide where best to add a sentence.

The vocabulary focus is on academic words and phrases related to:

- botany, the scientific study and categorization of plants.

A Warm-up

A1 Complete tasks 1–3.

1. Make a list of three important food crops that grow in your country or in another country that you know about.
2. Share your list with other students. Then listen to other students and add the crops they mention to your list.
3. What are the three most important crops on your list? Discuss why they are so important.

B Academic Vocabulary

B1 Complete definitions 1–8 with words from the passages. One answer has been done for you.

Trees have a hard, outer layer. This is known as bark. The bark protects trees from pests, which are organisms such as insects that can cause damage. Not all insects are pests. Some perform the vital function of transferring reproductive material between the male and female parts of a plant, a process known as pollination.

1. The word "bark" is defined in the passage as the _____hard, outer layer_____ of trees.
2. The word "pests" is defined as _____, such as insects.
3. "Pollination" occurs when _____ is transferred between male and female parts of a plant.

Most plants grow in soil – the upper layer of earth that is usually a mixture of dead organisms, small pieces of rock, and mud. Their roots spread underground in the soil to anchor the plant. They also absorb water and nutrients, the substances that all organisms need to survive.

4. The word "soil" is defined as a mixture of _____ that forms the upper layer of earth.
5. A plant's "roots" absorb water and vital substances, and _____ in the soil.
6. The word "nutrients" is defined as _____ require for survival.

Plants have various types of specialist tissues, which are groups of cells with a similar form and function. Among the most important tissues are those that can convert the sun's energy into sugars, a process called photosynthesis

7. The word "tissues" is defined as groups of cells that share a _____.
8. "Photosynthesis" is the process by which plant tissues turn _____.

C Analyzing Insert Text Questions

All Insert Text questions follow the same pattern. On the screen you will see one or two paragraphs from the passage. The paragraph(s) will contain four squares at the start or end of some sentences. Usually, these sentences are next to each other in the paragraph(s). You will also see a new sentence in bold and the question will ask you which is the best square in the passage at which to add the new sentence, as in this example:

Look at the four squares [■] that indicate where the following sentence could be added to the passage.

You will see a sentence in bold font here that can be added to the passage.

Where would the sentence best fit?

Click on a square [■] to add the sentence to the passage.

When you click on one of the squares with your mouse, the screen will change to show you the new sentence added at that position in the paragraph. You can change your answer as many times as you like by clicking on a different square.

If the new sentence is added to the passage at the correct position:

- phrases in the new sentence will logically relate or refer to words or phrases in the sentence before and/or after it.
- the whole paragraph will show cohesion – each sentence will logically follow from the previous sentence.

If the new sentence is added to the passage at one of the three incorrect positions:

- phrases in the new sentence will not relate or refer to matching words or phrases in the previous or next sentence.
- the cohesion of the paragraph may be lost – the new sentence may break a connection between two sentences that are logically related to one another.

C1 Answer Insert Text question 1 based on the reading passage below. Then discuss your answer with a partner.

A Swedish scholar Carl Linnaeus is most famous now for developing and popularizing the scientific system of naming known as binomial nomenclature. **B** During his lifetime, however, Linnaeus was better known for his many publications (most of which were written in Latin) on botany in general and the plants of Scandinavia in particular. **C** Among these are *Fundamenta Botanica* (first published in 1736), *Genera Plantarum* and *Flora Lapponica* (both 1737), *Flora Svecica* (1745), *Philosophica Botanica* (1751), and *Species Plantarum* (1753). **D**

1. Look at the four squares (■) that indicate where the following sentence could be added to the passage.

   This system allows a species to be scientifically classified by assigning it a two-part name.

   Where would the sentence best fit? Choose position **A**, **B**, **C**, or **D**.

C2 Write in the letter of the position, A–D, that completes these reasons why the wrong answers are incorrect. One answer has been done for you.

- Position ___*A*___ is not the best position at which to add the new sentence because the phrase "This system" in the new sentence refers to something already mentioned, but this position is at the start of the paragraph, so nothing has already been mentioned.
- The new sentence cannot be added at position _____ because the sentences before and after this position are linked and should not be separated: the sentence before includes "publications" and the sentence after includes "published."
- Position _____ is not where the new sentence should be added because no word or phrase in the new sentence relates to a word or phrase in the sentence before this position.

D Mastering Insert Text Questions – Recognizing the Function of a Sentence

Sentences with different functions are more likely or less likely at certain positions within a paragraph. If you can recognize the function of a sentence, you may be able to answer Insert Text questions more easily and quickly.

🔊 Track 3 **D1** Take notes as you listen to an experienced teacher talk about Insert Text questions. Then use your notes to answer questions 1 and 2.

1. What does the teacher NOT say about using sentence functions to answer Insert Text questions?
   A The function of a sentence may help you decide likely positions for the answer, but not the exact position.
   B Some types of sentences are much more common in the TOEFL test than other types.
   C Any type of sentence can appear anywhere in a paragraph, but some positions are unlikely.
   D If the function of a sentence is not obvious, try to answer the question using other strategies.

2. The teacher discusses likely positions within a paragraph for sentences with a particular function. Indicate which positions the teacher says are common for each function. One answer has been done for you.

Function	Near start of paragraph	Middle of paragraph	Near end of paragraph
Adding a detail or example			
Comparing or contrasting ideas			
Defining a term or concept			
Expressing a conclusion			
Introducing a topic	✓		

D2 Work with a partner to complete tasks 1–3.

1. Five functions of a sentence are shown in exercise **D1**. Make a list of some other sentence functions you know.
2. Look at your list of functions from task 1 and say at which position(s) in a paragraph they are commonly found.
3. Share your list of functions and common positions with other students. Then listen to their lists and take notes.

D3 What function, A–E, matches each sentence, 1–5? Work with a partner. One answer has been done for you.

1. Infections like these can affect the economy, so it can be seen that plant pathology is an important field of study. __D__
2. Rice ragged stunt virus and bacterial leaf blight, for instance, are both pathogens that can affect rice crops. ____
3. Many insects and other pests also affect the health of plants, but plant pathologists do not study these factors. ____
4. Various types of disease-causing pathogens affect plants, including fungi, parasites, viruses, and bacteria. ____
5. Plant pathology is the name given to the study of diseases that are caused by such organisms. ____

   A Adding a detail or example
   B Comparing or contrasting ideas
   C Defining a term or concept
   D Expressing a conclusion
   E Introducing a topic

D4 Put the sentences from exercise **D3** in the correct order to make a logically-organized paragraph about plant pathology. Work with a partner.

E Mastering Insert Text Questions – Focusing on Context Clues

The new sentence and the sentences marked by the four squares (■) will contain words or phrases – context clues – that can help you decide the best position at which to add the new sentence. Finding context clues in the new sentence that match or refer to clues in the passage is a key skill for answering Insert Text questions accurately.

E1 **Which word or phrase in these paragraphs does each highlighted phrase refer to? Underline the word or phrase and draw an arrow connecting it to the matching highlighted phrase. One answer has been done for you.**

The plant kingdom can be divided into two broad groups of seed-bearing plants: angiosperms and gymnosperms. The former differ from the latter in several ways, most notably in having an enclosed seed and in having flowers. There are almost 250,000 species of angiosperms in total, many of which are important sources of food, resources such as wood, or medicine.

The plant kingdom also contains some species that do not bear seeds. These include bryophytes, such as mosses, and pteridophytes, such as ferns. These species reproduce using spores, which are capsules of genetic information with a protective coating. They are carried by the wind or transported in some other way to a different location. When a spore lands in a suitable one, it begins to grow, creating a copy of the parent organism.

E2 **Answer questions 1–5 about sentences A–F. Work with a partner.**

1. Which words in sentence B refer to "trees" in sentence A? Find two answers.
2. Which phrase in sentence C gives an example of "leaf shape" mentioned in sentence B?
3. Which word in sentence D refers to "Coniferous trees" in sentence C?
4. Which adjectives in sentence E contrast with the word "thin" in sentence C? Find two answers.
5. Could you move sentence F to position E, and sentence E to position F? Why or why not?

A　Typically, trees are defined as a plant with a long woody stem, called a trunk, that supports branches and leaves.
B　Common ways of classifying them are by leaf shape and by the hardness or softness of their wood.
C　Coniferous trees typically keep their thin, needle-like leaves throughout the year.
D　They also typically produce light-colored soft wood that is easily worked.
E　Broadleaf trees have broader, flatter leaves that, except in tropical climates, usually fall to the ground in autumn.
F　They typically have hard, dense wood that is strong and durable but difficult to work with.

E3 **Use context clues to help you choose the best answer from the box to fill the blanks at positions A–H. One answer has been done for you.**

Plants are both affected by and affect their **A** _____environment_____ in various ways. Plants turn sunlight into energy through the process of photosynthesis. As such, the availability of **B** _____ is a significant environmental factor. Only certain species can grow on **C** _____ floors, for example, which receive little illumination from the sun because of the surrounding trees. Soil is another critical factor. Factors that affect which plants can grow, such as the quantity of nutrients and pH value, all differ from one type of **D** _____ to another. Finally, climate has a big impact, too, with average **E** _____ and rainfall being particularly important factors. In terms of how they impact their environs, some plants produce chemicals that can influence which other **F** _____ of plants can grow nearby. And because carbon dioxide is taken up and **G** _____ is emitted during photosynthesis, plants have an effect on the global **H** _____ , too.

atmosphere	forest	oxygen	species
environment	light	soil	temperature

TEST TACTIC

To check your answer, say the relevant part of the passage in your mind but either replace the highlighted word with your answer (for Reference questions) or add the new sentence at your chosen position (for Insert Text questions). If the passage sounds unnatural, you might have made a mistake.

F Mastering Insert Text Questions – Recognizing Cohesion and Coherence

Well-written paragraphs are coherent – each sentence logically follows from the previous one – and cohesive – words in one sentence refer back or forward to words in other sentences. Recognizing coherence and cohesion is a valuable skill for Insert Text questions as it can help you decide where best to add the new sentence.

F1 Use context clues and the coherence and cohesion of each passage to decide the best place to add each bold sentence. Then discuss your answers with a partner. One answer has been done for you.

1. The best position in the passage at which to add this sentence is position ___C___.

    Scientific analysis of resin shows that it contains compounds that are toxic to a variety of organisms that eat plant tissues.

    A Natural resin is a sticky liquid secreted by various species of plants, especially coniferous trees like pines, firs, and cedars, that hardens and becomes solid over time. **B** Its specific function is uncertain, but it is likely that, at least in part, resin serves to protect the plant from pests. **C**

2. The best position in the passage at which to add this sentence is position _____.

    There are two types of sap: phloem sap, which flows from sources of carbohydrate to tissues that require them, and xylem sap, which moves from the roots of the plant to its leaves.

    A Plant sap is a watery fluid that transports water and nutrients throughout the tissues and organs of vascular plants. **B** Some xylem saps are used by humans as a source of food, including maple syrup, which is the processed xylem sap of certain species of maple tree. **C**

3. The best position in the passage at which to add this sentence is position _____.

    There is strong evidence that latex has a defensive function.

    A Around one in ten flowering plants produce latex, a milky liquid composed of proteins, sugars, oils, and other substances. **B** It is often produced when a plant suffers tissue damage, such as when an insect begins consuming it, and it contains levels of defensive compounds much greater than other tissues. **C**

4. The best position in the passage at which to add this sentence is position _____.

    Mucilage, a thick, glue-like liquid produced by plants, is often used either as a base for adhesives or in food and medicine.

    A In the plant kingdom, some carnivorous plants use the stickiness of mucilage to trap insects. **B** In other plants its functions include storing water or food, helping seeds to germinate or disperse, or protecting damaged tissues. **C**

F2 Work with a partner to complete this table of reasons why the sentences in exercise F1 cannot be added at some positions in the passage. Note that one wrong position is wrong for two reasons. Two answers have been done for you.

Reason why the new sentence cannot be added at some positions	Position
It adds details about a topic *before* the topic has been introduced or defined.	1A
It introduces or defines a topic *after* details about that topic have been mentioned.	
It separates two sentences that are coherent and logically related.	1B

G Analyzing Reference Questions

Reference questions ask you to identify which word or phrase in the passage refers to a highlighted word. The key word will be highlighted in the question, too. The key word or phrase may be a pronoun (such as "they" or "it"), a determiner (such as "the other" or "several"), or a noun phrase (such as "that idea" or "the situation").

The word "_____" in the passage refers to

The phrase "_____" in the passage refers to

The phrase "_____" in the passage refers to the concept of

The correct answer to Reference questions:

- will make sense, be correct English, and will not change the meaning of the passage if it replaces the highlighted word.

In contrast, incorrect answers:

- will not make sense, or will make sense, but change the meaning of the passage if they replace the highlighted word.

G1 **Answer Reference questions 1 and 2. Then discuss your answers with a partner.**

Piper nigrum is a flowering vine native to certain countries in South Asia that bears clusters of fruit which are called peppercorns when dried. Once so valuable that they were known as black gold and sometimes used as a form of money, peppercorns are still widely used in the cuisine of many cultures.

1. The word "they" in the passage refers to
   A countries
   B clusters
   C peppercorns
   D cultures

When Columbus set sail from Spain in 1492 on the journey that resulted in the discovery of the American continent, his intention and that of his financial backers was actually to find a westward route to the Indies – as the lands of South and Southeast Asia were known – which were the only known source of valuable spices like pepper and cloves that were eagerly sought by European consumers. Columbus' hope was that finding a westward route would make trading these commodities easier and therefore more profitable.

2. The phrase "these commodities" in the passage refers to
   A consumers
   B spices
   C lands
   D backers

G2 **Indicate which phrases, 1–8, from the passages in exercise G1 helped you answer that exercise. One answer has been done for you.**

1. a flowering vine	☐ Helpful	☑ Not helpful
2. when dried	☐ Helpful	☐ Not helpful
3. so valuable	☐ Helpful	☐ Not helpful
4. black gold	☐ Helpful	☐ Not helpful
5. set sail from Spain	☐ Helpful	☐ Not helpful
6. the American continent	☐ Helpful	☐ Not helpful
7. westward route	☐ Helpful	☐ Not helpful
8. pepper and cloves	☐ Helpful	☐ Not helpful

H Mastering Reference Questions – Focusing on Context Clues and Cohesion

As with Insert Text questions, a key skill for answering Reference questions is recognizing cohesion and context clues in the passage. These can help you decide which answer the highlighted word or phrase refers to.

H1 Circle the expressions in passages 1–4 that either refer to or give an example of the highlighted word. One answer has been done for you.

1. The study of fungi – (mushrooms, yeasts, and molds) – is often considered a subfield of botany even though (they) are not classified as plants. One major difference is that (their) cell walls are made from chitin, not cellulose like plants.

2. A number of common foods are technically fruits even though they are often considered to be vegetables. Among these items are avocados, eggplants, which are actually a type of berry, cucumbers, which are from the same family as melons, tomatoes, and even olives, which means that, strictly speaking, olive oil is a fruit juice.

3. Bamboo, which is native to every populated continent except Europe, is the largest member of the grass family. It grows extremely quickly and many species are both strong and durable, factors that have led to its use for a wide variety of purposes including as a construction material, as a food or medicine, and as a raw material for making paper and textiles. The plant also has a symbolic role in many Asian cultures.

4. *The Day of the Triffids* by John Wyndham is a classic science fiction story from the 1950s. The triffids referred to in the title are a fictional species of large, venomous, mobile plant that often attacks humans. The tale describes the efforts of a small group of people who have survived a natural disaster to find a place to live that is safe from triffids.

H2 Use context clues and cohesion clues to answer questions 1–4. If none of the answers is correct, write your own.

Several species of acacia trees in Africa and Central America have developed symbiotic relationships with ants. The insects live in hollow thorn-like appendages on the branches of the tree. They also acquire nutrients from the tree. In return, they provide the tree with some measure of protection against predation by other insects or herbivorous organisms. Some species of ants will also attack the leaves of plants that are growing near acacias and that might compete with them for resources.

1. The word "they" in the passage refers to
    A nutrients
    B branches
    C insects
    D _your answer_

2. The word "them" in the passage refers to
    A ants
    B leaves
    C plants
    D _your answer_

A genus of plants known as seed ferns (scientific name *Glossopteris*) evolved during the Permian period, which lasted from roughly 299 to 252 million years ago. Fossil discoveries show they were woody, seed-bearing, grew up to 30 meters (33 yards) in height, and had broad, tongue-shaped leaves. They became a dominant species during the Permian but went extinct at the end of that period. Seed fern fossils have been discovered in every southern continent. This evidence led several scholars to suggest that all of the world's landmasses were once joined as one massive supercontinent known as Gondwana before separating and moving to their current positions on the surface of the Earth, a theory that is now known to be correct.

3. The word "They" in the passage refers to
    A years
    B discoveries
    C leaves
    D _your answer_

4. The phrase "This evidence" in the passage refers to
    A the extinction of seed ferns at the end of the Permian
    B the discovery of seed fern fossils on many continents
    C the joining of all Earth's landmasses into a single continent
    D _your answer_

▌ Test Challenge

11 Practice Insert Text and Reference questions by answering questions 1–10. Try to finish in 15 minutes or less so as to get realistic practice for the test. Use this checklist of skills that you studied in this unit as a guide.

For Insert Text questions

☑   Decide which positions are likely and unlikely based on the function of the new sentence.

☑   Find words or phrases in the new sentence that match context clues in the passage.

☑   Look for cohesion and coherence in the passage to decide where best to add the new sentence.

For Reference questions

☑   Focus on context clues, cohesion, and coherence to decide which answer matches the highlighted expression.

Carnivorous Plants

All plants derive energy from sunlight through the process of photosynthesis, but must get vital nutrients from their surroundings. Carnivorous plants typically live in nutrient-poor soils and, as a result, have evolved a number of ways to trap insects and other small organisms that are a good source of these minerals. Two types of carnivorous plants, sundews and butterworts, have leaves covered with sticky mucilage that glistens in sunlight. Insects that are attracted to the shimmering light become trapped on the leaves. **A** Pitcher plants are another type of carnivorous plant. They attract insects with bright colors and sweet nectar or water at the bottom of a pitcher-shaped leaf that traps the insect and prevents it from escaping. **B** Bladderworts are aquatic carnivorous plants that capture small organisms through the use of suction powered by differential pressure: when a prey species brushes against special membranes, a trapdoor opens that sucks in both the prey and the surrounding water. **C** The final type of carnivorous plant is the venus flytrap, which has specialist leaves that snap closed when an insect touches them and remain closed until it dies. **D**

1. The phrase "these minerals" in the passage refers to
    Ⓐ small organisms
    Ⓑ nutrient-poor soils
    Ⓒ carnivorous plants
    Ⓓ vital nutrients

2. Look at the four squares (■) that indicate where the following sentence could be added to the passage.

    In all cases, once the prey has been trapped, carnivorous plants digest it and obtain its nutrients.

    Where would the sentence best fit? Choose position **A**, **B**, **C**, or **D**.

TEST TACTIC

For Reference questions, the answers are listed in the order they appear in the passage. In most cases answer A will be the answer that is farthest away from the highlighted expression. Knowing that the answers are in order may help you find them more quickly and save time.

Miracle Fruit

Three different types of plant that have the capacity to alter taste perception in humans are known colloquially as "miracle fruit." **A** All three plants are being studied by food scientists to learn more about their active ingredients and to determine if these are suitable for being used as food additives or as medicines. **B** The most widely known of these is *Synsepalum dulcificum*, a berry that grows in parts of tropical West Africa. **C** It contains a protein molecule called miraculin, which activates sweet receptors on the tongue in the presence of acid. **D** Miraculin makes sour foods and beverages taste sweet for up to an hour after consumption. Chewing the seeds of the fruit of *Thaumatococcus danielli* has the same effect. Their covering contains a protein called thaumatin, which is approximately 3,000 times sweeter than sugar and which affects the tongue so that sour flavors taste sweet until the effect wears off. *Gymnema sylvestre*, an herb native to India and Sri Lanka, also sometimes goes by the name "miracle fruit," although this is a misnomer as its leaves rather than its fruit affect taste. Unlike the other two species, *G. sylvestre* suppresses sweet tastes.

3. Look at the four squares (■) that indicate where the following sentence could be added to the passage.

   The berry itself does not have a high sugar content, however, and does not taste particularly sweet when eaten.

   Where would the sentence best fit? Choose position **A**, **B**, **C**, or **D**.

4. The word these in the passage refers to
   - Ⓐ three plants
   - Ⓑ food scientists
   - Ⓒ active ingredients
   - Ⓓ food additives

5. The word this in the passage refers to
   - Ⓐ name
   - Ⓑ India
   - Ⓒ herb
   - Ⓓ tongue

Tree Trunks

A The trunk of a tree is made up of five basic layers. **B** From the outside to the inside, these are the outer and inner bark, the vascular cambium layer, the sapwood, and the heartwood. **C** Together they provide protection, structural support, and transportation of water, nutrients, and food to all of its branches, leaves, and cells. **D**

Outer bark consists of dead cells that protect against moisture loss as well as environmental damage from weather, natural phenomena, and pests. Inner bark, the cells of which die and become outer bark as they are pushed outwards by a tree's growth, is a layer of tube-shaped cells called phloem. These act as pipes for the transportation of carbohydrates from the leaves, where they are made during photosynthesis, to the rest of the tree.

Beneath the inner bark is the vascular cambium layer, the only part of the trunk that grows. The cambium cells continually divide inward to form new wood and outward to form new bark. **E** This is regulated by growth hormones called auxins that are released by leaf buds each spring. **F**

The two inner layers of the trunk are collectively known as the xylem. **G** Sapwood is the newly-created wood formed by the cambium. **H** It consists of living cells that conduct water and minerals from the roots to the leaves, branches, and upper parts of a tree. As the cambium continues to produce new sapwood, the older, inner layers of that material die and are converted into heartwood. This layer is usually darker than the sapwood and consists of cellulose fibers bound with a complex compound called lignin. Lignin provides enough strength for the heartwood cells to continue supporting mature trees from within even though they are no longer alive.

6. Look at the four squares (■) that indicate where the following sentence could be added to the passage.

   The latter is named for its location at the center of the trunk and not because it is any more important to the tree than the other layers; indeed, some species of trees do not form heartwood at all.

   Where would the sentence best fit? Choose position **A**, **B**, **C**, or **D**.

7. The word "its" in the passage refers to
   - (A) layer
   - (B) bark
   - (C) tree
   - (D) trunk

8. The word "This" in the passage refers to
   - (A) the death of inner bark cells caused by growth
   - (B) the transportation of carbohydrates from the leaves
   - (C) the division of cells in the cambium layer
   - (D) the release of auxins from leaf buds each year

9. Look at the four squares (■) that indicate where the following sentence could be added to the passage.

   After release these are transported to the rest of the tree's cells along with sugars via the phloem layer.

   Where would the sentence best fit? Choose position **E**, **F**, **G**, or **H**.

10. The word "they" in the passage refers to
    - (A) mature trees
    - (B) heartwood cells
    - (C) cellulose fibers
    - (D) inner layers

Next Steps

Topics related to botany are common in the reading section of the TOEFL Test. You may also have questions about these subjects in the other sections. As a result, learning more about botany, as well as practicing key skills for Insert Text and Reference questions, may raise your overall test score.

To learn more about botany and vocabulary related to this discipline:

1. Find an online museum (sometimes called a virtual museum) that has exhibitions or tours related to botany. Useful search phrases that may help you find interesting sites are "virtual museum plants" and "online museum botany".
2. Use your computer to visit or tour the online exhibition. When you hear or see an unfamiliar word on the site, use your dictionary to check its meaning. If you think the word is likely to be useful for botany, study it in more detail.

To practice a key skill for Insert Text and Reference questions:

1. Find an academic or news article in English related to botany (or another subject that you find interesting).
2. Read the article once to understand the main ideas, but do not worry about the meaning of every word.
3. Read the first paragraph of the article again and highlight the first pronoun or determiner that you find.
4. Now scan the first paragraph and look for words or phrases that the highlighted word refers to.
5. Repeat steps 3 and 4 for the other pronouns and determiners in the first paragraph and again for the other paragraphs.

Unit Focus

There are ten types of reading questions in the TOEFL Test, including two types of "reading to learn" questions: Fill in a Table questions and Prose Summary questions. These questions test your understanding of how ideas in the passage are related to other ideas. Fill in a Table questions ask you to match answer choices to one of several categories, and Prose Summary questions ask you to choose the answers that accurately summarize key ideas in the passage. Unlike other reading questions, which are worth just one point, reading to learn questions are worth up to three points. You need to learn and practice several key skills to answer these questions, including:

- recognizing answers that restate or contradict ideas in the passage.
- recognizing answers that look similar to the passage, but are not mentioned in it.
- distinguishing between answers that restate major and minor ideas from the passage.

The vocabulary focus is on academic words and phrases related to:

- Earth science, the scientific study of Earth, including sub-disciplines like geography and geology.

A Warm-up

A1 Complete tasks 1 and 2 with a partner.

1. Write the name of one geographical landform, like a lake, river, mountain, or desert, from each continental area, A–F.

A Africa	C Australasia	E North America
B Asia	D Europe	F South America

2. Share your list and knowledge of each landform with other students. Then listen to their lists.

B Academic Vocabulary

B1 Choose the best definition, A–H, for words 1–8, which are related to Earth science. When you have finished, check your answers in a dictionary. One answer has been done for you.

1. atmosphere _____ _the mixture of gases, including oxygen and nitrogen, that surrounds Earth_ _____
2. climate _____
3. continent _____
4. erosion _____
5. eruption _____
6. glacier _____
7. precipitation _____
8. sediment _____

A   a large area of land that may be divided into two or more countries
B   a mass of ice that often moves slowly and does not fully melt each year
C   fine material that slowly sinks to the bottom of a sea, lake, or river
D   the weather that occurs in a region over a period of time
E   drops or crystals of water in the atmosphere that fall to Earth
F   the mixture of gases, including oxygen and nitrogen, that surrounds Earth
G   the gradual wearing down of rock or soil by water, wind, or other causes
H   the violent release of materials such as lava, rocks, ash, and gas from a volcano

C Analyzing Fill in a Table Questions

You can recognize Fill in a Table questions from their detailed directions, as in this example:

Directions: Select the phrases that correctly describe _____ and _____.
Two of the phrases will NOT be used. **This question is worth 3 points.**

Below the directions you will see two or three categories and space for five answers. You will also see a list of six or more answer choices, at least one of which will not match any of the categories. Each correct answer choice will match only one of the categories.

Fill in a Table questions are worth up to 3 points. To get 3 points, you need to choose all five correct answers and assign them to the correct category. To get 2 points, you must choose and correctly assign four answers, and to get 1 point you must choose and correctly assign three answers. Choosing and assigning zero to two correct answers is not worth any points.

The five correct answers to Fill in a Table questions:

- restate ideas that are mentioned in the passage and that match one of the category headings.

In contrast, the one or two answers that are incorrect and should not be used:

- might use words from the passage, but express an idea that is not mentioned in the passage.
- might restate an idea from the passage, but not an idea that matches any of the categories.
- might look similar to an idea from the passage, but contradict or change one or more key details.

C1 **Read the passage. Then select the phrases that correctly describe each category. One of the phrases will NOT be used.**

Scientists use one scale to measure earthquakes, and a different one for volcanic eruptions. The Moment Magnitude Scale (MMS), which was developed in the 1970s as a replacement for the older Richter Scale, assigns a value from 1 to 10 according to how much energy an earthquake releases. The scale is logarithmic, meaning that each point on the scale represents ten times less energy than the point above it. The Volcanic Explosivity Index (VEI) measures the power of a volcanic eruption on a nine-point scale from 0 to 8. From VEI 0 to VEI 2, each level represents 100 less power than the one above it. From VEI 2 to VEI 8, the scale is logarithmic like the MMS. An eruption's VEI level is determined both by how long it lasts and how powerful it is in terms of how much material is ejected.

Moment Magnitude Scale

-
-

Volcanic Explosivity Index

-

Both Moment Magnitude Scale and Volcanic Explosivity Index

-
-

A   The scale was designed as a substitute for an older scale.
B   The scale measures only how much energy is released by an event.
C   The scale can help scientists decide when an event is likely to occur.
D   All or most points on the scale represent ten times the power of the point below.
E   The scale can be used to measure nine or more levels of event.
F   The scale measures both the duration and intensity of an event.

> **TEST TACTIC**
>
> In some reading passages, key ideas are discussed in separate paragraphs, but in other passages key ideas are compared and contrasted within the same paragraph. Recognizing how a passage or paragraph is organized can help you find the answers to Fill in a Table questions more quickly and easily.

D Mastering Fill in a Table Questions – Analyzing the Answer Choices

To answer Fill in a Table questions, you need to practice several key skills. These include recognizing answers that are not mentioned in the passage, recognizing answers that restate or contradict the passage, and deciding which category an answer matches.

🔊 Track 4 **D1** **Take notes as you listen to an experienced teacher discuss Fill in a Table and Prose Summary questions. Then use your notes to answer questions 1 and 2.**

1. What does the teacher say about Fill in a Table and Prose Summary questions? *Choose two answers.*
   A They are worth several points so it is important to save time to answer them well.
   B They are harder than other questions, so students should answer them carefully.
   C Fill in a Table questions are not as common as Prose Summary questions.
   D Most students find it difficult to improve their ability to answer these questions.

2. The teacher discusses some strategies for answering Fill in a Table questions. Put the strategies in the order that the teacher mentions them. One answer has been done for you.

1.
2.
3.
4. Eliminate this answer choice if it contradicts the information in the relevant section of the passage.
5.

A Eliminate this answer choice if it contradicts the information in the relevant section of the passage.
B Skim and scan the passage to find the relevant section that matches one of the answer choices.
C Scan the relevant section to decide which category the answer matches and then select your answer.
D Eliminate this answer choice if the information is not mentioned anywhere in the passage.
E Decide if the answer choice restates or contradicts the information in the relevant section.

D2 **Use skimming and scanning to decide if each statement, 1–4, is Mentioned or Not mentioned in this passage. One answer has been done for you.**

Valleys are formed when the flowing waters of a river or stream cut down through the underlying rock and soil over thousands of years. They typically have a V shape when seen in cross-section, although a valley that forms in an arid area with hard underlying rock may form a steep-sided canyon. If the climate later becomes cold enough for glaciers to form and one moves downhill along the path of a typical river valley, the shape of the valley changes significantly. The glacier erodes the gentle slopes of the valley making them steeper. The floor of the valley is also affected and becomes wider than before. If the glacier then melts, the former V shape will have become the characteristic U shape of a glaciated valley. Some of the glacial meltwater may remain in the bottom of the valley, forming one or more ribbon lakes, which are named for their long, thin shape.

1. V-shaped valleys are neither as steep nor as wide as U-shaped valleys.
   ☑ Mentioned   ☐ Not mentioned
2. Canyons may form when a river runs through a dry area with hard rock.
   ☐ Mentioned   ☐ Not mentioned
3. Most V-shaped valleys eventually become U-shaped valleys.
   ☐ Mentioned   ☐ Not mentioned
4. Erosion caused by glaciers may lead to the formation of rivers.
   ☐ Mentioned   ☐ Not mentioned

D3 Use skimming and scanning to decide if each statement, 1–4, Restates or Contradicts this passage. One answer has been done for you. When you have finished, rewrite the statements that contradict the passage so that they restate it.

Scientists distinguish several different kinds of precipitation. The term *drizzle* is used when drops of water in the atmosphere with a diameter less than 0.5 millimeter fall as precipitation. Drizzle is the most frequent form of precipitation over wide areas of the planet, though the drops of water that form drizzle are often so small that the precipitation evaporates before reaching the ground. Another form of precipitation is rain, which makes up a significant part of the moisture that forms the planet's water cycle. When the temperature is cold, several different varieties of precipitation may form. Sleet is one, although the meaning of the term depends on location. In some countries, sleet means snow mixed with rain that partially melts when it falls to Earth. In other regions, sleet is a mixture of snow, ice pellets, and freezing rain. When atmospheric water vapor freezes to form ice crystals, it is called snow. If the water vapor forms irregular lumps of ice at least 5 millimeters across instead of crystals, it is known as hail, while graupel, or soft hail, is the name given to precipitation composed of smaller ice pellets mixed with tiny ice crystals.

1. Drizzle may not always fall to Earth's surface.
   ☑ Restates   ☐ Contradicts
2. Rain is the most common form of precipitation.
   ☐ Restates   ☐ Contradicts
3. Precipitation in the form of rain constitutes a small part of the water cycle.
   ☐ Restates   ☐ Contradicts
4. Sleet, snow, hail, and graupel all form under cold conditions.
   ☐ Restates   ☐ Contradicts

D4 Match these statements to their category by choosing the correct heading for categories 1 and 2 from A–D.

The Mississippi River is the longest river in the United States, and one of the three or four longest rivers in the world. Its source is Lake Itasca in north-central Minnesota, and from there it wends in a generally southward direction to its delta on the Gulf of Mexico. The Mississippi is divided into Upper, Middle, and Lower portions, with the divisions occurring at its confluences with the Missouri River and Ohio River respectively. Other tributaries include the Red, Arkansas, and Tennessee Rivers. A number of large settlements are located along the river and depend on it economically to a greater or lesser extent, including St. Louis, Memphis, and New Orleans.

1. _____

   • Its source is in northern Minnesota.
   • It flows southwards past some major cities.
   • It meets the ocean at the Gulf of Mexico.

2. _____

   • The Middle Mississippi starts where the Mississippi River meets the Missouri River.
   • The Lower Mississippi runs from the confluence with the Ohio River to the Gulf Mexico.

A   Main divisions of the Mississippi River
B   Major rivers in the United States of America
C   Physical characteristics of the Mississippi River
D   The general route of the Mississippi River

TEST TACTIC

Be careful with answer choices to Fill in a Table questions that both restate the passage clearly and match one of the categories very obviously. Obvious answers like these sometimes contradict a detail in the passage, so make sure you read all the answers carefully to avoid making mistakes.

D5 **Use the skills you have learned to answer this Fill in a Table question by selecting the answers, A–G, that correctly describe each category. Two of the answers will NOT be used. One answer has been done for you.**

When a volcano erupts, hot liquid rock called lava is often produced. Three broad classes of lava are known: mafic, felsic, and intermediate. Mafic lava is rich in iron and magnesium and erupts at very hot temperatures. It has a low viscosity, so eruptions of mafic lavas may flow long distances. Mafic lavas with very high levels of magnesium that erupt at temperatures as high as 1,600 degrees Celsius are called ultramafic. Felsic lavas are rich in elements including silica and aluminum, and are usually highly viscous and may erupt at temperatures 300 degrees lower than mafic lavas. Because of their viscosity, they typically do not flow for long distances except when they erupt at higher-than-usual temperatures. Intermediate lavas, as their name implies, possess characteristics halfway between felsic and mafic lavas. Chemically they contain fairly high levels of iron, magnesium, silica, and aluminum and erupt at temperatures between 750 and 950 degrees Celsius. They also have a viscosity level between that of the other two types of lava.

TEST TACTIC

If you are running out of time to answer a Fill in a Table question, focus on completing the category with the most answers accurately. Then assign the remaining answers using your common sense. This will often give you at least 1 point without taking too much time.

Mafic and ultramafic lavas
• Their low level of viscosity means they may flow for long distances.
•

Felsic or intermediate lavas
•
•
•

A   Their low level of viscosity means they may flow for long distances.
B   They erupt at low temperatures because they are rich in magnesium and iron.
C   They may be formed when lava eruptions from two types of volcano combine.
D   They contain high levels of the elements aluminum and silica.
E   They contain a wider variety of chemical elements than other types of lava.
F   They typically erupt at higher temperatures than other lavas.
G   Eruptions that occur under normal conditions rarely flow great distances.

E Analyzing Prose Summary Questions

You can also recognize Prose Summary questions from their detailed directions:

Directions: An introductory sentence for a brief summary of the passage is provided below. Complete the summary by selecting the THREE answer choices that express the most important ideas in the passage. Some sentences do not belong in the summary because they express ideas that are not presented in the passage or are minor ideas in the passage. **This question is worth 2 points.**

Below the directions you will see a sentence summarizing a key idea from the passage and space for three other sentences. You will also see a list of six answer statements, three of which also summarize a key idea from the passage. You will get 2 points for choosing all three right answers, 1 point for two right answers, and 0 points for one or zero right answers.

The three correct answers to Prose Summary questions:
• restate major ideas from the passage (sometimes by combining information from two paragraphs).
• are related to the overall main idea of the passage, which you can easily recognize from the title of the passage.

In contrast, the three incorrect answers:
- may restate a minor idea from the passage.
- may restate a point from the passage, but contradict one or more key details.
- may use words from the passage, but express an idea that is not mentioned in the passage.

E1 **Answer this Prose Summary question. Discuss your answers with a partner when you have finished.**

Portolan charts are a type of map intended for marine navigation. They were first made in Italy in the late thirteenth century, and then later in Spain and Portugal, and were in use from roughly 1275 to 1500 A.D. They differ in several ways from earlier maps. For one thing, portolans typically show specific marine regions in detail, often the coasts of the Mediterranean, Black Sea, or Atlantic Ocean, whereas many other maps showed the whole world (such maps are collectively known as *mappae mundi*) or one region, but with a focus on countries, not seas. In addition, portolans were drawn by pilots or navigators with first-hand knowledge of a region. Other maps were generally drawn by scholars who had never visited the places they were depicting. Further, portolans were designed for real-world navigation and depicted coastal features realistically as well as compass directions and, sometimes, typical wind directions. The Carta Pisana, the oldest surviving portolan, shows the Black Sea and Mediterranean coasts in enough detail that it could be used today even though it was made over 700 years ago. At the time of their creation and use, portolans provided information that was very valuable because it allowed sailors and traders to travel safely. They were so valuable, in fact, that the Spanish and Portuguese governments apparently considered them to be state secrets.

Directions: An introductory sentence for a brief summary of the passage is provided below. Complete the summary by selecting the THREE answer choices that express the most important ideas in the passage. Some sentences do not belong in the summary because they express ideas that are not presented in the passage or are minor ideas in the passage.

> **Portolan charts were a type of map intended to be used for safe sea travel.**
>
> •
>
> •
>
> •

A   Portolan charts were drawn by scholars and professional map-makers.
B   Individual portolan charts often show the coastlines of multiple bodies of water.
C   The information shown on portolan charts was considered to be of great value.
D   Old maps that depict the whole world are known as *mappae mundi*.
E   Portolans include information of use to sailors such as wind directions.
F   Portolan charts accurately show the features of the coasts they depict.

E2 **Complete descriptions 1–3 of the *wrong* answers from exercise E1. One answer has been done for you.**

1. Answer _____A_____ is wrong because it contradicts a key detail from the passage.
2. Answer _____ is wrong because it summarizes a minor idea from the passage.
3. Answer _____ is wrong because it describes a point that is not mentioned in the passage.

F Mastering Prose Summary Questions – Analyzing the Answer Choices

As with Fill in a Table questions, a key skill for answering Prose Summary questions is recognizing whether answers contradict or restate the passage. Another skill is recognizing if an answer restates a major or minor idea in the passage.

🔊 Track 5   **F1** **Take notes as you listen to an experienced teacher. Then use your notes to choose the best statement, A–C, to complete the steps for answering Prose Summary questions.**

Step 1	First, skim and scan the _____
Step 2	Next, compare the _____
Step 3	Finally, re-read the _____

A   relevant section and decide if the answer choice is a major or minor idea in the passage. If it is a minor idea, eliminate this answer. If it is a major idea, choose this answer.
B   answer choice to the relevant section of the passage and decide if the answer restates or contradicts the passage. If it contradicts the passage, eliminate this answer.
C   passage to find the section that gives information about an answer choice. If you cannot find a relevant section, eliminate this answer choice.

F2 **Match each answer choice, A–E, to the correct category. Then compare answers with a partner. One answer should NOT be chosen because it describes information that is not mentioned in the passage.**

Gaius Plinius Caecilius Secundus, or Pliny the Younger, was a Roman lawyer and writer. He is famous mainly for writing a large number of letters that constitute an excellent historical record of important events in Roman history. For geographers, two of Pliny's letters written to his friend the famous Roman historian Tacitus are especially interesting because they give a detailed account of the eruption of Mount Vesuvius in the year 79 A.D. This eruption apparently caused the death of Pliny's uncle, the noted Roman writer Pliny the Elder.

In these two letters, Pliny gives a clear, detailed account of the eruption. He describes the shape, height, and color of the ash cloud formed by the eruption. He also details the fall of hot ash, pumice, and rocks blackened by heat. He describes how the ash began to pile up "like snowdrifts" and reduced visibility and made breathing difficult. He also references numerous earthquakes that followed the eruption. Pliny's account is so vivid and accurate that modern volcanologists use the term Plinian eruption to describe volcanic eruptions of this type.

Answers that restate information in the passage
•
•

Answers that contradict information in the passage
•
•

A   The eruption of Mount Vesuvius caused hot ash and heated rocks to fall to the ground.
B   Unlike his uncle, Pliny the Younger did not see the eruption of Vesuvius himself.
C   Pliny the Younger's account of the eruption was imprecise in a number of ways.
D   Pliny the Younger knew many well-known Romans including the historian Tacitus.
E   According to Pliny the Younger, people felt earthquakes after Vesuvius erupted.

F3 Decide if statements 1–8 summarize a Major point or Minor point about the following passages. Major points usually match the overall main idea (as shown by the title of the passage) and describe a general point rather than a specific detail. One answer has been done for you.

Soil Formation

Soil is formed from parent materials that are weathered, transformed, transported, and then deposited to make the soil. Parent material can be classified as residual, transported, or cumulose. Residual materials are minerals that are formed from the original bedrock. Transported materials have been moved from one place and deposited in another place by the action of water, wind, ice, or gravity. And cumulose materials are organic parent materials that have grown in place and then accumulated to form a soil.

1. Soils are formed from up to three types of parent material.   ☑ Major   ☐ Minor
2. Ice and liquid water can relocate parent materials of soil.   ☐ Major   ☐ Minor

Sedimentary Rocks

Sedimentary rocks are formed when particles of material are deposited within bodies of water, such as oceans and lakes, or at the Earth's surface. Over time, the level of deposited material builds up, and pressure from the mass of the overlying material transforms the lowest-lying sediments into solid layers of rock. Although different types of sedimentary rocks, including sandstones, limestones, shales, and conglomerates, cover a large proportion of Earth's crust, they are underlain by igneous and metamorphic rocks, and scientists generally estimate that sedimentary rocks account for less than 10% of the total volume of the crust.

3. Pressure transforms particles and sediment into rock layers.   ☐ Major   ☐ Minor
4. Sedimentary rocks form a small proportion of Earth's crust.   ☐ Major   ☐ Minor
5. Scientists have to estimate some data about sedimentary rocks.   ☐ Major   ☐ Minor

Ansel Adams

Ansel Adams was among the most important and influential American photographers of the twentieth century. He photographed a wide variety of subjects, but he is best-known for his high-contrast, wide-format black and white landscape pictures with a wide tonal range. Many of his most famous pictures, such as *The Tetons and the Snake River* and *Monolith, the Face of Half Dome*, show natural features like rock cliffs, granite domes, mountain peaks and ranges, forested river valleys and bare rock slopes, and lakes, waterfalls, rivers, and streams.

6. Ansel Adams is best known for his landscape photographs.   ☐ Major   ☐ Minor
7. Ansel Adams' photographs sometimes depict bare rock.   ☐ Major   ☐ Minor
8. Black and white photographs can have a wide range of tones.   ☐ Major   ☐ Minor

G Test Challenge

G1 Answer these Fill in a Table and Prose Summary questions. Try to finish in 12 minutes or less so as to get realistic practice for the test. Use this checklist of skills that you studied in this unit as a guide.

For Fill in a Table questions

☑ Eliminate answer choices that are not mentioned in the passage or that contradict it.

☑ Eliminate answers that paraphrase the passage but do not match any of the categories.

☑ Decide which category each of the remaining answers matches.

For Prose Summary questions

☑ Eliminate answer choices that are not mentioned in the passage or that contradict it.

☑ Decide if the remaining answers restate a major or minor idea in the passage; then choose the three major points.

TEST TACTIC

If you are not sure whether an answer choice restates a major or minor point in the passage, imagine deleting that point. If the passage still makes sense and the author's arguments are still clear, the answer probably describes a minor point.

TEST TACTIC

For Prose Summary questions, if two answer choices express opposite ideas, often one of those choices is right and one is wrong. For Fill in a Table questions, if two answers express opposite ideas, one might be right and one wrong, or the two choices might match different categories.

Glacial Inlets

The formation of glacial inlets occurs when a glacier melts and its characteristic U-shaped valley is submerged by a rise in sea level. Depending on the size and weight of the glacier that caused them, these glacial inlets may be significantly deeper than the floor of the adjacent sea, although the depth is usually less near the mouth of the inlet.

Two main types of glacial inlet are recognized by scientists, with names that come from the same linguistic root and so are extremely similar: fjords (or fiords) and fjards (fiards). Förden are a third type of glacial inlet that are found in one part of Germany and Denmark. These inlets share many characteristics, but also differ in several ways.

Fjords are typically found in mountainous areas and may have very high, steep sides. For example, the sides of Sognefjord in Norway rise vertically from the water for almost one thousand meters along parts of its length. The channel of the fjord may be relatively straight, but is more commonly winding, and often splits to form several branches, one of which is usually wider than the others. Fjords tend to be longer and narrower than fjards or förden. The longest fjord in the world, Scoresby Sund in Greenland, is over 350 kilometers in length.

Fjards are typically found in areas of lower relief and thus tend to be lower and less steep than fjords. Because of their low relief, fjards are often associated with features like salt marshes and mud flats that are not characteristic of fjords. They are usually irregular in shape and deep – though generally not as deep as fjords – with a shallow mouth.

1. **Directions:** Select the phrases that correctly describe each type of glacial inlet. One of the phrases will NOT be used. **This question is worth 3 points.**

Fjords

-
-

Fjards

-

Fjords and fjards

-
-

Ⓐ   Inlet channels may be shallower in some parts than others.
Ⓑ   Inlets are usually short and straight with few branches.
Ⓒ   Inlets may occur near low-relief features like mud flats.
Ⓓ   Channels are often steep-sided, winding, and branched.
Ⓔ   Inlets are formed when a glacial valley is submerged.
Ⓕ   Inlets typically occur in mountainous regions.

Naming Landforms

English has a huge number of words that either derive from or are loaned from other languages. One area of the language where this is especially true is names for natural features and landforms. Many of these words are English words originally, of course, but there are also words for landforms from languages as diverse as Arabic, Russian, Italian, Irish Gaelic, Greenlandic, and Old Norse.

There are several reasons for this inclusion in English of words from such a range of languages. Many natural features are found in some regions but not in others. English has words for features that are found in the British countryside, such as rivers, lakes, hills, mountains, cliffs, sand dunes, and so on. But to describe features that are less common or which do not occur at all, words from other languages are often used. For example, glaciers sometimes form concave depressions in mountains. These are relatively rare in England, but are common in other regions and can be called either a *cirque*, from French, a *corrie*, from Scottish Gaelic, or a *cwm*, pronounced /coom/, from Welsh. In a similar way, the names for types of lava like *a'a* and *pahoehoe* come from the Hawaiian language because these lavas are commonly found in the volcanic Hawaiian Islands.

During the period when the fields of geography and geology were becoming more scientific, these subjects were widely studied and taught in various European countries, including France, Germany, Spain, and Italy. As a result, if a scholar from one of those countries was the first to describe a landform in detail, words from that scholar's language may be used to name the landform even if it can be found in Britain. Examples include the Spanish word *cuesta* to describe a ridge with one gentle and one steep slope, the German word *dreikanter* to describe a rock shaped by wind-blown sand, and the French word *levee* to describe a natural or artificial embankment that controls river levels.

Finally, as with many academic subjects, scholars working in the Earth sciences often use classical languages to name features that are new to science, for which no local name could be determined, or which were described in classical sources. The word archipelago, meaning a chain of islands, comes from two Greek words meaning *chief* and *sea*. The name for metamorphic rocks also derives from Greek, in this case from a word meaning *to transform*, which describes the process that metamorphic rocks undergo; the names for igneous and sedimentary rocks, however, both come from Latin words that mean, respectively, *fiery* and *settling* or *sinking down*.

---

2. **Directions:** An introductory sentence for a brief summary of the passage is provided below. Complete the summary by selecting the THREE answer choices that express the most important ideas in the passage. Some sentences do not belong in the summary because they express ideas that are not presented in the passage or are minor ideas in the passage. **This question is worth 2 points.**

> **Many geographical landforms have names that come from languages other than English.**
>
> •
>
> •
>
> •

   Ⓐ   Scholars turn to ancient languages to name previously unknown landforms.

   Ⓑ   Mountainous regions that contain concave glacial depressions are not found in England.

   Ⓒ   Some names come from the European language that was first used to describe them.

   Ⓓ   Metamorphic rocks, whose name comes from Greek, have undergone a transformation.

   Ⓔ   Levees are a common feature along the banks of a number of rivers in France.

   Ⓕ   Names may come from a language native to the region where a landform is common.

TEST TACTIC

If you are running out of time to answer a Prose Summary question, quickly choose the three answers that are most directly related to the title of the passage and most general (rather than specific). This will often give you at least 1 point without taking much time.

Continental Drift

Looking at a map of the world, the shapes of some continents seem as if they fit together like a kind of giant puzzle. The first person to suggest in print that the continents had originally been joined and then had moved to their present locations was the Flemish map-maker and geographer Abraham Ortelius near the end of the sixteenth century. Other notables who suggested similar theories are the explorer Alexander von Humboldt, and geographer and scientist Antonio Snider-Pellegrini, both in the nineteenth century. A book by Snider-Pellegrini published in 1858 even included maps showing his impression of how the American and African continents had once been joined.

However, the idea was not taken seriously by scholars until Alfred Wegener, a German meteorologist and polar researcher, published the same idea in a 1912 article and 1915 book. Wegener's theory, which mirrored some similar, earlier theories though he developed his ideas independently, described what he termed *Kontinentalverschiebung*, which translates into English as "continental drift." In his works, in addition to noting the close 'fit' of the continents with one another, Wegener gave geological evidence. He noted that sedimentary rocks that share the same attributes are found in South America, Africa, Antarctica, India, and Australia. Wegener also noted that fossils of the same plants and reptiles could be found widely distributed over these same continental areas. Wegener argued that, when taken as a whole, his evidence strongly suggested that the current continents had once all been joined as one huge continent but had later separated and moved to their present positions on the surface of the Earth.

From the beginning, a few people accepted his ideas, but the predominant reaction was critical, with a number of influential geologists like Harold Jeffreys and George Gaylord Simpson attacking Wegener's views. In general, critics were not convinced by his evidence, which was viewed as being circumstantial rather than conclusive. Further, the forces that Wegener proposed as strong enough to move the continents – including pseudo-centrifugal force from the Earth's rotation – were calculated to be too weak to do so and no other mechanism that might be able to move continents was accepted. It has also been suggested there was bias against Wegener because he was mainly a meteorologist not a geologist and did not follow certain standard practices of the latter discipline.

By the 1950s, however, evidence from new discoveries began to change people's minds. Some rocks contain minerals like hematite that are magnetized by the Earth's magnetic field when they are formed. The polarity, strength, and orientation of the magnetism in these minerals can be used to determine when and where the rock was formed. Analysis of such minerals from rocks in India showed that they had been formed in the southern hemisphere and then moved north of the equator as Wegener had proposed. Additional paleomagnetic evidence suggested that the positions of Europe and North America, too, had changed. Then in the 1960s it became clear that the Earth was spreading apart at mid-ocean ridges where new crustal material was being formed. This process of seafloor spreading finally provided a mechanism for how continents move and proved Wegener's theory to most people's satisfaction. Sadly, Wegener died in 1930 and did not live to see his ideas widely accepted.

3. **Directions:** Select the phrases that correctly describe evidence relating to the theory of continental drift. Two of the phrases will NOT be used. **This question is worth 3 points.**

Evidence that Wegener initially presented

-
-
-

Evidence that persuaded other scientists

-
-

Ⓐ   Proof that Europe and North America had once been in the same location

Ⓑ   Information about the magnetic polarity of certain minerals in rocks

Ⓒ   Rocks found in diverse locations that share the same characteristics

Ⓓ   The way in which the shape of some continents seem to fit together well

Ⓔ   Recognition that Wegener's theories were previously suggested by other scholars

Ⓕ   The discovery that the seafloor is spreading and new crustal material is being formed

Ⓖ   Widely distributed fossilized remains from various species of organism

4. **Directions:** An introductory sentence for a brief summary of the passage is provided below. Complete the summary by selecting the THREE answer choices that express the most important ideas in the passage. Some sentences do not belong in the summary because they express ideas that are not presented in the passage or are minor ideas in the passage. **This question is worth 2 points.**

Note that in the real TOEFL Test, you will never have both a Prose Summary and Fill in a Table question about the same passage.

> **Alfred Wegener's theory of continental drift was not accepted at first but was later proved correct.**
>
> •
>
> •
>
> •

Ⓐ   New scientific discoveries in the 1950s and 1960s led to Wegener's theory being accepted.

Ⓑ   Wegener's theory was criticized because it did not adequately explain how continents move.

Ⓒ   Alfred Wegener died before his theory of continental drift was widely accepted.

Ⓓ   Wegener's ideas were put forward in two works – an article and a book.

Ⓔ   A few people wrote books in support of Wegener's theory of continental drift.

Ⓕ   Alfred Wegener provided several geological examples in support of his theory.

Next Steps

Topics related to Earth science are very common in both the TOEFL reading and listening sections, so learning more about this subject, as well as practicing key skills for Fill in a Table and Prose Summary questions, may help you increase your overall test score.

To learn more about Earth science and vocabulary related to this discipline:

1. Read an article in your language about one aspect of Earth science to get some background knowledge about this topic.
2. Read an English article about the same topic to understand the main ideas, but do not try to understand every word.
3. Read the English article again and make a list of up to ten unfamiliar words that are directly related to the topic and that you think are important. If the article is about glaciers, for example, your list might include words like *moraine* or *crevasse* but not a word like *ice*, which is a familiar word, or *process*, which is not directly related to the topic of glaciers.

To practice key skills for Fill in a Table and Prose Summary questions:

1. Choose two articles in English about the same aspect of Earth science.
2. Pick one of the articles – call this article A – and scan it to find five major points and five minor points.
3. Read article B to see if it restates the major and minor points that you noted from article A.
4. Next, look for ideas in either article A or B that are not mentioned in the other article.
5. Finally, look for points in either article A or B that are contradicted in the other article.

Directions

This reading review test is intended to help you find out your strengths and weaknesses in reading. You will have 40 minutes to read two passages and answer 25 questions (worth 28 points). The passages and questions are designed to be at the same level as the ones you will see on the TOEFL Test. When you have finished, check your answers with your instructor or against the Answer Key. Then use the conversion chart on page 90 to convert your raw score to your likely score on the TOEFL Test.

Test

Read the two passages and answer questions 1–25. You have 40 minutes.

Parasites

Parasites are organisms that have specialized adaptations allowing them to live within (as endoparasites) or on (as ectoparasites) a much larger host organism for an extended period of time. This lifestyle benefits the parasite, typically by providing it with access to something it needs, such as nutrients or other vital resources. Traditionally, all parasite infections were believed to be non-mutual in that the relationship was detrimental to the host organism. Recent research studies, however, have provided evidence that in some cases parasites may actually confer health advantages on their hosts, too. Parasites are typically classified according to their life cycle and how they interact with their hosts.

Macroparasites have two main defining characteristics. As their name suggests, they tend to be large enough to be seen with the naked eye. In addition, their life cycle involves at least two different hosts: a primary host in which they reach maturity and may reproduce, and a secondary host in which the parasites complete one or more developmental stages in their life cycle. For example, schistosomiasis is caused by several species of parasitic trematodes, a kind of flatworm. The worms reach maturity in humans, who catch the infection after being exposed to water contaminated with freshwater snails. These snails act as the secondary host for the parasite. Some macroparasites, such as tapeworms, have even more complex life cycles and must complete various developmental stages in a sequence of different hosts. And in some cases, such as with the roundworm that causes trichinosis, the host may have both mature and juvenile parasites in different internal organs, thereby functioning as both the primary and secondary host to the parasite.

In contrast with macroparasites, microparasites are too small to be seen without a microscope. In addition, they typically live out their life cycle within a single host organism, and are usually transmitted directly between hosts of the same species without going through a secondary host. The main classes of microparasites are bacteria, protozoa, and fungi, all of which are single-celled organisms, as well as viruses, which are non-cellular. The bacterium that causes salmonella poisoning, for instance, is a microparasite. Based on size, the plasmodium protozoan that causes malaria is a microparasite, yet it shares a feature of macroparasites in that it needs two hosts: a mosquito and human or other animal.

In addition to their differences in size and typical life cycle, macroparasites and microparasites cause different kinds of infections. Those resulting from macroparasites tend to be chronic and develop slowly because of the relatively long generation times – measured in weeks or even months – of those organisms. Hosts that recover from an infection rarely develop immunity to it, although this can happen if a particular host has a very high parasite burden. By contrast, infections resulting from microparasites are often acute and come on quickly because of the much shorter generation time and higher reproductive rate of these parasites. Hosts that are infected and then recover from infections by microparasites often develop protective immunity against further infections in the future.

One further class of parasitic organism is the parasitoid. These organisms share many of the characteristics of true parasites – they live on or within a host organism, for instance, and require that host to complete part of their life cycle. However, a parasitoid infection often requires the death of the host organism. The ichneumon wasp is an example. Female wasps lay eggs on or inside a host. When the eggs hatch the larva feed on the host's dying or dead body until they mature and become adults. It is true that certain parasites do sometimes cause acute infections that are fatal to their host organisms, but this is not a required part of their life cycle. Indeed, when its host dies, a parasite typically dies, too.

1. Which of the following best expresses the essential information in the highlighted sentence in paragraph 1? Incorrect choices change the meaning in important ways or leave out essential information.
   Ⓐ Host organisms can live for an extended period when parasites have not adapted to them.
   Ⓑ Larger organisms can typically live with parasitic organisms for longer periods of time.
   Ⓒ Parasitic organisms have adapted to living on or inside a different organism called a host.
   Ⓓ The special adaptations of some organisms allow them to be ectoparasites or endoparasites.

2. The word "detrimental" in paragraph 1 most likely means
   Ⓐ communal
   Ⓑ beneficial
   Ⓒ detailed
   Ⓓ harmful

3. In paragraph 2, the author states that macroparasites usually
   Ⓐ have complex life cycles
   Ⓑ use snails as secondary hosts
   Ⓒ live within a host's internal organs
   Ⓓ reach maturity in humans

4. The word "juvenile" in paragraph 2 is closest in meaning to
   Ⓐ flexible
   Ⓑ young
   Ⓒ divisive
   Ⓓ paternal

5. The author mentions all of the following about microparasites EXCEPT:
   Ⓐ They are all single-celled organisms.
   Ⓑ They are not visible to the naked eye.
   Ⓒ They typically do not need a secondary host.
   Ⓓ They mainly cause acute problems in their host.

6. Why does the author mention the plasmodium protozoan in paragraph 3?
   Ⓐ To explain why microparasites which are bacteria, fungi, or viruses do not require two hosts
   Ⓑ To give an example of a parasite that can live within a single host or within more than one host
   Ⓒ To suggest that microparasites cause diseases in humans more often than macroparasites do
   Ⓓ To demonstrate that the categories of macroparasite and microparasite are not exclusive

7. What point does the author make about parasitic infections in paragraph 4?
   Ⓐ In general, macroparasitic infections do not affect their host rapidly.
   Ⓑ Infections caused by microparasites often last for weeks or even longer.
   Ⓒ Parasites with shorter generation times only rarely cause infections.
   Ⓓ Parasitic infections are likely to be less of a problem in the future.

8. The word "immunity" in paragraph 4 is closest in meaning to
   (A) capacity
   (B) imbalance
   (C) danger
   (D) resistance

9. What does the author imply in paragraph 5?
   (A) Severe parasitic infections usually kill the host.
   (B) Parasitoids do not die when their host does.
   (C) Mature parasitoids are generally not dangerous.
   (D) All parasitoid species infect a host by laying eggs.

10. The word "their" in paragraph 5 refers to
    (A) host organisms
    (B) acute infections
    (C) certain parasites
    (D) female wasps

11. Look at the four squares (■) that indicate where the following sentence could be added to the passage.

    More than 200 million people around the world are thought to suffer from schistosomiasis, making it a disease with significant socioeconomic effects.

    Where would the sentence best fit? Choose position **A**, **B**, **C**, or **D**.

    Macroparasites have two main defining characteristics. As their name suggests, they tend to be large enough to be seen with the naked eye. In addition, their life cycle involves at least two different hosts: a primary host in which they reach maturity and may reproduce, and a secondary host in which the parasites complete one or more developmental stages in their life cycle. **A** For example, schistosomiasis is caused by several species of parasitic trematodes, a kind of flatworm. **B** The worms reach maturity in humans who catch the infection after being exposed to water contaminated with freshwater snails. **C** These snails act as the secondary host for the parasite. **D** Some macroparasites, such as tapeworms, have even more complex life cycles and must complete various developmental stages in a sequence of different hosts. And in some cases, such as with the roundworm that causes trichinosis, the host may have both mature and juvenile parasites in different internal organs, thereby functioning as both the primary and secondary host to the parasite.

12. **Directions:** Select the phrases that correctly describe each type of parasitic organism. One of the phrases will NOT be used. **This question is worth 3 points.**

Macroparasites
•
•

Microparasites
•
•

Parasitoids
•

<table>
<tr><td>Ⓐ</td><td>Gain health benefits from their host</td></tr>
<tr><td>Ⓑ</td><td>Reproduce at a rapid rate</td></tr>
<tr><td>Ⓒ</td><td>Reach adulthood in their primary host</td></tr>
<tr><td>Ⓓ</td><td>Have a life cycle that is often fatal to their host</td></tr>
<tr><td>Ⓔ</td><td>Usually cause chronic infections in a host</td></tr>
<tr><td>Ⓕ</td><td>May be one of four classes of organism</td></tr>
</table>

Machu Picchu

Machu Picchu is the site of a ruined Inca city in the mountains of Peru roughly 80 kilometers (50 miles) from the city of Cusco, the ancient Incan capital. Archaeologists believe Machu Picchu was built during the period when the Incan Empire was at its strongest, most likely around 1450 A.D. It is not known for certain why the site was built, but the most widely accepted theory is that Pachacuti, the ninth ruler of the Incas, had it built as a royal estate. Evidence suggests that the site was occupied by a permanent population of around 300 people, but may have housed as many as 1,000 when the emperor visited. Machu Picchu was mostly abandoned in the 1530s or 1540s during the Spanish Conquest of the Incas, though the Spanish soldiers likely did not visit or know about the site. Archaeological data suggests that a few people may have continued to occupy the site until 1572, the year when the last Incan capital city was captured.

After it was abandoned, the site was forgotten except by local people. It became widely known only in the early years of the twentieth century when American academic Hiram Bingham III discovered and reported it as part of an expedition sponsored by Yale University. Bingham's name has become closely associated with the site, though it is possible that Machu Picchu was actually rediscovered as early as the 1860s or 1870s by two Germans, businessman Augusto Berns and engineer J. M. von Hassel. At least one map dating from 1874, for example, makes reference to the site. There are also claims that two British missionaries, Thomas Payne and Stuart McNairn, climbed up to Machu Picchu five years before Bingham first visited the site.

The layout and architecture of the site follow the natural terrain of the mountain on which Machu Picchu is built, with the site divided into two sectors, a heavily-terraced agricultural sector divided into upper and lower zones in the southeastern part of the site, and an urban sector in the northeastern part. The terraces allowed more of the mountain slopes to be devoted to farming; they also helped reduce the impact of soil erosion and protect against landslides. The fields had cleverly engineered channels to provide irrigation, with the water coming from natural springs. The agricultural setup ensured that the site was self-sufficient, with scholars estimating that farmers would have been able to grow enough food to feed several times the maximum number of people who ever lived at the site.

The urban sector has roughly 200 buildings situated around a large central square. The buildings to the west of the square mostly had a ceremonial or spiritual function, while those to the east were predominantly residential. The most famous buildings at the site include the Temple of the Sun, the Temple of Three Windows, the Temple of the Condor, and the Hitching Post of the Sun, or the Intihuatana Stone. These names are the ones given by modern scholars; the original names by which the Inca knew these structures, and indeed their original purpose, are not known. The urban sector also includes palatial homes for the rich as well as simpler homes for lower-class residents, fountains, storehouses, workshops, and possibly royal tombs.

One of the most striking features of Machu Picchu is its construction. The primary building material is granite blocks cut from nearby quarries. Granite is a hard rock that is difficult to cut to exact specifications even with modern tools. The Inca clearly did not have those, or even a system of writing, yet the stones were cut to exact measurements and then fitted to other stones using a technique called *ashlar* in which no mortar, a material normally used to bind bricks or blocks of stone together, was used. Buildings constructed using ashlar are generally extremely durable, an important point because the area where Machu Picchu is located is prone to earthquakes. At the time it was constructed, the Inca did not have draft animals like horses or donkeys, and there is no evidence that they used wheeled vehicles, so it is believed that all of the stones were cut, moved, and placed by teams of hundreds of workers.

13. Why was Machu Picchu probably built?
- (A)   To provide homes for 1,000 people
- (B)   To defend against attacking armies
- (C)   As a place where a ruler could stay
- (D)   To be a capital of the Incan Empire

14. The word "abandoned" in paragraph 1 is closest in meaning to
- (A)   deserted
- (B)   allocated
- (C)   assembled
- (D)   supported

15. What point does the author NOT make in paragraph 2?
- (A)   Hiram Bingham III was the first person to spread news about Machu Picchu widely.
- (B)   German businessmen tried to make money from Machu Picchu in the 1870s.
- (C)   For a long time the only people who knew about Machu Picchu were the ones living near it.
- (D)   Evidence suggests that Hiram Bingham III was not the first person to rediscover Mach Picchu.

16. The word "terrain" in paragraph 3 is closest in meaning to
- (A)   opportunity
- (B)   construction
- (C)   environment
- (D)   settlement

17. Select the TWO answer choices that describe the functions of the terraces mentioned in paragraph 3. *To receive credit you must select two answers.*
- [A]   To give protection against natural processes
- [B]   To create channels for transporting water
- [C]   To provide additional land for agriculture
- [D]   To increase the impact of human engineering

18. Which of the following best expresses the essential information in the highlighted sentence in paragraph 3? Incorrect choices change the meaning in important ways or leave out essential information.
- (A)   Farmers could grow enough food for themselves, but were not set up to grow sufficient food for the groups of scholars.
- (B)   The site at Machu Picchu did not have sufficient land or agricultural resources for the estimated maximum population.
- (C)   There was enough agricultural land and water to provide food for a larger population than could live at the site.
- (D)   Even when the maximum population lived at the site, experts believe farmers were able to feed them several times.

19. What does the author imply in paragraph 4?
- (A)   The Inca who lived at Machu Picchu built houses with many windows because the sun was important to them.
- (B)   Some buildings that are called temples by modern scholars may not originally have had a religious function.
- (C)   The palatial homes for rich residents of Machu Picchu are located to the west of the large central square.
- (D)   Most residences in the urban sector were constructed as close as possible to the large central square.

20. The word "those" in paragraph 5 refers to
    - Ⓐ granite blocks
    - Ⓑ nearby quarries
    - Ⓒ exact specifications
    - Ⓓ modern tools

21. The word "bind" in paragraph 5 most likely means
    - Ⓐ pressure
    - Ⓑ occupy
    - Ⓒ denote
    - Ⓓ connect

22. Why does the author mention the lack of horses and donkeys in paragraph 5?
    - Ⓐ To emphasize the impressive nature of the construction of Machu Picchu
    - Ⓑ To suggest that the construction of Machu Picchu proceeded rather slowly
    - Ⓒ To give an example of something that would have helped with construction
    - Ⓓ To explain why there is no evidence that the Inca used vehicles with wheels

23. The phrase "is prone to" in paragraph 5 is closest in meaning to
    - Ⓐ rapidly protects
    - Ⓑ largely avoids
    - Ⓒ hardly develops
    - Ⓓ often experiences

24. Look at the four squares (■) that indicate where the following sentence could be added to the passage.

    These were fed by the abundant rains the site received annually, particularly between October and April.

    Where would the sentence best fit? Choose position ■A, ■B, ■C, or ■D.

    The layout and architecture of the site follow the natural terrain of the mountain on which Machu Picchu is built, with the site divided into two sectors, a heavily-terraced agricultural sector divided into upper and lower zones in the southeastern part of the site, and an urban sector in the northeastern part. ■A The terraces allowed more of the mountain slopes to be used for farming; they also helped reduce the impact of soil erosion and protect against landslides. ■B The fields had cleverly-engineered channels to provide irrigation, with the water coming from natural springs. ■C The agricultural setup ensured that the site was self-sufficient, with scholars estimating that farmers would have been able to grow enough food to feed several times the maximum number of people who ever lived at the site. ■D

25. **Directions:** An introductory sentence for a brief summary of the passage is provided below. Complete the summary by selecting the THREE answer choices that express the most important ideas in the passage. Some sentences do not belong in the summary because they express ideas that are not presented in the passage or are minor ideas in the passage. **This question is worth 2 points.**

> **Machu Picchu is an important Inca site in the mountains of Peru.**
>
> -
> -
> -

- Ⓐ An American university sponsored expeditions to discover Machu Picchu in the 1860s and 1870s.
- Ⓑ Traditional Inca building methods could not be used at Machu Picchu because of the danger of earthquakes.
- Ⓒ Machu Picchu did not become known to the wider world until the early part of the twentieth century.
- Ⓓ The site at Machu Picchu has two zones, one for food production and one for housing and other purposes.
- Ⓔ Soldiers from Spain could not attack Machu Picchu because too many people were living at the site.
- Ⓕ The methods of construction used to build Machu Picchu are impressive given the technology at the time.

Score Conversion

Check your answers to questions 1–25. Then use this conversion chart to find out your approximate reading score range on the TOEFL Test.

Raw Score (out of 28)	Probable Level	Approximate Score Range
26–28		28–30
23–25	High	25–27
20–22		22–24
18–20	Intermediate	19–21
14–17		15–18
10–13		11–14
6–9	Low	7–10
3–6		3–6
0–2		0–2

Overview

The listening section measures your ability to understand conversations and lectures spoken in English. You will see and/or hear:

- Instructions to put on your headphones — less than 1 minute
- Directions for adjusting the volume of the sound you will hear through your headphones — about 1 minute
- Directions for the listening section — about 2 minutes
- Either two conversations and four lectures with 34 questions (if you had four passages in the reading section), or three conversations and six lectures with 51 questions (if you had three passages in the reading section) — 60–90 minutes

Your answers will be scored by a computer and your raw score will be converted to a scaled score from 0–30.

NOTES

- The conversations and lectures are divided into sets, with each set having one conversation and two lectures. You will have ten minutes to answer the 17 questions in each set. The clock does not count down while you are listening to the conversation and lectures.
- Each conversation lasts three minutes or longer. The speakers may be a student and a professor, or a student and a person who works at a college. The conversations are about typical issues for students, such as taking classes, using the library, or paying college fees.
- Each lecture lasts four minutes or longer. You may hear a monologue, in which only a professor speaks. You may also hear interactive lectures in which you will hear a professor plus comments and questions from one or two students. Monologues are often the first lecture in a set, and interactive lectures are often the second lecture in a set. Topics for lectures include typical subjects that students study at college.
- You may see up to eight different types of questions in the listening section, divided into three categories: basic comprehension questions, pragmatic understanding questions, and connecting information questions.
- If you have three sets (in other words, three conversations and six lectures), it is possible that the questions about one of the conversations and two of the lectures will NOT count towards your raw score. However, there is no way to know which conversation and lectures will not count, so you should answer all questions to the best of your ability.
- Most speakers in the listening section will speak with a North American accent, but you may also hear speakers from Australia, Great Britain, or New Zealand. These speakers will not have strong accents.

Detailed Guide

TEST TACTIC

Do not take off your headset during the listening section, even after a conversation or lecture finishes. Some of the questions require you to listen again to a replayed part of the talk.

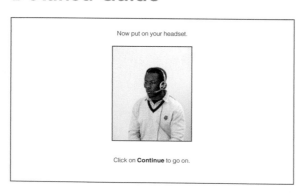

Now put on your headset.

Click on **Continue** to go on.

Before you begin the listening section you will see a screen telling you to put on your headset. You must use the headset in order to hear the conversations and lectures.

After you have put on your headphones, click on the button labeled **Continue**.

Next you will see instructions for changing the volume. Follow the instructions and adjust the volume so that you can hear the speaker clearly through your headset.

When you have set the volume at a comfortable level, click on the button labeled **Continue**. The speaker will keep repeating the message until you click this button.

Changing the Volume

To change the volume, click on the **Volume** icon at the top of screen. The volume control will appear. Move the volume indicator to the left or to the right to change the volume.

To close the volume control, click on the Volume icon again.

You will be able to change the volume during the test if you need to.

> You may now change the volume.
> When you are finished, click on Continue.

When you begin the listening section of the TOEFL Test, you will first see the directions for the whole section. You will hear a narrator read the directions aloud. You can change the volume while the narrator is speaking by clicking on the **Volume** button in the top right corner of the screen.

When you are ready to begin the test, click the button marked **Continue**.

Listening Section Directions

This section measures your ability to understand conversations and lectures in English.

The Listening section is divided into 2 separately timed parts. In each part you will listen to one conversation and two lectures. You will each conversation or lecture only **one** time.

After each conversation or lecture, you will answer some questions about it. The questions typically ask about the main idea and supporting details. Some questions ask about a speaker's purpose or attitude. Answer the questions based on what is stated or implied by the speakers.

You may take notes while you listen. You may use your notes to help you answer the questions. Your notes will **not** be scored.

If you need to change the volume while you listen, click on the **Volume** icon at the top of the screen.

In some questions, you will see this icon: ⌒ This means that you will hear, but not see, part of the question.

Some of the questions have special directions. These directions appear in a gray box on the screen.

Most questions are worth 1 point. If a question is worth more than 1 point, it will have special directions that indicate how many points you can receive.

You must answer each question. After you answer, click on **Next**. Then click on **OK** to confirm your answer and go on to the next question. After you click on **OK**, you cannot return to previous questions.

Next you will see a picture of two people on the screen, such as a student and a professor, or a student and a college librarian. A narrator will say who the people are and tell you to listen to their conversation.

The conversation will usually last at least three minutes. You will see a bar below the picture that shows how much longer the conversation will last. You may take notes while you listen to the conversation.

Usually the picture on the screen does not change during the conversation. However, in rare cases you might see a picture of a notebook with some words written on it.

After the conversation you will see a screen telling you to get ready to answer some questions. This screen will disappear automatically after a few seconds.

Then a question will appear on the screen and the narrator will read it aloud. Next the answer choices will appear. The timer will begin to count down as soon as the answer choices appear.

In total you will see five questions after each conversation. After you answer one question, the next one will appear and you will not be able to go back and change your answer to the previous question. When you have answered all five questions, the timer will stop and you will hear a lecture.

Now get ready to answer the questions.

You may use your notes to help you answer.

TOEFL Listening   VOLUME   HELP ?   OK   NEXT →

Question 1 of 17   HIDE TIME   00 : 09 : 46

Why does the student visit her professor?

○ To get help with an assignment

○ To submit a late piece of work

○ To return a book he borrowed

○ To explain that she will be absent

Before each lecture you will see a screen with the name of an academic subject, such as "History" or "Marine Biology." The narrator will then tell you to listen to a lecture from a class about this subject.

History

Then the screen will change and you will see a picture of a professor on the screen. The professor will speak about an academic topic, usually for at least four or five minutes but sometimes for longer. Sometimes you will hear comments or questions from a student, too. You will see a bar below the picture that shows how much longer the lecture will last.

You may take notes while you listen to the professor or other speakers.

convection

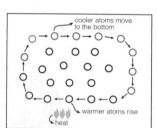

During the lecture the picture on the screen might change. If a student asks a question or makes a comment, the picture will usually show a close up of the student.

If the professor mentions an important detail, such as a name or date, you might see a picture of a chalkboard with this detail written on it. And if the professor explains a complex process or different aspects of a topic, you might see a diagram.

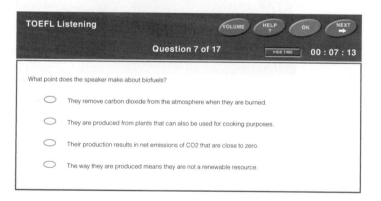

TOEFL Listening	VOLUME	HELP?	OK	NEXT ➡

Question 7 of 17   HIDE TIME   00 : 07 : 13

What point does the speaker make about biofuels?

○ They remove carbon dioxide from the atmosphere when they are burned.

○ They are produced from plants that can also be used for cooking purposes.

○ Their production results in net emissions of CO2 that are close to zero.

○ The way they are produced means they are not a renewable resource.

After each lecture you will see a screen telling you to get ready to answer some questions. This screen will disappear automatically after a few seconds.

Then a question will appear on the screen and the narrator will read it aloud. Next the answer choices will appear. The timer will begin to count down as soon as the answer choices appear.

In total you will see six questions after each lecture. After you answer one question, the next one will appear and you will not be able to go back and change your answer to the previous question.

When you have answered all six questions, the timer will stop and you will either hear the next lecture or see a screen telling you that this part of the listening section is finished. If you see this screen, You will have to click **Continue** to go on to the next part of the listening or the next part of the test.

TEST TACTIC

When the picture on the screen changes, it is usually a sign that the speaker is discussing a key point. So if the picture changes, concentrate hard, listen carefully, and take effective notes.

Most questions in the listening section ask you to choose one answer from four choices. To choose your answer, click on the answer or on the oval next to it. To change your answer, click on a different answer choice.

After you have chosen your answer, click on the **Next** button and then the **OK** button at the top right of the screen. After you have clicked **OK**, you will see the next question and you will not be able to go back or change your answer.

You cannot go on to the next question until you select an answer choice.

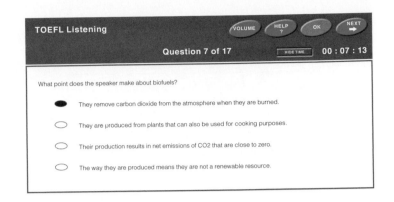

Some questions that ask you to choose one answer from four choices are replay questions. For these questions you will first see a message telling you to listen again to part of the conversation or lecture. Then you will see the picture of the speaker or speakers again and listen to part of the conversation or lecture. Next you will see a question on the screen plus an icon of some headphones. Finally you will listen again to a short part of the replayed part of the conversation or lecture. You will then see the answer choices and be able to answer the question in the normal way.

For some replay questions you will not see the picture of the speaker or speakers again, and you will only hear a replayed part of the conversation or lecture once.

Note that the time to answer questions will not count down while you listen to replayed parts of the conversation or lecture.

Listen again to part of the conversation.
Then answer the question.

Why does the professor say this? 🎧

     ◯ To remind the man that he already asked for an extension

     ◯ To express her surprise that the man could not find a book

     ◯ To give an example of something the man should probably do

     ◯ To emphasize her positive reaction to the man's idea

Some questions require you to choose two or three answers from four to six choices. These questions have special directions shown in a gray box.

To choose your answers, click on the box next to them. If you need to choose a different answer, click on the box next to an answer you have already selected to deselect it. Then click on the box next to a different answer.

You will only be able to go to the next question when you have chosen the required number of answers. If you choose too many or too few answers and then click on the **Next** and **OK** buttons, you will see a warning message.

Why does the man say he will be absent?

     ☐ He has an interview for a job.

     ☒ He has a medical appointment.

     ☒ He has to attend a meeting.

     ☐ He has to visit a family member.

RETURN TO QUESTION

You must select the EXACT number of choices before you can leave this question."

In the lecture, the professor discusses who had the right to vote in Athens in the fifth century B.C. Indicate whether these groups had the right to vote.

Click in the correct box for each answer.		
	Yes	No
Women who were married to male citizens		✓
Male citizens who had completed military training		
Male citizens of other city states in Greece		
Foreigners who had been granted citizenship of Athens		

Some questions ask you to decide which answers match which categories. These questions also have special directions shown in a gray box.

To mark your answers, click in the correct column. A check (✓) will appear. If you wish to change an answer, click again in the same column to clear your answer and then click in another column. You can change answers as often as you wish.

For most of these questions, each answer choice matches only one category. In some cases, however, an answer choice may match two categories.

You must assign every answer to a category before you will be able to click on the **Next** and **OK** buttons.

The professor mentions the typical stages in the flight of a model rocket. Put the stages in the correct order.

Drag the answer choices to the spaces where they belong. To remove an answer choice, click on it.

1	
2	
3	Coasting flight
4	
5	

- Powered ascent
-
- Slow descent
- Ejection charge
- Lift off

Some questions ask you to put events or steps in a process in order. These questions also have special directions shown in a gray box.

To answer these questions, drag the answer choices into the correct order. If you wish to change an answer, drag a different answer into the same space, or drag the original answer away from the table. You can change answers as often as you wish.

You must assign every answer to a position before you will be able to click on the **Next** and **OK** buttons.

After you have answered all of the questions in the listening section, you will have a break for ten minutes.

TEST TACTIC

Try to use some of your time during the ten-minute break after the listening section to prepare yourself for the speaking section. For example, you could think about the steps you need to follow to answer each type of speaking question.

Scoring

Your answers for the listening section will be scored by computer. For most questions, you will get 1 point for a correct answer, but some questions may have specific directions that say they are worth 2 or 3 points.

The computer will add up all of your correct answers to get your raw score. The maximum raw score depends on how many questions you had. The maximum raw score may be 34 points (if you listened to two conversations and four lectures) or 51 questions (if you listened to three conversations and six lectures).

After your raw score has been calculated, the computer will convert it to a scaled score from 0–30. ETS does not give specific information about how your raw score is converted to a scaled score from 0–30. However, it is likely that your raw score is calculated as a percentage of the maximum raw score, and your scaled score is then calculated as the same percentage of 30 (the maximum scaled score). So, for example, if your raw score is 24 points out of a maximum of 34 points, your percentage of correct answers is 70%. This would give you a scaled score of 70% of 30, or 21 points.

This chart shows an estimate of how many answers you need to get right in order to get a scaled score of 14–30.

Percentage Correct	Raw Score out of 34	Raw Score out of 51	Scaled Score
99–100%	34	50–51	30
95–98%	32–33	48–50	29
92–94%	31–32	47–48	28
89–91%	30–31	45–46	27
85–88%	29–30	43–45	26
82–84%	28–29	42–43	25
79–81%	27–28	40–41	24
75–78%	26–27	38–40	23
72–74%	24–25	37–38	22
69–71%	23–24	35–36	21
65–68%	22–23	33–35	20
62–64%	21–22	32–33	19
59–61%	20–21	30–31	18
55–58%	19–20	28–29	17
52–54%	18	27–28	16
49–51%	17	25–26	15
45–48%	15–16	23–24	14

When you receive your score from the TOEFL Test, you will get a score report. The report will give your scaled score in listening from 0–30, your listening level (High, Intermediate, or Low), plus a short description of the typical performance of students at that level.

Here are the levels and descriptions for listening that you might see on your score report:

Level (Scaled Score)	Your Performance
High (22–30)	Test takers who receive a score at the HIGH level, as you did, typically understand conversations and lectures in English that present a wide range of listening demands. These demands can include difficult vocabulary (uncommon terms, or colloquial or figurative language), complex grammatical structures, abstract or complex ideas and/or making sense of unexpected or seemingly contradictory information. When listening to lectures and conversations like these, test takers at the HIGH level typically can: • understand main ideas and important details, whether they are stated or implied; • distinguish more important ideas from less important ones; • understand how information is being used (for example, to provide evidence for a claim or describe a step in a complex process); • recognize how pieces of information are connected (for example, in a cause-and-effect relationship); • understand many different ways that speakers use language for purposes other than to give information (for example, to emphasize a point, express agreement or disagreement, or convey intentions indirectly); and • synthesize information, even when it is not presented in sequence, and make correct inferences on the basis of that information.
Intermediate (14–21)	Test takers who receive a score at the INTERMEDIATE level, as you did, typically understand conversations and lectures in English that present a wide range of listening demands. These demands can include difficult vocabulary (uncommon terms or colloquial or figurative language), complex grammatical structures and/or abstract or complex ideas. However, lectures and conversations that require the listener to make sense of unexpected or seemingly contradictory information may present some difficulty. When listening to conversations and lectures like these, test takers at the INTERMEDIATE level typically can: • understand explicitly stated main ideas and important details, especially if they are reinforced, but may have difficulty understanding main ideas that must be inferred or important details that are not reinforced; • understand how information is being used (for example, to provide support or describe a step in a complex process); • recognize how pieces of information are connected (for example, in a cause-and-effect relationship); • understand, though perhaps not consistently, ways that speakers use language for purposes other than to give information (for example, to emphasize a point, express agreement or disagreement, or convey intentions indirectly); and • synthesize information from adjacent parts of a lecture or conversation and make correct inferences on the basis of that information, but may have difficulty synthesizing information from separate parts of a lecture or conversation.

TEST TACTIC

Some listening question types are more common than others. To improve your listening score, focus on becoming better at answering Detail questions (see Unit 9), Gist questions (Unit 8), and Making Inferences questions (Unit 14) in that order.

Low (0–13)	Test takers who receive a score at the LOW level, as you did, typically understand the main idea and some important details of conversations. However, test takers at the low level may have difficulty understanding lectures and conversations in English that involve abstract or complex

ideas and recognizing the relationship between those ideas. Test takers at this level also may not understand sections of lectures and conversations that contain difficult vocabulary or complex grammatical structures.

Test takers at the LOW level typically can:

- understand main ideas when they are stated explicitly or marked as important, but may have difficulty understanding main ideas if they are not stated explicitly;
- understand important details when they are stated explicitly or marked as important, but may have difficulty understanding details if they are not repeated or clearly marked as important, or if they are conveyed over several exchanges among different speakers;
- understand ways that speakers use language to emphasize a point or to indicate agreement or disagreement, but generally only when the information is related to a central theme or is clearly marked as important; and
- make connections between the key ideas in a conversation, particularly if the ideas are related to a central theme or are repeated. |

Source: www.ets.org/Media/Tests/TOEFL/pdf/TOEFL_Perf_Feedback.pdf

Directions

This listening diagnostic test is intended to help you find out your strengths and weaknesses in listening. You will listen to two conversations and two lectures and answer 22 questions about them. The conversations and lectures are designed to be at the same level as the ones on the TOEFL Test. You may take notes while you listen. After each conversation, take 3.5 minutes to answer the questions. After each lecture, take 4.5 minutes to answer the questions. When you have finished, check your answers with your instructor or against the Answer Key. Then use the conversion chart on page 103 to find out your likely score on the TOEFL Test.

Test

Tracks 6–11   Listen to a conversation between a student and a university employee.

1. Why does the woman go to see the man?
   - (A) To resolve an issue with her resident advisor
   - (B) To apply for a new student identity card
   - (C) To arrange to move in with a new roommate
   - (D) To complain about issues in her residence

2. What can be inferred about the man when he says this?
   - (A) He is surprised at what the woman's resident advisor said to her.
   - (B) He thinks the woman misunderstood her resident advisor's words.
   - (C) He did not realize there was no waiting list for campus residences.
   - (D) He thinks the woman is using humor to discuss her resident advisor.

3. Listen again to part of the conversation. Why does the student say this?
   - (A) She is concerned that she might not be able to switch rooms.
   - (B) She wants the man to come with her to McMaster Residence.
   - (C) She feels that the man was not listening to her carefully.
   - (D) She thinks her explanation might have confused the man.

4. What do the speakers say about McMaster Residence? *Choose two answers.*
   - [A] Some students have had issues using their computers in the residence.
   - [B] The residence is coeducational, but individual floors are segregated by gender.
   - [C] It has a more convenient location than the woman's current residence.
   - [D] All of the students who live there share a room with a roommate.

5. How soon could the woman move into her new residence?
   - (A) By the end of the day
   - (B) Before the weekend
   - (C) After five or six days
   - (D) By the end of the year

🔊 Tracks 12–18   Listen to part of a lecture in a sports science class.

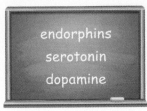

6. What does the professor mainly discuss?
   - (A) The reasons why runner's high affects some people but not others
   - (B) The origin and causes of the physical sensation called runner's high
   - (C) The effects of some naturally produced chemicals on runners' brains
   - (D) The ways in which runner's high reduces physical and psychological pain

7. The professor discusses some effects of runner's high. Indicate which of these effects he mentions.

	Yes	No
Feelings of happiness		
Improved brain activity		
Increased levels of doubt		
Reduced sensitivity to pain		

🎧 8. Listen again to part of the lecture. What does the professor imply?
   - (A) Non-runners can experience runner's high.
   - (B) Runner's high can lead to physical pain and discomfort.
   - (C) Certain chemicals can block the effects of runner's high.
   - (D) Low intensity activity can cause runner's high.

9. What point does the professor make about psychological factors?
   - (A) Scientists have proven that they help people achieve exercise goals.
   - (B) There is some doubt whether they are affected by runner's high.
   - (C) They are hard to evaluate scientifically because they are subjective.
   - (D) They are unrelated to the physical factors that runners experience.

10. What does the professor say about persistence hunting? *Choose two answers.*
   - [A] It still occurs among certain societies of hunter-gatherers.
   - [B] It reinforces traditional methods of hunting and foraging.
   - [C] Animals that are adapted for running often engage in it.
   - [D] It involves hunting prey for a long time over long distances.

🎧 11. Listen again to part of the lecture. Why does the professor say this?
   - (A) To indicate that the point he is about to make is not proven
   - (B) To suggest that nobody has a likely theory about runner's high
   - (C) To emphasize that scientists are still researching the topic
   - (D) To argue that some theories make more sense than others

 Tracks 19–24   Listen to a conversation between a student and his professor.

12. What do the speakers mainly discuss?
       Ⓐ   Ideas that the man does not understand
       Ⓑ   Why the man has fallen behind in class
       Ⓒ   How the man can study more effectively
       Ⓓ   Some reading that the professor assigned

13. What does the man say about the teaching assistant?
       Ⓐ   Her response was not very helpful.
       Ⓑ   She is not available to see him.
       Ⓒ   She asked him to wait a few days.
       Ⓓ   She is worried about his work.

14. Listen again to part of the conversation. Why does the professor say this?
       Ⓐ   She thinks the man has been studying in the wrong way.
       Ⓑ   She is worried that the man will not accept her advice.
       Ⓒ   She wants to encourage the man to think in a positive way.
       Ⓓ   She does not want the man to think she is criticizing him.

15. What does the man say about his study habits? *Choose two answers.*
       Ⓐ   He enjoys discussing ideas with others.
       Ⓑ   He does not like to study in silence.
       Ⓒ   He only rarely studies in the library.
       Ⓓ   He usually prefers to learn on his own.

16. What is the student likely to do next?
       Ⓐ   Discuss his theories with the professor
       Ⓑ   Speak to the teaching assistant
       Ⓒ   Start or join a study group
       Ⓓ   Visit the campus medical center

 Tracks 25–31   Listen to part of a talk in an Earth sciences class.

Parícutin

17. What does the professor mainly discuss?
       Ⓐ   The development of knowledge about volcanoes
       Ⓑ   Effects of the eruption of volcanoes on villagers
       Ⓒ   Mexican volcanoes that erupted in the 1940s
       Ⓓ   The chronology of the eruption of one volcano

18. The professor discusses the eruption of a volcano. Put the events in the order in which they occurred.

First	
Second	
Third	
Fourth	

- Ⓐ The eruption caused a fissure to form in a farmer's field.
- Ⓑ Volcanic material formed a cone approximately 50 meters tall.
- Ⓒ Local people heard the sounds of subterranean earthquakes.
- Ⓓ Very high clouds of ash and smoke formed in the sky.

19. What does the professor say about the eruption of Parícutin?
- Ⓐ It lasted approximately 52 years from start to finish.
- Ⓑ The first year of the eruption was the most explosive.
- Ⓒ It was more violent than 90% of other volcanoes.
- Ⓓ Its quiet phase lasted for approximately six months.

20. What can be inferred about the professor when she says this?
- Ⓐ She is surprised that airlines diverted flights to let passengers view the eruption.
- Ⓑ She imagines that airline passengers were not happy when their flights were diverted.
- Ⓒ She does not believe airline passengers would have had a good view of the eruption.
- Ⓓ She feels that airline passengers these days would not be interested in seeing an eruption.

21. What point does the professor make about the data collected about Parícutin?
- Ⓐ Data collected early in the eruption was more valuable than later data.
- Ⓑ The photographic data was especially useful as a tool for detailed analysis.
- Ⓒ The data enhanced scientific understanding of volcanoes in general.
- Ⓓ The data became helpful when scientists analyzed it with a computer.

22. What does the professor imply when she says this?
- Ⓐ Parícutin is an example of a cinder cone volcano.
- Ⓑ Scientists from around the world studied Parícutin.
- Ⓒ Scholars reached few conclusions about Parícutin.
- Ⓓ Cinder cone volcanoes are not very common.

Score Conversion

Check your answers to questions 1–22. Give yourself one point for each fully correct answer. Then use this conversion chart to find out your approximate listening score range on the TOEFL Test.

Raw Score (out of 22)	Probable Level	Approximate Score Range
20–22		28–30
18–20	High	25–27
16–18		22–24
13–16	Intermediate	18–21
10–13		14–17
7–10		10–13
4–7	Low	5–9
0–3		0–4

Unit Focus

There are seven types of listening questions in the TOEFL Test. These include gist questions, which are classified as "basic comprehension" questions. You will see two types of gist questions in the TOEFL Test: Gist-content questions ask you about the main idea of the conversation or lecture; and Gist-purpose questions ask you the reason why the speakers are having a conversation or, sometimes, why a professor mentions a particular idea during a lecture. You will see a gist question after almost every conversation or lecture, often as the first question. You will learn several key skills to answer gist questions in this unit, including:

- listening and taking notes about the main ideas of a conversation or talk.
- recognizing why the speaker or speakers are discussing a particular topic.
- analyzing answer choices to decide if they are likely or unlikely.

The vocabulary focus is on campus and academic words and phrases related to:

- doing, submitting, and getting a grade for coursework that a professor has assigned.
- biology, the study of living organisms, and related sub-disciplines like biochemistry.

A Warm-up

A1 Work with a partner to complete tasks 1–3. Spend three minutes on each task.

1. Make a list of topics that a student might discuss with a professor, a librarian, a sports coach, and a study counselor.
2. Make a list of reasons why a student might visit a tutor's office, a university cafeteria, a bookstore, and a computer lab.
3. Share your lists with another pair of students and listen to their ideas.

B Campus Vocabulary

B1 Read this article giving advice to new college students. Then answer questions 1–6 about the highlighted expressions.

Advice for New Students

Life at college can be wonderful. There are so many people to meet and things to do that it can be hard to focus on your studies. However, studying is your reason for going to college, so it is important to maintain a good grade point average (GPA) by working hard and submitting your work by the due date. If you do not understand how to do an assignment, discuss the issue with your tutor during his or her office hours. If you need more time to research and finish a term paper, your tutor might be willing to give you an extension. If there is a serious medical reason why you need additional time, you might be eligible for an incomplete, which will give you until the middle of the next semester to submit your work.

1. Which highlighted expressions mean a task that students need to complete for homework? *Choose two answers.*
2. Which highlighted expression means the date or time by which homework or coursework must be handed in?
3. Which highlighted expressions mean extra time to finish homework beyond the original deadline? *Choose two answers.*
4. Which highlighted expression means the average of all the final marks a student has received for completing college courses?
5. Which highlighted expression means a period when students do not need an appointment to speak to a professor?
6. Which highlighted expression means to read and study a subject in order to write or give a presentation about it?

C Analyzing Gist-content and Gist-purpose Questions

All gist questions focus on the gist, that is, the main idea or main purpose, of the listening, but the two types of gist questions look slightly different. Gist-content questions ask about the main subject of the conversation or lecture and usually begin with *What*, as in these examples. Gist-content questions are common after both conversations and lectures:

> What do the speakers mainly discuss?
>
> What is the main topic of the lecture?
>
> What aspect of _____ does the professor mainly discuss?

Gist-purpose questions, on the other hand, ask why the two speakers are talking or why a professor mentions a particular idea. They usually begin with *For what reason* or *Why*, as in these examples. Gist-purpose questions are common after conversations, but less common after lectures:

> For what reason does the man visit _____?
>
> Why does the student visit the _____?
>
> Why does the professor mention _____?

The correct answer to Gist-content and Gist-purpose questions usually:

- describes something that was either discussed throughout the conversation or lecture or mentioned several times.
- paraphrases information from the conversation or lecture rather than repeating the speakers' words.

In contrast, incorrect answers to both types of gist questions often:

- repeat or restate words from just one part of the conversation or lecture.
- include words from the conversation or lecture, but incorrectly summarize its main point.

C1 Read this script from a conversation between a student and her professor. Then complete tasks 1 and 2.

Student	Professor? Could I check two things about the assignment for Biology 208? The paper should be 1,000 words and you need it next Friday, right?
Professor	No, and no. There's a term paper due at the end of the semester that needs to be 1,000 words, but this assignment should only be 500 words. And the due date is actually this Friday, not next Friday.
Student	*This* Friday? I'm not sure I can finish by then ... er, could I get an extension?
Professor	Sorry, Jodie, but no. I don't give extensions unless a student is sick and, well, you seem pretty healthy... Besides, it's only Tuesday, so you've got a few days.

1. Why did the student go to see her professor?
   A To receive an assignment
   B To confirm some information
   C To ask for an extended due date
   D To explain that she is sick

2. Underline words in the script that helped you answer question 1. Work with a partner.

C2 Complete these descriptions of the wrong answers from exercise C1 by writing in the letter of each wrong answer.

1. The student did not know she needed extra time before going to see her professor, so answer _____ cannot be right.
2. Answer _____ cannot be correct as the student does not mention this and because the professor says she is healthy.
3. The student asks her professor about an assignment she has already received, so answer _____ must be wrong.

TEST TACTIC

The main topic of conversations is often about how to solve a minor problem that the student has. When you listen, take careful notes whenever one speaker discusses a problem or a solution to a problem. Often these notes will help you answer a Gist-content or Gist-purpose question.

D Mastering Gist-content and Gist-purpose Questions – Recognizing Topic Markers

Sometimes a speaker may use a phrase (called a topic marker) to introduce the main point of the lecture or conversation. Recognizing topic markers is a valuable skill for gist questions because after using the topic marker phrase, the speaker usually goes on to discuss the main idea in more detail.

Tracks 32–37 **D1** **Listen to excerpts (short parts) from six conversations and lectures. In which excerpt, 1–6, does a speaker use each topic marker, A–F? One answer has been done for you.**

Topic marker	Excerpt
A I wanted to find out...	
B I was hoping to ...	1
C Let's continue our discussion of ...	
D Now let's turn to ...	
E Today we're going to talk about ...	
F We're going to be covering ...	

Tracks 32–37 **D2** **Listen again to the excerpts from exercise D1 and take notes. Then use your notes to answer questions 1–6.**

1. In excerpt 1, why does the man go to see his professor?
   A   To get some help with an assignment   B   To submit a paper before the deadline

2. In excerpt 2, what does the professor say the main topic of the lecture will be?
   A   An important molecule   B   Common names in biology

3. In excerpt 3, what does the professor say she will mainly discuss?
   A   How the heart, lungs, and liver differ   B   The functions of internal organs

4. In excerpt 4, why does the woman talk to the man?
   A   To ask for information about her grades   B   To request a new student ID number

5. In excerpt 5, what does the professor say the main topic of the lecture will be?
   A   Genetic material   B   The cell nucleus

6. In excerpt 6, what does the professor say he will mainly discuss?
   A   Different methods of reproduction   B   How mammals and birds differ

E Mastering Gist-content and Gist-purpose Questions – Listening for Repeated Information

The gist of a conversation or lecture is something that the speakers discuss several times throughout the conversation or lecture. As a result, recognizing and making a note of repeated information may help you to recognize the right answer to Gist-content and Gist-purpose questions.

E1 **Use these notes about a lecture to answer question 1 (a Gist-content question) and question 2 (Gist-purpose).**

cell division → two types for cells with nucleus
1   meiosis for reproduction of organism
step one – parent cell copies mixed up DNA
parent cell divides into two
step two – DNA in new cells changes
both cell and DNA split
daughter cells get ½ of DNA

2   mitosis for reproduction of cells
       parent cell copies DNA in own nucleus
       parent cell divides = usually 100% copy
           errors rare

also binary fission for cells without nucleus
read about bf before next week's class

TEST TACTIC

Sometimes the reason why a student visits a professor and the main topic they discuss differ. For example, a student might visit his tutor to borrow a book, but their conversation might focus on an assignment, not the book. To avoid errors, listen both for topic markers and repeated information.

1. What does the professor mainly discuss? (The answer will be something mentioned throughout the notes.)
   A   The reproduction of cells and organisms
   B   Complex changes to DNA within cells
   C   Two processes by which cells divide
   D   How parent and daughter cells differ

2. Why does the professor mention binary fission? (The answer will be mentioned in just one part of the notes.)
   A   To introduce the topic of the next class
   B   To contrast it with mitosis and meiosis
   C   To explain the process of binary fission
   D   To describe the function of a cell nucleus

)) Track 38   **E2** **Take notes as you listen to a student talk with his professor. Then use your notes to answer questions 1 and 2.**

1. How often do the speakers discuss each of these things? Put a check (✓) in the correct column.

	Once	Twice	Multiple Times
An assignment that the professor gave			
The due date of the assignment			
A recommended article			
An extension of the assignment's deadline			
A failing grade for the assignment			
A visit to the Study Skills Center			

2. Why did the student go to see his professor? (The answer will be something the speakers discuss multiple times.)
   A   To ask her opinion of the Study Skills Center
   B   To understand why he failed an assignment
   C   To ask for extra time to complete a paper
   D   To get a suggestion for which article to read

F Mastering Gist-content and Gist-purpose Questions – Recognizing Unlikely Answers

Sometimes an answer choice expresses an idea that is not likely to be the main idea or purpose of the conversation or lecture. If you can recognize these unlikely answers, you will find it easier to choose the correct answer to gist questions.

F1 **Check (✓) the box if you think each answer to example gist questions 1 and 2 is Likely or Unlikely. Note that you do not need to listen to anything to complete this task. One answer has been done for you.**

1. Why does the student go to see her professor?
   A   To ask the professor to do some research for her   ☐ Likely   ☑ Unlikely
   B   To ask for advice about how to write a term paper   ☐ Likely   ☐ Unlikely
   C   To discuss a difficult academic theory   ☐ Likely   ☐ Unlikely
   D   To talk about the professor's new office   ☐ Likely   ☐ Unlikely

2. What does the professor mainly discuss in the lecture?
   A   The results of an important biological experiment   ☐ Likely   ☐ Unlikely
   B   Why the government should invest in biotechnology   ☐ Likely   ☐ Unlikely
   C   The best way for students to complete an assignment   ☐ Likely   ☐ Unlikely
   D   Several important concepts in biotechnology   ☐ Likely   ☐ Unlikely

F2 Match each Unlikely answer from exercise **F1** to one of descriptive reasons 1–4. One answer has been done for you.

Reasons

1. It is unlikely a student would visit a professor in order to have a whole conversation about this topic.
2. It is unlikely that a student would ask a professor for this, and unlikely that a professor would agree to it.
3. In lectures in the TOEFL Test, professors rarely express personal views about political or social topics.
4. Professors typically give lectures to discuss academic theories, concepts, and so on, not to explain homework.

Answer A from question 1 in exercise F1 matches reason 2.

G Mastering Gist-content and Gist-purpose Questions – Analyzing the Answer Choices

The correct answer to a gist question usually paraphrases or summarizes the words that the speaker(s) use. Incorrect answers, on the other hand, often repeat words that the speaker(s) use. So being able to recognize answers that restate the listening is an important skill for answering Gist-content and Gist-purpose questions correctly.

TEST TACTIC

The academic subject of the talk may help you decide if an answer choice is likely or unlikely. For example, the main idea of a lecture about physics might be Einstein's scientific theories, but is unlikely to be Einstein's personal relationships because those are unrelated to physics.

G1 Read these partial scripts from a conversation and a lecture. Then answer questions 1 and 2 by choosing the answer choice that restates or summarizes the professor's words.

Professor	Come in, Ben. I wanted to talk to you about the paper you handed in. I'm afraid I can't give you a grade because you didn't cite the sources for your ideas.
Student	What do you mean? I included a bibliography like you requested.
Professor	There's a bibliography, yes, but you didn't say which ideas came from which sources. It's not enough just to give a list of the books you read, you also need to attribute ideas to the person who came up with them.
Student	You mean that if an idea comes from the writer of one book, I need to say that it comes from her?
Professor	Exactly ... Can you add that information and resubmit the paper by tomorrow?

1. Why did the professor ask to see the student?
   A To ask him to add a bibliography to his paper
   B To get him to explain his ideas in more detail
   C To suggest some useful sources of ideas to him
   D To have him say where his arguments came from

Professor	Last week we discussed DNA. Today we're going to talk about another nucleic acid – ribonucleic acid, or RNA. First let's see how RNA and DNA differ. You all remember that DNA is a double helix, right? Well RNA is a single-stranded molecule not a double-stranded one. Another difference is that RNA's four bases are guanine, cytosine, and adenine, but instead of having thymine like DNA, RNA has uracil. And finally, as its name suggests, RNA contains the monosaccharide ribose rather than deoxyribose, which is in DNA. OK, so let's move on to discuss the vital roles that RNA plays within the body.

2. What is the main purpose of this part of the talk?
   A To describe the bases that make up DNA and RNA
   B To compare two different kinds of nucleic acid
   C To talk about the vital roles of RNA in the body
   D To remind students about the structure of DNA

Track 39 **G2** **Listen to part of a lecture in a biochemistry class and choose one word from answers A—F to fill blanks 1—6 in these notes.**

elements → 92 natural / 25 essential for living [1.]
        plants + animals need different [2.]
4 elements most important → 95% of most organisms
        hydrogen, carbon, nitrogen, oxygen
        carbon in every cell → organic [3.]
7 elements major importance
        phosphorus, sulfur, calcium, potassium
        sodium, magnesium, chlorine
trace elements → only need in tiny [4.]
        organisms need them for [5.]
        e.g., humans have 75mg of copper (less than single grain rice)
        too little → [6.]   / too much → poison

A amounts
B elements
C health
D heart disease
E molecules
F organisms

G3 **Use the notes from exercise G2 to answer questions 1 and 2.**

1. What does the professor mainly discuss?
   A How many and which elements exist naturally
   B Which substances are necessary for life
   C How to recognize which molecules are organic

2. Why does the professor mention copper?
   A To illustrate the importance of trace elements for health
   B To show that not every species requires every trace element
   C To define trace elements in a way students will understand

H Academic Vocabulary

H1 **Look at these partial scripts from some of the lectures you have heard in this unit. Answer questions 1—8 with a word from each script.**

Professor   Today we're going to talk about the most important molecule in biology. It's sometimes referred to as "hydrogen oxide" ...

1. Which noun in the partial script above means a group of atoms that are bonded together?

Professor   We're going to be covering the functions of the major internal organs of mammals, such as the heart, lungs, and liver ...

2. Which noun means body parts of plants or animals that have a specific function?

Professor   Carbon can be found in all living cells: it is, after all, the element that determines whether a molecule is organic, meaning related to life, or inorganic ...

3. Which noun means the smallest units of an organism that have a structure and specific function?
4. Which noun means a substance like carbon that cannot be changed into another substance?

Professor   Let's continue our discussion of the nucleus of the cell. Last class we talked about its structure – the outer membrane, the pores, the genetic material inside it ...

5. Which noun means the central part of a living cell?
6. Which adjective describes material that is related to genes and DNA?

Professor   Now let's turn to methods of reproduction that animals use. There are two basic methods – giving birth to live offspring, as almost all mammals and a few fish do ...

7. Which noun means the action of producing a child?
8. Which noun means the child of a person or animal?

▌ Test Challenge

I1 **Practice some Gist-content and Gist-purpose questions. While you listen, cover the questions and take notes. Then use your notes and memory to answer questions 1–6. Use this checklist of skills that you studied in this unit as a guide.**

While you listen to the conversations and lectures

☑ Listen for topic marker phrases and make careful notes of what the speakers say immediately after you hear one.

☑ Take notes when you hear repeated information, especially information that is mentioned throughout the talk.

When you answer the questions

☑ Avoid answers that describe an idea that is unlikely to be the main idea or purpose of the talk.

☑ Remember that answers that repeat several words from the talk are often distractors.

🔊 Tracks 40–41 Listen to a conversation between a student and a university employee.

1. Why does the man go to see the university employee?
   - Ⓐ To ask for help with a minor medical problem
   - Ⓑ To get formal approval to miss an upcoming exam
   - Ⓒ To learn whether his exam is on Thursday or Friday
   - Ⓓ To pick up a letter about his student record

🔊 Tracks 42–43 Listen to a talk in a biology class.

 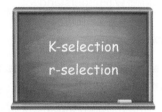

K-selection
r-selection

2. What main topic does the professor discuss?
   - Ⓐ What students should study for a midterm exam
   - Ⓑ The level of parental care that species provide
   - Ⓒ Different strategies for reproductive success
   - Ⓓ Environmental selection among mammals

🔊 Tracks 44–45 Listen to part of a lecture in a history of science class.

3. What is the professor mainly discussing?
   - Ⓐ Scientific discoveries in the early twentieth century
   - Ⓑ The importance of Crick and Watson's theory
   - Ⓒ The use of X-rays to take pictures of molecules
   - Ⓓ The history of the discovery of DNA's structure

Tracks
46–47 Listen to a conversation between a student and her professor.

4. What do the two speakers mainly discuss?
   (A) The student's part-time job
   (B) The student's attitude in class
   (C) Why the student has poor grades
   (D) Ways to gain academic confidence

Tracks
48–49 Listen to part of a talk in a biotechnology class.

5. Why does the professor talk about farming?
   (A) To describe an overlooked aspect of biotechnology
   (B) To recommend a number of uses of biotechnology
   (C) To discuss successful methods biotechnologists have used
   (D) To give an example of the dangers of biotechnology

Tracks
50–51 Listen to a lecture in an introduction to biological sciences class.

6. What is the main purpose of the lecture?
   (A) To contrast the characteristics of plants and animals
   (B) To explain how living cells respond to the environment
   (C) To give a clear definition of respiration and organization
   (D) To describe the characteristics of living organisms

Next Steps

Topics related to biology are common in the listening section of the TOEFL Test. You may also have questions about this subject in the other sections of the test. As a result, learning more about biology, as well as practicing key skills for Gist-content and Gist-purpose questions, may raise your overall test score.

To learn more about biology and vocabulary related to this discipline:

1. Do an Internet search for "key concepts in biology" and choose a topic that sounds interesting from the search results.
2. Read an article about this topic just once. After reading, make a list of questions about this topic that are unclear to you.
3. Read a different article about the same topic just once. Write answers to as many of the questions on your list as you can. Then make a new list of questions that are unclear (or still unclear) to you.
4. Read other articles about the same topic until you can write answers to all of the questions on your list.
5. Review the answers that you wrote to your questions and make a list of vocabulary you used in your written answers. Study these words in detail until you are confident that you will remember the meaning and normal usage of each word.

To practice a key skill for Gist-content and Gist-purpose questions:

1. Listen once to a television or radio news broadcast, such as a story about business, politics, sports, or science.
2. Take notes as you listen. Focus on noting down information that is repeated throughout the broadcast.
3. Review your notes. Then use your notes and your memory to write a one or two-sentence summary of the broadcast. For example, if you listened to a news story about a woman who helped some people in trouble, your summary might be: *A woman helped some people escape from a burning building. Police officers said she probably saved several lives.*

Unit Focus

There are seven types of listening questions in the TOEFL Test. These include Detail questions, which are the most common question type. You will see one to three Detail questions, which are classified as "basic comprehension" questions, after each lecture and conversation. Detail questions test your comprehension of major points from the listening. For most questions you must choose one correct answer from four choices, but sometimes you will have to choose two or three correct answers from four to six choices. You will learn several key skills to answer Detail questions in this unit, including:

- listening for information in a conversation or lecture that answers a question like *who*, *where*, or *what*.
- listening for the way in which various points in a conversation or lecture are related to one another.
- recognizing and taking notes about the major points of a conversation or lecture.

The vocabulary focus is on campus and academic words and phrases related to:

- people who hold academic and administrative positions that students often meet and deal with at college.
- astronomy, the scientific study of objects in space (beyond Earth's atmosphere) and the universe as a whole.

A Warm-up

A1 Work with a partner to complete tasks 1–3.

1. Write four questions that ask something about astronomy or space that you would like to know. For example, you might write *How old is the universe?* or *What are stars made of?* Work together to write grammatically correct questions.
2. Listen to the questions that other students wrote. If you can answer any of their questions, share your knowledge.
3. Read your questions to other students. Take notes as you listen to their answers.

B Campus Vocabulary

B1 Choose the best phrase from answers A–H to complete sentences 1–8. Each sentence helps you understand the meaning of one of the highlighted expressions. One answer has been done for you.

1. Speak to your academic advisor if you need answers to academic ___questions___ such as which classes to take.
2. If you want to play college _____, the coach is the person who will decide if you are good enough and train you.
3. Visit a counselor if you are having personal _____ and want some advice about how to solve or deal with them.
4. If you ever need to speak to the person in _____ of academic matters at your college, that person is the dean.
5. All of the instructors at a college or in a particular _____ at a college are known collectively as the faculty.
6. When you attend _____ and seminars, make sure that you listen carefully to the points that the professor makes.
7. In order to find out information about your academic _____ or how to register for classes, speak to a registrar.
8. If you need help understanding a _____ that an instructor discussed in class, speak to the teaching assistant.

A charge	C lectures	E questions	G sports
B department	D problems	F record	H theory

C Analyzing Detail Questions

Detail questions ask you about major ideas that the speaker or speakers discuss in the conversation or lecture:

What does the professor say about _____?

Why did the _____ begin?

According to the woman, how was _____ formed?

Some Detail questions ask you to choose two or three correct answers from four to six choices, as in this example:

What are the effects of _____? *Choose two answers.*

The correct answer to a Detail question usually:

- describes a major idea from the conversation or lecture rather than a minor point.
- paraphrases information from the conversation or lecture rather than repeating the speakers' words.

In contrast, incorrect answers to Detail questions:

- may paraphrase or repeat words that describe a minor point from the conversation or lecture.
- sometimes use words from the conversation or lecture but describe information that was not mentioned by any speaker.
- may contradict information that a speaker mentions during the conversation or lecture.
- may restate a major or minor point from the conversation or lecture that does not answer the question.

TEST TACTIC

If a Detail question asks you to choose two or three answers, you cannot move on to the next question until you have chosen that many answers. As a result, it is not possible to get a question wrong because you did not notice that you needed to choose multiple answers.

C1 Read this script from a lecture in an art history class. Then answer question 1.

Professor   As we discussed last week, Vincent Van Gogh was fascinated, obsessed even, with depicting color on the canvas. He also went through a period where he was particularly interested in the effects of night and the nocturnal on light and color. Several of his more famous works are paintings of the night sky, including *Starry Night Over the Rhone* and *The Starry Night*. He painted the first of these by night and described it in a letter to his brother using phrases like "the aquamarine field of the sky" and "sparkling green and pink stars." Even though it was painted from life, Van Gogh used a bit of artistic license. The painting depicts the constellation Ursa Major, but in fact he was looking south when he painted it and this constellation would only have been visible to the north. Unlike *Starry Night Over the Rhone*, Van Gogh painted *The Starry Night* from memory. As such, it's not intended to be an accurate portrayal of the night sky. Despite this, some have noted that parts of the painting resemble actual features found in space such as a whirlpool galaxy or interstellar gas cloud. Van Gogh almost certainly knew nothing about these features, however, so again they should be attributed to artistic license.

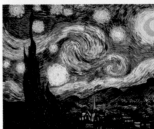

1. What points does the professor make about Van Gogh? *Choose three answers.*
   A He was inspired to paint night scenes after reading letters from his brother.
   B He sometimes painted nocturnal scenes from life, sometimes from memory.
   C He used his imagination to portray the features and colors of the night sky.
   D He believed that painting images of the night sky would make him famous.
   E He painted night scenes because of his interest in how night affects colors.
   F He lived and worked in a region where the sky to the north was rarely visible.

C2 Underline clues in the wrong answers that help you recognize why that answer is wrong. Then work with a partner to write short explanations as in this example:

Example   The phrase "letters from his brother" is a clue because the lecture says Van Gogh sent letters to his brother, not received letters from him.

D Mastering Detail Questions – Recognizing Details as You Listen

Detail questions typically begin with words like *what, who, where, when,* and so on. As you listen to the conversations and lectures, you may notice that a speaker is talking about what happened, who did something, or where or when something began. Make a note of information like this that seems to answer a question, as it may help you answer Detail questions.

D1 Look at these example notes from a lecture and conversation. Which question, A–F, does each circled point answer?

Hubble (space telescope → orbiting Earth) since 1990
many problems before and after launch
    original plan to launch in 1983 (but delayed)
    new plan to launch in 1986 (but shuttle disaster)
    launched in 1990 but (mirror had wrong shape)
    astronauts had to fix mirror in space
Hubble now (produces amazing images of planets + stars)
    estimate (of $400 million wrong = actually $10 billion+)

A   How much has it cost?
B   What does it do?
C   What will somebody do?
D   What problems occurred?
E   What is it and where is it?
F   When was it given?

Woman   need extra time to do assignm about Hubble
Man   why? (Assignment set 2 weeks ago)
W   sorry but play for college softball team
         (will play in final of softball tournament
         team traveling 2 days before deadline)
         coach said must get permission from prof to play
M   understand + give permission + good luck!

🔊 Tracks 52–55 **D2** Take notes as you listen to some excerpts (short parts) from conversations and talks. Then use your notes to answer questions 1–4. To get realistic practice for the test, cover the questions and answers while you listen.

1. What information does the woman give in Excerpt 1?
   A   What the man should say to the dean
   B   Who the man's academic advisor is
   C   How the man can attend the conference
   D   Why the man is not able to see the dean

2. What does the man discuss in Excerpt 2? *Choose two answers.*
   A   How gas giant planets are formed
   B   What Saturn's rings are made of
   C   Which planets have ring systems
   D   Why Saturn's rings are well developed

3. What does the woman talk about in Excerpt 3? *Choose two answers.*
   A   What happened during the Space Race
   B   Which country won the Space Race
   C   When and why the Space Race ended
   D   What benefits the Space Race brought

4. What do the speakers discuss in Excerpt 4?
   A   The purpose of the staff training session
   B   Why an office on campus is currently closed
   C   The time when the woman's training will finish
   D   When the woman will meet the registrar

E Mastering Detail Questions – Noticing How Ideas Are Connected

Detail questions sometimes focus on how two points or ideas are related, so a key skill for detail questions is to listen for and make a note of information that explains the relationship between two ideas. To do this effectively, listen for expressions that introduce common relationships between ideas.

E1 Work with a partner to complete tasks 1 and 2.

1. Add expressions A–H to the correct column in the table. One answer has been done for you.
2. Add at least one more expression to each of the four categories.
3. Add the title "Example" to the blank column. Then add matching expressions like "such as".

Cause or Effect	Contrast	Similarity	Sequence	
The reason is … … because of …	but … … unlike … However, …	Similarly, … Another …	After that, … Then, …	

A However, …
B Until finally, …
C In the same way, …
D To begin, …
E As a result of …
F due to …
G A related point …
H Instead of …

Tracks 56–59 **E2** Take notes as you listen to some excerpts from conversations and talks. Then use your notes to answer questions 1–4 by checking (✓) the right box. One answer has been done for you.

1. Which relationship between ideas does the woman discuss in Excerpt 1?
   ☐ Contrast   ☑ Similarity
2. Which relationship between ideas does the woman discuss in Excerpt 2?
   ☐ Example   ☐ Cause/Effect
3. Which relationship between ideas does the man discuss in Excerpt 3?
   ☐ Similarity   ☐ Time
4. Which relationship between ideas does the speaker woman in Excerpt 4?
   ☐ Cause/Effect   ☐ Contrast

F Mastering Detail Questions – Noticing Details Mentioned as Part of a List

Some Detail questions ask you to choose two or three answers that are mentioned during a conversation or talk. These questions may ask about information that is mentioned as part of a list even though this information may describe minor points from the talk. A useful skill for Detail questions is listening and making a note of information that is mentioned as part of a list.

Track 60 **F1** Take notes as you listen to excerpts from a conversation and lecture. Then use your notes to answer questions 1 and 2.

1. What help can the International Student Center provide? *Choose two answers.*
   A Study guidance geared towards overseas students
   B Information about how to do assignments more quickly
   C Advice on how to make friends with other students
   D Suggestions for dealing with feelings of homesickness

2. According to the man, what is found in the vacuum of space? *Choose two answers.*
   A Particles called neutrinos
   B Atoms of hydrogen
   C High-density particles
   D Many kinds of matter

G Mastering Detail Questions – Recognizing Major and Minor Points

The majority of Detail questions ask about major details from the conversations and lectures, not minor points. So a useful skill for answering Detail questions is deciding whether information that a speaker mentions is a major or minor point.

 Tracks 52–55   **G1** **Listen again to some excerpts you have already heard. As you listen, take notes. Then use your notes to answer questions 1–4. Use the checklists to help you.**

Major points	☑	may be discussed for a period of time.
	☑	may be mentioned more than once.
	☑	are often related to the main idea of the talk.
Minor points	☑	may be important if mentioned as part of a list.
	☑	are often discussed just once and for a short time.
	☑	may be unrelated or weakly related to the main idea.

1. Which of these points from excerpt 1 is a major point, and which is a minor point?
   A The man needs to see the dean.
   B The man has an academic advisor.

2. Which of these points from excerpt 2 is a major point, and which is a minor point?
   A Several planets are surrounded by rings.
   B Planetary rings are formed of dust and ice.

3. Are these two points from excerpt 3 both major points or both minor points?
   A Government spending on the Space Race was high, but had positive benefits.
   B The Space Race was a period of competition between the US and the USSR.

4. Are these two points from excerpt 4 both major points or both minor points?
   A The woman is uncertain why the registrar's office is not open.
   B There was no sign on the door of the registrar's office.

H Mastering Detail Questions – Analyzing the Answer Choices

Most correct answers to listening questions in the TOEFL Test, including Detail questions, paraphrase what the speaker(s) say. Therefore, recognizing answers that restate words from the conversations and lectures is a key listening skill.

Tracks 56–59   **H1** **Take notes as you listen again to some of the excerpts from conversations and lectures that you have already heard. Then use your notes to answer questions 1–4.**

1. What major point does the woman make in excerpt 1?
   A Hearing deeper sounds makes people think colors are darker.
   B Redshift changes how light moves towards or goes past objects.
   C When the wavelength of light is longer its color looks more red.

2. What does the professor say about larger optical telescopes in excerpt 2?
   A They are not an important tool for astronomers these days.
   B They have proportionally smaller lenses than other telescopes.
   C They can gather more light than smaller instruments.

3. According to excerpt 3, what happens when a star dies? *Choose two answers.*
   A After first getting smaller, a dying star gets larger.
   B During the red giant phase, carbon and helium separate.
   C The planetary nebula phase causes the star to contract.
   D In its final stages, the star will get smaller and cooler.

4. What point does the speaker make in excerpt 4?
   A Astronomers need formal training to make significant observations.
   B Simple tools and techniques can be used to do useful work in astronomy.
   C Major discoveries in astronomy require the use of costly equipment.

Tracks 56–59 **H2** **Listen again to the excerpts from exercise H1 and complete tasks 1–5. One answer has been done for you.**

1. In excerpt 1, does the woman repeat or paraphrase the words "looks more red?"
   ☐ Repeat   ☑ Paraphrase

2. In excerpt 2, does the woman repeat or paraphrase the words "smaller instruments?"
   ☐ Repeat   ☐ Paraphrase

3. In excerpt 3, does the man repeat or paraphrase the words "dying star?"
   ☐ Repeat   ☐ Paraphrase

4. Also in excerpt 3, does the man repeat or paraphrase the words "smaller and cooler?"
   ☐ Repeat   ☐ Paraphrase

5. In excerpt 4, does the woman repeat or paraphrase the words "simple tools?"
   ☐ Repeat   ☐ Paraphrase

I Academic Vocabulary

I1 **Choose the correct phrase, A–H, to complete definitions 1–8 of some useful highlighted words related to astronomy. One answer has been done for you.**

1. A constellation is a group of stars that, as seen from Earth, forms a _____pattern_____ or shape that has meaning for humans.
2. A massive cluster of _____, planets, satellites, dust, and gas is a galaxy. The universe has billions of galaxies.
3. Gravity is the force that a heavy object, that is one with large mass, exerts on a nearby _____ with less mass.
4. Gravity causes planets to go around, or orbit, stars; it also causes stars to orbit the _____ of their galaxies.
5. Planets are bodies in space – made of _____ or gas – that orbit a star but do not shine with internal light
6. A satellite is a body in space, like a moon or _____, that orbits a larger body. Many satellites have elliptical orbits.
7. The _____ plus the planets like Earth, Mars, and Jupiter that orbit it are collectively known as the solar system.
8. Astronomers view the universe through a device known as a telescope. Many different _____ of telescopes exist.

A centers   C object   E rock   G stars
B kinds   D pattern   F spacecraft   H sun

J Test Challenge

J1 Practice answering these Detail questions. While you listen, cover the questions and take notes. Then use your notes and memory to answer questions 1–8. Use this checklist of skills that you studied in this unit as a guide.

While you listen to the conversation and lectures

☑ Listen for and make a note of information in the talks that answers questions like *who*, *where*, *how*, *what*, or *why*.

☑ Make a note when one of the speakers discusses information that explains how two ideas are connected.

☑ Listen for and make a note of major points from the talk – these are often points that are related to the main idea.

When you answer the questions

☑ Be careful of answers that describe a minor point from the talk, unless the question asks you to choose two or three answers.

☑ Remember that correct answers often paraphrase the words and phrases that you heard in the talks.

🔊 Tracks 61–63   Listen to a conversation between a student and a university employee in a Careers Office on campus.

1. What does the man want?
   - Ⓐ A high-paying job for just a few weeks
   - Ⓑ Information about getting a good job after graduation
   - Ⓒ A part-time job on campus for a few hours each week
   - Ⓓ A job that gives him a chance to travel

2. What kind of experience does the man have? *Choose two answers.*
   - Ⓐ He has worked in the Housing Office.
   - Ⓑ He has lived overseas for several years.
   - Ⓒ He can speak more than one language.
   - Ⓓ He has impressive computer skills.

🔊 Tracks 64–67   Listen to part of a talk in an astronomy class.

  terrestrial planets  Ganymede  dwarf planets

3. What are two characteristics of the terrestrial planets? *Choose two answers.*
   - Ⓐ All four planets are close to each other in size.
   - Ⓑ They are low in mass but have a high density.
   - Ⓒ They are found in the outer solar system.
   - Ⓓ They do not have many natural satellites.

4. What point does the professor make about Ganymede?
   - Ⓐ It has more than 60 natural satellites.
   - Ⓑ It is surrounded by a planetary ring system.
   - Ⓒ It is like a terrestrial planet in some ways.
   - Ⓓ It is located close to the planet Mercury.

5. What does the professor say about dwarf planets? *Choose two answers.*
   - [A] Before 2006 they were known by a different classification.
   - [B] They are typically 25% smaller than true planets.
   - [C] Not all astronomers agree on how to classify them.
   - [D] They orbit gas giant planets rather than the sun.
   - [E] A number of them have been discovered recently.

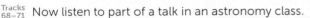 Now listen to part of a talk in an astronomy class.

Fermi paradox

6. What is the Fermi paradox?
   - (A) An important discussion about the nature of nuclear physics
   - (B) An argument among astronomers about the size of a galaxy
   - (C) An estimate of the time it would take to travel between stars
   - (D) A question about why humans have not met intelligent aliens

7. What does the professor say about Earth?
   - (A) It is similar to some planets that orbit other stars.
   - (B) It is an average planet that orbits an average star.
   - (C) It might have conditions for life that are out of the ordinary.
   - (D) It is a rare planet because multi-cellular life is common.

8. What points does the professor make about the search for intelligent life? *Choose two answers.*
   - [A] Humans are not spending enough time and money on the search.
   - [B] Humans have not been searching for intelligent life for very long.
   - [C] Humans may not be searching for the right types of evidence.
   - [D] Humans are not intelligent enough to recognize hidden evidence.

Next Steps

Topics related to astronomy are common in the listening section of the TOEFL Test. You may also have questions about this subject in the other sections of the test, especially the reading section. As a result, learning more about astronomy, as well as practicing key skills for Detail questions, may raise your overall test score.

To learn more about astronomy and vocabulary related to this discipline:

1. Choose a science fiction movie or a documentary about space or space exploration that sounds interesting to you. Make sure that the movie you choose has English subtitles.
2. While you are watching, make a note of any unfamiliar words you see in the subtitles. Pause the movie if necessary.
3. After watching, check the unfamiliar words in your dictionary. If they are related to astronomy, study them carefully.

To practice a key skill for Detail questions:

1. Listen once to a television or radio news broadcast, such as a story about space, business, politics, sports, or astronomy.
2. Take notes as you listen. Focus on taking notes about the major points of the story and how those points are connected.
3. Read a news article about the same story. Compare the details in the article with your notes. Give yourself two points for every correct detail in your notes, but take away one point for each wrong detail. Write down your final points total.
4. Repeat steps 1–3 with a different news story. Try to increase your points total each time you do this self-study activity.

Unit Focus

There are seven types of listening questions in the TOEFL Test. These include Understanding the Function of What Is Said questions, which are classified as "pragmatic understanding" questions. Function questions test if you can recognize a speaker's motivation, or reason, for saying something. The motivation will not be stated directly, so you will have to use indirect clues to choose the correct answer. You will have a Function question after most conversations and lectures. This unit will teach you several key skills to answer Function questions, including:

- listening for expressions that tell you why a speaker is talking.
- using contextual information to understand why a speaker is talking.
- evaluating answer choices and eliminating unlikely options.

The vocabulary focus is on campus and academic words and phrases related to:

- the cost of studying and living at a university in North America and other words related to students' finances.
- art, including architecture, painting, and sculpture, and art history, the study of how art has developed over time.

A Warm-up

A1 Work with a partner to complete tasks 1–3.

1. Think of an artist from your country or one whose work you admire. Tell your partner some information about this artist.
2. Listen to your partner tell you some information about an artist. Take notes as you listen.
3. Share the information that your partner told you with the rest of the class. Then listen to other students talk. Finally, tell your partner which artist interests you most and why.

B Campus Vocabulary

B1 Read this article giving financial advice to new college students. Then answer questions 1–8.

These financial tips and reminders will help you enjoy a stress-free time while you are a student here at Fillmore Tech College. First, remember you will need to pay tuition for your classes and fees for other college services. You will also need $8,000–$12,000 per year for living expenses like housing, food, transportation, utilities, entertainment, and so on. We offer various types of financial aid for students in financial need, including a limited number of scholarships: check our website for more details. Staff in the bursar's office can also help you apply for a student loan and work out a repayment schedule, or provide information about work-study programs that offer a guaranteed part-time position on campus.

1. Which word in the article means a university official whose office has responsibility for dealing with financial matters?
2. Which word means money that students have to pay to a college for general services rather than for tuition?
3. Which phrase is a general name for financial support that students can receive if they cannot afford to pay for college fully?
4. Which phrase describes additional expenses related to living at college that students have?
5. Which phrase means money that college students who need funds can borrow, but must repay later?
6. Which word means financial support that students in need can apply for, but do not need to repay later?
7. Which word means the payment that students make in order to be allowed to attend classes?
8. Which phrase describes a program that helps college students find a job working on campus?

C Analyzing Function Questions

Function questions ask why a speaker said something. Most of these questions are replay questions. This means you will listen to an excerpt (short part) of the whole conversation or lecture you have just heard. Next you will see a question on the screen. You will then hear all or part of the excerpt again. Here are some examples of the question you will see on the screen before part of the conversation or lecture is replayed:

> Why does the professor say this?
>
> Why does the woman ask this?
>
> What does the student mean when she says this?

Some Function questions are not replay questions. These questions describe and ask about a specific part of the conversation or lecture, as in these examples:

> Why does the student mention having to visit _____?
>
> Why does the professor mention the difficulty of _____?

The correct answer to Function questions:

- describes the most likely reason why the speaker said something.
- rarely includes the same words or phrases that the speaker used.

In contrast, incorrect answers to Function questions:

- may describe an unlikely reason for the speaker to say something.
- may restate the literal meaning of the speaker's words, but not explain why he or she used those words.
- often repeat the same words or phrases that the speaker said.

TEST TACTIC

The correct answer to Function questions is usually not something a speaker expresses directly. So, for example, if a man says, "I'm late for class," the function of his words is probably to say that he must leave soon, not to say that he is late.

C1 Read this script from a conversation between a student and his professor. Then answer questions 1 and 2.

Student	Do you have a minute, Professor? I wanted to ask you about our seminar last Monday. I didn't really understand the argument you made about vanishing points.
Professor	Well, I guess I can explain again, but I'm curious why you didn't ask me in class. I can appreciate your not wanting to interrupt a lecture, but the whole purpose of a seminar is to discuss ideas and clear up things you don't understand.
Student	I thought I understood it in class, but then I did some of the reading you assigned, and realized that actually I had the wrong idea.
Professor	OK, now I get why you didn't ask me before. I'll gladly help you, but I've got an appointment in a few minutes, so could you come back at 12 o'clock?

isn't it? I was going to attend Professor Cheung's talk
12, so could I come see you after that?

ing as well, so seeing you after would be ideal.

ays the highlighted words?
he difference between seminars and lectures.
upt either lectures or seminars with questions.
asking questions and discussing the subject.
ve asked for clarification during the class.

vords?

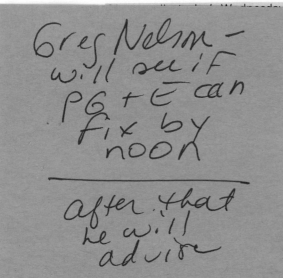

Greg Nelson —
will see if
PG+E can
fix by
noon

after that
he will
advise

D Mastering Function Questions – Listening for Functional Expressions

Sometimes a speaker will use an expression that helps you understand why he or she is speaking. For instance, if a speaker says, "the reason is that" or "because," it is clear that he or she is giving a reason for something. Recognizing these and other functional expressions and taking notes when you hear them are both key skills for Function questions.

Track 72 **D1** Take notes as you listen to an experienced teacher talk about Function questions. Then use your notes and memory to put answers A–F in the order the teacher says them. The first answer has been done for you.

Common Function	Functional Expressions
1. give an example	
2.	
3.	
4.	
5.	
6	

A clarify information
B compare or contrast
C define something
D give a reason
E give an example
F give some advice

Track 72 **D2** Complete tasks 1 and 2.

1. Use your notes and memory to add the example functional expressions the teacher mentions to the table in exercise **D1**.
2. Listen again to the experienced teacher's talk and correct your answers to task 1.

Tracks 73–78 **D3** Listen to some excerpts from conversations and lectures. After each excerpt, add the functional expression you hear to the table in exercise **D1**.

D4 Work with a partner to think of other functional expressions that match each common function listed in exercise **D1**. Add the expressions to the table. Then share your ideas with other students.

E Mastering Function Questions – Recognizing the Function from Context

The context, or situation, in which a speaker is talking can also help you recognize the function of his or her words. The context may be the main idea of the whole conversation or lecture, information a speaker has just mentioned, or even the academic subject the lecture is about.

E1 Add at least three of the functions from exercise **D1** that you think are likely functions a speaker would have in contexts 1-4. Then discuss your ideas with a partner. One answer has been done for you.

Context	Likely Functions
1. A university employee tells a student how to get financial aid.	clarify information, give a reason, give some advice
2. A professor discusses art movements in the twentieth century.	
3. A professor talks about the influence of the Bauhaus school.	
4. A professor explains how to recognize Islamic and Buddhist art.	

TEST TACTIC

If a speaker uses an expression you know, but which you cannot recognize the function of, ask yourself, "When or where would I use this expression?" Thinking in this way will often help you understand the function of the expression.

E2 Listen to excerpts from two conversations and two lectures. After each excerpt, use the context to help you decide what the speaker is likely to do next. Then discuss your answers with a partner. One question has been answered for you.

Tracks 79–82

1. Listen to part of a conversation in a college library. What is the man likely to do next?
   A Advise the woman not to study at cafés in town in the future   ☐ Likely ☑ Unlikely
   B Tell the woman she has to buy a replacement copy of the lost book   ☑ Likely ☐ Unlikely
   C Suggest that the woman telephone the café where she lost the book   ☑ Likely ☐ Unlikely

2. Listen to part of a lecture in an art history class. What is the woman likely to do next?
   A Describe other paintings like *The Night Watch* that are known to be   ☐ Likely ☐ Unlikely
      by Rembrandt
   B Explain what terms to use when a work cannot definitely be attributed   ☐ Likely ☐ Unlikely
      to an artist
   C Discuss how Rembrandt and other artists created their most   ☐ Likely ☐ Unlikely
      famous paintings

3. Listen to part of a conversation in a finance office. What is the woman likely to do next?
   A Talk about other financial aid options the man has   ☐ Likely ☐ Unlikely
   B Explain why the student was not eligible to apply   ☐ Likely ☐ Unlikely
   C Ask the student to describe his academic record   ☐ Likely ☐ Unlikely

4. Listen to part of a lecture in a geology class. What is the professor likely to do next?
   A Discuss different artists who used lapis lazuli   ☐ Likely ☐ Unlikely
   B Compare natural and artificial paint colors   ☐ Likely ☐ Unlikely
   C Talk about ways lapis lazuli is used these days   ☐ Likely ☐ Unlikely

E3 Listen to longer excerpts from the conversations and lectures in exercise **E2**. Take notes and decide whether answer A, B, or C, is the correct answer to each question in that exercise.

Tracks 83–86

F Mastering Function Questions – Recognizing Why a Speaker Says Something

Listening to the words a speaker uses and thinking about the context can help you understand a speaker's reason for saying something. To do this more effectively, ask yourself questions as you listen, such as *Why is the speaker saying this?* or *What does the speaker want the listener(s) to understand?*

F1 Listen to excerpts from two conversations and two lectures. As you listen to each excerpt, think about why the speaker is talking and what he or she wants the listener(s) to understand. Then answer the question.

Tracks 87–90

1. Listen to excerpt 1. What does the man mean?
   A He is sorry for missing an important deadline.
   B It is too late to submit a financial aid application.

2. Listen to excerpt 2. Why does the woman say this?
   A To explain why she lives on campus
   B To recommend living off-campus

3. Listen to excerpt 3. Why does the man say this?
   A To give examples of well-known buildings
   B To contrast two meanings of a particular term

4. Listen to excerpt 4. Why does the woman say this?
   A To encourage students to attend an event
   B To compare the works of several famous artists

Tracks 91–94 **F2** **Listen to some excerpts from different conversations and lectures. As you listen, think about why the speaker is saying this and what he or she wants the listener(s) to understand. Then write down your ideas. One answer has been done for you.**

1. Listen to excerpt 1. Why does the man ask this? _____ *to clarify information* _____
2. Listen to excerpt 2. Why does the woman say this?_____
3. Listen to excerpt 3. Why does the woman say this?_____
4. Listen to excerpt 4. Why does the man say this?_____

Tracks 95–98 **F3** **Listen to longer versions of the conversations and lectures from exercise F2. Take notes and check your answers to that exercise.**

G Mastering Function Questions – Evaluating the Answer Choices

A key skill for Function questions is to recognize common reasons why answer choices are wrong. If you can recognize these reasons, you can avoid choosing incorrect answers. Another key skill is using common sense to decide if an answer choice is likely or unlikely to be correct.

Tracks 99–105 **G1** **Listen to excerpts from a conversation and two lectures. Then mark each answer as Correct or Incorrect. One answer has been done for you.**

Listen to a conversation in the Finance Office.

1. Listen again to part of the conversation. What does the man mean?
   A He does not like the words the woman uses.   ☐ Correct   ☑ Incorrect
   B His grades are not as good as he would like.   ☑ Correct   ☐ Incorrect
   C He would rather apply for a part-time job.   ☐ Correct   ☑ Incorrect

Listen to part of a discussion in an art history seminar.

2. Why does the speaker talk about the meanings of the name of the painting?
   A To give additional supporting evidence for his point of view   ☐ Correct   ☐ Incorrect
   B To suggest that students should study Italian and French   ☐ Correct   ☐ Incorrect
   C To help students understand which painting he is discussing   ☐ Correct   ☐ Incorrect

Listen to part of a lecture about Chinese art.

3. Listen again to part of the lecture. Why does the woman say this?
   A To suggest that bamboo represents the summer   ☐ Correct   ☐ Incorrect
   B To contrast how quickly bamboo and other plants grow ☐ Correct   ☐ Incorrect
   C To explain why bamboo is both strong and flexible   ☐ Correct   ☐ Incorrect

4. Listen again to part of the lecture. What does the woman mean?
   A People are usually surprised when plum blossoms appear.   ☐ Correct   ☐ Incorrect
   B During winter, people look forward to the arrival of spring.   ☐ Correct   ☐ Incorrect
   C Cold weather and snow cause plum trees to produce blossoms.   ☐ Correct   ☐ Incorrect

TEST TACTIC

A speaker's intonation may sometimes help you understand his or her reason for speaking. For example, if a professor says some words in the form of a question, but her intonation falls at the end of the sentence rather than rises, she is probably emphasizing a point rather than asking a question.

Tracks 106–111 **G2** **First decide if the answers to questions 1–3 are likely or unlikely. Then listen to three excerpts and choose the right answer to each question.**

1. What reason does the student have for saying this to her professor?
   A To motivate her professor to give her more information
   B To tell her professor to read a particular book
   C To ask her professor for more information about a topic

2. What reason does the professor have for saying this to his students?
   A To define the meaning of an unfamiliar expression
   B To say something interesting to prevent boredom
   C To contrast aspects of two different cultures

3. What reason does the professor have for saying this to her student?
   A She wants the students to study the topic more after class.
   B She needs to clarify the meaning of a question before answering it.
   C She feels she should apologize for not speaking more clearly.

H Academic Vocabulary

H1 Choose the best highlighted word from definitions A–H to complete descriptions of three famous artworks. One answer has been done for you.

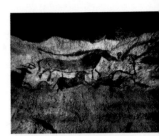

This work, part of the cave paintings at the famous Lascaux Caves in southwestern France, shows a typical scene of horses, deer, and cattle. The animals are painted in mineral 1. ___pigments___ like red and yellow ochre as well as 2. _____. The cave art at Lascaux is believed to have been painted more than 17,000 years ago.

Da Vinci's *Mona Lisa* is arguably the most famous example of a painting in the portraiture genre. It was most likely painted between 1503 and 1506 during the 3. _____. The 4. _____ was painted in oil on a wooden panel and is believed to be an image of Lisa Gherardini, the wife of a Tuscan merchant.

Monet's *Impression, Sunrise* painted in oil on 5. _____ in the year 1872 is a 6. _____ painting of the harbor at Le Havre in northern France. The small ship in the 7. _____ contrasts with the expanse of sea and sky painted in the loose brush strokes typical of Impressionism. Indeed, the Impressionist 8. _____ was named for this work.

A A canvas is a piece of stretched fabric – usually linen or cotton – on which artists paint using oil or acrylic paints.
B In art, charcoal can refer either to a black or dark gray form of carbon used for drawing, or a drawing done in charcoal.
C The foreground is the part of a painting, photograph, or view that appears closest to the observer.
D A painting or other work of art that shows a wide view of a natural scene is called a landscape.
E A style of art adopted by a group of artists who agree on certain artistic principles is called a movement.
F Pigments are substances that can be added to a liquid such as ink or paint to give it color.
G A portrait is a work of art such as a painting or photograph that focuses on the subject's face.
H The Renaissance was a movement in Europe from the fourteenth to seventeenth centuries marked by cultural and artistic changes.

I Test Challenge

I1 Practice some Understanding the Function of What Is Said questions. While you listen, cover the questions and take notes. Then use your notes and memory to answer questions 1–6. Use this checklist of skills that you studied in this unit as a guide.

While you listen to the conversation and lectures
- ☑ Listen for functional expressions like "for example" or "in my view" that tell you a speaker's reason for speaking.
- ☑ Ask yourself questions while you listen such as *Why is she saying this?* to better understand the speaker's motivation.

When you answer the questions
- ☑ Remember that wrong answers often repeat a speaker's words or paraphrase the literal meaning of his or her words.
- ☑ Use common sense to judge which answers are likely based on the context of the talk and based on real life.

TEST TACTIC

Many Function questions have answers that begin with infinitives (e.g., "to explain" or "to describe"). In some cases you can quickly eliminate an answer because it has an infinitive that obviously does not match the conversation or lecture.

Tracks 112–114 Listen to a conversation between a student and his professor.

1. Listen again to part of the conversation. What does the professor mean when she says this?
   - (A) The student's behavior is likely to cause trouble.
   - (B) The student has missed the deadline to cancel.
   - (C) It is a shame the student will not be able to help.
   - (D) The art show will be successful without his help.

2. Listen again to part of the conversation. Why does the professor say this?
   - (A) To describe the organization of the committee to the man
   - (B) To explain why she cannot guarantee a job for the man yet
   - (C) To clarify some important information the man did not know
   - (D) To imply that she needs help dealing with the committee

Tracks 115–117 Listen to part of a lecture in an art history class.

3. Listen again to part of the lecture. Why does the professor say this?
   - (A) To remind students they should read their course books before class
   - (B) To imply the names of the Group of Seven members are unimportant
   - (C) To let students know they do not need to copy down all of the names
   - (D) To encourage students to listen to his views more carefully

4. Listen again to part of the lecture. Why does the professor say this?
   - (A) To emphasize the typical subject of Group of Seven paintings
   - (B) To explain why most Group of Seven paintings show Algonquin Park
   - (C) To give an example of a typical painting by the Group of Seven
   - (D) To suggest Algonquin School is a better name than Group of Seven

Tracks 118–120 Listen to part of a talk in a paleontology class. The professor is discussing prehistoric art.

Chauvet Cave

Aurignacian period

5. Listen again to part of the lecture. What does the woman mean?
   - (A) Most caves have images of human figures as well as predators.
   - (B) She is shocked that images of predatory animals were painted.
   - (C) There is no such thing as a typical prehistoric cave painting.
   - (D) Caves with prehistoric art rarely have paintings of predators.

6. Why does the professor discuss DNA analysis of horse bones and teeth?
   - (A) To prove that the majority of artists at Chauvet Cave were female
   - (B) To support the argument that cave artists painted actual animals
   - (C) To explain why horses are painted more often than other animals
   - (D) To demonstrate that scientific analysis can explain artistic techniques

Next Steps

Topics related to art and art history are common in the TOEFL Test, especially in the reading and listening sections. As a result, learning more about these subjects, as well as practicing key skills for Understanding the Function of What Is Said questions, may raise your overall test score.

To learn more about art and art history and vocabulary related to these disciplines, create some word chains:

1. Think of a basic word you know that is related to art or art history. For example, you might choose the word "paint."
2. Write the word at the top of a piece of paper. Also write its definition and its part of speech, such as noun or verb.
3. Think of a word that is connected to the previous word in the chain. For example, a word connected to "paint" might be "brush." (If you cannot think of a word connected to the previous word, do some research.)
4. Write this new word on the paper below the previous word. Include its definition and grammar information, too.
5. Repeat steps 3 and 4 until you have filled up the paper. If you do this every day, you will soon build your vocabulary.

To practice key skills for Understanding the Function of What Is Said questions:

1. Choose a short article or advertisement in a newspaper or magazine and try to understand the function of each sentence. For example, is the writer trying to express an opinion, suggest an action, give an example, or something else?
2. Repeat step 1 with different texts until you are confident you can recognize the function of most written sentences.
3. Watch a movie in English and pause it every few minutes. Think about what the speaker has just said and try to understand the function of his or her words.
4. Repeat step 3 with different movies until you are confident you can recognize the function of most spoken sentences.
5. Listen to academic lectures about art or another subject. You can find free lectures using the Internet. Pause the lecture every few minutes. Think about what the speaker has just said and think about the function of his or her words.

Unit Focus

There are seven types of listening questions in the TOEFL Test. These include Understanding the Speaker's Attitude questions, which are classified as "pragmatic understanding" questions. Attitude questions test how well you can recognize the opinion, attitude, or feelings of a speaker from his or her words and tone of voice. You will see several Attitude questions when you take the TOEFL Test, though you will probably not have one after every conversation or lecture. You will learn several key skills to answer Attitude questions in this unit, including:

- recognizing whether a speaker's tone of voice is positive or negative.
- recognizing and taking notes on directly and indirectly stated opinions and preferences.
- listening for and taking notes when a speaker discusses the opinion of somebody else.

The vocabulary focus is on campus and academic words and phrases related to:

- choosing which classes to take, and attending required and optional classes.
- literature, the study of written works that have artistic value including novels, short stories, poems, and dramas.

A Warm-up

A1 First add two emotions to this list. Then write down as many situations as possible in which you might feel emotions 1–8. Work with a partner. When you have finished, share your list with other students.

1. anxious
2. apologetic
3. disappointed
4. doubtful
5. interested
6. optimistic
7. _your idea_
8. _your idea_

A2 Complete sentences 1–4 using words from exercise **A1** or other words you know that describe how people feel. When you have finished, share your answers with other students and listen to their answers.

1. Last time I bought something expensive I felt _____ because _____
2. When I have to do homework I usually feel _____ because _____
3. Next time I take the TOEFL Test I think I will feel _____ because _____
4. If they have to talk in public, a lot of students feel _____ because _____

B Campus Vocabulary

B1 Choose the best word from choices A–H to complete definitions 1–8. Use a dictionary to check the meaning of any unfamiliar words.

1. The academic subject that a student at university chooses to specialize in studying is called a(n) _____.
2. A(n) _____ is an academic field that college students study which requires taking fewer courses than a major.
3. To get a degree, students must take a number of required _____ in subjects like English, math, and science.
4. Unlike core classes, which are compulsory, _____ classes are ones that students can choose to take.
5. Some classes have _____ courses which students must take before they can enroll in those specific classes.
6. _____ are classes for a small number of students who are expected to share ideas and participate actively.

7. When students pass a class they receive a certain number of _____ that are needed in order to graduate.

8. To _____ a class means to attend lectures, but not to do assignments, take exams, or receive credits.

A audit   C credits   E major   G prerequisite

B core classes   D elective   F minor   H seminars

C Analyzing Attitude Questions

Attitude questions typically ask about the opinion, attitude, or feelings of a speaker as in the examples below.

> What is the student's opinion about _____?
>
> How does the student feel about _____?
>
> What can be inferred about the professor's attitude towards _____?
>
> What point of view does the professor express about _____?

A few Attitude questions are replay questions, meaning you will hear an excerpt (short part) of the conversation or lecture again. In rare cases, an Attitude question may ask how certain a speaker is about something.

The correct answer to an Attitude question:

- may paraphrase an opinion that a speaker mentions directly.
- may summarize an opinion that a speaker expresses indirectly.
- matches a speaker's intonation – positive opinion for a positive tone of voice, for example.

In contrast, incorrect answers to Attitude questions may:

- repeat some of the words that a speaker used but not summarize or paraphrase his or her opinion.
- describe an opinion that is expressed by a person other than the person the question mentions.
- refer to a speaker's attitude towards a different idea than the one that the question asks about.

TEST TACTIC

Speakers may express opinions and feelings either directly or indirectly. Attitudes may be expressed directly, too, but it is more common for them to be expressed using indirect language or through a speaker's tone of voice.

C1 Use these scripts from a conversation and a lecture to answer questions 1 and 2.

Student Excuse me, Professor? I really appreciate your agreeing to let me audit your modern poetry class, but I've decided not to audit the class after all. I'm taking a lot of credits this semester as it is, you see, and I don't want to overstretch myself.

Professor I see. Well, it sounds like you've made the decision for a good reason.

Student Thanks, Professor. I thought you might be mad at me for changing my mind.

1. How did the student feel before visiting his professor?
    A Concerned
    B Agreeable
    C Reasonable
    D Sorrowful

Professor I'd like to continue our discussion of classic English novels by talking about one of my favorite books, *The History of Tom Jones, a Foundling* by English novelist Henry Fielding. It's told in the first person, which gives it an immediacy that is still fresh even though it was published in 1749. It's a picaresque novel, so it doesn't have much of a plot compared to modern novels, but it's an exciting work that tells of the amusing adventures of the main character – named Tom Jones, obviously.

2. What is the professor's opinion of the novel *Tom Jones*?
    A She feels it is not as enjoyable as modern novels because it has no plot.
    B She believes that certain aspects of the story are too obvious.
    C She thinks it is an enjoyable work with several positive qualities.
    D She considers it to be a humorous story that is no longer popular.

D Mastering Attitude Questions – Recognizing Positive and Negative Intonation

A speaker's tone of voice can help you understand his or her opinion, attitude, or feelings about something. As a result, listening for and taking notes when a speaker uses positive or negative intonation is a key skill that can help you answer Understanding the Speaker's Attitude questions.

Tracks 121–122 **D1** Follow the notes below as you listen to excerpts from a conversation and a lecture. Circle and label the notes when you hear a speaker use either positive or negative intonation. One example has been done for you.

TEST TACTIC

In addition to suggesting a positive or negative view, a speaker's tone of voice can indicate specific emotions or feelings. For example, intonation can indicate humor, frustration, preference, dislike, certainty, doubt, surprise, shock, and so on.

Woman	*positive* Modern (poetry seminar sounds good) → want take next semester
	Not taken prerequisite class
	Researched modern poetry in high school + will major in literature
	Want permission to take the class
Man	Not possible to take seminar without prerequisite
	Students without prereq have difficult time no permission
	Woman can audit class if she wants
Woman	Not thought about audit but good idea → thanks

Plot devices → situation / event / object / character moves story forward
    Necessary and found in every story BUT can be too obvious and not believable
Deus ex machina (DEM) = plot device with bad reputation
    Miraculous event that saves lives of protagonists e.g., arrival of hero
    DEM often criticized because not believable / natural / creative
    May be accepted by readers (or not noticed) if DEM follows from story
    Rescue of children in Lord of the Flies is natural example of DEM

Tracks 123–126 **D2** Listen to some excerpts from conversations and lectures. Does each speaker use positive or negative intonation?

1. Speaker 1   ☐ Positive   ☐ Negative
2. Speaker 2   ☐ Positive   ☐ Negative
3. Speaker 3   ☐ Positive   ☐ Negative
4. Speaker 4   ☐ Positive   ☐ Negative

Tracks 127–128 **D3** Listen to an excerpt from a conversation and lecture. As you listen, take notes about the speakers' intonation. After the first excerpt, answer questions 1 and 2. After the second excerpt, answer questions 3 and 4.

1. In excerpt 1, what is the professor's attitude to the student's question?
   A Disappointed
   B Apologetic

2. In excerpt 1, how does the student sound at the end of the conversation?
   A Confused
   B Surprised

3. In excerpt 2, how does the professor sound when he first mentions *Animal Farm*?
   A Critical
   B Interested

4. In excerpt 2, how does the professor sound at the end of the lecture?
   A Frustrated
   B Enthusiastic

E Mastering Attitude Questions – Recognizing Directly-Stated Opinions

In conversations and lectures in the TOEFL Test, speakers sometimes directly state their opinions or preferences about a subject. It is important to recognize and take accurate notes when a speaker expresses an opinion or preference because these notes may help you choose the correct answer to Attitude questions.

Tracks 129–134 **E1** Listen to six speakers use common expressions to state their feelings directly. As you listen, put a check (✓) in the column to show who uses each expression. Note that speakers 4 and 6 use two expressions. One answer has been done for you.

	Speaker 1	Speaker 2	Speaker 3	Speaker 4	Speaker 5	Speaker 6
1. It seems to me that …						
2. For me, …						
3. My view is that …						
4. From my point of view, …						
5. My preference is for …	✓					
6. In my experience, …						
7. I'd say that …						
8. I'm convinced that …						

E2 Make a list of other common expressions for stating your opinion or preference. Work with a partner. When you have finished, share your ideas with other students.

Tracks 135–136 **E3** Listen to an excerpt from a conversation and lecture and take notes about opinions that the speakers express. Then use your notes and memory to answer questions 1–5. Choose the answers that restate the speakers' opinions.

1. In excerpt 1, what is the professor's opinion of the student?
   A She would be successful if she decided to focus on literature.
   B She has recently begun to ask excellent questions in class.
   C She needs to participate more actively during lessons.

2. In excerpt 1, what is the student's attitude when the professor gives his opinion about her ability?
   A She is disappointed.
   B She is overjoyed.
   C She is surprised.

3. In excerpt 1, what is the professor's opinion of the student's essay?
   A It has both good points and bad points.
   B It is well organized but not long enough.
   C It deserves a higher grade than a B minus.

4. In excerpt 2, what is the professor's opinion about the *Satyricon* and *Golden Ass*?
   A They should not be classified as novels.
   B The works are very different from each other.
   C The works are shorter than other novels.

5. In excerpt 2, what is the professor's opinion about the novel *Don Quixote*?
   A It differs from modern picaresque novels.
   B It is an interesting, influential work.
   C It is the best book ever written.

F Mastering Attitude Questions – Recognizing Implied Opinions

In some conversations and lectures speakers imply their opinions rather than stating them directly. It is important both to recognize opinions that are mentioned indirectly and to take accurate notes when you hear one because some Attitude questions ask about indirectly-expressed opinions.

F1 Use the underlined phrases in this partial script to answer question 1.

Professor	I wanted to talk to you about our seminar class. <u>At the beginning of the semester your assignments were great, and you participated actively and made some great points in class, and, well, I was wondering what's changed.</u>
Student	I'm sorry, Professor. I had to start doing a part-time job about a month ago, and since then I've been tired all the time and it's been much harder to make time to prepare adequately for class and do the assignments.
Professor	I had a feeling it was something like that. <u>Look, I don't want to worry you, but this is a core class and unless you can find a better way to balance your time, you might have to take this class again next semester.</u>

1. What two opinions does the professor express indirectly? *Choose two answers.*
   A The student should find a full-time job not a part-time one.
   B There is a chance that the student might fail the class.
   C The student's participation has not been good recently.
   D The student makes good choices about balancing her time.

TEST TACTIC

Sometimes a speaker's words and tone of voice might contradict each other. For example, a speaker might say, "Well, that's just great," but use a tone of voice that indicates frustration. In general, tone of voice is more likely to indicate a speaker's true feelings.

F2 Use this partial script from an academic lecture to answer question 1. Then underline the words and phrases that helped you choose the answers. Compare your ideas with a partner when you have finished.

Professor	Epic poems, such as Homer's *Odyssey* and *Iliad* and Virgil's *Aeneid*, are long narrative poems that tell of heroic deeds. Classical epics share five conventions, but before I discuss them, let me clarify a couple of points. You'll see complicated lists of additional characteristics in some of the articles on your reading list, but the five conventions are the core of what defines an epic. Also, my focus is on Greek and Latin epics, so you won't be able to apply all of these ideas to epics in other languages, such as Sumerian or Akkadian epics like *Gilgamesh* or Sanskrit epics like *Mahabharata*, OK?

1. What two opinions does the speaker express indirectly? *Choose two answers.*
   A Not all epic poems are narrative poems that tell heroic stories.
   B Some scholars give a complicated definition of epic poems.
   C Epic poems in Greek are better than epics in other languages.
   D Not all epic poems share the same set of conventions.

🔊 Tracks 137–138 **F3** Listen to an excerpt from a conversation and a lecture. As you listen, take notes about the opinions that the speakers imply. Then use your notes and memory to answer questions 1 and 2.

1. What two opinions does the woman express indirectly in excerpt 1? *Choose two answers.*
   A The man should speak to his professor about the situation.
   B The problem will permanently affect the man's academic record.
   C The man's professor has not filled out records for the class.

2. What two opinions does the man express indirectly in excerpt 2? *Choose two answers.*
   A The *kigo*, or seasonal reference, in haiku poems is usually not a poetic phrase.
   B Syllables in English do not always match syllables in Japanese.
   C The concept of a *kireji*, or cutting word, may not be clear to listeners.

G Mastering Attitude Questions – Recognizing Different People's Opinions

In some conversations and lectures, two different speakers express opinions, or one speaker mentions the opinions of other people as well as his or her own point of view. Attitude questions may ask about the opinions of various people, not just the speaker, so being able to recognize which person holds which opinion is a key skill for these questions.

Tracks 139–140 **G1** **Listen to excerpts from two lectures. As you listen, take notes about opinions that the speakers discuss and about who holds those opinions. Then use your notes and memory to answer questions 1 and 2.**

1. Listen to excerpt 1 and take notes. Then put a check (✓) in the correct column to show who holds each opinion. One answer has been done for you.

Opinions about *The Love Song of J. Alfred Prufrock* by T.S. Eliot	Reviewers	Student	Professor
It is emotionally powerful.			✓
It is shocking and non-poetic.			
It causes feelings of discomfort.			

2. Listen to excerpt 2 and take notes. Then match each opinion to the person who holds or held it.

Opinions about French author Jules Verne	Contemporary critics	European academics	Professor
Jules Verne was a serious writer worthy of academic study.			
The works of Jules Verne were popular, but not high quality.			
Verne's writing style was new, but influenced other writers.			

H Academic Vocabulary

H1 **Which answer, A–H, best completes definitions 1–8 of the highlighted words, which are all related to literature? One answer has been done for you.**

1. In literature, criticism can be defined _____ as discussion about the qualities of a novel, poem, or play. _____
2. A narrative is the account or story _____
3. Novels are long works _____
4. The plot of a story is the sequence _____
5. Poetry is the general name given _____
6. The term prose describes writing that is similar _____
7. The protagonist is the main character _____
8. When a book is published, it is made available _____

A as discussion about the qualities of a novel, poem, or play.
B for distribution and sale in printed or electronic form.
C in a fictional narrative such as a novel, epic poem, or drama.
D of a sequence of events told in the order that they occurred.
E of events in a fictional work, such as a story, play, or movie.
F of imaginative fiction that often have a complicated plot.
G to literary works written in verse rather than in prose.
H to normal spoken language, such as an essay or news article.

TEST TACTIC

Although correct answers generally paraphrase a speaker's words rather than repeat them, many correct answers repeat one or two words. For example, a speaker might say, "in my view her theory is mistaken," and the correct answer might be "The professor's view is that the woman's theory is incorrect."

▌ Test Challenge

11 **Practice some Understanding the Speaker's Attitude questions. Cover the questions and take notes as you listen. Then use your notes and memory to answer questions 1–6. Use this checklist of skills that you studied in this unit as a guide.**

While you listen to the conversation and lectures

☑ Take notes when a speaker uses positive or negative intonation.

☑ Take notes when a speaker expresses an opinion directly or indirectly.

☑ Take notes when a speaker discusses another person's point of view.

When you answer the questions

☑ Look for answers that paraphrase directly-expressed opinions and accurately summarize implied opinions.

☑ Be careful not to choose answers that repeat information from a talk but do not paraphrase a person's opinion.

🔊 Tracks 141–143 Listen to a conversation between a student and a professor.

1. What is the professor's attitude to helping the student?
   - Ⓐ He is reluctant but willing to give her some guidance.
   - Ⓑ He thinks she should already have made a decision.
   - Ⓒ He feels that the decision she should make is obvious.
   - Ⓓ He is worried the student may not accept his advice.

2. What does the student say about creative writing?
   - Ⓐ She really enjoys writing film scripts.
   - Ⓑ It's not a subject that interests her.
   - Ⓒ It's something she can really focus on.
   - Ⓓ She finds it too literary and analytical.

🔊 Tracks 144–146 Listen to part of a discussion in a sociology class. The subject of the discussion is the Nobel Prize in Literature.

 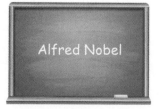

3. What does the professor think about the decisions of the Swedish Academy?
   - Ⓐ They are hardly ever controversial.
   - Ⓑ They show evidence of prejudice.
   - Ⓒ They often result in arguments.
   - Ⓓ They follow the terms of Nobel's will.

4. What does the professor think led to an improvement in the situation over the last 25 years?
    - Ⓐ Criticism of the Swedish Academy's decision in newspapers
    - Ⓑ Pressure from both female writers and writers from other continents
    - Ⓒ Improved decision-making by members of the Swedish Academy
    - Ⓓ An increase in the number of authors from non-European countries

Tracks
147–149 Listen to a part of a talk in an English literature class. The professor is discussing William Shakespeare.

 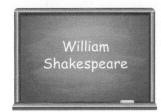 

5. What opinion does the professor say some people hold?
    - Ⓐ William Shakespeare was not a writer and did not come from Stratford.
    - Ⓑ There is little hard evidence that William Shakespeare died in 1616.
    - Ⓒ William Shakespeare must have had a very high level of education.
    - Ⓓ The literary works of William Shakespeare were written by someone else.

6. What is the professor's opinion about the authorship question? *Choose two answers.*
    - Ⓐ The arguments are powerful and believable but cannot be proved.
    - Ⓑ The absence of evidence supporting Shakespeare is a strong argument.
    - Ⓒ The evidence in favor of alternative candidates is weak.
    - Ⓓ The arguments are interesting but not supported by the evidence.

Next Steps

Topics related to literature are common in the listening section of the TOEFL Test. You may also have questions about this subject in the other sections of the test, especially the reading section. As a result, learning more about literature, as well as practicing key skills for Understanding Organization questions, may raise your overall test score.

To learn more about literature and vocabulary related to this discipline:

1. Think of an author you like or a famous writer from your country or another country.
2. Search the Internet for the author's name plus the phrase "critical analysis," as in "Shakespeare critical analysis".
3. Choose one of the websites from the search list that has a short article of roughly three to five paragraphs.
4. Read the article a couple of times to get an idea of the main points.
5. Read the article again and look for vocabulary related to the author's writings. Study these words carefully.

To practice a key skill for Understanding the Speaker's Attitude questions:

1. Listen to a radio program in English. (If there are no radio broadcasts in English in your area, search the Internet for "internet radio in English". Alternatively, listen to a television program but do not watch the screen while you listen.)
2. For the first five minutes while you listen, focus on listening to the speakers' intonation. Make notes of how that intonation helps you understand their point of view.
3. For the next five minutes, listen for and make a note of any opinions that the speakers express.
4. For the final five minutes, listen for and make a note of attitudes or feelings that the speakers express indirectly.
5. Repeat steps 1–4 for 15 minutes every day. Try listening to a different radio station or listen at a different time in order to hear a wide variety of speakers talk about a wide variety of topics.

Unit Focus

There are seven types of listening questions in the TOEFL Test. These include Understanding Organization questions, which are classified as "connecting information" questions. Organization questions test how well you can recognize either the organization of a lecture or the relationship between one concept and the main idea of the conversation or lecture. These questions are more common after lectures than conversations, but you will probably not see one after every lecture. This unit will teach you several key skills to answer Organization questions, including:

- recognizing why a speaker mentions a particular idea, point, or detail.
- recognizing how a particular idea, point, or detail relates to the whole conversation or lecture.
- recognizing common ways in which academic lectures are organized.
- taking effective notes and using those notes to eliminate incorrect answers.

The vocabulary focus is on campus and academic words and phrases related to:

- names for students at different stages of their education and for different categories of students.
- sociology, the study of human societies in general as well as individuals and groups within society.

A Warm-up

A1 **Complete sentences 1–5, which describe topics commonly studied by sociologists, with the correct ending, A–E.**

1. The study of crime _____
2. The study of education _____
3. The study of the family _____
4. The study of health _____
5. The study of technology _____

A focuses on issues like marriage and divorce, raising children, and relationships with relatives.
B involves identifying why people break the law and how society prevents or deals with law-breaking.
C focuses on understanding how things like illness, disability, and aging populations affect society.
D includes investigating the ways in which computers and the Internet have an impact on society.
E deals with issues like how learning both impacts and is impacted by the norms of a society.

B Campus Vocabulary

B1 **Use information from this passage to complete definitions 1–8 of the highlighted expressions. Two answers have been done for you.**

Undergraduate students at North American colleges typically study for four years to earn a degree. Undergraduates in their first year of study are called freshmen. Students in the other years of study are called sophomores, juniors, and seniors, respectively. Students who are taking graduate-level classes are usually called grad students. Students who originally enrolled at one college but are now studying at a different one are called transfer students, while exchange students are visiting from another college temporarily, usually for a semester or year.

1. An undergraduate is a student who _____ has not yet earned a degree. _____
2. A freshman is a student who _____ is in his or her first year of study. _____
3. A sophomore is a student who _____
4. A junior is a student who _____
5. A senior is a student who _____
6. A grad student is studying _____
7. A transfer student originally _____
8. An exchange student is _____

C Analyzing Organization Questions

There are two kinds of Organization questions. The most common kind asks you how one idea, example, or point that a speaker discusses is related to the whole lecture or conversation, as in these examples:

Why does the student mention _____?

Why does the lecturer talk about _____?

Why does the professor discuss _____?

The other kind of Organization question asks how all or part of a lecture is organized:

How does the professor organize her lecture?

How does the professor introduce the concept of _____?

The correct answer to an Organization question:

- usually describes how one idea, example, or point relates to the main idea of the conversation or lecture.
- may describe the way that the whole lecture is organized.
- will not be stated explicitly by any of the speakers during the conversation or lecture.

In contrast, incorrect answers to Organization questions:

- may summarize one idea, example, or point rather than explain how it relates to the whole conversation or lecture.
- may incorrectly describe the organization of the whole lecture.
- typically repeat or restate words from the conversation or lecture.

TEST TACTIC

The first kind of Organization question looks similar to Understanding the Function of What Is Said questions (see Unit 10). They differ in that Organization questions ask how the speaker's words relate to the subject of the talk, but Function questions ask how listeners would understand the speaker's words.

C1 **Use these scripts from a conversation and a lecture to answer questions 1 and 2.**

Woman	Excuse me? A professor told me that a book I need for an assignment is on the special reserve list, but I'm a transfer student and the special reserve system here is different from the one at my previous college.
Man	Oh, it's pretty simple. Instructors can put a book that many students are likely to need on special reserve. That means you can borrow it, but only for three days, and you'll have to go to the reserve desk to do so.
Woman	OK. Thanks, for the explanation. I'll go over to the reserve desk right now.

1. Why does the woman mention she is a transfer student?
   A To emphasize that it is important she gets a copy of the book soon
   B To explain why she doesn't understand the special reserve system
   C To point out that the library's systems are confusing for some students
   D To explain that she needs to borrow the book for longer than three days

| Professor | Although many of the major concepts and techniques of modern sociology have been known and used for thousands of years, sociology is a relatively modern discipline. French philosopher Auguste Comte felt that science could be used to analyze and understand the social world, and in 1838 he coined the name sociology. Later in the same century, three other influential thinkers – Karl Marx, Max Weber, and, especially, Emile Durkheim – developed the ideas that became the foundations of modern sociology. |

2. How does the professor organize his talk?
   A He contrasts different ideas about a subject.
   B He talks about events in the order they occurred.
   C He mentions problems and then gives solutions.
   D He discusses what led to acceptance of a theory.

D Mastering Organization Questions – Recognizing Why a Speaker Says Something

Most Organization questions ask why a speaker mentions a specific point. As a result, key skills to answer Organization questions include being able to recognize why a speaker mentions something, and identifying how a speaker's point is related to the whole conversation or lecture. As with all listening questions, taking effective notes is also important.

🔊 Track 150 **D1** **Take notes as you listen to an experienced teacher talk about answering Organization questions. Then use your notes to put points A–E in the order the teacher discusses them. One answer has been done for you.**

1. Take notes when a speaker gives a detailed example
2.
3.
4.
5.

A   Take notes when a speaker compares two things
B   Take notes when a speaker makes a digression
C   Ask "What is the speaker likely to talk about next?"
D   Take notes when a speaker gives a detailed example
E   Ask "Why is the speaker saying this information?"

🔊 Tracks 151–155 **D2** **Listen to five excerpts (short parts) from conversations and lectures and take notes. After each excerpt, answer the question. One answer has been done for you.**

1. What does the man do in excerpt 1?
    ☐ Gives an example   ☑ Compares two things   ☐ Makes a digression

2. What does the woman do in excerpt 2?
    ☐ Gives an example   ☐ Compares two things   ☐ Makes a digression

3. What does the man do in excerpt 3?
    ☐ Gives an example   ☐ Compares two things   ☐ Makes a digression

4. What does the woman do in excerpt 4?
    ☐ Gives an example   ☐ Compares two things   ☐ Makes a digression

5. What does the man do in excerpt 5?
    ☐ Gives an example   ☐ Compares two things   Makes a digression

D3 **Use these notes from part of a lecture to answer questions 1 and 2.**

Longitudinal study → observation of same data over period of time
Used in sociology to study events in life of people / organizations
Same people / organizations observed throughout study
Studies provide accurate results → easy to see changes over time
+ Results unaffected by cultural differences unlike other methods
Studies are expensive → sample size often small
Also take long time → participants drop out (attrition)

TEST TACTIC

While you are listening to a conversation or lecture, it can also be helpful to ask "How are the speaker's words connected to the main idea?" If you can recognize this connection, it may help you answer an Organization question.

1. Why does the speaker talk about cultural differences?
    A   To explain why one type of study takes a long time to do
    B   To compare one type of sociology study with other types

2. Why does the speaker mention the sample size of many longitudinal studies?
    A   To point out that cost and sample size are related
    B   To explain why these studies are rarely conducted

Tracks
156–159   **D4** Take notes as you listen to four excerpts from conversations and lectures. Then use your notes to answer questions 1–8.

Listen to part of a conversation between a student and his academic advisor. Then answer questions 1 and 2.

1. Why does the woman mention the lack of specialists in industrial sociology?
   A To emphasize the man should soon make a decision about what to specialize in
   B To explain why she thinks the student should apply to study at a different university

2. What is the woman likely to talk about next?
   A Faculty members at her university who specialize in industrial sociology
   B Colleges that offer good graduate programs in industrial sociology
   C Reasons why certain classes are offered at some schools but not others

Listen to part of a lecture in a sociology class. Then answer questions 3 and 4.

3. Why does the man mention the background of an author?
   A He wants to explain why students should be careful about accepting the theories in a book.
   B He wants students to know that the ideas in a book may not be expressed in familiar terms.

4. What is the man likely to discuss next?
   A He will probably explain what caused Jared Diamond to change from studying physiology to geography.
   B He is likely to summarize the main arguments in Jared Diamond's book *Guns, Germs, and Steel*.
   C He will most likely describe another book that he wants his students to read before the next class.

Listen to part of a lecture in an introductory social sciences class. Then answer questions 5 and 6.

5. Why does the professor mention several social science disciplines?
   A To highlight the importance of participant observation as a methodological tool
   B To argue that participant observation is both widely-used and simple to understand

6. What might the woman talk about next? *Choose two answers.*
   A Examples of well-known participant observation studies
   B Different types of research tools associated with anthropology
   C Examples of types of behavior researchers choose to observe

Listen to part of a discussion in a sociology seminar. Then answer questions 7 and 8.

7. Why does the woman mention developing regions?
   A To give an example of the types of societies that sociologists generally study
   B To clarify which types of families are more usual in which types of societies

8. What are the speakers likely to discuss next?
   A Possible causes and effects of a recent social development
   B Different ways sociologists study nuclear and extended families
   C How growing up with a single parent can have an effect on children

Tracks
156–159   **D5** Listen again to the excerpts from exercise **D4** and complete tasks 1 and 2.

1. Underline phrases with two or more words in the answer choices to exercise **D4** that repeat what a speaker says. For example, in excerpt 1 the woman says "make a decision," so you should underline these words in question 1, answer A.

2. In general, do right answers or wrong answers more often repeat phrases that a speaker says? Why do you think this is? Discuss with a partner. Then share your ideas with other students.

E Mastering Organization Questions – Recognizing Common Ways to Organize Lectures

Some Organization questions ask you how all or part of a lecture is organized. To answer these questions, it is important to know and be able to recognize common ways in which academic lectures are organized.

E1 **Choose the answer, A–E, that matches each description of a way to organize a lecture. Then compare answers with a partner. One answer has been done for you.**

Ways to organize lecture	Description
1. Cause and effect	
2. Chronological	
3. Problem and solution	
4. Contrast	The professor compares two different things or two aspects of one subject.
5. Topical	

A   The professor compares two different things or two aspects of one subject.
B   The speaker discusses events in the order they occurred, usually from earliest to latest.
C   The professor talks about several different aspects of a single topic or theory.
D   The lecturer focuses on the events or actions that made other events or actions happen.
E   The speaker discusses negative issues and how these issues might be resolved.

E2 **Look at these notes from two academic lectures. Then answer questions 1 and 2.**

TEST TACTIC

Typically, ideas that are connected are discussed close together. For example, if a man discusses both crime and poverty in the middle of a lecture, these topics are probably connected. However, if he discusses crime early in the lecture and poverty at the end, the topics are probably unconnected.

Questionnaires → common sociology research tool to get data
Two broad types of questionnaire used in sociology
1 Structured (also called closed → focus on closed questions)
        Good for quantitative info (e.g., how much / how often)
2 Unstructured (open → focus on open questions)
        Good for qualitative info (e.g., why / how / how feel)
Both types of questionnaire have advantages + disadvantages

1.   How is the lecture about questionnaires organized?
    A   The professor describes the causes of a particular activity.
    B   The lecturer discusses events in the order they occurred.
    C   The speaker compares two different aspects of one topic.

Structural functionalism → important theory in sociology
        Different aspects of society work together like organs in a body
        Body is strong + stable with each organ / weak + unstable without
Theory developed over time → Comte first suggested in mid 19 century
Developed more by Spencer and Durkheim in late 19 C
Theory refined in early / mid 20 C by Parsons (social action theory)
Modern refinements by Davis + Moore / Merton / Almond + Powell

2.   What organization does the lecture about structural functionalism have?
    A   Contrast
    B   Chronological
    C   Problem and solution

E3 Which way of organizing lectures from exercise **E1** would be the best way to organize lectures on academic topics 1–5? Why? Discuss with a partner.

1. Topic: the importance of the family in both industrial and agricultural societies
2. Topic: how government policies on prohibition led to a sharp increase in crime rates
3. Topic: the different roles and functions that several types of educational institutions have
4. Topic: the impact of aging populations on societies and ways to improve the situation
5. Topic: the growth of online communities since the development of the Internet

Tracks 160–164 **E4** Take notes as you listen to excerpts from five lectures. Then use your notes and memory to answer questions 1–10. Two answers have been done for you.

1. How is the lecture in excerpt 1 probably organized?
   ☑ Problem and solution   ☐ Cause and effect
2. What phrases from the lecture helped you answer question 1?
   bias and other problems / one solution
3. How is the talk in excerpt 2 probably organized?
   ☐ Topical   ☐ Contrast
4. What phrases helped you answer question 3?
5. How is the discussion in excerpt 3 probably organized?
   ☐ Chronological   ☐ Cause and effect
6. What phrases helped you answer question 5?
7. How is the talk in excerpt 4 probably organized?
   ☐ Contrast   ☐ Problem and solution
8. What phrases helped you answer question 7?
9. How is the lecture in excerpt 5 probably organized?
   ☐ Topical   ☐ Chronological
10. What phrases helped you answer question 9?

F Academic Vocabulary

F1 Read this passage about sociology. Use information from the passage to decide which word, A–H, best completes definitions 1–8. One answer has been done for you.

Like other social sciences, sociology is a broad discipline. At the micro level, it focuses on interactions among individuals, as well as on how the behavior of individuals both affects and is affected by society. Also important are concepts like agency and structure. On a larger scale, sociology is concerned with such things as social trends, cultural traditions and norms, bias against minority groups, the effects of technology on society, and interactions among groups, cultures, and organizations. Sociologists use various methods to gather data. For example, observers can measure and record events that occur, or researchers might conduct questionnaires, interviews, or experiments.

1. _____Bias_____ means either an irrational preference for or dislike of something or someone.
2. A specific person who is distinct from others in a group or society is a(n) _____.
3. _____ can be defined as a movement towards or away from some idea over time.
4. Specific ways of doing something – such as carrying out a plan or researching a topic – are called _____.
5. A(n) _____ occurs when two or more individuals, groups, or other institutions act with or talk to each other.
6. Sets of questions, usually with a choice of answers, designed to gather information about a subject are _____.
7. _____ is the way that a person acts in a particular situation, especially in terms of interacting with others.
8. A person who watches events or situations but usually does not participate in them is called a(n) _____.

A behavior	C individual	E methods	G questionnaires
B bias	D interaction	F observer	H trends

G Test Challenge

G1 Practice some Understanding Organization questions. While you listen, cover the questions and take notes. Then use your notes and memory to answer questions 1–6. Use this checklist of skills that you studied in this unit as a guide.

While you listen to the conversation and lectures

☑ Ask questions about what the speakers are saying, such as *Why is she saying this?* or *What will he say next?*

☑ Take notes when a speaker gives a detailed example, compares ideas, or talks about an idea that seems unrelated to the previous topic of discussion.

☑ Listen for how lectures are organized – does the speaker discuss various aspects of one topic, the causes or effects of something, or the chronological order in which events happened, for example?

When you answer the questions

☑ Remember that incorrect answers often paraphrase or repeat the words and phrases that you heard, but do not correctly describe the organization of the talk.

🔊 Tracks 165–167 Listen to a conversation between a student and a university official.

1. Why does the woman talk about credit hours?
   - Ⓐ To point out that most grad students are not eligible to become an exchange student
   - Ⓑ To explain why students with a weak academic record cannot become an exchange student
   - Ⓒ To remind the man to speak to his academic advisor before applying to the exchange program
   - Ⓓ To explain the main criterion for eligibility for applying to become an exchange student

2. Why does the woman mention London?
   - Ⓐ To say that the man would need permission if he wanted to apply there
   - Ⓑ To give an example of an exchange program for which good grades are needed
   - Ⓒ To point out that the man's grade point average is too low to apply there
   - Ⓓ To suggest that the man should think seriously about applying there

🔊 Tracks 168–170 Listen to part of a lecture in an introductory sociology class.

TEST TACTIC

In rare cases, Organization questions might be replay questions, which means which you will hear part of the lecture again. To answer these questions, you can use the same techniques as for Understanding the Function of What Is Said questions (see Unit 10).

3. How does the professor organize the lecture?
   - Ⓐ He contrasts the benefits of one theory with those of another theory.
   - Ⓑ He gives specific examples from society to support two arguments.
   - Ⓒ He defines two key concepts and then describes how they are related.
   - Ⓓ He introduces two phenomena and explains how one caused the other.

4. Why does the professor mention a sport team?
   - (A) To make a complex distinction easier for students to follow
   - (B) To argue that playing sports, like work, is an everyday activity
   - (C) To point out that rules and other structures control agency
   - (D) To clarify the relationship between work and physical activity

Tracks 171–173   Listen to part of a talk in a media studies class. The professor is discussing documentary films.

social issues
documentaries

5. How is the lecture organized?
   - (A) The professor compares successful documentary films with unsuccessful ones.
   - (B) The professor discusses one kind of documentary and then questions its social impact.
   - (C) The professor introduces a problem with documentaries and then describes a solution.
   - (D) The professor explains why documentaries have increased in popularity recently.

6. Why does the professor mention *The Thin Blue Line* by Errol Morris?
   - (A) To give an example of a documentary film that had a clear and measurable impact
   - (B) To demonstrate how a documentary can be supported by a social action campaign
   - (C) To explain why films by Michael Moore and Morgan Spurlock have not been effective
   - (D) To argue that even popular documentary films rarely influence other film-makers

Next Steps

Topics related to sociology are common in the listening section of the TOEFL Test. You may also have questions about this subject in the other sections of the test, especially the speaking section. As a result, learning more about sociology, as well as practicing key skills for Organization questions, may raise your overall test score.

To learn more about sociology and vocabulary related to this discipline:

1. Think of a topic related to society, such as crime, education, family, health, technology, tourism, work, and so on.
2. Make a list of words in your language that are related to this topic. Then use a dictionary to find the English translations.
3. Find a short Internet article about this topic in English and search the article for the words you translated in step 2.
4. Make a note of each word that you found in the article in step 3. Then study these words and learn how to use them.
5. Repeat steps 3 and 4 several times. Then think of a new topic related to society and repeat steps 2–4.

To practice a key skill for Understanding Organization questions:

1. Find some free academic lectures about sociology (or another subject that interests you) on the Internet. (The search phrases "free sociology lectures" or "free podcasts about sociology" should help you find some good sources of lectures.)
2. Begin listening to one of the lectures. If you find the speaker too difficult to understand, try a different lecture.
3. Take notes as you listen to the lecture. Then, after 60 to 90 seconds, pause the lecture.
4. While the lecture is paused, think about what the speaker just said. Then ask yourself these questions: (1) Why did the speaker say this? (2) How is the lecture organized? and (3) What is the speaker about to say next?
5. Repeat steps 3 and 4 until the lecture ends. (If the lecture is long, stop after 10–15 minutes and continue the next day.)

Doing this every day for 10 to 15 minutes will help you build key listening skills not only for Understanding Organization questions but also for other types of listening questions.

Unit Focus

There are seven types of listening questions in the TOEFL Test. These include Connecting Content questions, which are classified as "connecting information" questions. Connecting Content questions test how well you can recognize the relationship between ideas that a speaker discusses. You will see several of these questions when you take the TOEFL Test, but you will probably not have one after every conversation or lecture. You will learn and practice several key skills to answer Connecting Content questions in this unit, including:

- understanding how ideas, points, or details in a conversation or lecture are related to each other.
- making a note when a speaker assigns a concept or detail to a category.
- making a note when a speaker uses positive or negative language.
- making a note of events or steps in a process that a speaker mentions.

The vocabulary focus is on campus and academic words and phrases related to:

- living on campus in university-owned housing or off campus in privately-owned housing.
- political science, the study and analysis of government systems, political activity, and international relations.

A Warm-up

A1 Complete tasks 1 and 2 with a partner. Spend about five minutes on each task.

1. Make a list of words and phrases that describe politicians. Use a dictionary if you wish.
2. Are your words mostly positive or negative? Why do you think this is? Discuss with other students.

B Campus Vocabulary

B1 Choose a word or phrase from this notice to complete each sentence, 1–8. One answer has been done for you.

> **Important Announcements about Student Accommodation**
>
> - Beginning next term, every campus dormitory that is currently female-only or male-only will become coeducational. Resident advisors in each dorm will soon be holding information sessions to answer questions about this change.
> - As requested, students in off-campus housing may now purchase a meal plan.
> - The popular "roommate swap" board in the Housing Office is now available to access online at www.statecollege.educ/swap.

1. A building where students live and sleep when they are at college is called a ____dormitory____ (or dorm).
2. A dormitory where both male and female students live can be described as _____ (or coed).
3. _____ (or RAs) live in a dorm and provide help to other students living there.
4. Places where students live that are not located on the grounds of a college are known as _____.
5. A general word for all types of places to live, including dormitories and off-campus housing, is _____.
6. Students who need to discuss accommodation issues should go to the _____.
7. A _____ is a system that allows students to pay in advance for food they will eat at campus facilities.
8. A person who lives and sleeps in the same room, apartment, or house as somebody else is a _____.

C Analyzing Connecting Content Questions

There are three types of Connecting Content questions. In the first type, you will see a table with two categories – either *Yes* and *No*, or *Included* and *Not Included* – and four or five answer choices. Each answer matches only one category.

The second type of Connecting Content question is similar to the first type, but it may have more than two categories and the category names will vary according to the subject of the conversation or lecture. The speaker or speakers will mention the category names when they speak. In rare cases, one answer may match more than one category.

The third type of Connecting Content question usually asks you to put events or people in order from the earliest (or first) to the latest (or last). Sometimes you may have to put the steps in a process in the correct order. Note that for this third type of question, occasionally you will see instructions which state that one of the answer choices should not be used.

In general, you can correctly answer Connecting Content questions if you:

- take notes about the information and the category each time a speaker mentions an idea connected to a category.
- listen carefully for and make a note of positive and negative expressions when a speaker introduces a new idea.
- listen carefully and take notes when a speaker mentions the order in which steps or events should happen.

TEST TACTIC

Most answers to Connecting Content questions match just one category. An answer that matches "Yes" obviously cannot also match "No." In some cases, however, an answer might match two categories. For example, a politician might match both "Nineteenth Century Leaders" and "Twentieth Century Leaders."

Track 174 **C1** **Take notes as you listen to two students discuss a homework assignment. Then use your notes to answer questions 1–3.**

1. The speakers discuss the two Houses of the United States Congress. Indicate which statement describes each House.

	Lower House	Upper House
Each member serves a six-year term and may be re-elected.		
Different states have different numbers of members.		
The usual name is the House of Representatives.		

2. The speakers discuss Congress. Indicate which statements correctly describe the Senate.

	Yes	No
The number of senators per state does not depend on population.		
Senators meet in the south wing of the United States Capitol.		
There are 435 members in total.		

3. The speakers discuss the construction of the United States Capitol. Put the events in the order in which they occurred.

First	
Second	
Third	
Fourth	

- Government officials began meeting in the Capitol building before construction was complete.
- The Capitol building was used for government functions as well as church services.
- A competition was held to encourage designs for expansions to the Capitol building.
- The United States Congress met in locations including Philadelphia and New York.

C2 **Which question in exercise C1 matches each type of Connecting Content question described at the top of this page?**

D Mastering Connecting Content Questions – Recognizing Categories

One key skill for Connecting Content questions is recognizing and making a note when a speaker introduces a category. The speaker may name the category before discussing it, or give information about the category first and then name it.

D1 Look at this script from part of a conversation. Then answer questions 1–3. One answer has been done for you.

Student	I'm living in a dormitory, but my roommate is noisy and I can't study well, so I was thinking about moving.
Employee	OK, well, there are a few things you could do. The simplest option would probably be to transfer to a different dorm. That typically takes between one and two weeks. You could also transfer into a shared apartment on campus, but there's already a very long waiting list for those, so it might be months before you could do that. Your other option would be to move off-campus and find a place in town.
Student	If I wanted to move into off-campus housing, how long would that take?
Employee	Once you find a place you like, we can usually get the paperwork sorted out in two to three business days.

1. What is the first option that the employee mentions to the student? __transfer to a different dorm__

2. What is the second option that the employee mentions to the student? _____

3. What is the final option that the employee mentions to the student? _____

Tracks 175–178 **D2** Take notes as you listen to excerpts (short parts) from two conversations and two lectures. After each excerpt, use your notes to answer one of questions 1–4.

1. In excerpt 1, which assignments does the woman say the man must do? One answer has been done for you.

	Yes	No
Give a presentation		✓
Produce a case study		
Write a term paper		

2. In excerpt 2, which meal plans do the speakers discuss?

	Yes	No
Block plan		
Limited plan		
Value plan		

3. In excerpt 3, which types of trade agreement does the professor discuss?

	Yes	No
Bilateral agreements		
Multilateral agreements		
Trilateral agreements		
Unilateral agreements		

TEST TACTIC

Sometimes a speaker will use the word *category*. At other times, the speaker might say *class*, *classification*, *genre*, *group* or *grouping*, *kind*, *sort*, *type*, *variety*, or even *things*. When you hear any of these words, listen carefully and take notes. Your notes might help you answer a Connecting Content question.

4. In excerpt 4, which of these political systems does the professor discuss?

	Yes	No
Authoritarianism		
Democracy		
Federalism		
Monarchy		

E Mastering Connecting Content Questions – Matching Details to a Category

Another key skill that will help you answer Connecting Content questions quickly and accurately is recognizing and making a note when a speaker mentions either general information or specific details that are connected to a category.

E1 Look again at the script from part of a conversation in exercise **D1**. Then answer the Connecting Content question.

The speakers discuss options the student has for moving out of her current accommodation. Indicate how long each option would take. One answer has been done for you.

	Transfer to a different dormitory	Transfer into an on-campus apartment	Move out of university accommodation
Less than one week			✓
From one to two weeks			
More than four weeks			

Tracks 179–182 **E2** Listen again to the excerpts that you heard in exercises **D2** and add to the notes you already made. Then answer questions 1–4.

1. In excerpt 1, the speakers discuss assignments for a class. Indicate which details match each assignment.

	Term paper	Case study
Should be less than 1,000 words		
Must be submitted by week six of the course		
Can be delivered in the form of a presentation		

2. In excerpt 2, the speakers discuss meal plan options. Indicate which details match each kind of meal plan.

	Block plan	Value plan
Students can eat in any restaurant on campus.		
Students are limited to 10 plan meals per week.		
Students can eat as much as they like per meal.		

3. In excerpt 3, the professor discusses trade agreements. Indicate which description matches each type of agreement.

	Unilateral	Bilateral	Multilateral
Only one nation benefits from the agreement.			
All signing nations benefit from the agreement.			
The agreement applies only to the export of goods.			
The agreement applies both to imports and exports.			✓

4. In excerpt 4, the professor discusses different kinds of political systems. Indicate which description matches each system.

	Authoritarianism	Democracy	Monarchy
Some groups may have fewer rights than others.			
The government holds all of the power.			
Individual people have power to change government.			
The ruler has power as a result of his or her parents.			

F Mastering Connecting Content Questions – Recognizing Positive or Negative References

Another key skill for Connecting Content questions is to recognize and take notes when a speaker uses positive or negative words to describe an idea. This can help you decide whether the speaker includes or excludes this idea from a category.

◁)) Tracks 183–184 **F1** **Listen to a short conversation and a lecture and take notes. Then use your notes to answer questions 1 and 2.**

1. In the conversation, the speakers discuss the man's plans. Indicate which of these opinions the man holds. One answer has been done for you.

	Yes	No
He thinks some of the professor's colleagues are public law experts.		✓
He really enjoyed taking the professor's class last year.		
His term paper for the professor's class was very good.		
His family might be unhappy if he chose to study political science.		

2. In the lecture, the speaker discusses plurality voting. Indicate which of these points he makes.

	Yes	No
Citizens generally find plurality voting systems harder to understand than other systems.		✓
One criticism of plurality voting is that the winning party may not have majority support.		
With plurality voting, some citizens may feel that a vote for a minority party is a wasted vote.		
Roughly 40% of countries have adopted a proportional representation voting system.		
Countries with a proportional representation system tend to have few political parties.		

TEST TACTIC

Take notes when a speaker mentions a date connected with an idea, person, or event. If the speaker gives several dates, you may see a Connecting Content question that asks you to put answers in order. Taking careful notes when you hear dates will make such questions easier.

F2 Look at the answers to exercise **F1**. Match each *No* answer to one of reasons 1–3.
One answer has been done for you.

Reasons	*No* answers
1. A different person said this answer, not the person asked about in the question.	• Question 1, first answer •
2. This answer contradicts (says the opposite of) what the speaker actually said.	• •
3. This answer includes some of a speaker's words, but adds ideas he or she did not say.	• •

G Mastering Connecting Content Questions – Recognizing the Order of Events

To answer Connecting Content questions accurately, it may also be helpful to recognize and make a note when the speaker discusses either the order in which events occur or the order of steps in a process.

G1 Read these lecture notes. Then look at question 1. This question has already been answered, but some of the answers are in the wrong order. Work with a partner to put the answers in the right order.

TOPIC = women's suffrage (WS) = right to vote
often public <u>demo</u>nstrations before WS was allowed
first demo in France in late eighteenth century
    (C18)
<u>campaign</u> in C19 in USA by Susan B Anthony and
    others
    – neither polit camp successful at giving WS
WS in C18 + C19 in few places but limited +
    temporary
    – Sweden, Finland, few US States, Sierra Leone
New Zealand 1893 = first nation to give full WS
    – because of camp led by Kate Sheppard
    from 1891

Australia gave full WS in 1902 in federal elections
    – limits for aboriginal women in some states
Finland, Norway and Denmark first European
    countries
    – 1907, 1913, and 1915 respectively for full WS
after end World War I, many nations granted WS
    – UK in 1918 but only women over 30
    (men over 21)
    – USA 1920 / Spain 1931 / France + Japan
    1945
almost all countries now WS but limited some
    places

1. The professor describes the history of women's right to vote. In which order did these events occur?

First	Unsuccessful demonstrations for women's suffrage were held.
Second	A campaign led to the first nation granting full women's suffrage.
Third	Women were granted limited voting rights in some regions.
Fourth	Numerous countries chose to give women the right to vote.
Fifth	Several European countries gave women full voting rights.

G2 Discuss questions 1 and 2 with a partner.

1. What abbreviations (short ways of writing something) are used in the notes for exercise **G1**?
2. What other words or phrases in the notes could be abbreviated?

Tracks 185–186 **G3** **Listen to a conversation and lecture and take notes. Then use your notes to answer questions 1 and 2.**

1. The speakers discuss applying to become a resident advisor. Put the steps in the application process in order. One step should NOT be included. One answer has been done for you.

First	Attend an information session
Second	
Third	
Fourth	

- Attend an individual training session
- Attend an information session
- Attend a group interview
- Fill out and submit the application
- Wait for the application to be assessed

2. The professor discusses how laws are passed in the United States. Put the legislative steps in the correct order.

First	
Second	
Third	
Fourth	

- A committee discusses the bill and approves or rejects it.
- A member of Congress sponsors a bill or measure.
- If the bill is enrolled, the president can accept or veto it.
- Members of both chambers of Congress debate the bill.

H Academic Vocabulary

H1 **Work with a partner to decide which definition, A–H, matches the highlighted words in statements 1–6.**

1. A bilateral agreement between two states
2. A coalition of bureaucrats and military leaders
3. During an election citizens cast their vote
4. Legislation giving women the right to vote
5. Representatives elected to serve different regions
6. Senators vote to override the president's veto

A A contract between two (or more) people or countries is a(n) _____.
B An organized event at which people vote for a candidate is a(n) _____.
C A temporary political union between two or more parties is a(n) _____.
D Laws written and passed by an official body or government is _____.
E Nations or regions within a nation with their own government are _____.
F Non-elected officials who work for a government department are _____.
G Elected politicians whose role is to act on behalf of citizens are _____.
H The political power to reject a decision, law, or proposal is a(n) _____.

Tracks 187–192 **H2** **Listen to some short excerpts from conversations and lectures you have already heard. Which highlighted word from exercise H1 do you hear in each excerpt? One answer has been done for you.**

Excerpt 1 _____representatives_____   Excerpt 4 _____

Excerpt 2 _____   Excerpt 5 _____

Excerpt 3 _____   Excerpt 6 _____

Ⅰ Test Challenge

I1 Practice some Connecting Content questions. While you listen, cover the questions and take notes. Then use your notes and memory to answer questions 1–6. Use this checklist of skills that you studied in this unit as a guide.

While you listen to the conversation and lectures

☑ Listen carefully and take notes when a speaker mentions a category or a detail connected to a category.

☑ Listen carefully and take notes when a speaker expresses positive or negative ideas about something.

☑ Concentrate and take notes when a speaker discusses the order of events or steps in a process.

When you answer the questions

☑ Use your notes and memory to choose the correct categories or correct sequence for each answer.

🔊 Tracks 193–195 Listen to a conversation between a student and a university employee.

1. The speakers discuss a newly constructed dormitory. Indicate which benefits of this dormitory the speakers mention.

	Yes	No
The large number of available rooms		
The techniques used in its construction		
The relatively inexpensive cost of living there		
The convenience of its location for the man		

2. The speakers discuss two alternative housing options for the student. Indicate what the speakers say about each option.

	On-campus accommodation	Off-campus accommodation
Prices tend to be expensive		
Not constructed recently		
No coed accommodations		
Less convenient location		

Tracks 196–198 Listen to part of a lecture in an international relations class.

International Telegraph Union

League of Nations

United Nations

3. The speaker discusses the League of Nations. Indicate which of these answers were goals of the League of Nations.

	Yes	No
Find a way to end World War I quickly		
Maintain peace throughout the world		
Solve international disputes diplomatically		
Cooperate with governments to promote trade		

4. The speaker describes the events that led to the founding of the United Nations. Put the events in the order that they happened.

First	
Second	
Third	
Fourth	

- The League of Nations was founded to promote world disarmament.
- The United Nations Charter was drafted and signed in San Francisco.
- Members of the UN Security Council ratified the United Nations Charter.
- A group of allied countries discussed and signed the Atlantic Charter.
- Governments discussed and founded several international organizations.

Tracks
199–201 Listen to a lecture in an introduction to world literature class.

5. The professor discusses political satire. Indicate which of these traits the professor includes in her definition of satire.

	Included	Not included
Being humorous		
Being critical		
Being ironic		
Being indirect		

6. The professor mentions some examples of political satire. Put the names of these satirical authors in order of when they were writing, from the earliest time to the most recent.

First	
Second	
Third	
Fourth	

- Aristophanes
- Jonathan Swift
- Maurice Joly
- Niccolò Machiavelli

Next Steps

Topics related to political science are common in the listening section of the TOEFL Test. You may also have questions about this subject in the other sections of the test. As a result, learning more about political science, as well as practicing key skills for Connecting Content questions, may raise your overall test score.

To learn more about political science and vocabulary related to this discipline:

1. Read a few articles in your language about political science to get some background knowledge about this topic.
2. Search the Internet for websites that let you watch or listen to free academic lectures about political science. For example, you could search for "free political science lectures" or "free online political science videos".
3. Listen to each lecture several times and make a note of words and phrases that the speaker uses frequently.
4. Check these words in your dictionary and study and learn the most useful words related to political science.

To practice key skills for Connecting Content questions:

1. Watch an Internet video in which somebody compares or contrasts two or three things.
2. As you listen, make notes about the positive and negative points the speaker makes about each thing.
3. After you have watched the video, create two tables that summarize the positive and negative aspects of each thing.
4. You can also watch "how to" videos in which a speaker gives a step-by-step explanation of how to do something. Make notes while you watch. Then after the video finishes, use your notes to write a short summary of the process.

Unit Focus

There are seven types of listening questions in the TOEFL Test. These include Making Inferences questions, which are one type of "connecting information" questions. In Making Inferences questions, you have to understand or make a conclusion about something that a speaker mentions indirectly. These questions are relatively common, and you will probably have at least one Making Inferences question after each conversation and lecture. This unit will teach you several key skills to answer Making Inferences questions, including:

- recognizing how and when a speaker is expressing an idea indirectly.
- drawing a conclusion from ideas a speaker mentions or a conclusion about what a speaker is likely to do.
- recognizing whether an answer choice is mentioned directly, indirectly, or not mentioned at all.

The vocabulary focus is on campus and academic words and phrases related to:

- using textbooks as well as borrowing books and using the services of a university library.
- economics, the study and analysis of the production, distribution, and consumption of goods and services.

A Warm-up

A1 This diagram shows a simplified economic cycle. Label each box with one answer from A–D. (Check the meaning of those words in a dictionary, if necessary.) One answer has been done for you.

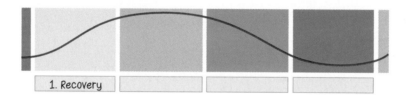

1. Recovery

A Depression
B Downturn
C Prosperity
D Recovery

B Campus Vocabulary

B1 Read the definitions of these highlighted expressions. Then choose the best expression to complete each blank in the conversation. One answer has been done for you.

A bibliography is a list of the books and articles that a student used for research while writing an assignment.

The list of all the books, journals, and other materials in a library that a user can borrow or consult is called the catalog.

The main book that students are assigned to read when they take a particular course is the coursebook or textbook.

An interlibrary loan is when a user requests a book from a different library because it is unavailable at his or her library.

A journal is a type of magazine that publishes specialist articles and information about one academic discipline.

The list of books and articles that a professor asks students to read for a course is called a reading list.

Professors can put books that are likely to be required by many students on a special reserve list in the library.

In a library, the stacks are the shelves where all of the books, journals, and other materials are stored.

Student	Could I talk to you about the grade you gave me for this paper, Professor? It was lower than I expected.
Professor	I gave you a low grade because your paper was half-finished, Joe. The only book listed in your 1. __bibliography__ is the 2. _____, so it looks like you didn't read any of the titles from the 3. _____ that I gave you.
Student	I wanted to do the reading, but I couldn't find the books from the list in the library 4. _____. And I couldn't read the 5. _____ article that you mentioned because that journal's not in the library's 6. _____. I requested the journal via 7. _____, but it didn't arrive from the other library in time.
Professor	The books are not in the stacks because I placed them on the 8. _____ list. I mentioned that in class, remember? I also said that I had copies of the journal article available in my office.
Student	Oh. I missed two classes because of illness, and I guess I missed some important information. Sorry.

C Analyzing Making Inferences Questions

Making Inferences questions ask you about information that is not directly stated by a speaker. Most Making Inferences questions include a word that refers to indirect information like "conclude," "imply," or "infer," as in these examples:

What can be concluded about the woman?

What does the professor imply about _____?

What can be inferred about _____?

Some Making Inferences questions are replay questions. This means you will hear an excerpt (short part) of the whole conversation or lecture you have just heard. Next you will see a question on the screen like one of the examples below. In most cases, you will then hear all or part of the excerpt again:

What does the student imply when he says this?

What does the professor imply about _____ when she says this?

The correct answer to Making Inferences questions:
- correctly describes an idea that one or both speakers mentioned indirectly.
- rarely repeats the same words or phrases that the speaker used.
- may describe how two or more details from the conversation or lecture are related.

In contrast, incorrect answers to Making Inferences questions:
- often repeat the same words or phrases that the speaker said.
- may restate or repeat an idea that one or both speakers mentioned directly.

TEST TACTIC

The right answer to Inference questions is usually related to the main idea or purpose of the talk. If you are unsure which answer to choose, ask "What's the main idea?" and "Which answer is most closely related to it?" These questions may help you choose the right answer.

C1 **Read these partial scripts from a conversation and a lecture. Then answer questions 1 and 2.**

Student	Excuse me, Professor. I'm not sure how to answer the assignment you set.
Professor	Have you done all the reading that I assigned?
Student	I read the chapters in the coursebook, but there are two titles on the reading list I haven't looked at yet.
Professor	Well, then your next step is clear, I think.

1. The professor implies that the student should
   A answer more clearly
   B complete the reading
   C return to the library
   D hand in the homework

Professor   There's a famous quotation by Adam Smith, the Scottish scholar who's often called the "father of modern economics," that I'd like to discuss. I don't remember Smith's exact words, I'm afraid, but he said something like, "What's prudent conduct for every private family is scarcely folly for a great kingdom." Now Smith was writing this over 220 years ago, at a time when the style was to convey one's ideas in a roundabout way, but his message is actually simple: ideas that make economic sense for a family also make economic sense for a country.

2. What does the professor imply about Adam Smith?
   A It is not important to know his exact words.
   B His ideas are interesting but old-fashioned.
   C His words do not express his concept directly.
   D He believed great kingdoms were rarely prudent.

D Mastering Making Inferences Questions – Listening and Taking Notes Effectively

The answers to Making Inferences questions are not stated directly during the conversations or lectures, so a key skill for answering these questions is to listen effectively and take notes when you think a speaker is expressing an idea indirectly.

🔊 Tracks 202–205 **D1** **Listen to four students talk about listening for inferences. Then match each person to the point they make, A–D. One answer has been done for you.**

Ahmed
Point __c__

Miki
Point _____

Jorgen
Point _____

Rosa
Point _____

A Some speakers express an idea indirectly by discussing an opposite idea.
B Some speakers express an idea indirectly by mentioning various points, but not explicitly stating a conclusion.
C Some speakers express an idea indirectly by talking about an idea that is related to the implied point.
D Some speakers express an idea indirectly by using a specific tone of voice.

🔊 Tracks 206–208 **D2** **Listen to some excerpts from conversations and lectures. Take notes as you listen. Then use your notes and memory to answer questions 1–6.**

1. In excerpt 1, what point does the woman make indirectly?
   A The reading list from her professor is hard to find.
   B A book she needs is not available in her college library.

2. How does she express this point?
   A She discusses an idea that is related to her implied point.
   B She mentions various points, but does not explicitly state a conclusion.

3. In excerpt 2, what does the man imply?
   A The prices of products and services do not generally go up.
   B If demand for a product decreases, its price often decreases, too.

4. How does he express this point?
   A He expresses an opposite idea.
   B He uses a specific tone of voice.

5. In excerpt 3, what point does the man make indirectly?
    A   Books are not easy to find in the library's stacks.
    B   He did not expect to be able to search the catalog.

6. How does he express this point?
    A   He talks about an idea that is related to his implied point.
    B   He uses a specific tone of voice.

D3 Use these notes from a conversation and lecture to answer questions 1 and 2. Then compare answers with a partner.

Prof How help?	Difficult to develop economic theories based on real data
Student Not follow ideas in coursebook	Real-world economic data often complicated + "messy"
P Whole book?	Economic models → easier to understand but limited
S No — chapters 3 + 4	Usually include variables / use mathematics + logic
P Please remind me	e.g., Leontief's input-output model (won Nobel prize)
S About Chicago school of economics	Types = stochastic (quantitative) / non-stochastic
P Like to help but very broad topic	Different types have different limitations

1. What can be inferred from the conversation? *Choose two answers.*
    A   The professor thinks the student should read the whole coursebook more carefully.
    B   The professor does not remember the contents of each chapter of the coursebook.
    C   The professor thinks the student is asking a question that is too general.
    D   The professor is not familiar with the ideas of the Chicago school of economics.

2. What does the professor imply in the lecture? *Choose two answers.*
    A   Non-stochastic economic models are not quantitative.
    B   People who use an economic model often win a Nobel prize.
    C   Models are developed by mathematicians, not by economists.
    D   Economists use models because real-world data is so complex.

D4 Take notes as you listen to excerpts from a conversation and two lectures. After each excerpt use your notes and memory to answer questions 1–3.

Tracks 209–211

1. What can be inferred from excerpt 1? *Choose two answers.*
    A   The process of applying for an interlibrary loan is complicated.
    B   The man already has scheduled activities on the weekends.
    C   The man needs a job that pays more than minimum wage.
    D   Jobs at the university library are popular among students.

2. What can be inferred from excerpt 2? *Choose two answers.*
    A   The depression phase occurs before the recovery phase.
    B   Some models of the business cycle are more complex than others.
    C   The name "economic cycle" is less common than "business cycle."
    D   Economic optimism is necessary for the recovery stage to begin.

3. What can be inferred from excerpt 3? *Choose two answers.*
    A   The professor asked the students to do some reading before class.
    B   A person's level of risk aversion determines how often he or she invests.
    C   A risk-seeking investor looks for high-risk, high-return investments.
    D   The students do not fully understand the concept of risk aversion.

TEST TACTIC

If you think a speaker is making a point indirectly, try underlining that section of your notes (or putting a sign in the margin of your notes). This will help you find implied ideas more easily later, and may help you reach conclusions based on the speaker's words.

E Mastering Making Inferences Questions – Reaching Conclusions

For some Making Inferences questions you will need to make a conclusion based on what you hear. You might have to come to a conclusion about a situation or theory, about a speaker's opinion, or about what a speaker is likely to do next. Typically, you will hear at least two pieces of information during a conversation or lecture to help you draw a conclusion.

E1 **Read this script from part of a lecture. Then complete tasks 1 and 2 with a partner.**

Professor   During a property bubble, real estate prices continue rising until they become so high that buyers can no longer afford them. The financial crisis of 2007–2012 was caused when property bubbles around the world burst. The "Lost Decade" in Japan, when the economy grew at a very slow rate, was also caused by a burst bubble, though in that case the bubble was related to the price of many assets, not just real estate.

1. What conclusions can you draw from the script? *Choose two answers.*
   A   Property bubbles can cause economic problems.
   B   Property bubbles can occur in any country.
   C   Slow economic growth rates can cause property bubbles.
   D   It is a good idea to buy a home during a property bubble.

2. Underline the words and phrases in the script that helped you answer task 1.

Tracks 212–214   **E2** **Listen to some excerpts from a conversation and two lectures. After each excerpt, answer the questions.**

Listen to part of a conversation. Can you make the following conclusion from the conversation?

1. The man's bibliography for an assignment included books he did not read.   ☐ Yes   ☐ No

Listen to part of a lecture about normative economics. Can you reach the following conclusions from the lecture?

2. Positive economics focuses on what actually happens in the economy, not on what should happen.   ☐ Yes   ☐ No

3. Social choice is the most important theory based on normative economics.   ☐ Yes   ☐ No

Listen to part of a lecture about import quotas. Can you come to the following conclusions from the lecture?

4. Without import quotas, domestic producers of a product cannot be successful.   ☐ Yes   ☐ No

5. Import quotas do not benefit either overseas producers or domestic consumers.   ☐ Yes   ☐ No

TEST TACTIC

It is relatively common for speakers to mention an indirect idea more than once and in more than one way. So when you look at your notes after listening, look for ideas that are repeated: these might indicate an implied idea.

F Mastering Making Inferences Questions – Analyzing the Answer Choices

The right answer to a Making Inferences question must describe an idea that the speaker implied, but the wrong answers often paraphrase an idea that the speaker directly states, or repeat some of the speaker's words but express an idea the speaker does not mention. Recognizing these different types of wrong answers is a key skill for Making Inferences questions.

F1 **Read these scripts for two Making Inferences questions that replay part of the talk. Then answer questions 1 and 2.**

Narrator   Listen again to part of the conversation. What does the student imply when she says this?

Student   I'm finding your economics class stimulating, but the reading list is longer than I expected. I had to get a part-time job this semester, and with my hours there plus the other classes I'm taking, there's never enough time.

Narrator   Listen again to part of the lecture. What does the professor imply when he says this?

Professor   I'd like to define some expressions that, judging from your recent papers, seem to be confusing to some of you. Economists typically use the word *monetary* when talking about things like the amount of money in circulation in the economy. They typically use *fiscal* when referring to government expenditures and tax revenues. In contrast, they generally use *financial* when the discussion is related to raising capital or providing funds. I hope that's clear and that you'll use these terms correctly in the future.

1. Put a check (✔) in the correct column to indicate which ideas the student implies and which she states directly.

	Implies	States directly
The woman is enjoying an economics class that she is taking.		
The woman needed to make some extra money this semester.		
Doing the reading for her economics class requires a lot of time.		

2. Put a check (✔) in the correct column to indicate which ideas the professor implies and which he states directly.

	Implies	States directly
Some of his students used some economics terms incorrectly in their assignments.		
The word *fiscal* is most often used to refer to government expenses and incomes.		
Economists generally use the words *fiscal* and *financial* with different meanings.		

Tracks
215–217   **F2** **Listen to some excerpts from a two conversations and a lecture. After each excerpt, answer the questions.**

Listen to part of a conversation. Does the man Imply, State, or Not mention ideas 1 and 2?

1. He thinks the price of the coursebook is expensive.
    ☐ Imply   ☐ State   ☐ Not mention

2. He will go to an off-campus bookshop to buy a used book.
    ☐ Imply   ☐ State   ☐ Not mention

Listen to part of a lecture. Does the woman Imply, State, or Not mention ideas 3 and 4?

3. GDP is the value of goods and services used by the population of a country.
    ☐ Imply   ☐ State   ☐ Not mention

4. Countries with a low GDP most likely do not have a healthy economy.
    ☐ Imply   ☐ State   ☐ Not mention

Listen to part of a conversation. Does the woman Imply, State, or Not mention ideas 5 and 6?

5. The library has been having problems with its computerized catalog recently.
    ☐ Imply   ☐ State   ☐ Not mention

6. The man will not be able to search the library catalog for about two hours.
    ☐ Imply   ☐ State   ☐ Not mention

G Academic Vocabulary

Track 218 **G1** **Listen to a speaker define these useful highlighted words related to economics. As you listen, fill in the missing phrases. One answer has been done for you.**

1. The word capital often means ___money or property___ that can be used to purchase or invest in something.
2. A consumer, like a customer, can be defined as a person who buys or uses _____.
3. Demand refers to the level of desire among consumers in _____ for specific goods and services.
4. Items that a company has produced in order for _____ them are called goods.
5. Productivity generally refers to how _____ and efficiently a business can produce goods.
6. A recession is defined as a relatively short period of time when the economy experiences a _____.
7. Resources, such as oil, water, capital, or workers, are the _____ assets a country or company has.
8. Supply typically refers to how much of a particular good or service is available in one market at a _____.

G2 **Discuss tasks 1–5 with one or two partners. When you have finished, share your ideas with other students.**

1. What is the relationship between the words *capital* and *capitalism*?
2. What are the verb forms of the words consumer, demand, productivity, and supply?
3. The words *goods* and *services* are often used together as a phrase. How do services differ from goods?
4. What word is used to describe a recession that is both long and serious?
5. What are some of the most important resources in your country? Why are they important?

H Test Challenge

TEST TACTIC

Do not choose an answer that you feel is true only because of your common sense or your existing knowledge of a subject. Unless an answer choice is supported by something that a speaker says or implies, it is unlikely to be correct.

H1 **Practice some Making Inferences questions. While you listen, cover the questions and take notes. Then use your notes and memory to answer questions 1–6. Use this checklist of skills that you studied in this unit as a guide.**

While you listen to the conversation and lectures

☑ Listen for signs that a speaker may be expressing an idea indirectly – such as describing an opposite idea, making several related points but not explicitly stating a conclusion, and so on – then take notes on what you hear.

When you answer the questions

☑ Use your notes and memory to draw conclusions from two or more related points that a speaker mentioned.

☑ Remember that incorrect answers often paraphrase or repeat a speaker's words and may express an idea that a speaker did not mention.

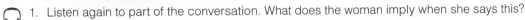

Tracks 219–221 Listen to a conversation in a university library.

 1. Listen again to part of the conversation. What does the woman imply when she says this?
- Ⓐ Undergraduates can borrow more than four interlibrary loan books.
- Ⓑ The man should register as a student at the university to get library access.
- Ⓒ Only university alumni can borrow books through interlibrary loan.
- Ⓓ The problem does not affect students at other universities.

2. What is the student likely to do next? *Choose two answers.*
- Ⓐ Apply to become a student at a distance-learning institution
- Ⓑ Apply for some books through the interlibrary loan scheme
- Ⓒ Apply for access to the library at Eastern State University
- Ⓓ Apply for a special card that lets him borrow up to six books

Tracks 222–224 Listen to part of a lecture in a European history class. The professor is talking about trade policies.

mercantilism

Anglo-Dutch Wars
1652–1784

 3. Listen again to part of the conversation. What does the woman imply when she says this?
- Ⓐ Politicians focused on gaining increased personal wealth.
- Ⓑ Voters supported politicians who wanted balanced trade.
- Ⓒ Opportunities for trade were limited by political policies.
- Ⓓ Politicians made decisions favoring economic gain.

4. What does the professor imply about mercantilism?
- Ⓐ Mercantilist policies were the cause of a majority of European wars between 1652 and 1784.
- Ⓑ Mercantilism led to the creation of profitable trading links between major European powers.
- Ⓒ Some nations that were once colonies still suffer the effects of former mercantilist policies.
- Ⓓ Not all governments understood the links between mercantilism and wealth accumulation.

🔊 Tracks 225–227 Listen to part of a talk in an economics class. The professor is discussing economic goals.

full employment

economic growth

economic stability

5. What does the author imply about economic goals?

    Ⓐ   In reality, governments are not likely to be able to achieve them.

    Ⓑ   In most cases, they are difficult to define, understand, and measure.

    Ⓒ   Microeconomic goals are often reached later than macroeconomic goals.

    Ⓓ   In general, governments care about them more than individuals do.

6. What can be inferred about economic stability?

    Ⓐ   Nations that have achieved it tend to experience fluctuations in production.

    Ⓑ   Achieving it gives both governments and individuals confidence in the future.

    Ⓒ   It is most often achieved by societies that adopt long-term economic plans.

    Ⓓ   Achieving it requires a focus on reducing the rates of inflation and deflation.

Next Steps

Topics related to economics are common in every section of the TOEFL Test, especially the reading, listening, and speaking sections. As a result, learning more about economics, as well as practicing key skills for Making Inferences questions, may raise your overall test score.

To learn more about economics and vocabulary related to this discipline:

1. Read a story related to business, finance, or economics in a newspaper or magazine. Highlight any unfamiliar words.
2. After you finish, make a list of the ten highlighted words that are used most frequently in the article.
3. Use an English-English dictionary to find out what these words mean and how they are typically used.
4. Search the Internet for articles that have the first word on your list *in their title*. (If you are using Google, you can do this by typing "intitle:" plus the word you want to find; for example, "intitle: distribution".)
5. Read some of the articles to see how the word is used. Then repeat step 4 with the other nine words on your list.
6. Repeat steps 2–5 about a different story related to business, finance, economics, and so on.

To practice key skills for Making Inferences questions:

1. Watch a television program in which a presenter interviews somebody such as a politician, actor, and so on.
2. As you watch, note down what the interviewee says. When he or she says something indirectly, underline your notes.
3. At the end of the interview, review your notes and write a summary of ideas that the interviewee expressed indirectly.
4. Repeat steps 1–3 with a different television program until you are confident that you can recognize inferences well.
5. Repeat steps 1–4, but this time either do not watch the screen while you listen, or listen to a radio interview.

Directions

This listening review test is intended to help you find out your strengths and weaknesses in listening. You will listen to two conversations and two lectures and answer 22 questions about them. The conversations and lectures are designed to be at the same level as the ones on the TOEFL Test. You may take notes while you listen. After each conversation, take 3.5 minutes to answer the questions. After each lecture, take 4.5 minutes to answer the questions. When you have finished, check your answers with your instructor or against the Answer Key. Then use the conversion chart on page 167 to find out your likely score on the TOEFL Test.

Test

Tracks 228–233 Listen to a conversation between a student and one of his instructors.

1. Why does the student visit his instructor?
   - Ⓐ To find out when her office hours are
   - Ⓑ To ask about a class he did not attend
   - Ⓒ To get her advice about his study plans
   - Ⓓ To explain why he will stop taking a class

2. What does the man say about the woman's class? *Choose two answers.*
   - Ａ He finds the workload too heavy.
   - Ｂ It is not one of his core classes.
   - Ｃ The class is very interesting.
   - Ｄ He was unable to register for it.

 3. Listen again to part of the conversation. What does the student imply when he says this?
   - Ⓐ He feels like he has too much work to do.
   - Ⓑ He registered for too many classes by mistake.
   - Ⓒ He will register for more classes next semester.
   - Ⓓ He is not sure whether to take the class or not.

4. Why does the instructor mention her time as an undergraduate?
   - Ⓐ To point out that many students experience similar issues
   - Ⓑ To emphasize that it is important to make decisions quickly
   - Ⓒ To explain why many students do not feel fully motivated
   - Ⓓ To suggest that the student's plan might not be the best one

5. What will the student most likely do next?
   - Ⓐ He will think about which class he should drop.
   - Ⓑ He will attend the professor's class.
   - Ⓒ He will find out about his core requirements.
   - Ⓓ He will drop the psychology class he is taking.

Tracks
234–240 Listen to part of a lecture in a United States History class.

William Henry
Harrison

Martin
Van Buren

Tippecanoe
and Tyler too

6. What is the main purpose of the lecture?
   - (A) To highlight the military career of William Henry Harrison
   - (B) To give the reasons for William Henry Harrison's death
   - (C) To describe William Henry Harrison's main political opponents
   - (D) To note some effects of William Henry Harrison's presidency

7. The professor discusses events in the life of William Henry Harrison. Put the events in the order in which they occurred.

First	
Second	
Third	
Fourth	
Fifth	

   - (A) He resigned his post as commander of an army.
   - (B) He lost and then won elections to become president.
   - (C) He became the governor of Indiana Territory.
   - (D) He held office as a senator of the United States.
   - (E) He retired from public life and settled on a farm.

8. What were some results of Harrison's time as governor of Indiana Territory? *Choose two answers.*
   - [A] The Territory lost a battle at Tippecanoe.
   - [B] The size of the Territory increased.
   - [C] Several officials resigned their posts.
   - [D] Hostility with Native Americans grew.

9. On what points was Martin Van Buren criticized during the 1840 presidential campaign?
   Choose two answers.
   - [A] His use of negative slogans
   - [B] His impact on the economy
   - [C] His affluent mode of life
   - [D] His violent military record

10. Listen again to part of the lecture. What does the professor imply?
   - (A) Slogans are a common feature of modern political campaigns.
   - (B) Relatively few wealthy politicians are successful at winning elections.
   - (C) Both Martin Van Buren and William Henry Harrison had nicknames.
   - (D) Martin Van Buren was unable to criticize William Henry Harrison's policies.

11. What happened to Vice President John Tyler after Harrison's death?
   - (A) He was president of the United States for almost four years.
   - (B) He became a respected member of Congress in 1841.
   - (C) He lost an emergency election to become the president.
   - (D) He held the post of acting president until Congress convened.

Tracks 241–246 Listen to a conversation between a student and a university employee.

12. For what reason does the woman visit the man's office?
    - (A) To ask about vegetarian meal options
    - (B) To learn about different meal plans
    - (C) To request a cancellation and refund
    - (D) To pay the fees for her meal plan

13. What do the speakers say about the café in the Student Center? *Choose two answers.*
    - (A) It is being remodeled, but will reopen soon.
    - (B) It offers good meal options for vegan students.
    - (C) Students with a meal plan cannot eat there.
    - (D) It is a popular meeting place for students.

14. Listen again to part of the conversation. What does the student imply?
    - (A) Her current diet is negatively affecting her health.
    - (B) The man does not know how vegan differs from vegetarian.
    - (C) She worries that the café will not offer salad every day.
    - (D) Most dining locations offer a poor selection for vegans.

15. Listen again to part of the conversation. What can be inferred about the student?
    - (A) She is not happy about what the man has told her.
    - (B) She thinks the man has given her wrong information.
    - (C) She believes the renovations are taking too long.
    - (D) She has changed her mind about the cancellation.

16. What will the student probably do next?
    - (A) Pay the administration fee
    - (B) Tell the man her decision
    - (C) Speak to her parents
    - (D) Apply for financial support

Tracks 247–253 Listen to part of a talk in a psychology class. The professor is discussing stress.

17. Listen again to part of the talk. What does the professor imply when she says this?
    - (A) Students may have forgotten that their exam is coming up.
    - (B) Students should study hard for the two weeks before their exam.
    - (C) Students might feel stress because their exam is coming up.
    - (D) Students are unlikely to have questions about stress on their exam.

18. What factors make a life change more stressful? *Choose three answers.*
- A How large the change is
- B How many people the change affects
- C How often the change happens
- D How long the change lasts
- E How unexpected the change is
- F How costly the change is to manage

19. What theory does the male student suggest about why change causes stress?
- A The brain equates change with potential danger.
- B People feel stress when they cannot focus on today.
- C Changes are not predictable, so people rarely feel safe.
- D Human bodies react when things change from good to bad.

20. The professor mentions three types of stressors. Indicate which characteristics match each type.

	Ambient stressors	Life stressors	Traumatic stressors
Are caused by things like work or relationships			
Are often unexpected and may involve violence			
May be caused by negative or positive events			
Affect multiple people at the same time			

21. What example of a routine stressor does the professor give?
- A Noise caused by construction work
- B Having a dispute with a manager
- C Driving to and from a hospital
- D Getting married and having a baby

 22. Listen again to part of the talk. What does the professor imply when she says this?
- A There are three causes of traumatic stressors.
- B Traumatic stressors cause high levels of stress.
- C Traumatic stressors have several characteristics.
- D Few people experience multiple traumatic stressors.

Score Conversion

Check your answers to questions 1–22. Give yourself one point for each fully correct answer. Then use this conversion chart to find out your approximate listening score range on the TOEFL Test.

Raw Score (out of 22)	Probable Level	Approximate Score Range
20–22		28–30
18–20	High	25–27
16–18		22–24
13–16	Intermediate	18–21
10–13		14–17
7–10		10–13
4–7	Low	5–9
0–3		0–4

Overview

The speaking section measures your ability to speak English effectively in academic settings. You will see and/or hear:

• Directions for adjusting the recording level of the microphone	about 1 minute
• Directions for the speaking section	about 2 minutes
• Independent Task 1 about a familiar topic, with 15 seconds to prepare and 45 seconds to respond	about 1 minute
• Independent Task 2 about a familiar topic, with 15 seconds to prepare and 45 seconds to respond	about 1 minute
• Integrated Task 3 about a campus situation, with 45 seconds to read a text, about 75 seconds to listen to a conversation, 30 seconds to prepare, and 60 seconds to respond	about 3.5 minutes
• Integrated Task 4 about academic course content, with 45 seconds to read a text, about 120 seconds to listen to a lecture, 30 seconds to prepare, and 60 seconds to respond	about 4.5 minutes
• Integrated Task 5 about a campus situation, with about 90 seconds to listen to a conversation, 20 seconds to prepare, and 60 seconds to respond	about 3 minutes
• Integrated Task 6 about academic course content, with about 120 seconds to listen to a lecture, 20 seconds to prepare, and 60 seconds to respond	about 3.5 minutes

Your spoken responses will be recorded and sent as digital files to human raters for grading. After all of your responses have been graded, your raw scores will be converted to a scaled score from 0–30.

NOTES

- Most speakers that you hear will speak with a North American accent, but you may also hear speakers from Australia, Great Britain, or New Zealand in some questions. These speakers will not have strong accents.
- Your responses will be recorded automatically. You do not need to press any buttons to start recording.

Detailed Guide

TEST TACTIC

Use the time when you are setting up your microphone to warm up your voice. Record yourself several times until you feel confident that you are speaking clearly and fluently. This might help you deliver better responses.

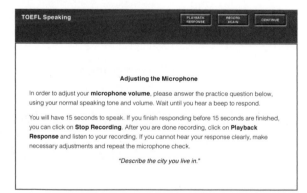

Before the speaking section begins you will need to set up the microphone you are using. The microphone will be connected to the headset, so you should wear your headset to get the best quality recording. Setting up the microphone will allow your voice to be recorded accurately and clearly.

To do this you will be asked to answer a practice question. Your answer to this question will not be scored.

When you answer, follow the directions on the screen and speak clearly but not too loudly or quietly. After recording, listen to your voice. If you are satisfied that your voice is clear and easy to hear, click the button marked **Continue**. If you want to record your voice again, click **Record Again**.

When you begin the speaking section of the TOEFL Test, you will first see the directions for the whole section. You will hear a narrator read the directions aloud. You can change the volume while the narrator is speaking by clicking on the **Volume** button in the top right corner of the screen.

When you are ready to begin the test, click the button marked **Continue**.

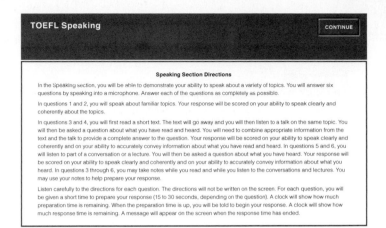

Before you see the first question, you will see a picture of a student wearing a headset and you will hear a narrator explain Speaking Task 1. You will not see the explanation on the screen. When the narrator finishes the explanation, this screen will disappear automatically.

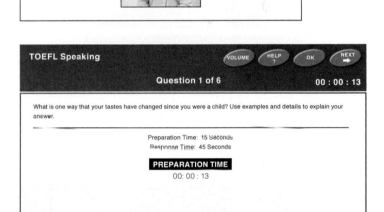

Next you will see the question for Speaking Task 1. A narrator will read the question aloud. Then a second voice will tell you to begin preparing your response. After that you will have 15 seconds to prepare. The amount of preparation time remaining will be shown on the screen.

After your preparation time is up, the second voice will tell you to begin speaking. You will have 45 seconds to speak. When you speak, make sure your voice is clear and you are speaking into the microphone. The amount of time remaining will be shown on the screen while you are speaking. When the time is up, the computer will automatically go on to the next question.

Next you will hear but not see an explanation of Speaking Task 2. Then you will see the Speaking Task 2 question on the screen. As with Task 1, you will hear a narrator saying the question. You will also hear a second voice telling you to begin preparing and then to begin speaking. You will have the same amount of preparation and response time for Speaking Task 2 as you do for Task 1.

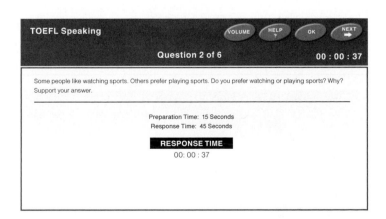

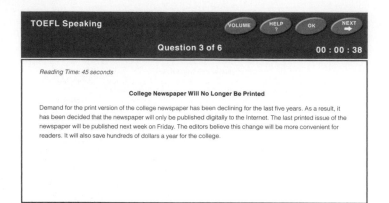

Next you will hear but not see an explanation of Speaking Task 3. Then you will see a short reading passage on the screen. The passage will describe a situation at a college campus. The narrator will briefly introduce the passage and tell you to read it.

You will usually have 45 seconds to read, but if the passage is shorter or longer than usual, you may have 40 seconds or 50 seconds. You may take notes about the passage while you read.

Next you will see a picture of two students on the screen and the narrator will tell you to listen to their conversation. The students will express their opinions about the situation described in the reading passage. One of the students will give detailed reasons for his or her views.

The conversation will usually last 60–90 seconds. You will see a bar below the picture of the people that shows how much longer the conversation will last. You may take notes while you listen to the conversation.

After the conversation you will first see a screen telling you to get ready to answer the question. This screen will disappear automatically after a few seconds. You will see this screen before Speaking Tasks 4, 5, and 6, too.

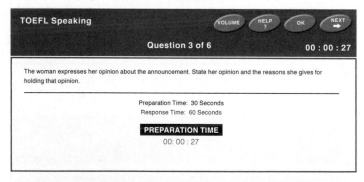

Then you will see the Speaking Task 3 question on the screen. The narrator will read the question aloud. Then a second voice will tell you to begin preparing your response. After that you will have 30 seconds to prepare. The amount of preparation time remaining will be shown on the screen. Then the second voice will tell you to begin speaking. You will have 60 seconds to speak. The amount of speaking time remaining will be shown on the screen.

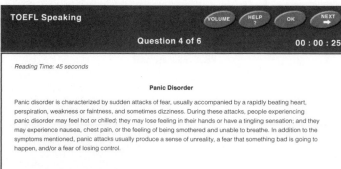

Next you will hear but not see an explanation of Speaking Task 4. Then you will see a short reading passage on the screen. The passage will give general information about an academic topic. The narrator will briefly introduce the passage and tell you to read it.

You will usually have 45 seconds to read, but if the passage is shorter or longer than usual, you may have 40 seconds or 50 seconds. You may take notes about the passage while you read.

Next you will see a picture of a professor on the screen and the narrator will tell you to listen to a lecture on the same topic as the passage. The professor usually gives specific information, such as examples or details, about the general topic described in the passage.

The lecture will usually last 60–90 seconds but may be longer. You will see a bar below the picture of the professor that shows how much longer the lecture will last. You may take notes while you listen to the lecture.

After the lecture you will see a question on the screen. As with Task 3, you will hear a narrator saying the question. You will also hear a second voice telling you to begin preparing and then to begin speaking. You will have the same amount of preparation and response time for Speaking Task 4 as you do for Task 3.

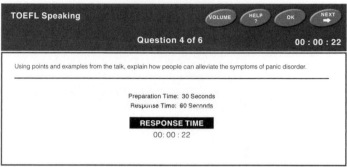

Next you will hear but not see an explanation of Speaking Task 5. Then you will see a picture of two people on the screen and the narrator will tell you to listen to their conversation. The speakers may be two students or one student and a professor or university employee. The speakers will discuss a problem that one or both of them have plus two possible solutions to the problem.

The conversation will usually last 60–90 seconds. You will see a bar below the picture of the people that shows how much longer the conversation will last. You may take notes while you listen to the conversation.

After the conversation you will see a question on the screen. The narrator will read the question aloud. Then a second voice will tell you to begin preparing your response. After that you will have 20 seconds to prepare. The amount of preparation time remaining will be shown on the screen. Then the second voice will tell you to begin speaking. You will have 60 seconds to speak. The amount of speaking time remaining will be shown on the screen.

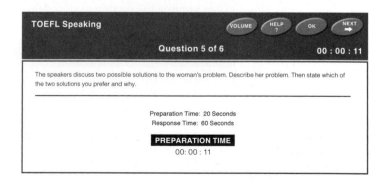

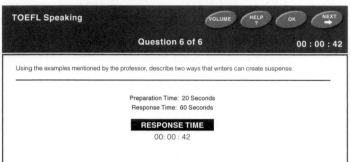

Next you will hear but not see an explanation of Speaking Task 6. Then you will see a picture of a professor on the screen. The narrator will tell you to listen to a lecture on an academic topic. The professor usually gives a general introduction to a topic and then discusses specific details or examples about it.

The lecture will usually last 90–120 seconds but may be longer. You will see a bar below the picture of the professor that shows how much longer the lecture will last. You may take notes while you listen to the lecture.

After the lecture you will see a question on the screen. As with Task 5, you will hear a narrator saying the question. You will also hear a second voice telling you to begin preparing and then to begin speaking. You will have the same amount of preparation and response time for Speaking Task 6 as you do for Task 5.

Scoring

Your six responses will be recorded and sent to ETS's Online Scoring Network. Your responses will be graded by three to six trained raters. No personal data is sent with each response, so the raters will not know your name, nationality, previous scores on the TOEFL Test, or any other personal details. The raters will not communicate with each other in any way about your responses.

Each rater will listen to your response and grade it holistically by focusing on the quality of your whole response. The rater will especially focus on your delivery, your language use, and how well you developed the topic. The rater will assign your response a grade from 0–4. The rater can only assign whole grades like 3, not half grades like 3.5.

When judging the quality of your delivery, the raters will focus on the following criteria for Speaking Tasks 1–6:

Score	Delivery – Speaking Tasks 1–6
4	The speech must be clear, fluent, and well-paced. There may be a few minor issues with intonation or pronunciation that do not affect the listener's ability to understand easily.
3	The speech must be generally clear and mostly fluent. There may be minor but obvious issues with intonation, pronunciation, and pacing. The listener may need to make an effort to understand.
2	The speech must be understandable if the listener concentrates. There may be serious issues with pronunciation, intonation, fluency, and pace. The listener may not understand all of the ideas.
1	The speech will have consistent problems with pronunciation, intonation, and pacing. There are likely to be long and frequent pauses within sentences and between sentences

When judging the quality of your language use, the raters will focus on the following criteria for Speaking Tasks 1–6:

Score	Language Use – Speaking Tasks 1–6
4	The speech must include a variety of simple and complex grammar structures and use vocabulary expressions effectively. If there are errors, they should be minor and must not confuse the listener.
3	The speech must use grammar and vocabulary effectively and automatically most of the time. The use of grammar and vocabulary may be limited to relatively simple structures, and may include errors that cause minor confusion for the listener.
2	The speech will demonstrate a limited ability to use grammar and vocabulary. The listener will usually understand simple ideas, but complex ideas will cause confusion or misunderstanding.
1	The speech will use a very limited range of grammar and vocabulary. The listener may not understand even simple ideas.

When judging the quality of your topic development, the raters will use slightly different criteria for Speaking Tasks 1 and 2 compared with Speaking Tasks 3–6:

Score	Topic Development – Speaking Tasks 1 and 2
4	The response must be well developed. Ideas should follow a logical sequence or be clearly related to each other.
3	The response must be reasonably well developed although the relationship between ideas may not be obvious. The development of some ideas may be limited, and general rather than specific.
2	The response should be connected to the topic but the development of ideas will be limited and sometimes unclear. There may be a lot of repetition, and the relationship between ideas may be unclear.
1	The response may seem unconnected to the topic except for very basic ideas. There may be a lot of repetition, including repetition of words and phrases from the question.

Score	Topic Development – Speaking Tasks 3–6
4	The response must be well developed. The ideas should be clearly relevant to the task and include specific details. Some details may be incorrect or omitted.
3	The response must be reasonably well developed. The ideas should be relevant to the task, but may be inaccurate, incomplete, or general rather than specific.
2	The response must include some relevant information, but will have obvious mistakes and missing information. Key details will be missing, unclear, or wrong. Ideas may not be clearly connected to each other.
1	The response will have very little relevant information. Most ideas will be unclear, wrong, or too general. There may be a lot of repetition, including repetition of words and phrases from the question.

To achieve a score of 4 points, a response must match all three descriptions at level 4 for delivery, language use, and topic development. To achieve 1, 2, or 3 points, a response must match or exceed at least two of the descriptions at that level. So, for example, a response that is at level 4 for delivery, level 4 for language use, but level 3 for topic development would score 3 points. And a response that is at level 2 for delivery, but level 3 for language use and topic development would also score 3 points.

Responses that are not in English or that are completely off the topic will receive a score of zero.

Your raw scores for each response are then converted to a scaled score from 0 to 30 points. ETS does not explain in detail how the raw scores are converted to a scaled score. However, this table, which is adapted from information published by ETS, shows how some example final scores would be converted to the 0–30 scale:

Scores for Individual Speaking Tasks						Average of all Speaking Tasks	Scaled Score
Task 1	Task 2	Task 3	Task 4	Task 5	Task 6		
4	4	4	4	4	4	4.00	30
4	4	4	4	4	3	3.83	29
4	4	4	4	3	3	3.66	28
4	4	4	3	3	3	3.50	27
4	4	3	3	3	3	3.33	26
4	3	3	3	3	3	3.16	24
3	3	3	3	3	3	3.00	23
3	3	3	3	3	2	2.83	22
3	3	3	3	2	2	2.66	20
3	3	3	2	2	2	2.50	19
3	3	2	2	2	2	2.33	18
3	2	2	2	2	2	2.16	17
2	2	2	2	2	2	2.00	15

TEST TACTIC

Confidence is one key to getting a better speaking score. To sound confident, sit up straight, use a slightly louder voice than usual, and smile as you talk. Breathing deeply several times before you begin speaking may also help.

When you receive your score from the TOEFL Test, you will get a score report. The report will give your scaled score in speaking from 0–30, your speaking level (Good, Fair, Limited, or Weak), plus a short description of the typical performance of students at that level. The descriptions will cover the three types of responses: Speaking about Familiar Topics (Speaking Tasks 1 and 2), Speaking about Campus Situations (Tasks 3 and 5), and Speaking about Academic Course Content (Tasks 4 and 6).

Here are the level descriptions for responses about familiar topics (Speaking Tasks 1 and 2):

Level	Your Performance
Good (3.5–4.0)	Your responses indicate an ability to communicate your personal experiences and opinions effectively in English. Overall, your speech is clear and fluent. Your use of vocabulary and grammar is effective with only minor errors. Your ideas are generally well developed and expressed coherently.
Fair (2.5–3.0)	Your responses indicate you are able to speak in English about your personal experiences and opinions in a mostly clear and coherent manner. Your speech is mostly clear with only occasional errors. Grammar and vocabulary are somewhat limited and include some errors. At times, the limitations prevent you from elaborating fully on your ideas, but they do not seriously interfere with overall communication.
Limited (1.5–2.0)	Your responses indicate some difficulty speaking in English about everyday experiences and opinions. Listeners sometimes have trouble understanding you because of noticeable problems with pronunciation, grammar and vocabulary. While you are able to respond partially to the questions, you are not able to fully develop your ideas, possibly due to limited vocabulary and grammar.
Weak (0–1.0)	Your responses are incomplete. They contain little or no content and are difficult for listeners to understand.

Here are the level descriptions for the responses about campus situations (Speaking Tasks 3 and 5):

Level	Your Performance
Good (3.5–4.0)	Your responses indicate an ability to speak effectively in English about reading material and conversations typically encountered by university students. Overall, your responses are clear and coherent, with only occasional errors of pronunciation, grammar or vocabulary.
Fair (2.5–3.0)	Your responses demonstrate an ability to speak in English about reading material and experiences typically encountered by university students. You are able to convey relevant information about conversations, newspaper articles and campus bulletins; however, some details are missing or inaccurate. Limitations of grammar, vocabulary and pronunciation at times cause difficulty for the listener. However, they do not seriously interfere with overall communication.
Limited (1.5–2.0)	Your responses indicate that you have some difficulty speaking in English about information from conversations, newspaper articles, university publications and so on. While you are able to talk about some of the key information from these sources, limited grammar and vocabulary may prevent you from fully expressing your ideas. Problems with pronunciation make it difficult for listeners to understand you at times.
Weak (0–1.0)	Your responses are incomplete. They include little or no information about the topic. Your speech is often difficult for listeners to understand, and the meaning is unclear.

And here are the level descriptions for the responses about academic course content (Speaking Tasks 4 and 6):

Level	Your Performance
Good (3.5–4.0)	Your responses demonstrate an ability to communicate effectively in English about academic topics typical of first-year university studies. Your speech is mostly clear and fluent. You are able to use appropriate vocabulary and grammar to explain concepts and ideas from reading or lecture material. You are able to talk about key information and relevant details with only minor inaccuracies.
Fair (2.5–3.0)	Your responses demonstrate that you are able to speak in English about academic reading and lecture material, with only minor communication problems. For the most part, your speech is clear and easy to understand. However, some problems with pronunciation and intonation may occasionally cause difficulty for the listener. Your use of grammar and vocabulary is adequate to talk about the topics, but some ideas are not fully developed or are inaccurate.
Limited (1.5–2.0)	In your responses, you are able to use English to talk about the basic ideas from academic reading or lecture materials, but, in general, you include few relevant or accurate details. It is sometimes difficult for listeners to understand your responses because of problems with grammar, vocabulary and pronunciation. Overall, you are able to respond in a general way to the questions, but the amount of information in your responses is limited and the expression of ideas is often vague and unclear.
Weak (0–1.0)	Your responses are incomplete. They include little or no information about the topic. Your speech is often difficult for listeners to understand, and the meaning is unclear.

Source: www.ets.org/Media/Tests/TOEFL/pdf/TOEFL_Perf_Feedback.pdf

TEST TACTIC

In general, it is better to use a variety of simple grammar and vocabulary structures accurately than to use complex grammar and vocabulary structures incorrectly. You are more likely to use unnatural language or make confusing errors when using complex structures.

Directions

This speaking review test is intended to help you learn your speaking strengths and weaknesses. You will answer six speaking tasks that are designed to be at the same level as the ones on the TOEFL Test. For some tasks you will listen to one or two speakers. You may take notes while you listen. For the most realistic practice, cover the questions when you listen, and record your answers when you speak.

Test

🔊 Tracks 254–255 **TASK 1 – SPEAKING ABOUT A FAMILIAR TOPIC**

Talk about a place that was important to you when you were a child. Describe the place and say why it was important to you. Give reasons and details to support your answer.

Preparation Time: 15 Seconds   Response Time: 45 Seconds

🔊 Tracks 256–257 **TASK 2 – SPEAKING ABOUT A FAMILIAR TOPIC**

Some college students prefer studying for assignments with other people. Other students prefer working on their own when they have an assignment. Which way do you prefer? Why?

Preparation Time: 15 Seconds   Response Time: 45 Seconds

🔊 Tracks 258–261 **TASK 3 – SPEAKING ABOUT A CAMPUS SITUATION**

A student wrote a letter to the university newspaper about a problem. Read the letter. You have 45 seconds to read the letter. Begin reading now.

Office Hours Problem

I've noticed a trend recently with regard to office hours. Not only do instructors seem to be reducing how much time they are available to see students, but often they come to their office late when they have office hours scheduled. I think the university should institute a policy to force all teaching staff to do a minimum number of office hours per week and find a way to enforce the policy. I'm sure I'm not the only student who feels frustrated by this situation.

Now listen to two students as they discuss the letter.

The man/woman expresses his/her opinion about the letter. State his/her opinion and explain the reasons he/she gives for holding that opinion.

Preparation Time: 30 Seconds   Response Time: 60 Seconds

🔊 Tracks 262–265 **TASK 4 – SPEAKING ABOUT ACADEMIC CONTENT**

Now read the passage about the conduction of heat. You have 45 seconds to read the passage.

The Conduction of Heat

In simple terms, heat conduction is the movement of heat (in the form of thermal energy) from one area to another. Heat naturally flows from a region of higher temperature to one of lower temperature until both areas reach roughly the same temperature, a condition known as thermal equilibrium. Conduction takes place in solids, liquids, and gases. It occurs when atoms and molecules interact with other atoms and molecules, transferring some of their energy in the form of heat. Conduction is the most significant means of heat transfer between solid objects. It is less significant between solids and liquids, and even weaker between solids and gases.

Now listen to a lecture on this topic in an introductory science class.

Using points and examples from the lecture, explain the conduction of heat between solids, liquids, and gases.

Preparation Time: 30 Seconds   Response Time: 60 Seconds

Tracks 266–269 **TASK 5 – SPEAKING ABOUT A CAMPUS SITUATION**

Now listen to a conversation between a man and a woman.

The speakers discuss two possible solutions to a problem. Describe the problem. Then state which of the two solutions you prefer and why.

Preparation Time: 20 Seconds   Response Time: 60 Seconds

Tracks 270–273 **TASK 6 – SPEAKING ABOUT ACADEMIC CONTENT**

Now listen to part of a talk in a biology class.

Using points and examples from the talk, summarize the two definitions of comorbidity that the professor discusses.

Preparation Time: 20 Seconds   Response Time: 60 Seconds

Score Conversion

Ask a teacher or native speaker to evaluate each response from 0–4. (If necessary, you can evaluate your responses yourself. See pages 172–175 of the Speaking Reference unit for the criteria for scoring.) Then add up the scores for each response to find your raw score and use this conversion chart to find out your approximate speaking score range on the TOEFL Test.

Raw Score (out of 24)	Probable Level	Approximate Score Range
21–24	Good	26–30
15–20	Fair	19–25
9–14	Limited	11–18
1–8	Weak	1–10

Unit Focus

In the speaking section of the TOEFL Test you will have six tasks. Speaking Task 1 is one of two independent tasks about familiar topics. The question will typically ask you to express an opinion about a person, place, object, activity, or event that you know. You will have 15 seconds to prepare your response and 45 seconds to speak. In this unit you will learn and practice several key skills to answer Speaking Task 1 questions effectively, including:

- learning and using a model answer that matches all Speaking Task 1 questions.
- thinking of and expressing relevant opinions and reasons clearly and directly.
- thinking of and talking about detailed examples that support your reasons.
- speaking clearly, fluently, and confidently without long pauses.

The vocabulary focus is on practical words and phrases related to:

- describing people, places, objects, activities, and events.

A Warm-up

A1 Work with a partner. Answer three speaking tasks from this chart each. When you answer, try to speak for up to 45 seconds without any long pauses. After each speech, give your partner some helpful feedback.

Describe one	helpful person relaxing place useful object enjoyable activity popular event	that you know and say why	he she it	is so	helpful. relaxing. useful. enjoyable. popular.

B Practical Vocabulary

B1 Choose the best answer, A–F, to complete this chart of descriptive adjectives that would be useful for answering Speaking Task 1 questions. Check a dictionary if any of the words have unfamiliar meanings.

Descriptive Adjective	Synonym	Antonym
1.	compassionate	Unkind
economical	inexpensive	2.
3.	inspiring	Boring
relaxing	4.	5.
time-saving	6.	Inefficient

A calming
B caring
C convenient
D costly
E exciting
F stressful

C Analyzing Speaking Task 1

There are four types of Speaking Task 1 questions that you might see in the TOEFL Test. These question types look slightly different from each other, but you can answer all of them in the same way.

The first type, which is the most common, asks you to talk positively about a person, place, object, event, or activity, as in this example:

Choose a _____ you enjoyed and say why you enjoyed it. Include examples and details in your response.

The second type of question is similar to the first type, but it asks you to talk negatively about someone or something:

What is one _____ that you do not enjoy? Give a reason and specific examples in support of your answer.

The third type asks you to talk about one option from a list of several choices:

Do you prefer _____ , _____ , or _____ ? Why? Provide specific details and examples in your answer.

The final type of question asks you to say what advice or recommendation you would give to another person:

A friend has asked your advice about _____ . What specific advice about _____ would you give your friend? Why? Include examples and details in support of your answer.

When the question appears on the screen, an announcer will read it. After that a second announcer will tell you to begin preparing your response. After 15 seconds, the second announcer will tell you to begin your response. The screen will show both the question and how much time remains during your preparation and speaking time.

To answer a Speaking Task 1 question effectively and get a good score, your response should:

- use language well – you need to use grammar and vocabulary naturally and effectively with few mistakes.
- be delivered well – your speech should be clear and fluent, with good pronunciation and few long pauses.
- develop the topic well – you need to give a well-organized response that directly answers the question.

Common problems when answering Speaking Task 1 questions that are likely to reduce your score include:

- poor language use – frequent mistakes, or vocabulary and grammar that are unnatural.
- poor delivery – unclear pronunciation or intonation, frequent or long pauses, or lack of fluency.
- poor topic development – a response that is disorganized, repeats ideas, or does not answer the question.

C1 Match questions 1–4 to one of the four types of Speaking Task 1 questions described above.

1. A friend is planning to visit your hometown. How would you recommend that your friend travel there? Why?
2. Would you prefer to attend a university in your hometown, one in another part of your country, or one overseas? Why?
3. What is one gift you received that you really liked? Describe the gift and say why you liked it.
4. What is one event you attended recently that you did not enjoy? Describe the event and say why you did not enjoy it.

C2 Look at this response to a Speaking Task 1 question. Then complete tasks 1–3.

It's hard to choose just one gift that I really like. However, if I had to pick one, it would be a tablet computer that my parents gave me. ~~This tablet is the gift that I like most.~~ The main reason is that my tablet is useful for studying. For example, with my tablet I can read books or connect to the Internet wherever I am. This means I can study at home, at a café, or at a friend's house, which is very convenient. ~~It is useful and convenient to study wherever I want.~~ So that's why I really like my tablet.

1. Which of the Speaking Task 1 questions from exercise **C1** does the response answer?
2. What is the problem with the two crossed out sentences (~~like this~~) in the response?
3. Practice saying the response until you can say it confidently and fluently. Do not say the crossed out sentences.

D Mastering Speaking Task 1 – Preparing an Effective Response

Thinking of and choosing an opinion, reason, and example that are all easy to talk about will help you get a good score for Speaking Task 1. However, you only have 15 seconds to prepare your response, so it is essential to make good decisions and to use your time effectively.

D1 Summarize the opinion, reason, and example from this response to a Speaking Task 1 question. One answer has been done for you.

> Choose a book you enjoyed reading and say why you enjoyed it. Include examples and details in your response.

It's hard to choose just one book that I enjoyed. However, if I had to pick one, it would be a book that helped me learn English effectively. The main reason is that this book helped me gain confidence. For example, before I got this book I thought I would fail an English exam that I had to take. But reading the book helped me understand English better and I became more confident, so I passed the exam with a high score. So that's why this book is one that I enjoyed reading.

Opinion _____

Reason _____

Example   _The speaker was worried about failing an English exam but a book gave her confidence and she passed._

D2 Look at this checklist for preparing an effective response for Speaking Task 1 questions. Then complete tasks 1 and 2.

> ☑ Your opinion, reason, and example should be familiar ideas that you have talked about before in English.
>
> ☑ You should be able to discuss the opinion, reason, and example using simple, easy-to-pronounce words.
>
> ☑ The opinion, reason, and example should directly answer the question and be connected to each other.

1. Do the opinion, reason, and example from exercise **D1** match each point in the checklist? Discuss with a partner.
2. Work with a partner to think of another opinion, reason, and example for the Speaking Task 1 question in exercise **D1**. Use the checklist as a guide.

D3 Complete tasks 1–5.

1. Take 15 seconds to think of an opinion, reason, and example for question A below.
2. After 15 seconds, use the checklist from exercise **D2** to judge your opinion, reason, and example. If you are satisfied that your ideas match each point in the checklist, go on to task 3; if not, repeat task 1.
3. Quickly write down the opinion, reason, and example that you thought of in task 1. Write in notes, not full sentences.
4. Repeat tasks 1–3 for Speaking Task 1 questions B–D below.
5. Share your ideas for Speaking Task 1 questions A–D with other students. Then listen to their ideas. Which are the best ideas? Why are they the best ideas?

A What is one subject that you do not enjoy studying? Give a reason and specific examples in support of your answer.

B Describe one person who has helped you in your life. Say who the person is and how he or she has helped you.

C A friend has asked your advice about an interesting topic to learn about. What topic would you recommend? Why?

D Do you prefer studying at home, in a café, or at a library? Why? Provide specific details and examples in your answer.

TEST TACTIC

If you want to make a note of your opinion, reason, and example during the 15 seconds of preparation time, that is OK. However, most people find that 15 seconds is enough time to think of ideas, but not enough time to write ideas down.

E Mastering Speaking Task 1 – Delivering a High-Quality Response

All Speaking Task 1 questions can be answered in the same way. As a result, using a template – a well-organized model answer that uses natural language – will help you avoid mistakes and deliver an effective, quality response in 45 seconds.

E1 What information, A–E, does each highlighted phrase in this template introduce? Use the response in exercise **D1** as a guide. One answer has been done for you.

It's hard to choose ...   1. _____ *a summary of the question* _____

However, if I had to pick one, it would be ...   2. _____

The main reason is that ...   3. _____

For example, ...   4. _____

So that's why ...   5. _____

A a detailed supporting example   D a summary of the question
B an easy-to-write-about opinion   E a clear and relevant reason
C a paraphrase of your opinion (optional)

E2 Write in the highlighted phrases from exercise **E1** to complete this response to a Speaking Task 1 question. One answer has been done for you.

> Choose a book you enjoyed reading and say why you enjoyed it. Include examples and details in your response.

1. It's hard to choose _____ only one book that I really liked. 2. _____ a book about choosing a career from my parents. 3. _____ this book helped me decide what to do with my life. 4. _____, when I was a high school student I wanted to work with cars, so I was planning to get a job as a mechanic. However, after reading the book I decided that working with cars would be tedious, so I changed my plan. 5. _____ I really enjoyed the book about choosing a career.

))) Track 274 **E3** Complete tasks 1 and 2.

1. Listen to a high-level student say the full response from exercise **E2** sentence by sentence. Repeat each sentence after you hear it. Try to match the speaker's intonation, rhythm, and pronunciation. Keep practicing until you can say the response confidently and fluently.
2. Work with a partner to practice saying the full response from **E2**. Each time your partner speaks, give him or her useful feedback about intonation, rhythm, and pronunciation.

E4 Write in the best answer, A–D, to complete blanks 1–4 in this Speaking Task 1 response. When you have finished, practice saying the completed response until you can say it fluently and confidently in 45 seconds or less.

> Describe one place you would like to go for a vacation. Support your answer with details.

It's hard to choose 1. _____. However, if I had to pick one, it would be
2. _____. The main reason is that 3. _____.
For example, when I was a student at high school and university, 4. _____ .
I would love to go and see the real buildings in Rome and learn more about the history and culture of that city. So that's why I would choose to visit Rome.

A taking a trip to Rome in Italy   C only one place to go for a vacation
B I read about the old buildings in Rome   D I find Roman history very stimulating

E5 Write a full response to this Speaking Task 1 question.

> What is one event you attended recently that you did not enjoy? Describe the event and say why you did not enjoy it.

It's hard to choose _____

However, if I had to pick one, it would be _____

The main reason is that _____

For example, _____

So that's why _____

E6 Practice saying your response from exercise **E5** until you can say it fluently and confidently in 45 seconds or less.

E7 Work with a partner to complete tasks 1–5. Use some of the words you studied in exercise **B1** in your responses.

1. Prepare a response to one of the Speaking Task 1 questions in this chart:

Describe one	person place object activity *your idea*	that you would like to that you do not want to you would recommend that a friend	meet. visit. buy. do. *your idea.*

2. Listen to the response that your partner prepared. Take notes if you like.
3. After listening, put checks (✔) in the YES or NO columns of the table below. Then give your partner feedback.
4. Say the response you prepared and get your partner's feedback. Try to get perfect feedback – YES in every column.
5. Fix any mistakes in your response that your partner noticed. Then repeat tasks 1–5 with several different partners.

Did your partner	YES	NO
Give an opinion that clearly and directly answers the question?		
Mention a reason that is directly relevant to the topic of the question?		
Give a supporting example that logically follows from the reason?		
Finish his or her response in less than 45 seconds?		
Use the template phrases accurately?		
Speak clearly, fluently, and confidently without long pauses?		

E8 How confident are you about answering Speaking Task 1 questions? Complete this short survey.

1. I think that I will be able to prepare my response well in 15 seconds.
   ☐ Yes   ☐ Maybe   ☐ No
2. I think that I will be able to remember the model language from the template.
   ☐ Yes   ☐ Maybe   ☐ No
3. I think that I will be able to add my own opinion, reason, and example to the template.
   ☐ Yes   ☐ Maybe   ☐ No
4. 4. I think that I will be able to deliver my speech fluently and confidently in 45 seconds.
   ☐ Yes   ☐ Maybe   ☐ No

E9 For each question in exercise **E8** that you answered Maybe or No, discuss with other students how you can improve and become more confident so that you could answer Yes.

TEST TACTIC

If you find that you cannot complete all five sections of the template in 45 seconds, do not worry about step 5. A concluding sentence is optional provided that your opinion, reason, and supporting example are clear.

F Test Challenge

Tracks 275–282 **F1** Answer *two* of questions 1–4. For each question, take 15 seconds to prepare and speak for no more than 45 seconds in order to get realistic practice for the test. Use this checklist of skills that you learned in this unit as a guide.

Note that in this book you will hear a beep at the end of your speaking time. In the TOEFL Test you will not hear this final beep; instead, you will see how much time is left on the screen.

- ☑ Make sure your opinion, reason, and example are familiar, match the topic, and logically support each other.
- ☑ Follow the template as closely as you can – this will help you deliver a well-organized, effective, natural response.

1. Describe an important event from your childhood. Explain why this event is important to you. Include specific examples.
2. Talk about a place you have visited that you did not like very much. Explain why you disliked this place.
3. Which of the following do you use most often: a digital camera, a cell phone, or a computer? Why? Give details and examples to support your response.
4. Your friend has asked for advice about how to become healthier. What advice would you give your friend? Support your answer.

F2 Prepare responses to the two questions from exercise **F1** that you have not answered yet. Say your responses to a partner in 45 seconds and give and receive feedback to help each other deliver better responses.

Next Steps

Descriptive adjectives are useful for answering Speaking Task 1, Speaking Task 2, and Writing Task 2 questions. You may also see or hear these words in the reading and listening sections of TOEFL. As a result, learning more descriptive words, as well as practicing key skills for Speaking Task 1 questions, may help you increase your TOEFL score.

To learn more descriptive adjectives:

1. Read an article in English once to understand the main ideas, but do not try to understand every word.
2. Read the article again and make a list of adjectives in the article that describe a person, place, idea, situation, or event.
3. Write sentences using the adjectives on your list, and then say your sentences aloud in a clear, confident voice. Writing and then saying the sentences will help you remember the adjectives.

To practice key skills for Speaking Task 1 questions:

1. Spend two minutes to make a list of as many different people as you can think of.
2. For the first person on your list, spend 15 seconds thinking of reasons and examples either why you like that person, why you dislike that person, or why you think another person should speak to that person. (Your reasons and examples do not have to be true, but they do have to be easy to talk about.)
3. Then take 45 seconds to give a speech based on your reasons and examples. Use the template from exercise **E1**.
4. Repeat steps 2 and 3 for the other people on your list.
5. Repeat steps 1–4, but this time make a list of places, objects, activities, or events.

Unit Focus

In the speaking section of the TOEFL Test you will have six tasks. Speaking Task 2 is one of two independent tasks about familiar topics. The question will ask you to express an opinion about a general topic like education, work, health, or free time activities. The topic will include two contrasting points of view, and you will need to say which one you think is better. You will have 15 seconds to prepare your response and then 45 seconds to speak. In this unit you will learn and practice key skills to answer Speaking Task 2 questions effectively, including:

- learning and using a model answer that matches all Speaking Task 2 questions.
- thinking of and expressing relevant opinions and reasons clearly and directly.
- thinking of and talking about detailed examples that support your reasons.
- speaking clearly, fluently, and confidently without long pauses.

The vocabulary focus is on practical words and phrases related to:

- education, work, health, and free time.

A Warm-up

A1 How many reasons can you think of that answer questions 1–4? Share your answers with other students and listen to their ideas. Which are the best ideas?

1. Do you prefer studying alone or with your friends? Why?

   I prefer studying with my friends because _____ *your reasons* _____

2. Which is better, working for a large company or working for a small company? Why?

   I think that working for a large company is better because _____ *your reasons* _____

3. Do you agree or disagree that regular exercise is the best way to maintain your health? Why?

   I agree that exercising often is the best way to stay healthy because _____ *your reasons* _____

4. Would you rather spend your free time watching television or reading a book? Why?

   I would rather relax in front of the television because _____ *your reasons* _____

B Practical Vocabulary

B1 Copy answers A–H to the category they match. One answer has been done for you.

Expressions related to education	Expressions related to free time activities
•	•
•	•

Expressions related to health	Expressions related to work
•	• earn a good salary
•	•

A earn a good salary D submit an assignment G get good grades
B stay in good shape E spend time with friends H find a good job
C take a few days off F maintain my health

C Analyzing Speaking Task 2

There are three types of Speaking Task 2 questions that you might see on the TOEFL Test. These question types look different from each other, but you can answer all of them in the same way.

For the first type of question, which is the most common, you must state which idea you prefer from two contrasting ideas and say why this is your preference. Here is an example of this type of question:

> Some people like to do _____. Other people like to do _____. Which do you prefer? Why? Support your answer with details and examples.

To answer the second type of question you must explain why you agree or disagree with a particular statement:

> Do you agree or disagree that _____? Why? Support your answer.

For the third type of question, you must say which of two contrasting ideas is better for other people and explain why you think so:

> Some people believe students should _____. Other people think students should _____. Which option do you think is better for students? Why?

When the question appears on the screen, an announcer will read it. After that a second announcer will tell you to begin preparing your response. After 15 seconds, the second announcer will tell you to begin your response. The screen will show both the question and how much time remains during your preparation and speaking time.

To answer a Speaking Task 2 question effectively and get a good score, your response should:

- use language well – you need to use grammar and vocabulary naturally and effectively with few mistakes.
- be delivered well – your speech should be clear and fluent, with good pronunciation and few long pauses.
- develop the topic well – you need to give a well-organized response that directly answers the question.

Common problems when answering Speaking Task 2 questions that are likely to reduce your score include:

- poor language use – frequent mistakes, or vocabulary and grammar that are unnatural.
- poor delivery – unclear pronunciation or intonation, frequent or long pauses, or lack of fluency.
- poor topic development – a response that is disorganized, repeats ideas, or does not answer the question.

TEST TACTIC

Lack of fluency – which often happens if you worry too much about grammar and vocabulary – is likely to affect your score, but minor language mistakes are not. So keep speaking, even if you realize that you have made a few small errors.

C1 **Match questions 1–3 to one of the three types of Speaking Task 2 questions described above.**

1. Some schools require students to wear a uniform. Other schools allow students to wear their own clothes. Which do you think is better for students? Why?
2. Some people enjoy spending free time alone. Others prefer to spend it with friends. What is your preference? Why?
3. Do you agree or disagree that speaking more than one language is a useful skill for people who work in a store? Why?

C2 **Look at this response to a Speaking Task 2 question. Then complete tasks 1–3.**

There are some advantages to spending _____ time with others. However, overall I feel that enjoying leisure time alone is better. The main reason is that I can save money. For example, when I am on my own I can do _____ activities like walking in the park or reading a library book. Doing _____ things is important for me these days because I don't have much money. In contrast, if I hang out with friends, usually we go out and I have to buy things like food, coffee, or movie tickets. So that's why I prefer spending my _____ time by myself.

1. Which word completes the response? (The same word is missing from all four blanks.)
2. Which of the Speaking Task 2 questions from exercise **C1** does the response answer?
3. Practice saying the response (with the missing word added to the blanks) until you can say it confidently and fluently.

D Mastering Speaking Task 2 – Preparing an Effective Response

Thinking of and choosing an opinion, reason, and example that are all easy to talk about will help you get a good score for Speaking Task 2. However, you only have 15 seconds to prepare your response, so it is essential to make good choices and use your time effectively.

Track 283 **D1** Listen to two students discuss preparing for Speaking Task 2 questions. What advice does the woman give the man? Check (✓) the correct column. One answer has been done for you.

	Yes	No
Choose the opinion that is easier to talk about even if it is not your real opinion.	✓	
Use stock reasons that match many topics, such as education, time, work, or health.		
Think of two contrasting examples – one that is positive and one that is negative.		
Make sure one example is about a person you know well, like a family member or friend.		

D2 Match each opinion and reason, A–D, to either question 1 or 2. One answer has been done for you.

1. Some people enjoy watching TV when they have free time. Others like going for walks. Which do you enjoy more? Why?
2. Some people learn best by reading books. Others prefer reading articles on a computer. What is your preference? Why?

A opinion – books / reason – slower to read on screen so books save time ___matches question 2___
B opinion – computers / reason – computer skills are essential for getting good job _____
C opinion – watching TV / reason – learn useful facts by watching documentaries _____
D opinion – walking / reason – walking is good exercise to stay healthy _____

D3 Complete tasks 1–3 with a partner.

1. Which two answers from A–D in exercise **D2** would be easiest for you to talk about? Why?
2. Which stock reason – education, time, work, or health – matches each reason given in answers A–D in **D2**?
3. Make a list of other reasons (including stock reasons) that would match each opinion in **D2**. Then share your ideas with the class. Which are the best reasons? Why are they the best reasons?

D4 Look at this example from a response to a Speaking Task 2 question. Then complete tasks 1 and 2.

For example, when I was a child I often read articles on a computer and this helped me develop excellent computer skills. Because of these skills, now I have a great job with a good salary. However, my friend only read books and did not develop good computer skills. Even though he is very smart and has a lot of academic knowledge, he does not have a good job.

1. Which opinion and reason – A, B, C, or D – from exercise **D2** does the example match?
2. With a partner, write three examples that match the other opinions and reasons from **D2**. Try to include a positive example that supports the opinion and a negative one about the other choice.

D5 Complete steps 1–5.

Step 1   Take 15 seconds to think of an opinion, reason, and example for question 1 below.
Step 2   Then decide if you are satisfied with your ideas. If yes, go to step 3; if not, repeat step 1.
Step 3   Quickly note down the opinion, reason, and example that you thought of in step 1.
Step 4   Repeat steps 1–3 for question 2 below.
Step 5   Share your ideas for questions 1 and 2 with other students. Then listen to their ideas. Which are the best ideas? Why are they the best ideas?

1. Some people want a job that pays well. Others would rather have a job that gives them plenty of time off. What kind of job would you prefer? Why?
2. Do you agree or disagree that universities teach students the skills they need to be successful in their careers? Why?

E Mastering Speaking Task 2 – Delivering a High-Quality Response

All Speaking Task 2 questions can be answered in the same way. As a result, using a template – a well-organized model answer that uses natural language – will help you avoid mistakes and deliver an effective, quality response in 45 seconds.

E1 **What information, A–E, does each highlighted phrase in this template introduce? One answer has been done for you.**

There are some advantages to ... 1. _____*a summary of the opinion you reject*_____

However, overall I feel that ... 2. _____

The main reason is that ... 3. _____

For example, ... 4. _____

So that's why ... 5. _____

A a paraphrase of your opinion (optional)
B a detailed supporting example
C a summary of the opinion you reject
D a clear and relevant reason for your opinion
E a summary of the opinion you choose

E2 **Write in the highlighted phrases from exercise E1 to complete this response to a Speaking Task 2 question. One answer has been done for you.**

Some people believe children should learn how to use a computer at school. Other people think young children should focus on learning academic subjects. Which do you think is better for children? Why?

1. _____*There are some advantages to*_____ children concentrating on academic subjects.
2. _____ children should learn computer skills at school.
3. _____ computer skills may help them get a good job in the future. 4._____ my sister had computer lessons at school and because her computer skills are good, she easily got a great job after graduating from university. In contrast, my cousin didn't learn about computers at school and he lacks good computer skills. For this reason, he can't find a good job now even though he's very smart. 5. _____ I think schools should teach children about computers.

)) Track 284 **E3** **Complete tasks 1 and 2.**

1. Listen to a high-level student say the full response from exercise **E2**. Repeat each sentence after you hear it. Try to match the speaker's intonation, rhythm, and pronunciation. Keep practicing until you can say each sentence confidently and fluently.
2. Work with a partner to practice saying the full response. Each time your partner speaks, give him or her feedback about intonation, rhythm, and pronunciation.

E4 Use your own words to complete two opposite responses to this Speaking Task 2 question. Then practice saying each response until you can say it confidently and fluently in 45 seconds or less.

Some people like to have a job with a high salary. Other people would rather get a job that gives them lots of free time. Which type of job would you like? Why? Support your answer.

There are some advantages to having a job that pays well. However, overall I feel that getting a job which allows me plenty of time off is preferable. The main reason is that _____

_____

_____

_____

_____ So that's why I would rather have a job that gives me lots of free time, not one with a high salary.

There are some advantages to a job that lets me have plenty of time off. However, overall I feel that a position that comes with a good salary is better. The main reason is that _____

_____

_____

_____

_____ So that's why I would prefer a job that pays well to one that offers a lot of free time.

E5 Work with a partner to complete tasks 1–5. Use some of the words you studied in exercise **B1** in your responses.

1. Prepare a response to *one* of these Speaking Task 2 questions:
   - Some students like to learn about science. Others would rather study literature or art. Which do you prefer? Why?
   - Do you agree or disagree that having several part-time jobs is better than having one full-time position? Why?
   - Some students choose to eat only fruits and vegetables. Others like eating meat and fish, too. Which do you prefer?
   - Some children like to spend free time watching movies. Others prefer to play with friends. Which is better? Why?

2. Listen to the response that your partner prepared. Take notes if you like.
3. After listening, put checks (✓) in the YES or NO columns of the table below. Then give your partner feedback.
4. Say the response you prepared and get your partner's feedback. Try to get perfect feedback – YES in every column.
5. Fix any mistakes in your response that your partner noticed. Then repeat tasks 1–5 with several different partners.

Did your partner	YES	NO
Give an opinion that clearly matches one of the choices from the question?		
Mention a reason that is directly relevant to the topic of the question?		
Give a supporting example that logically follows from the reason?		
Finish his or her response in less than 45 seconds?		
Use the template phrases accurately?		
Speak clearly, fluently, and confidently without long pauses?		

F Test Challenge

F1 **Answer *two* of questions 1–4. For each question, take 15 seconds to prepare and speak for no more than 45 seconds in order to get realistic practice for the test. Use this checklist of skills that you learned in this unit as a guide.**

Tracks 285–292

> ☑ Make sure your opinion, reason, and example are familiar, match the topic, and logically support each other.
>
> ☑ Follow the template as closely as you can – this will help you deliver a well-organized, effective, natural response.

This book uses a beep to indicate your speaking time is up. Remember that you will not hear this beep in the real test.

1. Some college students work part-time while they are studying. Others choose not to work so they can concentrate on their studies. Which do you think is better for students? Explain why.

2. Some people prefer doing outdoor activities in their free time. Others prefer spending their free time indoors. Which do you prefer? Include details and examples in your explanation.

3. At some colleges, students study just one subject in order to get a deep knowledge of that subject. At other colleges, students study various subjects in order to get a broad knowledge of many subjects. Which is better for students? Why?

4. Do you agree or disagree that it is healthier to live in a small town than in a big city? Why? Support your answer.

F2 **Prepare responses to the two questions from exercise F1 that you have not answered yet. Say your responses to a partner in 45 seconds and give and receive feedback to help each other deliver better responses.**

Next Steps

Expressions related to education, work, health, and free time are especially useful for answering Speaking Task 1, Speaking Task 2, and Writing Task 2 questions. These words may also appear in the other sections of TOEFL. As a result, learning other useful expressions related to these topics, as well as practicing key skills for Speaking Task 2 questions, may help you increase your overall TOEFL score.

To learn more expressions related to study, work, health, and free time:

1. Do an Internet search for "study tips", "work advice", "how to stay healthy", or "fun free time activities".
2. Read one of the articles that you find. While you read, make a list of words and phrases related to the topic.
3. Write sentences using these words and phrases. Then practice saying your sentences in a clear, confident voice. Writing and then saying the sentences will help you remember the words and phrases.

To practice key skills for Speaking Task 2 questions:

1. Spend a few minutes to make a list of pairs of opposite ideas. For example, your list might include things like summer and winter, or actions like working part-time and full-time.
2. Choose one pair of ideas from your list. Think of a reason and detailed supporting example why you like one of the items in the pair. Then think of a reason with supporting example why you dislike the opposite idea.
3. Use the template for Speaking Task 2 to give a 45-second response using the ideas you thought about in step 2. Record your speech. Then listen to the recording. If you are not satisfied for some reason, keep practicing until you feel satisfied.
4. Repeat steps 2 and 3 for the other pairs of opposite ideas on your list.

Unit Focus

In the speaking section of the TOEFL Test you will have six tasks. Speaking Task 3 is one of two integrated tasks about common campus situations that college students experience. You will first read a short passage about a situation at college. Then you will listen to two students discussing the same situation. After that you will be asked to summarize the opinion and supporting reasons of one of the students. In this unit you will learn and practice several key skills to answer Speaking Task 3 questions effectively, including:

- taking notes when you read a passage and listen to a conversation.
- using your preparation time effectively to organize your response.
- learning and using a template to deliver a clear, organized, effective response.
- speaking clearly and confidently, with natural pauses and emphasis.

The vocabulary focus is on campus words and phrases related to:

- places at college where students spend time.

A Warm-up

A1 Write a short response to questions 1–3. Use the example as a guide.

How would you feel if your college announced that
1. students could use the library 24 hours a day, seven days a week?
2. students would be charged $250 to pay for a new computer center?
3. students would no longer be allowed to use cell phones on campus?

Example   I would be unhappy if my college let students use the library 24 hours a day, seven days a week. The main reason is that I think my college would probably increase tuition fees to pay for it.

B Campus Vocabulary

B1 Use words from this conversation to complete sentences 1–8. One answer has been done for you.

Woman	Excuse me, I need to go to the International Student Office. I've got a map, but I'm new on campus and I'm not even sure where I am now.
Man	We're between the Student Center and the fitness center, which are, uh, these buildings on your map. See? So to get to the International Student Office, you'll need to go past the music auditorium, which is here on the map, and then the Health Services Center, here. OK?
Woman	Yeah, I see. And after that it looks like I just need to go a little bit farther past the dining hall and the Administrative Building. Thank you for the help.

1. The ___administrative building___ is where a student might go to collect administrative documents.
2. An _____ is a building where students can attend concerts or other events.
3. The _____ of a university is where all of the academic and administrative buildings are.
4. When students are hungry, they can eat at a _____, cafeteria, or restaurant.
5. A student who wants to work out could go for a run or go to the _____.
6. A doctor or nurse who works at a college probably sees patients at the _____.
7. If a student from another country has a problem, he or she should go to the _____.
8. A central place on campus where students can relax with friends is the _____.

C Analyzing Speaking Task 3

For Speaking Task 3 questions, you will first see a short reading passage on the screen and an announcer will briefly summarize the main idea of the passage. The passage, which may be an announcement, a newspaper article, or a letter, will discuss a new or changed situation at a college. The passage will include either reasons for or opinions about the new situation. You will usually have 45 or 50 seconds to read the passage, depending on its length.

After you read, the announcer will introduce a conversation in which a man and woman discuss the situation described in the passage. Both people will give their opinion, but one person – the main speaker – will give a longer opinion with more detailed reasons and supporting ideas. While you listen, take notes about the main speaker's opinion, reasons, and supporting examples.

After listening, you will see the question on the screen and the announcer will read it aloud. The question will look like this:

> The man expresses his opinion about _____. State his opinion and explain the reasons he gives for holding that opinion.

A second announcer will then tell you to begin preparing your response. You will have 30 seconds to prepare. The amount of preparation time remaining will be shown on the screen. After the preparation time, the second announcer will tell you to start speaking. You will have 60 seconds to speak. The amount of time remaining will be shown onscreen.

To answer a Speaking Task 3 question effectively and get a good score, your response should:
- use language well – you need to use grammar and vocabulary naturally and effectively with few mistakes.
- be delivered well – your speech should be clear and fluent, with good pronunciation and few long pauses.
- develop the topic well – you need to summarize the situation mentioned in the passage, state the main speaker's opinion, and summarize his or her supporting reasons.

Common problems when answering Speaking Task 3 questions that may reduce your score include:
- poor language use – frequent mistakes, or vocabulary and grammar that are unnatural.
- poor delivery – unclear pronunciation or intonation, frequent or long pauses, or lack of fluency.
- poor topic development – a response that does not clearly summarize the main speaker's point of view.

TEST TACTIC

Speaking Task 3 questions ask you to discuss only the main speaker's opinion and reasons. If you discuss other opinions, including *your* opinion, you will probably not have time to answer the question completely, which will reduce your score.

C1 Answer questions 1–4 by summarizing this passage and script. After you have summarized, say each answer clearly. One answer has been done for you.

The college is pleased to announce a series of free lectures to be held in the auditorium. The lectures will cover a range of non-academic topics, including politics, business, music, and art. There will be a lecture at 8 p.m. every Thursday in October.

Man	Great news about these new lectures in the auditorium, isn't it?
Woman	Really? They're not about academic subjects, so …
Man	Even though I'm not studying politics or business, I'm still interested, especially if I can learn about them for free. And I know *you're* interested in music and art. Plus, it's great the college is offering these events. Last year, a lot of people were unhappy because there were so few events on campus. If we go to these lectures, maybe the college will offer more events.
Woman	Hmmm. Good point. Maybe I'll go to one or two of them.

1. What does the college announce? _____ The college announces some free lectures. _____
2. How does the man feel about the announcement? _____
3. What is the first reason he gives for his feeling? _____
4. What is the second reason he gives? _____

D Mastering Speaking Task 3 – Reading the Passage

When you read the passage, you need to find and make a note of the main point of the passage plus any reasons, opinions, or details that support or explain the main point. If you have time, it can also be helpful to think about how students might react to the situation described in the passage.

D1 **These notes about the reading passage below mention the type of document, main idea, and supporting points. Underline the section(s) of the passage that match each point in the notes. One answer has been done for you.**

> student thinks procedure to start student clubs not good
> — should not have to be full-time student to start
> — should not have to find 50 members before start
> student wants college to change policy to start clubs

New Registration Procedure Needed for Student Clubs

I like chess so when I found there was no student chess club at the college, I wanted to start one. However, the procedure for registering student clubs makes that impossible. According to college policy, new clubs can only be founded by full-time students, and clubs will not be approved unless at least 50 students are interested in joining. I can see no reason why part-time students like me cannot start a club, and why must a club find potential members *before* it can be registered? I hope other students will join me in asking the college to reconsider its policy.

D2 **Work with a partner to predict how students might react to this passage. Use the examples as a guide. When you have finished, share your ideas with other students.**

Examples   I think students would support the writer because finding 50 interested students is too many.
Students might oppose the writer because part-time and full-time students should not have the same rights.

D3 **Complete tasks 1 and 2.**

1. Read these announcements and take notes. Use the sample notes in exercise **D1** as a guide.
2. Predict how students might react to the information in the announcements. When you have finished, discuss your predictions with a partner.

Improvements to Campus Exercise Facilities

The college is pleased to announce that the new fitness center in Murrow Hall is now complete and will be open starting March 1. The college now has state-of-the-art sporting facilities that are open 24 hours a day, seven days a week for use by academic staff, administrative staff, and students who have an athletic scholarship. Students without an athletic scholarship can either gain access to the new facilities by applying for a "Gym Access" card for just $50 per semester, or use existing exercise facilities at no charge.

New Bulletin Boards in Student Center

Last Monday students in the Student Center on campus were surprised to see that several new bulletin boards had been erected. At first the boards were empty, but within hours the first notices had been posted. When asked for comment, a college spokesperson said that the college hoped the bulletin boards would provide a central place for students to put up notices and advertisements. The spokesperson also said the bulletin boards would help make the campus look cleaner because notices posted elsewhere on campus would be taken down.

D4 Now use your notes and predictions from exercise **D3** to answer questions 1–6. Speak clearly and use full sentences when you answer.

1. What is the main situation described in the first passage?
2. What is the first supporting reason, opinion, or detail mentioned in the first passage?
3. What is the second supporting reason, opinion, or detail mentioned in the first passage?
4. What is the main situation described in the second passage?
5. What is the first supporting reason, opinion, or detail mentioned in the second passage?
6. What is the second supporting reason, opinion, or detail mentioned in the second passage?

E Mastering Speaking Task 3 – Listening to the Conversation

The conversation will typically last 60 to 80 seconds. While you are listening, take clear notes about both speakers' ideas, as well as the reasons and details they give. If you are confident you have recognized whether the main speaker is the man or woman, focus only on his or her words.

E1 Read these notes about a conversation in which two students discuss the letter about student clubs from exercise **D1**. Match each underlined abbreviation (short way to write something) to the full word, A–L. One answer has been done for you.

<u>M</u>	see letter about <u>stdnt</u> clubs?
<u>W</u>	saw it
M	agree <u>w/</u> stdnt = <u>cllg</u> should change policy
	cllg rule = <u>ft</u> + <u>pt</u> stdnts must be <u>eql</u>
	current club policy against cllg rules
W	not know rule
M	not make sense clubs need 50 stdnts <u>B4</u> registered
	clubs not cost cllg <u>$</u> so <u>#</u> members not matter
W	good point

A and _____
B before _____
C college _____
D (are) equal _____
E full-time _____
F man ____M____
G money _____
H number (of) _____
I part-time _____
J student _____
K with _____
L woman _____

TEST TACTIC

To recognize the main speaker, listen for the person who gives longer, more detailed explanations. If you find it hard to recognize the main speaker, take notes about both speakers and don't worry: the speaking prompt will say whether the main speaker was the man or woman.

Track 293 **E2** Take notes as you listen to two students discussing the letter about student clubs from exercise **D1**. Then complete tasks 1–3 with a partner.

1. Listen to the conversation to check your answers to exercise **E1**. Then compare answers.
2. What other words in the notes could be abbreviated? How would you abbreviate them?
3. What other abbreviations do you use when you take notes? Share your ideas with other students.

Track 294 **E3** Take notes as you listen to two students discussing the announcements from exercise **D3**. Then use your notes to write full sentences in answer to questions 1–4.

1. Who is the main speaker?
2. What is his or her opinion about the announcement?
3. What is the first reason the main speaker gives for his or her opinion?
4. What is the second reason that the main speaker gives?

Track 295 **E4** Take notes as you listen to two students discussing the newspaper article about bulletin boards in exercise **D3**. Then use your notes to answer questions 1–4. Speak clearly and use full sentences when you answer.

1. Who is the main speaker?
2. What is his or her opinion about the announcement?
3. What is the first reason the main speaker gives for his or her opinion?
4. What is the second reason that the main speaker gives?

F Mastering Speaking Task 3 – Preparing Your Response

Use your preparation time to circle and label the key points in the notes you made while reading the passage and listening to the conversation. This will help you deliver a well-organized response. If you have enough time, either add details to your notes from your memory or rehearse your speech.

F1 Label these notes by matching the correct label, D1–R2, with each circled point. One answer has been done for you.

student thinks procedure to start student clubs not good
– should not have to be full-time student to start
– should not have to find 50 members before start
(student wants college to change policy to start clubs)

M   see letter about <u>stdnt</u> want start chess club?
W   saw it
M   (agree w/ stdnt) = cllg should change policy
      (cllg rule = <u>ft</u> + <u>pt</u> stdnts must be eql)
      (current club policy against cllg rules)
W   not know rule
M   (not make sense clubs need 50 stdnts B4 registered)
      (clubs not cost cllg $ so # members not matter)
W   good point

D1 (supporting detail 1)
D2 (supporting detail 2)
MP (main point)
OP (main speaker's opinion)
R1 (main speaker's reason 1)
R2 (main speaker's reason 2)

F2 Circle the key points in your notes from exercises **E3** and **E4** and label them D1, D2, MP, OP, R1, and R2.

G Mastering Speaking Task 3 – Delivering Your Response

All Speaking Task 3 questions follow a similar pattern. This means that using a template – a well-organized model answer that includes natural language – will help you save time, avoid mistakes, and deliver an effective, high-quality response.

G1 This response to a Speaking Task 3 question uses a template. Which labeled key point from your notes follows each highlighted template phrase: D1, D2, MP, OP, R1, or R2? One answer has been done for you.

The man expresses his opinion of the arguments in the letter about college policy for registering a student club. State his opinion and the reasons he gives for holding that opinion.

The two people discuss 1. __MP__ a letter by a student about a changed policy for starting student clubs.

The man supports 2. _____ the student's viewpoint.

First, he states that 3. _____ the college has a rule that full-time and part-time students should be treated equally.

He then adds that 4. _____ the current policy about registering student clubs is against this rule.

Next, the man says that 5. _____ he doesn't understand why clubs need 50 potential members before being registered.

He goes on to say that 6. _____ clubs don't cost the college money, so the number of members doesn't matter.

Track 296 **G2** **Listen to a high-level student say this response and complete tasks 1–4.**

The two people discuss a letter by a student about changing the policy for starting student clubs. **The man supports** the student's viewpoint. **First, he states that** the college has a rule that full-time and part-time students should be treated equally. **He then adds that** the college's policy about registering student clubs is against this rule. **Next, the man says that** he doesn't think clubs need fifty potential members before they can be registered. **He goes on to say that** student clubs don't cost the college any money, so the number of members doesn't matter.

1. Mark the speaker's pauses on the response. Use / for a short pause and // for a longer pause.
2. Underline the words in the response that the speaker emphasizes (says strongly).
3. Note the pronunciation of difficult words. Practice saying these words until you are confident you can say them correctly.
4. Practice saying the response with a partner. Each time your partner speaks, give him or her useful feedback about pronunciation, pausing, and emphasis.

G3 **Complete tasks 1 and 2.**

1. Look at your notes from exercises **D3** and **E4** about the college fitness center. Use your notes to write a full response using the template. Two sentences have been written for you.
2. Practice saying your completed response until you can say it fluently and confidently in 60 seconds or less.

The man expresses his opinion of the announcement about the new fitness center. State his opinion and the reasons he gives for holding that opinion.

The two people discuss 1. _____ *an announcement about a new fitness center.* _____

The *man/woman supports/opposes* 2. _____ *the decision of the college.* _____

First, *he/she* points out that 3. _____

He/She then adds that 4. _____

Next, the *man/woman* says that 5. _____

He/She finishes by saying that 6. _____

G4 **Look at your notes from exercises D3 and E4 about the bulletin boards in the Student Center. Use your notes to prepare a spoken response to this question.**

The woman expresses her opinion about the addition of bulletin boards to the Student Center. State her opinion and the reasons she gives for holding that opinion.

G5 **Work with a partner to complete tasks 1–4.**

1. Listen to the response that your partner prepared in exercise **G4**. Take notes if you like.
2. After listening, put checks (✓) in the YES or NO columns of the table below. Then give your partner feedback.
3. Say the response you prepared and get your partner's feedback. Try to get perfect feedback – YES in every column.
4. Fix any mistakes in your response that your partner noticed. Then repeat tasks 1–4 with several different partners.

Did your partner	YES	NO
Clearly describe the main point of the reading passage?		
Clearly state the main speaker's opinion?		
Mention the main speaker's first reason with supporting details?		
Mention the main speaker's second reason with supporting details?		
Finish his or her response in less than 60 seconds?		
Use the template phrases accurately?		
Speak clearly, fluently, and confidently without long pauses?		

H Test Challenge

H1 Answer Speaking Task 3 questions 1–3. Take 45 seconds to read the passage. Then listen to the conversation. After listening, spend 30 seconds preparing your response and speak for no more than 60 seconds in order to get realistic practice for the test. Use the checklist of skills that you learned in this unit as a guide.

☑ Read the passage and take notes about the main idea plus supporting reasons and/or details.

☑ Listen to the conversation and note the main speaker's opinion and supporting reasons and ideas.

☑ Use the preparation time to circle and label key information in your notes.

☑ Use the template to make sure your response is well-organized and natural, and speak clearly and fluently.

1. State University is planning to upgrade its library facilities. Read an announcement from the university about this plan.

Announcement from the University President

State University has decided to upgrade the library facilities available on campus. Over the next year, a new library will be constructed that will have double the number of books available for borrowing compared with the current library, as well as state-of-the-art computer facilities. It will also have over 500 individual study rooms that will be available for student use. Because the cost of constructing the new library will be high, all full-time students will be charged a one-time Library Improvement Fee of $100.

🔊 Tracks 297–300 Now listen to two students as they discuss the announcement.

The man/woman expresses his/her opinion about the announcement. State his/her opinion and explain the reasons he/she gives for holding that opinion.

2. A student wrote a letter to City College's newspaper about a suggested improvement to the college. Read the letter.

New Food Options Needed on Campus

I've studied at City College for two years and basically it's a great place to study. However, there's one area that could really be improved, and that's the quality of food served at the restaurants and cafeterias available on campus. Currently, students only have access to dining halls serving fast food. They're cheap, but the food's unhealthy, low-quality, and almost every dish has meat. I think that a modern college should offer students healthier options like salad bars, vegetarian cafés, and juice bars. I'd also like to see the dining halls serving dishes from other countries.

🔊 Tracks 301–304 Now listen as two students discuss the letter.

The man/woman expresses his/her opinion about the suggestion in the letter. State his/her opinion and explain the reasons he/she gives for holding that opinion.

3. A university is changing the hours of operation at its Health Services Center. Read the notice about these changes.

Change to Hours of Operation at the Health Services Center

In response to rising costs and falling demand, the university has decided to slightly reduce the hours when the Health Services Center will operate. Instead of offering evening services on Mondays, Wednesdays, and Thursdays, evening services will now be offered on Fridays only. In addition, the Health Services Center will no longer be open on the weekend. These changes are effective immediately. Students who need medical assistance when the Health Services Center is closed have the choice of attending several clinics located in town, details of which are available at the Health Services Center.

 Now listen to two students as they discuss the notice.

The man/woman expresses his/her opinion about the decision stated in the notice. State his/her opinion and explain the reasons he/she gives for holding that opinion.

Next Steps

Speaking Task 3 questions often focus on places that students go to on campus. You may also hear vocabulary related to these places in Speaking Task 5 or during conversations in the listening section. As a result, learning words related to campus places, as well as practicing key skills for Speaking Task 3, may help you increase your overall test score.

To learn more about vocabulary related to campus locations:

1. Visit the website of a college and search for "campus map". Print out the map (or look at it on the screen if you prefer).
2. For each place on the campus map, make a list of people who might work there or go there.
3. Make a second list of what the people who work or go to that place would do when they are there.
4. Then think about possible changes to that place and how those changes might affect students positively or negatively. For example, if the place is a Computer Center, one possible change is that the computers would be upgraded. This would benefit students because upgraded computers work faster. Another change is the hours of operation might be reduced. This would be bad for students because the Computer Center might be closed when they needed to go there.

To practice key skills for Speaking Task 3 questions:

1. Listen to a radio broadcast in which people can phone in to give their opinion about a topic. (You can use the Internet to search for "phone-in radio shows" in your area or phone-in radio shows that you can listen to online.)
2. When somebody gives an opinion about a topic, listen and take notes on the person's opinion and reasons.
3. Spend 30 seconds reviewing your notes. Then give a spoken summary of the opinion and reasons that you heard. If you repeat this activity often, you should find your ability to answer Speaking Task 3 questions will improve.

Unit Focus

In the speaking section of the TOEFL Test you will have six tasks. Speaking Task 4 is one of two integrated tasks about academic content. You will first read a short passage about one aspect of an academic topic. Then you will listen to a professor discussing the same topic. After that you will be asked to explain how the professor's words relate to the reading. In this unit you will learn and practice several key skills to answer Speaking Task 4 questions effectively, including:

- taking notes when you read a passage and listen to a conversation.
- using your preparation time effectively to organize your response.
- learning and using a template to deliver clear, organized, effective responses.
- speaking clearly and confidently, with natural pronunciation and intonation.

The vocabulary focus is on academic words and phrases related to:

- psychology, the scientific study of how the human mind functions and how humans behave in different situations.

A Warm-up

A1 Read this short description of two types of motivation. Then complete tasks 1 and 2.

In psychology, extrinsic motivation describes external factors that make people act, such as peer pressure, parental pressure, or desire for money. An example would be a person learning how to use a computer in order to get a better job. Intrinsic motivation, on the other hand, is motivation that comes from within. So a person choosing to learn about computers because of an innate, or natural, interest in technology would be an example of intrinsic motivation.

1. Write about a time when you did something as a result of extrinsic motivation. Explain what you did and why you did it. Then write about a time when you did something because of intrinsic motivation. Again, say what you did and why.
2. Read your answers to the class. Then listen to other students' answers. What motivating factors are most common?

B Academic Vocabulary

B1 Write in the best answer, A–H, to complete definitions 1–8 of the highlighted words. Then compare answers with a partner. One answer has been done for you.

1. To analyze something, like why a person behaves in a certain way, is to examine it carefully in order to explain it .
2. Characteristics, also known as traits, are the recognizable _____
3. A conscious action is one that a person is deliberately doing; _____
4. A strong wish to do something, especially if that wish occurs _____
5. A person who plays an active part in an event, activity, or _____
6. The word perception is used to describe using one's senses, _____
7. A rational belief is one that is based on logic and clear thinking; _____
8. A person's values, or beliefs, are the emotional principles and _____

A an irrational one is based on emotions and feelings.
B an unconscious action is one that a person is unaware of.
C certain way, is to examine it carefully in order to explain it.
D experiment is called a participant.
E features of an individual's personality.
F standards that are very important to that person.
G such as the sense of sight, to understand something.
H suddenly, is called an impulse.

C Analyzing Speaking Task 4

For Speaking Task 4 questions, you will first see a reading passage on the screen and an announcer will mention its main topic. The passage often gives an overview of one aspect of an academic subject, such as defining an idea or introducing a topic. Depending on the length of the passage, you will have 45 or 50 seconds to read it and take notes.

Next, the announcer will introduce a lecture about the same topic. The person giving the lecture will typically give some specific examples that illustrate the general idea or situation mentioned in the passage. While you listen, take notes about the points, details, and examples that the speaker discusses.

After listening, you will see the question on the screen and hear the announcer say it. The question will be similar to one of these examples:

Using points and examples from the lecture, explain how _____ affects _____.

Using examples the speaker mentions, explain how _____ can cause _____.

Using examples from the talk, explain how _____ and _____ are related.

A second announcer will then tell you to begin preparing your response. You will have 30 seconds to prepare. The amount of preparation time remaining will be shown on the screen. After the preparation time, the second announcer will tell you to start speaking. You will have 60 seconds to speak. The amount of time remaining will be shown onscreen.

To answer a Speaking Task 4 question effectively and get a good score, your response should:
- use language well – you need to use grammar and vocabulary naturally and effectively with few mistakes.
- be delivered well – your speech should be clear and fluent, with good pronunciation and few long pauses.
- develop the topic well – you need to answer the question clearly and discuss details and examples from the lecture.

Common problems when answering Speaking Task 4 questions that are likely to reduce your score include:
- poor language use – frequent mistakes, or vocabulary and grammar that are unnatural.
- poor delivery – unclear pronunciation or intonation, frequent or long pauses, or lack of fluency.
- poor topic development – not talking about specific aspects of the topic, or not answering each part of the question.

TEST TACTIC

If you notice a word in the passage that is used frequently, think about its pronunciation and say it in your mind several times. This will help you hear and understand this word during the lecture. It will also help you say that word accurately and naturally during your response.

C1 Read this short passage and script. Then answer questions 1–4. Speak clearly and in full sentences when you answer.

Peer pressure is the name given to the influence that members of a social group or individuals can have on others. This influence may cause a person to act in certain ways or adopt certain values, even if those actions and values are not what that person would normally do or believe.

Professor   We tend to think of peer pressure as exerting a negative influence, and often it does, but sometimes it's positive. Let me give you an example. I read about a small town near the college where over 95% of household waste is recycled. Why? Well, apparently a few families began recycling more, which made their neighbors feel that they should recycle more, which caused other neighbors to recycle even more, until the whole town was recycling almost everything possible. Without the peer pressure exerted by their neighbors, it's likely that the residents of this town would recycle at a level closer to the national average of just 34% of household waste.

1. Does the reading passage give a general or specific description of peer pressure?
2. Does the professor talk about an example of positive or negative peer pressure?
3. According to the professor, how and why did people in the small town change their behavior?
4. According to the professor, how would people in the town probably act if they did not experience peer pressure?

D Mastering Speaking Task 4 – Reading the Passage

When reading the passage, you need to make a note of its main point. Typically, this is a definition or explanation of an academic principle or theory. You also need to take notes on any specific details that add information about the main point. Remember to leave room on your note paper so you can take notes from the lecture, too.

D1 Read this passage from a typical Speaking Task 4 question. Then answer questions 1 and 2.

Confirmation Bias

When people are presented with a theory, argument, or opinion that is in line with their own views, they are more likely to read or listen to it, accept it as true, and remember it. Conversely, people typically ignore, reject, or forget theories, arguments, or opinions that they personally oppose. These tendencies, known as confirmation bias, are stronger for emotional issues and for beliefs that people hold deeply. Confirmation bias can cause people to make poor decisions if they ignore, reject, or forget evidence that their opinion is not the best one.

---

1. Which summary, A–C, of the main point of the passage is too general, which one is too detailed, and which one is good?

    A Confirmation bias (CB) = people accept ideas or arguments they read or hear when they match something they already believe but ignore ideas, theories, and so on they do not personally believe
    B Confirmation bias (CB) = people easily accept opinions they believe but reject ones they don't
    C Confirmation bias (CB) = people usually accept some opinions but not others

2. Which of these notes, A–E, about the passage are useful? Check (✓) the correct box. Then compare your answers with a partner and discuss why each note is either useful or not useful.

A People can read or listen to theories, arguments, and opinions	☐ Useful	☐ Not useful
B CB stronger about emotional topics	☐ Useful	☐ Not useful
C CB stronger about issues people believe strongly	☐ Useful	☐ Not useful
D People with CB can make poor decisions because of CB	☐ Useful	☐ Not useful
E People may ignore, reject, or forget opinions and evidence	☐ Useful	☐ Not useful

D2 Take notes about the main points and supporting details of these two passages from Speaking Task 4 questions. When you have finished, compare notes with a partner.

The NIMBY Principle

In principle, people tend to support development projects, such as the construction of a railway line, which they feel would benefit their community. However, if the development will affect them directly because it will occur close to where they live, they often oppose it. This is known as the NIMBY principle, with "NIMBY" standing for "not in my back yard." Construction projects likely to be opposed as a result of the NIMBY principle are factories or other industrial buildings, power stations, prisons, airports, and even projects that seem positive like schools or hospitals.

Social Psychology

Broadly speaking, the focus of social psychology is the study of how and under what conditions human thoughts, drives, beliefs, and behaviors are affected by other people. Social pyschologists also focus on related ideas such as the ways in which human perception and interaction are influenced by other people and by society. Social psychology theories are based on empirical, experimental data and cover a broad range of topics including individual and group behavior, and both positive and negative aspects of social behavior including leadership, conformity, and prejudice.

E Mastering Speaking Task 4 – Listening to the Lecture

In the lecture, which usually lasts from 75 to 90 seconds but may be longer, the speaker usually gives specific examples of the idea described in the reading passage, or explains how the idea applies to specific situations. While listening, take well-organized notes about the speaker's points on the same piece of paper as your notes about the reading passage.

E1 Read this short passage about taking notes for Speaking Task 4 questions. Then discuss questions 1–3 with a partner.

TEST TACTIC

Before listening, think of an abbreviation for the main point of the passage. For example, you might use *CB* if the main point is confirmation bias, or *PP* for peer pressure. When you listen, write this abbreviation when the lecturer makes a point that directly relates to the reading.

Effective Note-taking for Speaking Task 4 Questions

- You will not have time to write down every word you hear, so focus on writing only key words.
- If you can recognize how an idea is related to the main point of the reading passage, mention it in your notes.
- Use abbreviations – short ways to write words, like + for *and* or *bc* for *because* – to save time.
- Use arrows to show how two points are related to each other, such as to show that one thing caused another thing.
- Indent (leave space at the left edge) notes that are related to a note above them so the connection is easy to see later.

1. Which of the suggestions about note-taking from the passage do you already do?
2. Which *two* of the suggestions do you think are the most useful? Why?
3. Are these suggestions useful for other TOEFL questions, not just Speaking Task 4? Why or why not?

E2 Look at these reading and listening notes from part of a Speaking Task 4 lecture. Then complete tasks 1 and 2 with a partner.

READING	LISTENING
confirmation bias (CB) = people accept opinions they believe but reject ones they don't	prof + wife discuss vacation plans
	wife suggest go NYC but prof not want NYC
CB stronger about emotional topics	bc ngtv opin
CB stronger about issues people believe strongly	→ emotional experience as child
People with CB make poor decisions due to it	wife showed brochures + told recommendations
	prof reject pstv points + focus on ngtv = CB

1. The listening notes contain eight different abbreviations. Circle each abbreviation and write the full word.
2. The notes contain some unabbreviated long words like *emotional, experience, brochures,* and *recommendations.* How could you abbreviate these words?

🔊 Track 309–310 **E3** **Listen to the lecture that the notes in exercise E2 are about and complete tasks 1 and 2.**

1. Read the listening notes as you listen to part one of the lecture. Listen carefully for the full form of each abbreviation.
2. Complete the notes as you listen to part two of the lecture.

🔊 Track 311 **E4** **Look at your notes from the passage about the NIMBY principle in exercise D2. Then listen to a lecture on the same topic and take notes on the same piece of paper. Then use your notes to complete tasks 1 and 2.**

1. Did you use abbreviations when you took notes? Why or why not?
2. Overall, were you satisfied with the notes you took? Why or why not?

🔊 Track 312 **E5** **Look at your notes from the passage about social psychology in exercise D2. Then listen to a lecture on the same topic and take notes on the same piece of paper.**

F Mastering Speaking Task 4 – Preparing Your Response

Unlike questions for Speaking Task 3 and Speaking Task 5, questions for Speaking Task 4 do not follow a standard pattern. For this reason, you need to analyze the question carefully in order to understand what you need to say and how best to organize your response. After reading the question, use the remaining time to circle and label key points in your notes.

F1 **Write a description for how to answer Speaking Task 4 questions 1–3. Use the example as a guide.**

Using points and examples from the lecture, explain how confirmation bias affects the decisions people make.

Example   To answer this question, I would need to:
• Use information from the lecture in my response.
• Explain how confirmation bias influences people's decisions.

1. Using examples from the lecture, explain how confirmation bias affects people's behavior and how people can overcome this bias.
2. Using points and examples from the talk, explain how intrinsic and extrinsic motivation differ.
3. Using the example of recycling from the talk, explain what peer pressure is and how it affects people's behavior.

F2 **The key points in this Speaking Task 4 response have been underlined and labeled KP1–KP8 (KP stands for "key point"). Work with a partner to circle and label the notes below that match each key point. One answer has been done for you.**

Using points and examples from the lecture, explain how confirmation bias affects the decisions people make.

The reading introduces the concept of <u>confirmation bias</u>.[KP1] In summary, this is when <u>people prefer information that matches their opinions</u> [KP2] and <u>make bad decisions because of this preference</u>.[KP3] The professor gives <u>a personal example</u> [KP4] of this concept. First, he says that <u>his wife wanted a vacation in New York, but he did not want to go there because of a negative experience in New York when he was a child</u>.[KP5] Next, he mentions that <u>he rejected information about New York that did not match his negative opinion of that city</u>.[KP6] Finally, he states that <u>he and his wife vacationed in Miami instead of New York, but this was a bad decision</u>.[KP7] This example shows how <u>confirmation bias affected the professor's decision</u>.[KP8]

```
READING
       KP1
(confirmation bias) (CB) = people accept opinions they
        believe but reject ones they don't
CB stronger about emotional topics
CB stronger about issues people believe strongly
People with CB make poor decisions due to it
```

```
LISTENING
prof + wife discuss vacation plans
        wife suggest go NYC but prof not want NYC bc ngtv opin
        → emotional experience as child
wife showed brochures + told recommendations
prof reject pstv points + focus on ngtv points = CB
couple go Miami not NYC → bad experience
too hot + storm →  stay in hotel
```

F3 Analyze Speaking Task 4 questions 1 and 2 to understand what you need to do and how to organize your answers. Then circle and label key points in the notes you made about the NIMBY principle and social psychology from exercises **E4** and **E5**.

1. Explain how the examples that are mentioned by the professor demonstrate the NIMBY principle.
2. The speaker describes an experiment by Solomon Asch. Explain why this is a typical social psychology experiment.

G Mastering Speaking Task 4 – Delivering Your Response

Using a template – a well-organized model answer that includes natural language – will help you save time and deliver an effective, high-quality response for Speaking Task 4 questions. The Task 4 template has to be more flexible than for some other speaking questions, however, because Speaking Task 4 questions do not follow a standard pattern.

G1 Choose the function, A–E, that matches each highlighted template phrase in this response. Note that one function matches three phrases. One answer has been done for you.

The reading introduces the concept of ...   1.   _____introduce the main point from the reading passage._____

In summary, this is ...   2. _____

The professor gives a personal example of this concept.   3. _____

First, he says that ...   4. _____

Next, he mentions that ...   5. _____

Finally, he states that ...   6. _____

This example shows how ...   7. _____

A   Summarize the main point from the reading passage.
B   Summarize a point from the lecture that answers the question.
C   Give a very general overview of the focus of the lecture.
D   Introduce the main point from the reading passage.
E   Summarize how the example from the lecture answers the question.

🔊 Track 313 **G2** **Complete tasks 1 and 2.**

1. Listen to a high-level student say the full response from exercise **F2** sentence by sentence. Repeat each sentence after you hear it. Try to match the speaker's intonation, rhythm, and pronunciation. Keep practicing until you can say the response confidently and fluently.
2. Work with a partner to practice saying the full response from exercise **F2**. Each time your partner speaks, give him or her useful feedback about intonation, rhythm, and pronunciation.

G3 **Work with a different partner to answer questions 1–5.**

1. How would you change the template phrases in exercise **G1** if the professor were a woman?
2. How would you change the first template phrase if the reading passage defined an idea?
3. How would you change the third template phrase if the speaker gave a non-personal example?
4. How would you change the third and last template phrases if the speaker gave two examples?
5. What would you do if the speaker mentioned two points or four points instead of three?

G4 **Write a full response to this Speaking Task 4 question. Use the notes you made and labeled in exercise F3. Then practice saying your completed response until you can say it fluently and confidently in 60 seconds or less.**

Explain how the examples that are mentioned by the professor demonstrate the NIMBY principle.

The reading introduces the concept of _____

In summary, this is _____

The professor gives a personal example of this concept. _____

First, she says that _____

Next, she mentions that _____

Finally, she states that _____

This example shows how _____

G5 **Prepare a full response to this Speaking Task 4 question. Use the template and the notes you made and labeled in F3.**

The speaker describes an experiment by Solomon Asch. Explain why this is a typical social psychology experiment.

G6 **Work with a partner to complete tasks 1–4.**

1. Listen to the response that your partner prepared in exercise **G5**. Take notes, if you like.
2. After listening, put checks (✓) in the YES or NO columns of the table below. Then give your partner feedback.
3. Say your response from exercise **G5** and get your partner's feedback. Try to get perfect feedback – YES in every column.
4. Fix any mistakes in your response that your partner noticed. Then repeat tasks 1–3 with several different partners.

Did your partner	YES	NO
Clearly introduce and summarize the main point of the reading passage?		
Give a general overview of the focus of the lecture?		
Summarize points from the talk that answer the question?		
State explicitly how information from the talk answers the question?		
Finish his or her response in less than 60 seconds?		
Use the template phrases accurately?		
Speak clearly, fluently, and confidently without long pauses?		

H Test Challenge

H1 Answer Speaking Task 4 questions 1–3. Take 45 seconds to read the passage. Then listen to the lecture. After listening, spend 30 seconds preparing your response and then speak for no more than 60 seconds in order to get realistic practice for the test. Use this checklist of skills that you learned in this unit as a guide.

> ☑ Read the passage and take notes about the main point plus supporting reasons and/or details.
>
> ☑ Listen to the talk and make a note of the points that the speaker makes, especially if they relate to the passage.
>
> ☑ Use the preparation time to analyze the question and then circle and label key points in your notes.
>
> ☑ Speak clearly and fluently, and use the template to make sure your response is well-organized.

1. Now read the passage about sunk-cost bias. You have 45 seconds to read the passage. Begin reading now.

This book uses a beep to indicate your speaking time is up. Remember that you will not hear this beep in the real test.

Sunk-cost Bias

Past investments of time or money that cannot be recovered are known as sunk costs. People tend to think about sunk costs when making decisions, but this can lead to poor decisions because of so-called sunk-cost bias. A person who has already invested time or money in a project, for example, may decide to continue investing so as not to waste the initial, non-recoverable investment. This is fine when continued investment is likely to be beneficial, but in cases where continued investment is a bad risk, the rational decision would be to stop investing.

🔊 Tracks 314–317 Now listen to a lecture on this topic in a business studies class.

Using points and examples from the talk, explain how sunk-cost bias can cause people to make irrational decisions.

2. Now read the passage about defense mechanisms. You have 45 seconds to read the passage. Begin reading now.

Defense Mechanisms

Sigmund Freud, often known as the father of psychoanalysis, developed the theory of defense mechanisms. These are psychological strategies that allow people to function normally by protecting them from situations and events that could cause emotional distress and anxiety. Defense mechanisms may also protect people against inappropriate impulses. Typically, defensive strategies are unconscious – the brain adopts them automatically rather than as a result of conscious thought – but in some cases people will consciously choose to use one or more strategies

---

🔊 **Tracks 319–321** Now listen to part of a lecture on this topic in a psychology class.

Using details from the talk, explain why denial and rationalization are examples of defense mechanisms.

3. Now read the passage about the halo effect. You have 45 seconds to read the passage. Begin reading now.

The Halo Effect

If one characteristic of an individual, such as his physical appearance or behavior, is viewed positively, people are very likely to assume – without any evidence – that the same individual has other positive characteristics, such as kindness or intelligence. The reverse holds true as well: individuals with one less desirable trait are often seen as having other negative characteristics, again despite there being no evidence for that. This cognitive bias is called the halo effect, and it applies not just to individuals, but to organizations, countries, and products, too.

🔊 **Tracks 322–325** Now listen to a lecture on the same topic in a marketing class.

Using points and examples from the talk, explain how companies try to take advantage of the halo effect.

Next Steps

Speaking Task 4 and Task 6 questions are often about some aspect of psychology. This topic is also very common in the reading and listening sections of the TOEFL Test. As a result, learning words related to psychology, as well as practicing key skills for Speaking Task 4, may help you increase your overall test score.

To learn more vocabulary related to psychology:

1. Search the Internet for an online dictionary of psychological terms. (Search for "psychology dictionary" or similar.)
2. Read the definitions to find one that describes something you would like to learn more about.
3. Search the Internet for a longer article about the definition that sounds interesting. As you read the article, make a list of words related to psychology that are important for understanding the article.
4. Repeat steps 1–3 a few times each week. (When you are satisfied that your knowledge of psychology vocabulary has improved, try searching for an online dictionary about a different academic subject and then repeat the steps.)

To practice key skills for Speaking Task 4 questions:

1. Listen to one of the lectures from the listening section of this book that you have already studied. Take notes as you listen. Pause the audio after about 90 seconds.
2. Quickly look at your notes and number the points you want to summarize in the order you will say them.
3. Give a speech in which you summarize what the speakers said. Use phrases from steps 3–6 of the Speaking Task 4 template in your summary.
4. Repeat steps 1–3 for the next 90 seconds of the lecture. Then repeat again for the rest of the lecture.

Unit Focus

In the speaking section of the TOEFL Test you will have six tasks. Speaking Task 5 is one of two integrated tasks about common campus situations that college students experience. You will first listen to a conversation between two people. They will discuss a minor problem that one or both of them are having as well as possible solutions to the problem. Then you will be asked to summarize the problem and say which of the possible solutions you think is better and why. In this unit you will learn and practice several key skills to answer Speaking Task 5 questions effectively, including:

- taking clear, effective notes when you listen to a conversation.
- using your preparation time effectively to organize your response well.
- learning and using model phrases to deliver a clear, natural response.
- speaking clearly and confidently, with natural pronunciation and intonation.

The vocabulary focus is on campus words and phrases related to:

- important events, times, and periods during a typical academic year.

A Warm-up

A1 What would you do if you had problems 1–4? Write one solution for each problem. Use the example as a guide. When you have finished, compare answers with other students.

1. I find it hard to study because my roommate listens to loud music all the time.
2. I make a lot of mistakes in English when I write an essay or speak to my professors.
3. I eat too much unhealthy food because there are only fast-food restaurants on campus.
4. I live a long way from campus and it takes me more than one hour each day to get to class by bus.

Example   I would ask my roommate to play music less often and more quietly.

B Campus Vocabulary

B1 Match one of the definitions, A–H, to each phrase, 1–8. One answer has been done for you.

1. career fair	A a ceremony at which students receive a degree for successfully completing their studies
2. field trip	B a period of 15–18 weeks (one half of an academic year) during which students attend college
3. graduation	C an academic period when students can choose to take classes instead of taking a long vacation
4. midterm	D a trip made by students or researchers in order to get firsthand knowledge about a place
5. semester	E a vacation from college that typically lasts one week when some students go away with friends
6. spring break	F an event at which new students can learn important information about life at college
7. student orientation	G an event at which students can meet prospective employers and learn about job opportunities
8. summer session	H an exam that takes place approximately halfway through an academic semester or term

C Analyzing Speaking Task 5

For Speaking Task 5 questions, you will first hear a conversation between two people – either two students or a student and a university employee such as a tutor, professor, or administrator. The people will first talk about a problem that one or both of them are having. Then they will discuss two possible solutions to the problem. While you listen, takes notes about the problem and the two solutions. The conversation is usually between 60 and 90 seconds in length.

After listening, you will see the question on the screen and an announcer will read it aloud. The question will look like this:

> The students discuss two possible solutions to their problem. Describe the problem. Then state which of the two solutions you prefer and explain why.

A second announcer will then tell you to begin preparing your response. You will have 20 seconds to prepare. The amount of preparation time remaining will be shown onscreen. After the preparation time, the second announcer will tell you to begin speaking. You will have 60 seconds to deliver your response. The amount of time remaining will be shown onscreen.

To answer a Speaking Task 5 question effectively and get a good score, your response should:
- use language well – you need to use grammar and vocabulary naturally and effectively with few mistakes.
- be delivered well – your speech should be clear and fluent, with good pronunciation and few long pauses.
- develop the topic well – you need to summarize the problem and both state and explain the solution you prefer.

Common problems when answering Speaking Task 5 questions that may reduce your score include:
- poor language use – frequent mistakes, or vocabulary and grammar that are unnatural.
- poor delivery – unclear pronunciation or intonation, frequent or long pauses, or lack of fluency.
- poor topic development – not summarizing the problem or not explaining the reasons for your preferred solution.

C1 Use information from this script of a conversation from Speaking Task 5 to write full sentences in answer to questions 1–5 below. One sentence has been written for you.

Woman	Hi, James. Everything OK?
Man	Oh, hi, Maria. I've got a midterm on Friday, and I agreed to join a review session with a couple of classmates on Thursday. But I've just learned that one of my professors has organized a field trip on the same day.
Woman	So you're not sure whether to go on the field trip or join the study session?
Man	Right. I considered asking my friends to do a study session on Wednesday not Thursday, but I know they'd both need to miss classes in order to do that.
Woman	Well, there'll be other field trips later in the year, won't there? You could join the study session this time and go on the next field trip.
Man	Hmm... it's worth thinking about, but this field trip is to a place I'd really like to visit. It's really unlikely my professor will arrange another field trip to the same place.

1. What is the problem?   <u>The man's problem is that a study session and field trip are at the same time.</u>
2. Which option should he take?   <u>In my view, he should</u>
3. Why should he do this?   <u>The main reason is that</u>
4. Which option should he reject? <u>In contrast, I don't think he should</u>
5. Why should he reject it?   <u>This is because</u>

C2 Practice saying your sentences from exercise **C1**. Keep practicing until you can say them fluently and confidently.

D Mastering Speaking Task 5 – Listening to the Conversation

The conversation will typically last between 60 and 90 seconds. First, the speakers will describe a problem. Then they will discuss two suggestions for how to solve the problem. While you listen, take well-organized notes on the problem, the suggestions for solving the problem, and any positive or negative comments a speaker makes about each suggestion.

◁)) Tracks 326–329 **D1** **Take notes as you listen to four conversations from Speaking Task 5 questions. Then use your notes to complete this table. One answer has been done for you.**

	Who has the problem?	What is the problem?
Conversation 1	☐ Man ☑ Woman ☐ Both	She wants to go away with friends but has to do some schoolwork
Conversation 2	☐ Man ☐ Woman ☐ Both	
Conversation 3	☐ Man ☐ Woman ☐ Both	
Conversation 4	☐ Man ☐ Woman ☐ Both	

◁)) Tracks 326–329 **D2** **Listen again to the conversations from exercise D1 and take notes. Then answer questions 1 and 2.**

1. Indicate in which conversation a speaker uses each expression to introduce a suggestion. Place a check (✔) in the correct box. One answer has been done for you.

	Conversation 1	Conversation 2	Conversation 3	Conversation 4
Have you thought about				
Maybe we could				
What I would do is				
Why don't you	✓			

2. Indicate in which conversation a speaker makes each suggestion. Place a check (✔) in the correct box. One answer has been done for you.

	Conversation 1	Conversation 2	Conversation 3	Conversation 4
Do her assignments and then take a break	✓			
Find out dates and times for other orientations				
Try to start the internship later				
Visit the Housing Office				

TEST TACTIC

Good responses usually describe the problem in detail. When you listen, take as many notes as you can about the problem so you can describe it well. For example, saying "the woman has an interview and study session scheduled for 3 p.m." is better than "the woman has a schedule problem."

◁)) Track 330 **D3** **Listen to a conversation from a Speaking Task 5 question and fill in the missing details in these notes.**

```
W   prof asked two people help at conf on Mon + Tue
    [1.                    ] per day → want to?
M   cannot → already volun at [2.              ] orientation
W   volun just one day + conf other day?
M   other people [3.                  ] → not want to do same
W   ask orientation organizer for payment?
M   organizer complains about small event [4.                ]
```

D4 Use the notes from exercise **D3** to answer questions 1–6. When you have finished, compare answers with a partner.

1. What is the problem and who has it?
2. What is the first suggestion the woman makes?
3. What does the man say about this suggestion?
4. What is the woman's second suggestion?
5. What does the man say about this suggestion?
6. The word "professor" is abbreviated to "prof." What other words are abbreviated in the notes?

Tracks 331–332 **D5** Listen to two more Speaking Task 5 conversations. Take notes as you listen. Use the notes in exercise **D3** as a guide.

E Mastering Speaking Task 5 – Preparing Your Response

Use your 20 seconds of preparation time first to circle and label up to five key points in your notes: the problem, the two suggestions, and any reaction that a speaker has about either suggestion. Then decide which of the two suggestions you will choose to be the preferred suggestion you discuss in your response.

E1 Label the five circled key points in these notes with one label from A–E. One answer has been done for you.

```
W   prof asked two people help at conf on Mon + Tue
         $100 per day → want to?                          prob   The problem the speakers discuss
M   cannot → already volun at student orientation         S1     The first suggestion by a speaker
W   volun just one day + conf other day?                  S2     The second suggestion by a speaker
M   other people drop out → not want to do same           R1     Reaction about the first suggestion
W   ask orientation organizer for payment?                R2     Reaction about the second suggestion
M   organizer complains about small event budget
```

Track 333 **E2** Take notes as you listen to a man and woman talking. Then match suggestions 1–4 to the person who makes them. One answer has been done for you.

1. If one suggestion is on a familiar topic you have talked about before, choose that suggestion.
   ☑ Man   ☐ Woman
2. If you have better notes about one suggestion than the other, choose that suggestion.
   ☐ Man   ☐ Woman
3. If you do not understand one suggestion well, choose the other suggestion.
   ☐ Man   ☐ Woman
4. If it might take a long time to talk about one suggestion, choose the other suggestion.
   ☐ Man   ☐ Woman

E3 Complete tasks 1 and 2.

1. Look at the notes from exercise **E1**. Choose one of the two suggestions as your preferred suggestion. Label your preferred suggestion either "S1+" or "S2+."
2. Tell a partner why you would choose this suggestion as your preferred suggestion.

E4 Complete tasks 1–5.

1. Look at the first set of notes you made in exercise **D5**. Circle five key points in those notes.
2. Label the key points *prob, S1, S2, R1,* and *R2,* for problem, suggestion 1, and so on.
3. Decide which one of the two suggestions is your preferred suggestion. Label it *S1+* or *S2+.*
4. Tell a partner why you would choose this suggestion as your preferred suggestion.
5. Repeat tasks 1–4 about the second set of notes you made in exercise **D5**.

E5 Work with a partner to think of *both* a positive and a negative reason for each solution for problems 1 and 2. When you have finished, share your ideas with other students. One answer has been done for you.

If neither speaker gives a reaction to one of the suggestions or if your notes about the speakers' reactions are not clear, it may be helpful to think of your own reasons why a suggestion is a good idea or a bad idea. You can then use your reasons instead of the speakers' reasons in your response.

Problem 1	A student needs a full-time summer job to make money but also needs to attend summer session.
Solution 1	Get a part-time job instead of a full-time job • Positive – She can make some money and still study • Negative – She might not make enough money
Solution 2	Get a full-time job and take evening classes during the summer • •

Problem 2	A student wants to attend a career fair, but doesn't have time to type up an updated resume.
Solution 1	Go to the career fair with an out-of-date resume and mention his latest experience in person • •
Solution 2	Type up an updated resume quickly on the morning of the career fair and go to the fair late • •

F Mastering Speaking Task 5 – Delivering Your Response

All Speaking Task 5 questions follow a similar pattern. This means that using a template – a well-organized model answer that includes natural language – will help you save time, avoid mistakes, and deliver an effective, high-quality response.

F1 Choose the best answer from A–E to complete this partial response to a Speaking Task 5 question. The template phrases in the response are highlighted. One answer has been done for you.

The speakers discuss two possible solutions to the man's problem. Describe his problem. Then state which of the two solutions you prefer and why.

The man has a problem because 1. _____

The speakers discuss a couple of possible solutions to this problem.

In my view, the man should 2. _____

The main reason is that 3. _____

In contrast, I don't think he should 4. _____ drop out as a volunteer (S1) _____

This is because 5. _____

A   drop out as a volunteer. (S1)
B   even though the event budget is small, he might get some money. (R2)
C   he volunteered at an orientation so he cannot work at a conference. (prob)
D   other people have dropped out and the man does not want to do the same thing. (R1)
E   speak to the organizer of the student orientation and try to get paid for his time. (S2+)

TEST TACTIC

It does not matter which suggestion or reason you choose to talk about because there is no right or wrong answer. Choosing the suggestion and reason that you find easier to talk about will help you give a better response.

Track 334 **F2** **Listen several times to a high-level student say this response. As you listen, complete tasks 1–4.**

The man has a problem because he volunteered at an orientation so he cannot work at a conference. The speakers discuss a couple of possible solutions to this problem. In my view, the man should speak to the organizer of the student orientation and try to get paid for his time. The main reason is that even though the event budget is small, he might get some money. In contrast, I don't think he should drop out as a volunteer. This is because other people have dropped out and the man does not want to do the same thing.

1. Mark the speaker's pauses on the response. Use / for a short pause and // for a longer pause.
2. Underline the words in the response that the speaker emphasizes (says strongly).
3. Note the pronunciation of difficult words. Practice saying these words until you are confident you can say them correctly.
4. Practice saying the response with a partner. Each time your partner speaks, give him or her useful feedback about pronunciation, pausing, and emphasis.

F3 **Work with a partner to complete tasks 1 and 2.**

1. Rewrite the response from exercise **F2** using the other suggestion as the preferred suggestion. One sentence has been written for you.

The man has a problem because _____

The speakers discuss a couple of possible solutions to this problem.

In my view, the man should _____ drop out as a volunteer. _____

The main reason is that _____

In contrast, I don't think he should _____

This is because _____

2. Say the new response to your partner. Give each other useful feedback about pronunciation, pausing, and emphasis.

F4 **Complete tasks 1–3.**

1. Use your notes from conversation 1 of exercise **D4** to write a full response to the question below. One sentence has been written for you.
2. Practice saying your completed response until you can say it fluently and confidently in 60 seconds.
3. Say your response to a partner and listen to his or her feedback. Then listen to his or her response and give feedback.

The speakers discuss two possible solutions to the man's problem. Describe his problem. Then state which of the two solutions you prefer and why.

The man has a problem because _____ he cannot focus on studying for his midterm exams. _____

The speakers discuss a couple of possible solutions to this problem.

In my view, the man should _____

The main reason is that _____

In contrast, I don't think he should _____

This is because _____

F5 Use your notes from conversation 2 of exercise **D5** to write a full response to this question. One sentence has been written for you.

The speakers discuss two possible solutions to a problem the woman has. Describe the problem. Then state which of the two solutions you think she should adopt. Explain why.

The woman has a problem because <u>she has made plans and cannot go on a field trip that interests her.</u>

The speakers discuss a couple of possible solutions to this problem.

In my view, the woman should _____

The main reason is that _____

In contrast, I don't think she should _____

This is because _____

F6 Work with a partner to complete tasks 1–4.

1. Listen to the response that your partner prepared in exercise **F5**. Take notes, if you like.
2. After listening, put checks (✓) in the YES or NO columns of the table below. Then give your partner feedback.
3. Say your response from exercise **F5** and get your partner's feedback. Try to get perfect feedback – YES in every column.
4. Fix any mistakes in your response that your partner noticed. Then repeat tasks 1–3 with several different partners.

TEST TACTIC

When you are speaking, keep an eye on how much time is left. If you are almost out of time, you can cut the final part of the template (or even the final two parts) and still get a reasonably good score.

Did your partner	YES	NO
Clearly and correctly state who has the problem?		
Clearly and correctly describe the problem?		
Explain which suggestion he or she prefers and why?		
Explain which suggestion he or she does not prefer and why?		
Finish his or her response in less than 60 seconds?		
Use the template phrases accurately?		

G Test Challenge

G1 Answer Speaking Task 5 questions 1–3. After listening, spend 20 seconds preparing your response and speak for up to 60 seconds in order to get realistic practice for the test. Use the checklist of skills that you learned in this unit as a guide.

☑ Listen to the conversation and take notes on the problem, the suggestions, and comments about the suggestions.

☑ Use the preparation time to decide which suggestion you prefer and to circle and label key information in your notes.

☑ Speak clearly and fluently, and use the template to make sure your response is well organized and natural.

🔊 Tracks 335–338 1. Listen to a conversation between two students.

This book uses a beep to indicate your speaking time is up. Remember that you will not hear this beep in the real test.

The speakers discuss two possible solutions to a problem. Describe the problem. Then state which of the two solutions you prefer and why.

Tracks 339–342 2. Listen to a conversation between a man and a woman.

The speakers discuss two possible solutions to a problem. Describe the problem. Then state which of the two solutions you prefer and why.

Tracks 343–346 3. Listen to a conversation between a student and a professor.

The speakers discuss two possible solutions to a problem. Describe the problem. Then state which of the two solutions you prefer and why.

Next Steps

Speaking Task 5 questions often deal with important events and times during the academic year. You may also hear vocabulary related to this topic in Speaking Task 3 and during conversations in the listening section. As a result, learning words related to this topic, as well as practicing key skills for Speaking Task 5, may help you increase your overall test score.

To learn more vocabulary related to important events, times, and periods during a typical academic year:

1. Visit the website of a university or college that you are interested in attending or that you know about.
2. Use the search feature of that website to find articles that include some of the campus vocabulary from exercise **B1** on page 208 of this unit.
3. Read the articles and see how the words from **B1** are used. Then find other words in the article that are related to important events and times during the academic year. Study these words in order to understand their meaning and usage.

To practice key skills for Speaking Task 5 questions:

1. Search the Internet for "problems students have at university" or "common problems for college students".
2. Read one of the articles you find and take notes about the problems and two possible solutions to each problem. (If you cannot find two solutions in the article, think of possible solutions yourself.)
3. Imagine a person is having a problem that you researched in step 2. Use the template for Speaking Task 5 to make a speech that describes the problem, explains your preferred solution, and explains why another solution is not as good.
4. Repeat steps 1–3 often so that you become confident talking about problems using the template for Speaking Task 5.

Unit Focus

In the speaking section of the TOEFL Test you will have six tasks. Speaking Task 6 is one of two integrated tasks about academic content. You will first hear a short lecture about one aspect of an academic topic. Then you will be asked to summarize the key ideas from the lecture. In this unit you will learn and practice several key skills to answer Speaking Task 6 questions effectively, including:

- taking clear, effective notes when you listen to an academic lecture.
- using your preparation time effectively to organize your response well.
- learning and using model phrases to deliver a clear, natural response.
- speaking clearly and confidently, with natural pronunciation and intonation.

The vocabulary focus is on academic words and phrases related to:

- business studies, including the study of economics, finance, management, and marketing.

A Warm-up

◁)) Track 347 **A1** **Listen to parts of several academic lectures and take notes. Then use your notes to complete statements 1–5. You can either paraphrase or repeat each speaker's words. One answer has been done for you.**

Macroeconomics is concerned with 1. _____ the performance of the whole economy. _____

Microeconomics, on the other hand, focuses on 2. _____

_____

Loss leaders are 3. _____

Direct marketing involves 4. _____

A sole proprietorship is a business 5. _____

B Academic Vocabulary

B1 **Which answer, A–H, matches each highlighted word in sentences 1–4? Compare answers with a partner when you have finished. Then use a dictionary to confirm your answers.**

1. In a typical recession, consumers try to save money by spending less and by choosing cheaper alternatives to luxury brands.
2. In highly competitive industries, the difference between making a profit and losing money may come down to how much marketing a company does and to the loyalty of its customers.
3. There is a great deal of competition in business these days, but small, family-run businesses can succeed if they offer services that consumers really want.
4. In theory, the stockholders in a corporation have the power to hire and fire executives, although in practice, stockholders almost always approve the recommendations of the corporation's board members about hiring and firing.

A products that are sold under a particular name
B Work that is done by employees to help customers
C Making products sound attractive to increase sales
D Senior business managers with a lot of responsibility
E A financial benefit from selling or doing something
F People who buy goods or services from a company
G People who have partial ownership in a corporation
H The act of trying to be or do better than someone else

C Analyzing Speaking Task 6

For Speaking Task 6 questions, an announcer will first introduce a lecture about an academic topic. During the lecture, the speaker will usually explain a theory or idea, discuss a problem and its causes or solutions, or describe a process. The speaker will also generally give specific examples that make his or her points clear and easy to understand.

After listening to the lecture, you will see the question on the screen and hear the announcer say it. The question will be similar to one of these examples:

Using the examples mentioned by the speaker, explain how _____ and _____ differ.

Using points and examples from the lecture, compare the two kinds of _____ that the professor discusses.

Using the example of _____, explain the concept of _____ and say why _____.

A second announcer will then tell you to begin preparing your response. You will have 20 seconds to prepare. The amount of preparation time remaining will be shown onscreen. After the preparation time, the second announcer will tell you to begin speaking. You will have 60 seconds to deliver your response. The amount of time remaining will be shown onscreen.

To answer a Speaking Task 6 question effectively and get a good score, your response should:

- use language well – you need to use grammar and vocabulary naturally and effectively with few mistakes.
- be delivered well – your speech should be clear and fluent, with good pronunciation and few long pauses.
- develop the topic well – you need to answer the question clearly by mentioning details and examples from the lecture.

Common problems when answering Speaking Task 6 questions that are likely to reduce your score include:

- poor language use – frequent mistakes, or vocabulary and grammar that are unnatural.
- poor delivery – unclear pronunciation or intonation, frequent or long pauses, or lack of fluency.
- poor topic development – paraphrasing information from the talk poorly, or not answering each part of the question.

> ### TEST TACTIC
> As with Speaking Task 4 questions, all the information you need to answer Speaking Task 6 questions will be given in the lecture. You do not need any previous knowledge of the topic to be able to understand or speak about what you hear.

C1 Answer questions 1–4 based on this script from a Speaking Task 6 lecture. Write full sentences when you answer. One answer has been done for you.

Professor Inflation can be defined as a continuing increase in the price of goods or services over a period of time. If the rate of inflation is low, inflation may be viewed positively as it signifies a growing economy. Indeed, some economists believe a permanently low and stable inflation rate may reduce the risk and seriousness of recessions. If the rate is high, however, its effects become increasingly severe because people's earnings do not increase at the same level as inflation. So although goods and services cost more than they used to, people have about the same amount of money as they did before. Obviously, they cannot buy as many goods and services if those goods and services are more expensive, so demand goes down, making a recession likely.

1. How does the professor define inflation?
   The professor defines inflation as a continuing increase in the price of goods and services over a period of time.

2. What level of inflation is viewed positively? Why?
   _____

3. What level of inflation is viewed negatively? Why?
   _____

4. How might inflation lead to a recession?
   _____

D Mastering Speaking Task 6 – Listening to the Lecture

The lecture usually lasts 75 to 90 seconds. As you listen, take clear, well-organized notes about key ideas, concepts, theories, details, and examples that the speaker discusses.

Track 348 **D1** Take notes as you listen to an experienced teacher talk about Speaking Task 6. Then use your notes to put suggestions A–D in the order the teacher says them. One answer has been done for you.

First	Always make a note when the speaker defines or explains concepts, theories, principles, or issues
Second	
Third	
Fourth	

A   Take notes about information that explains how one thing has had an effect on another thing.

B   Make a note of information about how two things are different from each other or how one thing has changed over time.

C   Always make a note when the speaker defines or explains concepts, theories, principles, or issues.

D   Pay close attention to words that signal that the speaker is about to give an example or supporting detail.

Track 348 **D2** Listen again to the experienced teacher's advice. Take notes as you listen. Then write in missing expressions 1–4.

Expressions that explain how one thing has had an effect on another thing	• as a result of … • 1.
Expressions that show how two things are different or how one thing has changed	• at first …, but later … • 2.
Expressions that indicate definitions or explanations of important ideas	• this can be defined as … • 3.
Expressions that signal the speaker is giving an example or supporting details	• to illustrate … • 4.

D3 Complete tasks 1 and 2 with a partner.

1.   Add some other expressions to the categories in exercise **D2**.

2.   Share your ideas from task 1 with other students and listen to their ideas. Make a note of any expressions not in your list.

D4 Use this script from a Speaking Task 6 lecture to fill in missing details 1–6 in the notes on the next page. Work with a partner.

Professor   In business, "integration" typically means creating efficiency. Today I'll discuss two distinct types of integration. First is vertical integration, which is when one company controls two or more steps in the production process of an item. For example, a global company might control three steps in the production of clothes: first, the clothes are made in its own factories. Next, the clothes are shipped using its own transportation company. And finally, the clothes are sold to customers in its own stores. Typically, businesses get an advantage from vertical integration because it allows them to reduce costs and avoid delays in the supply chain. Horizontal integration, on the other hand, is when one company controls two or more companies that offer the same, or a very similar, product. So, for instance, a manufacturing company might sell two brands of televisions in different ways. It might sell one brand of TVs, call them brand A, in retail stores, and sell another brand, brand B, only through online channels. Companies usually engage in horizontal integration to get more market share.

```
integ = create efficiency = 2 types
  ┌─────────────────────┐
  │ 1.                  │
  └─────────────────────┘
        = one company controls 2+ steps in production of item
        eg global comp controls 3 steps in producing clothes
            (1) make clothes in ┌──────────────────┐ / (2) transportation / (3) sell in shops
                                │ 2.               │
                                └──────────────────┘
            →  advantages: reduced ┌──────────────┐ and fewer delays
                                   │ 3.           │
                                   └──────────────┘
  ┌─────────────────────┐
  │ 4.                  │
  └─────────────────────┘
        = one comp controls 2+ comp selling same product
        eg manuf comp sells 2 brands of ┌──────────────┐
                                        │ 5.           │
                                        └──────────────┘
            (1) brand A in stores / (2) brand B online
            →  advantages: increased ┌────────────┐ share
                                     │ 6.         │
                                     └────────────┘
```

D5 Write the full form of these abbreviations (short ways to write something) that are used in the notes in exercise **D4**. One answer has been done for you.

1. integ _____integration_____
2. 2+ _____

3. comp _____
4. manuf _____

D6 Discuss with a partner the best way to abbreviate words 1–6 from the notes in D4.

1. production
2. global
3. transportation

4. advantages
5. reduced
6. increased

))) Track 349 **D7** Read these partial notes about a Speaking Task 6 lecture. Then listen to the lecture and add missing notes 1–5.

```
stagflation = combine stagnation + inflation
stag  = high inflat + low econ growth = ┌──────────────────────┐
                                        │ 1.                   │
                                        └──────────────────────┘
      = global stag in 70s (caused by increased oil prices)
         → led to ┌──────────────────────┐
                  │ 2.                   │
                  └──────────────────────┘
stag  = historically hard for governments to break out
      = few policies against inflat ┌──────────────────┐
                                    │ 3.               │
                                    └──────────────────┘
      = policies that do work ┌──────────────────┐
                              │ 4.               │
                              └──────────────────┘
      = global stag from 70s ┌──────────────────┐
                             │ 5.               │
                             └──────────────────┘
```

D8 Read this short passage. Then complete tasks 1–4 with a partner.

Taking notes is a key skill both for the listening section of the TOEFL Test and the Integrated Speaking and Writing questions. Like most skills, the more you practice it, the easier it will become and the more you will improve. Research shows that boring practice is less effective than enjoyable practice, so when you practice taking notes, try to do so in an interesting, creative, fun, or unusual way to get the best possible results.

1. Make a list of some interesting, creative, fun, or unusual ways to practice taking notes.
2. Decide which are the three most interesting or useful ideas on your list.
3. Share your best three ideas with other students and listen to their ideas. Take notes as you listen.
4. Choose the note-taking ideas that are the most interesting for you, and practice them as often as you can.

TEST TACTIC

When you are taking notes, pay close attention to the beginning of the lecture. The speaker usually discusses the main subject or purpose of the talk within the first 10–15 seconds and then typically goes on to discuss two aspects of this topic.

E Mastering Speaking Task 6 – Preparing Your Response

You only have 20 seconds to prepare your response, so you will not have time to write out a detailed plan for your speech. First you should analyze the question carefully to understand what information a well-organized response should include. Use the remaining time to circle the key points in your notes that you will talk about and to label those points in the order you will mention them.

E1 Analyze Speaking Task 6 questions 1–3. What information do you need for an effective response to each question? Some answers have been done for you. Use these answers as a guide.

1. Using points and examples from the talk, compare the two types of business integration that the professor discusses.

> To deliver a good response to this question, I should:
>
> ☑ Mention and define business integration, which is the main topic of the lecture.
> ☑ Introduce and define the first type of integration that the speaker mentions.
> ☑ Summarize details and / or examples about the first type of integration.
> ☑ Introduce and define the second type of integration that the speaker mentions.
> ☑ _____

2. Using the examples mentioned by the professor, say how sole proprietorships and partnerships are different.

> To deliver a good response to this question, I should:
>
> ☑ Mention and define two types of businesses, which is the main topic of the lecture.
> ☑ Define what a sole proprietorship is.
> ☑ _____
> ☑ Contrast the definition of a partnership with the definition of a sole proprietorship.
> ☑ _____

3. Using points and examples from the lecture, explain the ways in which direct marketing benefits organizations.

> To deliver a good response to this question, I should:
>
> ☑ Mention and define direct marketing, which is the main topic of the lecture.
> ☑ _____
> ☑ _____
> ☑ Introduce the second benefit of direct marketing that the speaker mentions.
> ☑ _____

E2 The notes about integration on the next page have nine circled Key Points (labeled KP1–KP9). Match the Key Points to the steps required to deliver a good response to question 1 in exercise **E1**. One answer has been done for you.

1. _____ ☑ Mention and define business integration, which is the main topic of the lecture.
2. KP2 / KP3 ☑ Introduce and define the first type of integration that the speaker mentions.
3. _____ ☑ Summarize details and/or examples about the first type of integration.
4. _____ ☑ Introduce and define the second type of integration that the speaker mentions.
5. _____ ☑ Summarize details and/or examples about the second type of integration.

```
KP1   (integ = create efficiency = 2 types)
KP2   (vertical)
KP3        = (one company controls 2+ steps in production of item)
      eg  global comp controls (3 steps in producing clothes)
KP4             (1) make clothes in factories / (2) transportation) / (3) sell in shops
KP5        → advantages: (reduced costs and fewer delays)
KP6   (horizontal)
KP7        = one comp controls 2+ comp selling same product)
      eg  manuf comp (sells 2 brands of TVs)
KP8             (1) brand A in stores / (2) brand B online)
KP9        → advantages: (increased market share)
```

E3 Look at these notes and Speaking Task 6 question. Then complete tasks 1 and 2.

```
stagflation = combine stagnation + inflation
stag   = high inflat + low econ growth = bad for econ
       = global stag in 70s (caused by increased oil prices)
         → led to recession in many countries
stag   = historically hard for governments to break out
       = few policies against inflat work against stag
       = policies that do work take money + time
       = global stag from 70s lasted over 10 years
```

Using points and examples from the lecture, explain what stagflation is and say how it can affect the economy.

1. Analyze the question and decide what information you need to include in your response to the question about stagflation. (You will not have time to write out your ideas as you did in exercise **E1**, but thinking about the information before you speak will help you deliver an organized response.)
2. Circle and label information in the notes that you think should be a Key Point.

F Mastering Speaking Task 4 – Delivering Your Response

It is not always possible to use a template – a well-organized model answer that includes natural language – for Speaking Task 6 questions because the questions vary. However, if you prepare a well-organized response, in most cases you can use model phrases to deliver effective, high-quality responses to Speaking Task 6 questions.

F1 Which Key Points, KP1–KP9, from the notes in exercise **E2** are summarized in each sentence of this response? Some sentences include information from two Key Points. One answer has been done for you.

KP1	The professor discusses two types of integration, which helps businesses be efficient.
_____	First, she talks about vertical integration, which is when a company controls several steps in producing an item.
_____	She gives the example of a company that controls three steps in the production of clothes.
_____	She goes on to say that vertical integration reduces costs and delays.
_____	Next, she discusses horizontal integration, which is when a company controls companies selling the same product.
_____	She mentions the case of a company that controls two companies that both sell televisions.
_____	She then points out that horizontal integration increases market share.

TEST TACTIC

To paraphrase something you did not hear clearly, introduce it with "The speaker says something like …" or "The professor mentions something along the lines of …" A native speaker would often use one of these phrases, so using them will help you sound natural.

🔊 Track 350 **F2** **Complete tasks 1 and 2.**

1. Listen to a high-level student say the model answer from exercise **F1**. Repeat each sentence after you hear it. Try to match the speaker's intonation, rhythm, and pronunciation. Keep practicing until you can say each sentence confidently.
2. Work with a partner to practice saying the full response from exercise **F1** several times. After your partner speaks, give him or her useful feedback about intonation, rhythm, and pronunciation.

F3 **Use the notes about stagflation from exercise E3 to write a response to this Speaking Task 6 question.**

> Using points and examples from the lecture, explain what stagflation is and say how it can affect the economy.

The professor discusses _____

He defines this as _____

First, he talks about _____

He goes on to explain that _____

Next, he discusses _____

He then points out that _____

F4 **Work with a partner to complete tasks 1–4.**

1. Listen to the response that your partner prepared in exercise **F3**. Take notes, if you like.
2. After listening, put checks (✔) in the YES or NO columns of the table below. Then give your partner feedback.
3. Say your response from exercise **F3** and get your partner's feedback. Try to get perfect feedback – YES in every column.
4. Fix any mistakes in your response that your partner noticed. Then repeat tasks 1–3 with several different partners.

Did your partner	YES	NO
Summarize the main purpose of the lecture?		
Give a detailed paraphrase of key points from the lecture?		
Finish his or her response in less than 60 seconds?		
Use model phrases from the model answer accurately?		
Speak clearly, fluently, and confidently without long pauses?		
Organize his or her answer in a clear, logical way?		

G Test Challenge

G1 **Answer Speaking Task 6 questions 1–3. After listening, spend 20 seconds preparing your response and speak for up to 60 seconds in order to get realistic practice for the test. Use the checklist of skills that you learned in this unit as a guide.**

☑ Listen to the talk and make clear, detailed, well-organized notes of the points that the speaker makes.

☑ Use the preparation time to analyze and understand the question. Then circle and label key details in your notes.

☑ Speak clearly and fluently, and use the model phrases to make sure that your response sounds natural.

This book uses a beep to indicate your speaking time is up. Remember that you will not hear this beep in the real test.

Tracks 351–354 1. Now listen to part of a lecture in a business studies class.

Using points and examples from the lecture, describe the two types of free software that the professor discusses.

Tracks 355–358 2. Now listen to part of a talk in a marine biology course.

Using points and examples from the talk, explain what fish farming is and say why cobia is a suitable species for farming.

Tracks 359–362 3. Now listen to part of a discussion in a law seminar.

Using points and examples from the seminar, describe the legal responsibilities of a corporation.

Next Steps

Speaking Task 6 questions are often about some aspect of business or marketing. These topics are common in the other sections of the TOEFL Test, too. As a result, learning words related to business and marketing, as well as practicing key skills for Speaking Task 6, may help you increase your overall test score.

To learn more about vocabulary related to business and marketing:

1. Read the headline of a newspaper article about business or marketing.
2. Based on the headline, predict some words you will see in the article.
3. Read the article once to understand the main ideas. Then read it again and search for the words you predicted.
4. Read the article again and search for words related to business you did not predict you would see.
5. Study the words you found in steps 3 and 4. Learn their meanings as well as how to use them.

To practice key skills for Speaking Task 6 questions:

1. Listen to about 90 seconds of a radio broadcast or online talk about business (or any other subject that interests you).
2. As you listen, take clear, detailed, well-organized notes of the points that the speaker makes.
3. After listening for about 90 seconds, spend 20 seconds labeling your notes and preparing to speak.
4. Then deliver a 60-second talk using the model phrases that you learned in this unit. Your talk should summarize the main purpose of the broadcast and paraphrase the points that the speaker discusses. Record yourself giving the talk.
5. After you have finished, listen to the recording of your speech. Make a note of things you could improve next time.
6. Repeat steps 1–4. Try to avoid making the same mistakes that you noticed in step 5 when you listened to your recording.

Directions

This speaking review test is intended to help you learn your speaking strengths and weaknesses. You will answer six speaking tasks that are designed to be at the same level as the ones on the TOEFL Test. For some tasks you will listen to one or two speakers. You may take notes while you listen. For the most realistic practice, cover the questions when you listen, and record your answers when you speak.

Test

🔊 Tracks 363–364 **TASK 1 – SPEAKING ABOUT A FAMILIAR TOPIC**

What is one food that you do not enjoy eating? Why? Support your answer with specific details and examples.

Preparation Time: 15 Seconds   Response Time: 45 Seconds

🔊 Tracks 365–366 **TASK 2 – SPEAKING ABOUT A FAMILIAR TOPIC**

Some people like going out to a theater to watch a movie. Other people prefer watching movies at home. Which way of watching movies do you prefer? Why? Support your response.

Preparation Time: 15 Seconds   Response Time: 45 Seconds

🔊 Tracks 367–370 **TASK 3 – SPEAKING ABOUT A CAMPUS SITUATION**

State University is canceling events on campus. Read the notice about this cancellation. You have 45 seconds to read the notice. Begin reading now.

Campus Events Canceled

Two students were taken to hospital last week because of trouble at an event on campus. In response to this situation, the university has decided to cancel all events on campus until further notice. The university council feels that this action, which is effective immediately, is necessary to ensure the safety of all students. The university council will meet with the student association and representatives from student clubs and organizations in November to discuss the situation and find a permanent solution.

Now listen as two students discuss the notice.

The man/woman expresses his/her opinion about the notice. State his/her opinion and explain the reasons he/she gives for holding that opinion.

Preparation Time: 30 Seconds   Response Time: 60 Seconds

TASK 4 – SPEAKING ABOUT ACADEMIC CONTENT

Tracks 371–374

Now read the passage about geoarchaeology. You have 45 seconds to read the passage. Begin reading now.

Geoarchaeology

Geoarchaeology is a collaborative, interdisciplinary approach to the study of archaeology. It involves the use of analytical techniques and theoretical and practical concepts from multiple disciplines such as geography, geology, and even sciences like chemistry or physics to answer questions and solve problems in archaeology. These questions and problems include such issues as the human and environmental factors that are involved in site formation, the reconstruction of ancient climates and environments, the use of chronometric tools to date artifacts, and the sourcing of materials and artifacts.

Now listen to part of a lecture on this topic in an archaeology class.

Using the example of obsidian artifacts that the professor discusses, explain how trace element analysis helped answer an archaeological question.

Preparation Time: 30 Seconds   Response Time: 60 Seconds

TASK 5 – SPEAKING ABOUT A CAMPUS SITUATION

Tracks 375–378

Now listen to a conversation between a man and a woman.

The speakers discuss two possible solutions to a problem. Describe the problem. Then state which of the two solutions you prefer and why.

Preparation Time: 20 Seconds   Response Time: 60 Seconds

TASK 6 – SPEAKING ABOUT ACADEMIC CONTENT

Tracks 379–382

Now listen to part of a talk in a public health class.

Using points and examples from the talk, say what vaccination is. Then say how attitudes towards vaccination have changed over time.

Preparation Time: 30 Seconds   Response Time: 60 Seconds

Score Conversion

Ask a teacher or native speaker to evaluate each response from 0–4. (If necessary, you can evaluate your responses yourself. See pages 172–175 of the Speaking Reference unit for the criteria for scoring.) Then add up the scores for each response to find your raw score and use this conversion chart to find out your approximate speaking score range on the TOEFL Test.

Raw Score (out of 24)	Probable Level	Approximate Score Range
21–24	Good	26–30
15–20	Fair	19–25
9–14	Limited	11–18
1–8	Weak	1–10

Overview

The writing section measures your ability to write English in an academic setting. You will see and/or hear:

• General directions for the writing section	about 2 minutes
• Specific instructions for the first writing task based on reading and listening	about 2 minutes
• Integrated Writing Task 1 based on reading and listening, with three minutes to read a passage, 2–3 minutes to listen to a lecture about the same topic, and 20 minutes to type your response	about 26 minutes
• Independent Writing Task 2 based on knowledge and experience	30 minutes

Your typed responses will be recorded and sent as digital files to human raters for grading. After both of your responses have been graded, your raw scores will be converted to a scaled score from 0–30.

NOTES

- You must type your responses. Handwritten answers are not allowed.
- You will not be able to continue working on your responses after the time is up.
- Your responses will be saved automatically when your time is up. You do not need to do anything to save your work.

Detailed Guide

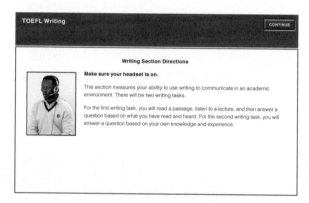

When you begin the writing section of the TOEFL Test, you will first see the directions for the whole section. You will hear a narrator read the directions aloud. You can change the volume of the narrator's voice while he is speaking by clicking on the **Volume** button in the top right corner of the screen.

When you are ready to go on, click the button marked **Continue**.

Next you will see specific directions for Writing Task 1. You will hear a narrator read the directions aloud. You can change the volume of the narrator's voice if you wish.

When you are ready to begin the writing test, click the button marked **Continue**.

TEST TACTIC

Because you must type your responses, learning to type quickly and accurately using a computer keyboard is a key skill for the TOEFL Test. You can find many effective, free typing tools on the Internet.

After the directions, you will see a reading passage on the left side of the screen. The passage typically has 230–300 words. You will have three minutes to read this passage. You can take notes on your scratch paper while you are reading.

A timer in the top right corner of the screen will show you how much reading time is left.

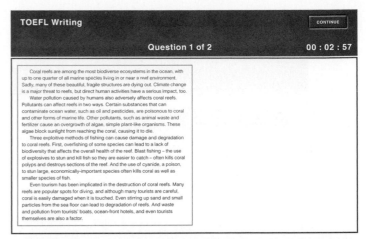

Next the reading passage will automatically disappear and you will see a picture of a professor on the screen. The narrator will tell you to listen to a lecture on the same topic as the reading passage. Then you will hear a professor deliver a lecture. The lecture will typically last between two and three minutes. You will see a bar below the picture that shows how much longer the lecture will last. You will only hear the lecture one time. You can take notes while you are listening.

While the professor is talking, you can change the volume, if necessary.

After the lecture, you will see a screen telling you to get ready to answer the question. This screen will disappear automatically after a few seconds.

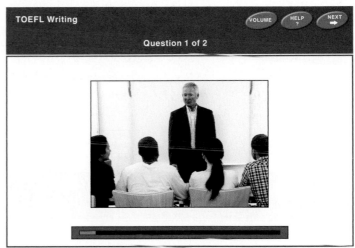

Then the screen will change and you will see the reading passage again. You will see the writing question on the screen, too, and the narrator will read the question aloud.

You will then have 20 minutes to plan and type a response to the question. While you are typing, you will be able to refer to your notes and see the reading passage, but you will not be able to listen again to the lecture.

As you type your response, your words will appear on the right side of the screen next to the reading passage. The number of words you have written will appear above your response. Generally, an effective response to Writing Task 1 will contain 150–225 words.

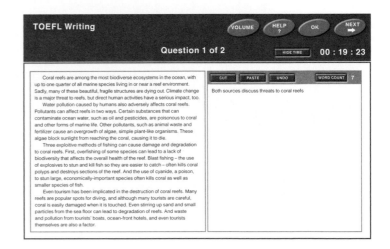

You will see several on-screen buttons that you can click to perform copy and paste functions. To use the **Cut** button, first select some text with your mouse. Then click the button. The selected text will be deleted from the screen and copied in the computer's memory. You can then click the **Paste** button to insert this copied text at a different position in your response.

If you make a mistake at any point, such as deleting a word or phrase, you can click the **Undo** button. This may help you recover from the mistake.

At the top of the screen you will see a toolbar with various buttons as well as the time remaining. You can choose to hide the amount of time remaining, if you prefer, by clicking the **Hide Time** button. If you change your mind, click the **Show Time** button.

Clicking the **Help** button will give you information about how to use the writing tools. If you click this button, the timer will count down while you look at the help information.

The Next button allows you to finish your response to Writing Task 1 and go on to Writing Task 2. If you click this button, you will see a warning message. You will have a choice of clicking **Return** to continue writing your response, or **Continue** to go on to the next task. Note that your time will continue to count down while you look at this message.

When your response time is over, the computer will automatically show you the directions for Writing Task 2.

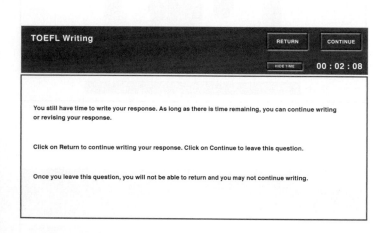

When your time is up for Writing Task 1, you will see the directions for Writing Task 2. You will not hear a narrator read these directions aloud.

When you are ready to go on, click the **Continue** button in the top right corner of the screen to begin the task.

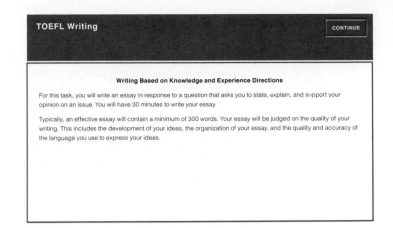

After the directions, the screen will change and you will see the question for Writing Task 2 on the screen. You will not hear a narrator read the question aloud.

You will then have 30 minutes to plan and type a response to the question. The time remaining will be shown at the top right of the screen below the **Next** button.

Typing your response to Writing Task 2 works the same as for Writing Task 1. You will see a count of how many words you have typed. Typically an effective response to Task 2 questions will have close to 300 words. You will have access to the same tools – **Cut**, **Paste**, and **Undo** – as well as the **Help** button.

If you finish typing your response before the 30 minutes is over, you can click on the **Next** button to finish the test. If there is still time remaining you will see the same warning message as for Writing Task 1 and you will be asked to confirm that you wish to end the test by clicking the **Continue** button.

When the test is over you will see a screen showing the end of the test. You will then have a chance to submit your score or cancel it.

Scoring

Your two responses will be sent electronically to ETS, the organization that develops the TOEFL Test. Each response will then be graded by a certified human rater and by a computerized automated scoring system.

Your responses to the integrated writing task and independent writing tasks will be sent to different human raters. No personal data is sent with either response, so the raters will not know your name, location, gender, previous scores on the TOEFL Test, or other personal details. The raters will not communicate with one other in any way about your responses.

After receiving your response, the rater will grade it holistically by focusing on the quality of your whole response. Typically, he or she will spend 60 to 90 seconds reading and evaluating your response. The rater will use the scoring rubrics described below to assign a grade from 0–5. The rater can only assign whole grades like 4, not half grades like 4.5.

When judging your response to the integrated writing task based on reading and listening, the rater will focus on the following criteria:

Score	Integrated Writing Task 1
5	A response at this level: • explains clearly how the main information from the lecture relates to information in the reading. • is typically well organized and fully developed. • generally has no more than a few minor errors that do not confuse the rater.
4	A response at this level: • should explain how most of the main ideas from the lecture relate to the reading, although some details may be missing, or slightly inaccurate or unclear. • may have frequent or obvious minor mistakes in grammar and vocabulary, although these mistakes should not seriously confuse the rater.
3	A response at this level: • typically summarizes some key details from the lecture and explains how they relate to the reading, but details are often incorrect or missing, and connections between the two sources are frequently unclear. • may have numerous obvious grammar and vocabulary mistakes that make it somewhat hard for the rater to understand the writer's ideas.
2	A response at this level: • may summarize some relevant information from the lecture, but many details are likely to be missing, very unclear, or very inaccurate. In addition, details of how the lecture and passage are related may be unclear. • may have numerous major problems with grammar and vocabulary that make it hard for the rater to understand the writer's ideas.
1	A response at this level: • generally includes very little information from the lecture, and does not show how the lecture and passage are connected. • typically has so many errors of all kinds that it is extremely hard for the rater to understand any of the writer's ideas.

A score of zero is given to blank responses, ones that are not written in English, ones that only copy words from the reading passage, or ones that only present the student's opinion about the topic, not the opinions in the passage and the lecture.

When judging your response to the independent writing task based on knowledge and experience, the rater will focus on the following criteria:

Score	Integrated Writing Task 2
5	A response at this level: • answers the question effectively with ideas that are clearly explained and fully developed. • is typically well organized and includes explanations and supporting examples that are coherent. • uses a variety of vocabulary expressions and grammar structures well and naturally, though it may have a few minor errors that do not confuse the rater.
4	A response at this level: • answers the question reasonably well, though some ideas may not be fully developed. • is generally well organized and supports ideas with effective explanations and examples, although some connections between ideas may not be clear. • uses a range of vocabulary expressions and grammar structures well, though it will likely have some obvious mistakes that are unlikely to confuse the rater.
3	A response at this level: • answers the question but is unlikely to be fully developed. • is reasonably well organized and includes some supporting details and examples, but ideas may not be clearly explained or connected to each other. • may use a limited range of accurate vocabulary and grammar structures, but is also likely to use language inconsistently and make mistakes that sometimes confuse the rater.
2	A response at this level: • usually has limited development and does not fully answer the question. • is not well organized and does not provide enough supporting details and examples. • has numerous obvious grammar and vocabulary mistakes that are likely to confuse the rater.
1	A response at this level: • is under developed and does not answer the question effectively. • is not organized and includes little or no detail relevant to the topic. • has serious and frequent errors.

A score of zero is given to blank responses, ones that are not written in English, or ones that are completely off topic.

TEST TACTIC

The scoring criteria do not specify that you need to use advanced grammar or vocabulary to get a good score. In fact, unless you are a very high-level student, using advanced language will probably reduce your score because you are more likely to make errors that confuse the reader.

In addition to certified human raters, your two responses will be assessed by a computerized scoring system called the e-rater engine developed by ETS. Like the human raters, e-rater will assign a score for each response from 0–5 but can only assign whole grades, not half grades. E-rater works in the following way:

The e-rater engine predicts essay scores based on features related to writing quality, including grammar, usage, mechanics, style, organization, and development. The computational methodology underlying the system is NLP (natural language processing), which identifies and extracts linguistic features from electronic text.
Source: www.ets.org/Media/Home/pdf/AutomatedScoring.pdf

Next, your scores for each response from the human rater and e-rater are compared. In most cases, the score from the human rater and from e-rater are the same or within one point of each other. So, for example, the human rater might assign a score of 4 points and e-rater might assign a score of 3, 4, or 5 points. In these cases, your final score for this response will be the average of the two scores. So, for example, if the human rater assigned a score of 4 points for your integrated writing response and e-rater assigned a score of 5 points, your final score for this task would be 4.5 points.

In rare cases, the scores from the human rater and e-rater differ by two or more points. So, for example, the human rater might assign a score of 3 points, but e-rater might assign a score of 5 points. In these cases, a second human rater will grade your response, and your final score for this task will be the average of all three scores. So, for instance, if the two human raters both assigned a score of 3 points for your independent writing response but e-rater assigned a score of 5 points, your final score for this task would be 3.67 points.

TEST TACTIC

As with most skills, regular practice is one key to becoming better at writing for the TOEFL Test. If you have enough time, write a TOEFL essay each day. If your time is limited, write three perfect sentences every day. That means sentences with no grammar, vocabulary, or spelling errors.

Your final score for the writing section is the average of the final scores for your two responses. So, for example, if you received an averaged final score of 3.5 points for the integrated task and an averaged final score of 4.0 points for the independent task, your final raw score for the writing section would be 3.75 points. This score is then converted to a scaled score from 0 to 30 points.

ETS does not explain in detail how the raw scores are converted to a scaled score. However, this table shows how some example final scores would be converted to the 0–30 scale:

Final Score – First Task	Final Score – Second Task	Final Score – Average	Scaled Score
5.00	5.00	5.00	30
4.50	5.00	4.75	29
4.50	4.50	4.50	28
4.00	4.50	4.25	27
3.50	4.50	4.00	25
3.50	4.00	3.75	24
3.00	4.00	3.50	22
3.00	3.50	3.25	21
2.50	3.50	3.00	20

When you receive your score from the TOEFL Test, you will get a score report that not only gives your scaled score in writing from 0–30, but also describes your performance for the two written responses (Good, Fair, or Limited). The report will also give a short description of the typical performance of students at that level.

Here are the levels and descriptions for the integrated writing task based on reading and listening:

Level	Scaled Score	Your Performance
Good (4.0–5.0)	24–30	You responded well to the task, relating the lecture to the reading. Weaknesses, if you have any, might have to do with: • slight imprecision in your summary of some of the main points; and/or • use of English that is occasionally ungrammatical or unclear.
Fair (2.5–3.5)	17–23	You responded to the task, relating the lecture to the reading, but your response indicates weaknesses such as: • an important idea or ideas may be missing, unclear, or inaccurate; • there may be unclarity in how the lecture and the reading passage are related; and/or • grammatical mistakes or vague/incorrect uses of words may make the writing difficult to understand.
Limited (1.0–2.0)	1–16	Your response was judged as limited due to: • failure to understand the lecture or reading passage; • deficiencies in relating the lecture to the reading passage; and/or • many grammatical errors and/or very unclear expressions and sentence structures.

And here are the levels and descriptions for the independent writing task based on knowledge and experience:

Level	Scaled Score	Your Performance
Good (4.0–5.0)	24–30	You responded with a well-organized and developed essay. Weaknesses, if you have any, might have to do with: • use of English that is occasionally ungrammatical, unclear or • unidiomatic, and/or • elaboration of ideas or connection of ideas that could have been stronger.
Fair (2.5–3.5)	17–23	You expressed ideas with reasons, examples and details, but your response indicated weaknesses, such as: • you may not provide enough specific support and development for your main points; • your ideas may be difficult to follow because of how you organize your essay or because of the language you use to connect your ideas; and/or • grammatical mistakes or vague/incorrect uses of words may make the writing difficult to understand.
Limited (1.0–2.0)	1–16	You attempted to express your opinion, but your response indicates notable deficiencies, such as: • your response contains insufficient detail; • your ideas and your connections of ideas are difficult to understand because of many grammatical errors and/or very unclear expressions and sentence structure; and/or • your response is only marginally related to the question that was asked.

Source: www.ets.org/Media/Tests/TOEFL/pdf/TOEFL_Perf_Feedback.pdf

Directions

This writing diagnostic test is intended to help you find out your strengths and weaknesses in writing. You will complete two writing tasks in 50 minutes. The total time required for the test is approximately 56 minutes. The tasks are designed to be at the same level as the ones you will see on the TOEFL Test. For the first task you will listen to a lecture. For the most realistic practice, cover the question when you listen. You may take notes while you listen. If possible, type your answers. When you have finished, ask a teacher to evaluate both responses from 0–5 or do it yourself. Then use the conversion chart on page 235 to convert your raw scores to your likely score on the TOEFL Test.

Test

TASK 1 – WRITING BASED ON READING AND LISTENING

For this task, you will read a passage about an academic topic. You will have three minutes to read. You may take notes on the passage while you read. You will then listen to a lecture about the same topic. While you listen you may also take notes. You may use your notes to help you answer the question.

You will then write a response to a question that asks you about the relationship between the lecture you heard and the reading passage. Try to answer the question as completely as possible using information from the reading passage and the lecture. The question does not ask you to express your personal opinion. Your response will be judged on the quality of your writing and on the completeness and accuracy of the content. Typically, an effective response will be 150 to 225 words.

Now read this passage. You have three minutes to read.

According to popular belief, in 1271 Italian merchant Marco Polo, together with his father and uncle, began a 24-year round-trip journey to China. After his return to Venice in 1296, Marco Polo wrote an influential account of his travels. Analysis of those writings, however, suggests that he might not have visited China at all, and that the details of his journey described in the book were copied from other sources.

One point that suggests Marco Polo did not visit China is his silence on aspects of Chinese culture that would have been surprising to Europeans. For example, his book does not make any reference to drinking tea, using chopsticks to eat, printed books, the Chinese system of logographic writing, or the use of trained sea birds to catch fish.

Polo's book is also silent on massive construction projects that would have amazed European travelers. The Great Wall of China existed at the time when Polo visited China, but his book makes no mention of it at all.

One final point is that Marco Polo says he and his relatives held important roles in the Mongol court. However, there are no references to Marco Polo or his father or uncle in Chinese documents from that time, a surprising omission because important officials were often mentioned in court documents. So again, it is hard to avoid the conclusion that Marco Polo did not, in fact, visit China.

Tracks 383 Now listen to a lecture on the topic you just read about.

You now have 20 minutes to plan and write your response. You may see the reading passage again while you write.

Summarize the points made in the lecture you just heard, being sure to specifically explain how they cast doubt on points made in the reading passage.

TASK 2 – WRITING BASED ON KNOWLEDGE AND EXPERIENCE

In this task you will demonstrate your ability to write an essay in response to a question that asks you to express and support your opinion about a topic or issue. Your essay will be scored on the quality of your writing. This includes the development of your ideas, the organization of your essay, and the quality and accuracy of the language you use to express your ideas. Typically, an effective essay will contain a minimum of 300 words.

Read the question below. You have 30 minutes to plan, write, and revise your essay.

Do you agree or disagree with the following statement?

Clear, effective communication is the most important element of any successful relationship between people.

Support your answer with reasons and specific details.

Score Conversion

Ask a teacher or native speaker to evaluate both responses from 0–5. (If necessary, you can evaluate your responses yourself. See pages 230–233 of the Writing Reference unit for the criteria for scoring.) Then add up the score for each response to find your raw score and use this conversion chart to find out your approximate writing score range on the TOEFL Test.

Raw Score (out of 10)	Probable Level	Approximate Score Range
10	Good	30
9		27
8		24
7	Fair	21
6		18
5		15
4	Limited	12
3		8
2		6
1		3

Unit Focus

In the writing section of the TOEFL Test you will have two tasks. Task 1 is called the integrated writing task. There are three types of Task 1 questions that all require a slightly different response. For Challenge questions, the most common type, you will need to explain how information from a lecture contrasts with information from a reading passage. In this unit you will learn key skills and a model answer that will help you write effective responses to Challenge questions, including:

- taking notes about the main points when you first see the reading passage.
- taking detailed notes about ideas in the lecture that are related to ideas in the reading.
- learning natural model phrases to write an effective introduction and three body paragraphs.
- avoiding common problems like copying phrases directly from the reading passage.

The vocabulary focus is on academic words and phrases related to:

- different aspects of society.

A Warm-up

A1 Do you agree or disagree with these quotations about society? Write your opinion and reason. Then talk with a partner and summarize his or her opinion and reason. Discuss each quotation with a different partner.

"The saddest aspect of life ... is that science gathers knowledge faster than society gathers wisdom."
ISAAC ASIMOV

1. I _____*agree / disagree*_____ with this quotation about society because _____*give the reason*_____.
   My partner _____*agrees / disagrees*_____ with Isaac Asimov's words because _____*give the reason*_____.

"I think the teaching profession contributes more to ... society than any other single profession."
JOHN WOODEN

2. I _____*agree / disagree*_____ with this quotation about society because _____*give the reason*_____.
   My partner _____*agrees / disagrees*_____ with John Wooden's words because _____*give the reason*_____.

B Academic Vocabulary

B1 Choose the best word from answers A–H to complete sentences 1–8. If necessary, check the meaning of the words in a dictionary. One answer has been done for you.

1. A commercial or business activity that many people do is often described as a(n) ____industry____.
2. A(n) _____ is something, such as a lack of money or place to live, that causes difficulty for somebody.
3. A(n) _____ is an organization or place such as a university or bank that plays an important role in society.
4. A situation, especially one that affects society, that people are concerned about is called a(n) _____.
5. A person's _____ towards something or somebody is how he or she feels about that thing or person.
6. _____ is the condition of not having enough money to pay for basic needs like food or clothing.
7. A program of action or plan that a government or group follows to change a situation is called a(n) _____.
8. _____ is the condition of accepting other people's views about subjects like religion or politics.

A attitude	C industry	E issue	G poverty
B hardship	D institution	F policy	H tolerance

c Analyzing Writing Task 1 — Challenge Questions

For Writing Task 1, you will first see a reading passage on the screen. The passage will be between 230 and 300 words long and will present three ideas, arguments, theories, or examples related to an academic topic. You will have three minutes to read the passage and take notes.

After three minutes, the passage will disappear from the screen and an announcer will tell you to listen to a lecture on the same topic. The lecture will last two to three minutes, and you will only have one chance to listen to it, so you should take notes as you listen. In almost every case, the speaker will discuss ideas, arguments, theories, or examples that challenge the three ideas from the passage. In these cases you will have a Challenge question like one of the examples below.

After listening, the writing task will appear on the screen and the announcer will read it aloud. You will then have exactly 20 minutes to prepare and type your response. During this time you will be able to see the passage again.

Challenge questions usually include a specific word or phrase like "challenge" or "different from" that makes it clear that the ideas in the passage and the lecture contrast with each other, as in these examples:

Summarize the points made in the lecture, explaining how they contrast with arguments made in the reading passage.

Summarize the points made in the lecture you just heard, being sure to explain how they are different from the points made in the reading passage.

Occasionally, however, a Challenge question may include the phrase "respond to," as in this example:

Summarize the points made in the lecture, explaining how they respond to specific points in the reading passage.

To answer Writing Task 1 Challenge questions effectively and get a good score, it is important to:

- paraphrase, summarize, or quote the ideas and supporting details that the speaker discusses in the lecture.
- give a clear, detailed explanation of how each point from the lecture differs from a point in the reading passage.
- use model paragraphs with natural phrases so your response is well-organized and has few mistakes.

One common problem that can reduce your score when answering all types of Writing Task 1 questions is:

- copying sentences from the reading passage rather than paraphrasing or summarizing the ideas in the passage.

C1 Circle the word or phrase in Writing Task 1 questions 1–5 that tells you each question is a Challenge question. One answer has been done for you.

1. Summarize the points made in the lecture, being sure to explain how they (challenge) the points made in the reading.
2. Summarize the points made in the lecture you just heard, explaining how they oppose specific points made in the reading passage.
3. Summarize the points made in the lecture you just heard, being sure to specifically explain how they cast doubt on points made in the reading passage.
4. Summarize the speaker's points from the lecture, being sure to explain how they differ from the points made in the reading passage.
5. Summarize the points made in the lecture you just heard, being sure to state how they contradict specific points made in the reading passage.

TEST TACTIC

In general, it is best to paraphrase or summarize the reading passage in your response. However, if you often make mistakes when paraphrasing or summarizing, or are slow at doing it, you will probably not reduce your score if you copy a few words and phrases directly from the reading.

D Mastering Writing Task 1 – Reading the Passage

A key skill is to recognize information in the passage that will help you understand the lecture. You will see the passage again after the lecture, so you do not need to understand every word when you first see it. However, you *do* need to make a note of the writer's main view about the topic (usually given in paragraph 1) as well as the three main points that he or she makes (usually given in the final three paragraphs). When you take notes, use abbreviations to save time.

D1 Reading passages for Writing Task 1 questions are usually organized in the same way as this example. Answer questions 1–4 after reading the example passage.

We read a great deal these days about a crisis in American education, and statistics do show that American students are often no better than average at things like reading, ability to use technology, and knowledge of science and mathematics. A reason often given for this is that low pay for teachers means the quality of many teachers is not as good as it could be. One way to solve this crisis would be to pay teachers based on their ability and performance.

The current system of experience-based pay means that teachers know they will get paid the same whether they put in a lot of work or a little work in any given year. This leads to a situation where some teachers do the minimum amount of work. Performance-based pay would lead to enhanced effort and performance by teachers.

Further, there is a direct and measurable link between the quality of instruction that students receive and their results as measured by how much they have learned. If teachers work harder and teach better because doing so will improve their pay, students are going to learn more and show improved levels of performance and achievement.

Another issue is that many smart people do not choose to become teachers because pay and conditions for teachers are not very good. Offering teachers higher pay for better performance would undoubtedly attract higher numbers of good quality, smart people into the profession, and this would improve student results, too.

1. Which answer describes how the reading passage is organized?
   A The first two paragraphs give the writer's opinions about the topic; the last two paragraphs give other people's opinions.
   B The first paragraph gives the author's opinion; the other paragraphs discuss specific details related to the author's view.

2. Which paragraph explains why some intelligent people do not go into teaching?
   Paragraph   ☐ 1   ☐ 2   ☐ 3   ☐ 4

3. Which paragraph notes a link between teacher effort and student performance?
   Paragraph   ☐ 1   ☐ 2   ☐ 3   ☐ 4

4. Which paragraph explains why some teachers do not work as hard as they could?
   Paragraph   ☐ 1   ☐ 2   ☐ 3   ☐ 4

D2 Look at these notes about the reading passage in exercise **D1**. Then discuss and answer questions 1–5 with a partner.

MV	crisis in US educ = only average perf by students (S) performance-based pay (PBP) for teachers (T) would solve
P1	PBP → more effort + better perf by T
P2	PBP → improved perf + achievem by S
P3	PBP → more good quality people become T

1. What abbreviations (short ways to write something) are used in the notes to mark the writer's main view and the three main points?
2. What abbreviations are used in the notes for the words *education*, *performance*, and *achievement*?
3. What do the abbreviations *S*, *PBP*, and *T* in the notes stand for? How do you know?

TEST TACTIC

After you finish taking notes about the three main points in the passage, use any remaining time to predict what the speaker might say in the lecture. Most Writing Task 1 questions are Challenge questions, so the best idea is to focus on how the speaker might challenge the reading.

D3 Read this passage and take notes. Use the notes in exercise **D2** as a guide. Complete the task in three minutes.

> Poverty is a global issue, and some have argued that a financial transaction tax – often called a Robin Hood tax – is the answer. Such a tax would involve levying a small fee of about 0.05% on all transactions between financial institutions. It is claimed that this tax might raise billions of dollars in revenue each year that could be used to fight poverty around the world. Reducing poverty is a worthwhile goal, to be sure, but a financial transaction tax is not the way to achieve it.
>
> First, a financial transaction tax would reduce profits of pension and other retirement funds, so retired people who rely on these funds would see a reduction in their income. In other words, a tax intended to reduce poverty would make some of society's most vulnerable people poorer.
>
> It is also argued that a financial transaction tax would only affect financial institutions, not consumers. However, history shows that businesses usually pass on higher costs to customers. So if such a tax were introduced, customers would see price increases for bank services, which again would lead to financial hardship for many.
>
> Finally, a financial transaction tax would probably lead to job losses in the finance industry. Cities like New York where finance is a major source of employment could also see job losses in industries that support the financial sector. A recent study suggests 1% of all private sector jobs might be lost. So again, a Robin Hood tax would contribute to poverty, not reduce it.

E Mastering Writing Task 1 – Listening to the Lecture

While you listen to the lecture, take detailed notes about the speaker's points. You will not have time to note every word the speaker says, so focus on ideas that relate to the three main points in the reading passage. Use abbreviations to save time.

E1 Read this script from a lecture about performance-based pay for teachers. Then decide if statements 1–6 are true or false. Rewrite the answers you mark false so that they are correct. One answer has been done for you.

Professor	People claim there's an education crisis these days and that giving teachers higher pay for better performance will solve it. But a closer look suggests that performance-based pay may not be such a good idea.
	Think back to the reading. The writer says that teachers would work harder under a system of merit-based pay. It's possible this is true, but impossible to be sure since no studies have been done to prove it. However, numerous studies have shown that offering more money is generally a poor way to motivate people to work harder.
	The writer also argues that performance-based pay for teachers will lead to better student results. Students might perform better, but not necessarily due to better teaching. Why? Well, offering workers more money for better results makes some people "cheat" the system and find ways to get better results without doing better work. There's every reason to think the teaching profession would be the same.
	Finally, studies have shown that many people become teachers to help others and be creative, not for monetary gain. So performance-based pay is likely to mean that many people who care more about money than about inspiring students decide to become teachers. But teachers like that are unlikely to solve the education crisis.

1. The lecture has the same organization as the reading passage in exercise **D1**. ☑ True ☐ False
2. The speaker's overall opinion about the topic is given at the end of the lecture. ☐ True ☐ False
3. The speaker's opinion about the topic is opposite to the opinion in the reading. ☐ True ☐ False
4. In the lecture, the speaker never mentions the reading passage directly. ☐ True ☐ False
5. The speaker discusses the same points as the reading and in the same order. ☐ True ☐ False
6. The speaker disagrees with some points from the reading, but agrees with others. ☐ True ☐ False

🔊 Track 384 **E2** **Listen to an experienced teacher talk about Writing Task 1. In which order does the teacher mention each point about taking notes? One answer has been done for you.**

> When you take notes while listening to the lecture, it is a good idea to:
>
> ☑ Use abbreviations to take notes more quickly and use the time more effectively   _____
>
> ☑ Copy the speaker's words directly or paraphrase them, whichever is easier for you   _____
>
> ☑ Take as many notes as you can about ideas that are related to points in the reading   _First_

🔊 Track 385 **E3** **Listen to the first half of the lecture about performance-based pay for teachers. As you listen, read the notes below. Then answer questions 1–3.**

MV	Some think PBP will solve educ crisis, but not good idea
P1	Possible T work harder if get PBP but no studies prove it Other studies show more $ does not motiv people work harder

1. Do the notes mainly paraphrase the lecture or copy the speaker's words directly?
2. What abbreviations used in the notes are also used in the reading notes in exercise **D2**?
3. What abbreviations for "money" and "motivate" are used in the notes?

🔊 Track 386 **E4** **Complete tasks 1 and 2. Use the checklist in exercise E2 and the partial notes in exercise E3 as a guide.**

1. Listen to the second half of the lecture from exercise **E3**. Complete the notes in **E3** as you listen.
2. Listen to a lecture about a financial transaction tax. Take notes as you listen.

F Mastering Writing Task 1 – Writing an Effective Response

TEST TACTIC

For Writing Task 1, there is generally no need to plan how you will answer the question. The model paragraphs you will learn in this unit are designed to have a logical structure, and the ideas you mention should follow the order of the ideas in the reading and lecture.

Your response should begin with an introduction and then have three body paragraphs, one for each matching point in the passage and lecture. You do not need a conclusion. Writing Task 1 questions follow a standard pattern. As a result, it is possible to use the same standard body paragraph three times with only minor changes.

F1 **Read this sample response to the reading passage and lecture about performance-based pay for teachers. Then write short answers to questions 1–8.**

Both sources discuss the issue of giving performance-based pay to teachers. This piece of writing will summarize how the points that the writer discusses are challenged by the speaker.

The writer first claims that teachers would work harder if they received performance-based pay. The speaker states that no academic studies prove that this is true. He goes on to state that other studies show that paying people more money is often not a good way to motivate them to work. This is one way that the lecture challenges the reading.

The writer next says that student results would improve if teachers got merit-based pay because teachers would teach better. The speaker argues that results would not improve because of better teaching. He continues by arguing that some teachers may find ways to cheat. This is another way that the lecture casts doubt on the reading.

The writer then asserts that more smart people will become teachers if they receive performance-based pay. The speaker makes the point that few people become teachers because they want a high salary. He then says that performance-based pay might cause people who love money to become teachers. This is the final way that the lecture contradicts the reading.

1. The introduction (first paragraph) has two sentences. Which sentence is a transition sentence?
2. In the introduction, which sentence describes how the ideas in the lecture relate to ideas in the passage?

3. In the introduction, which sentence gives a short summary of the main idea of the passage and lecture?
4. Body paragraph 1 has four sentences. Which sentence describes how the lecture relates to the passage?
5. In body paragraph 1, which sentence summarizes a point from the reading passage?
6. In body paragraph 1, which sentence summarizes the speaker's view about the point from the reading passage?
7. In body paragraph 1, which sentence gives information that supports the speaker's view?
8. Do body paragraphs 2 and 3 have the same organization as body paragraph 1?

F2 **Complete this response to a Writing Task 1 Challenge question using either the notes below or your own notes from exercise D3 (reading) and task 2 of exercise E4 (lecture).**

Reading Notes	Lecture Notes
MV Robin Hood tax (RHT) = 0.05% on financial transactions	MV RHT has advans
RHT → raise money to reduce world poverty but disadvantages	P1 RHT is only 0.05% so low cost to retired people Couple with $5000 per month have just $25 less
P1 RHT → reduce pension profits → retired people become poor	P2 Not all banks would increase costs / customers could switch banks
P2 RHT → banks increase costs → customers have financial problems	Also conditions of RHT could say banks not allowed pass on costs
P3 RHT → financial industry cuts jobs → other industries cut jobs too	P3 Any new tax leads to job losses, but usu temporary situation Governm could use $ raised by RHT tax to help people who lose jobs

Summarize the points made in the lecture, being sure to explain how they challenge the points made in the reading passage.

Both sources discuss _____
This piece of writing will summarize how the points that the writer discusses are challenged by the speaker.

The writer first claims that _____
The speaker states that _____
She goes on to state that _____
This is one way that the lecture challenges the reading.

The writer next says that _____
The speaker argues that _____
She continues by arguing that _____
This is another way that the lecture casts doubt on the reading.

The writer then asserts that _____
The speaker makes the point that _____
She then points out that _____
This is the final way that the lecture contradicts the reading.

G Mastering Writing Task 1 – Avoiding Common Problems

In your response, you need to refer to the reading passage as well as the lecture, but copying phrases and ideas directly from the reading may reduce your score. As a result, learning how to paraphrase ideas from the passage is a key skill.

G1 **Study the three examples of paraphrasing on the next page. Then use the examples to help you paraphrase the two short reading passages. One answer has been done for you.**

☑ A paraphrasing technique that rarely leads to mistakes is changing the order of clauses or phrases within a sentence.

Example   There is a crisis in American education.
→ American education is in crisis.

☑ Another technique that does not lead to many mistakes is changing the grammatical form of words in the original.

Example   Merit-based pay for teachers would lead to better performance.
→ Teachers would perform better if they were paid based on their merit.

☑ A final effective paraphrasing technique, but one that can lead to errors, is using synonyms for words in the original.

Example   There is a link between quality of instruction and students' results.
→ There is a connection between teaching quality and learners' grades.

There are three reasons why bullying is a less serious problem these days than it was in the past. First, many schools have implemented a zero-tolerance policy on bullying, so bullies may be expelled from school for a first offense. Second, educators receive much better training these days, so they can stop or prevent bullying before it happens. And third, social attitudes towards bullying have changed, which means that fewer people think it is acceptable or do it.

1. The writer first claims that _people who bully can be made to leave school because of zero-tolerance policies._
2. The writer next says that _____
3. The writer then asserts that _____

Frankly, it's ridiculous to argue there is less bullying now than in the past. First, studies have shown that zero-tolerance policies have had almost no impact on how much bullying occurs. Second, more bullying is taking place away from school where educators can do nothing to stop it no matter how much training they have. And third, social attitudes have always been against bullying, but a comparison of data from 1970, 1990, and 2010 shows that bullying is actually on the rise.

4. The writer first claims that _____
5. The writer next says that _____
6. The writer then asserts that _____

H Test Challenge

H1 **Practice writing a Challenge question by completing the Writing Task 1 question on page 243. First spend three minutes reading the passage at the top of that page. Then listen to the lecture. Finally, take exactly 20 minutes to write or type your response. Use the checklist of skills you studied in this unit as a guide.**

Before you begin writing

☑ Scan the passage and make a note of the main view and the three points, ideas, or theories that the writer gives.

☑ Listen to the lecture and take notes; focus especially on points that are related to the three points from the reading.

While you are writing

☑ Write an introduction that summarizes the topic of the reading and lecture, and the relationship between the sources.

☑ Write three body paragraphs that describe in detail how points discussed in the lecture relate to ideas in the reading.

Although there are relatively few of them on the roads currently, electric cars offer a range of benefits both for individuals and for society. As a result, it would make sense for governments to offer subsidies to auto makers to produce electric vehicles, and for auto makers to prioritize the manufacture of these vehicles.

A key benefit of electric vehicles is their low cost of operation. The average journey by car in the United States is about ten miles. According to one study, the cost to drive a gasoline-powered car that distance is around $1.60, but the cost of a ten-mile trip in an electric car is under 50 cents. An average driver would save hundreds of dollars a year with an electric car.

Another benefit for individuals is the convenience offered by electric cars. All types of cars need to be refueled, but electric cars can easily be refueled simply by plugging them in and recharging their batteries. This can be done at home. Refueling a gasoline-powered car, on the other hand, requires going to the gas station, a trip which itself burns fuel.

And the environmentally-friendly nature of electric vehicles is well known. Unlike gasoline-powered vehicles, electric ones do not burn fossil fuels for energy, and release no harmful gases like carbon monoxide or carbon dioxide into the atmosphere. These gases have been linked to climate change and health issues, so electric cars are both cleaner and safer.

Track 388 Now listen to a lecture on the topic you just read about.

Summarize the points made in the lecture you just heard, being sure to specifically explain how they cast doubt on points made in the reading passage.

Next Steps

You may have questions and topics related to society in every section of the TOEFL Test. In consequence, learning more vocabulary about this topic, as well as practicing key skills for Writing Task 1 questions, may raise your overall test score.

To learn and practice more vocabulary related to society:

1. Make a list of things you like and things you dislike about your society.
2. Do some research in English to compare the things you like about your society with the same things in other societies.
3. Do some research in English to come up with ideas for improving the things you dislike about your society.
4. While you are doing your research, make a note of and study any new words and expressions that you notice.

To practice a key skill for Writing Task 1 questions:

1. Listen to a talk that is about three minutes long. (If a talk is too long, listen to part of it.) Take notes as you listen.
2. Use your notes to write five sentences that accurately repeat what the speaker says in the talk. Listen again, if necessary, so you can write the sentences perfectly.
3. Write paraphrases of the five sentences. Use the three paraphrasing techniques that you learned in this unit.
4. If you repeat steps 1–3 every day, you will become better at paraphrasing, which is a key skill for all three types of Writing Task 1 questions and several speaking questions, too.

WRITING • Integrated Writing Task 1 — Problem-Solution Questions

Unit Focus

In the writing section of the TOEFL Test you will have two tasks. Task 1 is called the integrated writing task. There are three types of Task 1 questions that all require a slightly different response. For Problem-Solution questions, you will need to explain how a lecture gives solutions to problems or answers to questions mentioned in a reading passage. In this unit you will learn key skills and a model answer that will help you write effective responses to Problem-Solution questions, including:

- taking notes about the main points when you first see the reading passage.
- taking detailed notes about ideas in the lecture that are related to ideas in the reading.
- learning natural model phrases to write an effective introduction and three body paragraphs.
- avoiding common problems like incorrectly summarizing information from the lecture.

The vocabulary focus is on academic words and phrases related to:

- the environment.

A Warm-up

A1 Complete tasks 1–4.

1. Spend three minutes making a list of some environmental problems that affect your country or that you know about.
2. Share your list with a partner. Then listen to your partner's list and take notes about any problems not on your list.
3. With your partner, discuss and make a note of some possible solutions to the environmental problems on your lists.
4. Share your list of problems and possible solutions with other students. Then listen to their list of problems and solutions.

B Academic Vocabulary

B1 Expressions A–H are defined below. Work with a partner to choose the best expressions to complete statements 1–4. Two answers have been done for you.

1. Some studies show the use of pesticides in __agriculture__ to stop insects destroying crops may harm local _____.
2. Many people argue that burning __fossil fuels__ for energy may lead to a global increase in the average daily _____.
3. As the _____ of a city grows, the amount of light, noise, and atmospheric _____ those people generate also grows.
4. When people cut down trees and other _____, research shows that nearby _____ are more likely to flood.

A agriculture – the practice of farming, including growing crops
B fossil fuels – sources of energy like coal and oil that are buried in the ground
C pollution – something that makes air or water dirty or unsafe
D population – the number of people who live in a city or region
E temperature – how hot or cold the weather is at a particular time
F vegetation – plants, such as trees, bushes, grasses, and so on
G waterways – a body of water like a river that boats can travel on
H wildlife – a general word for the wild animals that live in a region

C Analyzing Writing Task 1 – Problem-Solution Questions

For Writing Task 1, you will first see a reading passage on the screen. The passage will be between 230 and 300 words long and will present three ideas, arguments, theories, or examples related to an academic topic. You will have three minutes to read the passage and take notes.

After three minutes, the passage will disappear from the screen and an announcer will tell you to listen to a lecture on the same topic. The lecture will last two to three minutes, and you will only have one chance to listen to it, so you should take notes as you listen. In some cases, the speaker will present solutions to problems that the reading passage discusses, or answers to questions that the reading passage asks. In these cases you will have a Problem-Solution question like one of the examples below.

After listening, the writing task will appear on the screen and the announcer will read it aloud. You will then have just 20 minutes to prepare and type your response. During this time you will be able to see the passage again.

Problem-Solution questions typically include a phrase like "address the problems" or "answer the questions," as in these examples:

> Summarize the points made in the lecture you just heard, being sure to specifically explain how they address the problems discussed in the reading passage.

> Summarize the points made in the lecture, being sure to say how they answer the questions raised in the reading passage.

To answer Writing Task 1 Problem-Solutions questions effectively and get a good score, it is important to:
- paraphrase, summarize, or quote the ideas and supporting details that the speaker discusses in the lecture.
- give a detailed explanation of how each point from the lecture responds to a question or problem in the passage.
- use model paragraphs with natural phrases so your response is well-organized and has few mistakes.

One common problem that can reduce your score when answering all types of Writing Task 1 questions is:
- incorrectly summarizing points from the lecture either by making language errors or by misunderstanding the speaker's views.

C1 Decide if Writing Task 1 questions 1–5 are Problem-Solution questions or Challenge questions (see Writing Unit 21). One answer has been done for you.

1. Summarize the points made in the lecture, explaining how they respond to specific issues in the reading passage.
   ☑ Problem-Solution   ☐ Challenge
2. Summarize the points made in the lecture you just heard, being sure to specifically explain how they cast doubt on points made in the reading passage.
   ☐ Problem-Solution   ☐ Challenge
3. Summarize the points made in the lecture, being sure to explain how they oppose specific points made in the reading passage.
   ☐ Problem-Solution   ☐ Challenge
4. Summarize the points made in the lecture you just heard, being sure to explain how they offer solutions to problems discussed in the reading passage.
   ☐ Problem-Solution   ☐ Challenge
5. Summarize the points made in the lecture you just heard, making sure you explain how they answer issues mentioned in the reading passage.
   ☐ Problem-Solution   ☐ Challenge

TEST TACTIC

In rare cases, a Problem-Solution question may use a phrase like "respond to issues." This can be confusing because "respond to" is also used in Challenge questions. However, if the passage discusses problems or asks questions, and the lecture mentions solutions or gives answers, it is a Problem-Solution question.

D   Mastering Writing Task 1 – Reading the Passage

A key skill is to recognize information in the passage that will help you understand the lecture. You will see the passage again after the lecture, so you do not need to understand every word when you first see it. However, you *do* need to make a note of the writer's main view about the topic (usually given in paragraph 1) as well as the three main points that he or she makes (usually given in the final three paragraphs). When you take notes, use abbreviations to save time.

D1 Read the checklist, the passage about the urban heat island effect, and the notes about the passage. Then discuss questions 1 and 2 with a partner.

When you take notes from the reading passage, you should:

☑ Label your notes so you can easily recognize the writer's main view and three main points

☑ Note only the writer's main view and three main points, not background information or supporting details

☑ Use abbreviations (short ways to write something) in your notes in order to save time

A phenomenon known as the urban heat island effect means cities are often significantly warmer than surrounding areas, especially at night. This is because the materials like concrete and steel used in the construction of city buildings trap heat during the day and release it at night. This phenomenon has a number of environmental effects.

As many cities are hotter than surrounding areas, residents of those cities use more electricity during the summer to keep cool. The cost of this usage – for fans, air conditioners, and refrigerators – may be as much as $100 million per year in a city like Los Angeles. And as energy production is rarely pollution-free, there is an environmental cost, too.

The urban heat island effect can also have a harmful effect on bodies of water within and near cities. When rain falls on a city, stored heat is transferred to the water. This warmed water flows into streams, rivers, and lakes and raises their temperature, which can stress or even kill wildlife. In one example, rainfall over Cedar Rapids, Iowa led to a large increase in the temperature of water in a nearby stream that killed many fish.

In addition to the environmental impact, the urban heat island effect can cause summer heat waves to last longer and be more severe. This leads to health issues, including an increase in the mortality rate – that is, the number of deaths. This issue is particularly significant in cities with a large seasonal variation in weather like Chicago and New York.

MV   urban heat island effect (UHIE) → effects on environm
       UHIE caused by city construction materials trapping heat
P1   UHIE → more use of elec → high annual $ / more pollut
P2   UHIE → nearby rivers etc. → raises temp → harms wildlife
P3   UHIE → heat waves longer + hotter → increases deaths

1. What information in the notes is unnecessary because it gives background information?
2. What abbreviations are used in the notes? What does each abbreviation stand for?

D2 Read this passage and take notes. Use the checklist in exercise D1 as a guide. Complete the task in three minutes.

A cultural symbol in many places, lions are currently listed as a vulnerable species by the International Union for the Conservation of Nature. Since the 1950s, it is estimated that the number of lions in Africa has fallen by a factor of ten to 20. If the situation does not improve, the species may face extinction.

A major cause of the decline in population of lions is hunting. Some of the hunting is done by local farmers protecting their livestock, but the bigger problem is hunting for trophy specimens by wealthy foreign tourists who are willing to pay significant amounts to shoot a lion. And because tourist dollars are an important source of income for many people in the regions where lions live, the rate at which lions are hunted for sport is only likely to increase.

Another cause is habitat loss. Growing human populations mean people are living and farming in areas that were previously uninhabited. This means less space both for lions and their prey. Unlike other big cats, lions only do well in areas with a high prey density. In areas with lower prey density, lion populations become fragmented and shrink.

A final problem facing lions is related to the first two issues. As lion populations and habitats are affected by hunting and human settlements, and as individual groups of lions become isolated from one another, the genetic diversity of each group of lions becomes more limited. Over time this leads to a so-called population bottleneck, meaning that the number of animals left for breeding may be too small for the species as a whole to survive.

TEST TACTIC

Even if you find the reading passage hard to understand, do not worry. You will see the passage again during the 20 minutes of writing time. During the first three minutes of reading time, focus on finding and noting the three main points, ideas, questions, or problems.

E Mastering Writing Task 1 – Listening to the Lecture

While you listen to the lecture, take detailed notes about the speaker's points. You will not have time to note every word the speaker says, so focus on ideas that relate to the three main points in the passage. Use abbreviations to save time.

Track 389 **E1** **Listen to three students talk about strategies they use when taking notes. Match each speaker, A–C, to one strategy.**

Strategy 1	The three points the speaker discusses in Writing Task 1 will be in the same order as the points in the reading. This knowledge helps you predict what the speaker will discuss next.	Speaker _____
Strategy 2	Just after the lecture finishes, you might have a good memory of the speaker's words. If so, do not start writing immediately, but take a little time to add to your lecture notes before your memory fades. This will help you summarize the lecture more effectively.	Speaker _____
Strategy 3	Although note-taking is difficult, the more you practice it, the easier it will become. So practice taking notes often, such as when you watch TV or listen to the radio.	Speaker _____

Track 390 **E2** **Take notes as you listen to a lecture about the urban heat island effect. Then copy three answers from A–D to complete these unfinished notes. One of the answers does not match the unfinished notes.**

MV UHIE affects people + environm BUT ways to reduce
P1 1. _____
    Painting roofs light color also reduces
P2 2. _____
    Also use green roofs to soak up H₂0 before
P3 3. _____
    Many cities have places for cooling and education

A Reducing heat in city reduces danger for people
B Planting trees + grass reduces heat in city
C Teaching people about cost of elec reduces effect
D Use materials to let H_2O cool before flow into river

Track 391 **E3** **Take notes as you listen to a lecture about the declining population of lions. Use the checklist below and the notes in exercise E2 as a guide.**

You will only have one chance to listen to the lecture, so you should

☑ Take as many notes as you can about ideas that are related to points in the reading

☑ Use abbreviations (short ways to write something) in your notes in order to save time

☑ Copy the speaker's words directly or paraphrase them, whichever is easier for you

F Mastering Writing Task 1 – Writing an Effective Response

Your response should begin with an introduction and then have three body paragraphs, one for each matching point in the passage and lecture. You do not need a conclusion. Problem-Solution questions are similar to Challenge questions, so you can use the same standard paragraphs you learned for Challenge questions with only minor changes to four sentences.

F1 Look at this outline response to a Writing Task 1 Challenge question (see Writing Unit 21). Then use the example in the first paragraph of the response as a guide to complete tasks 1 and 2.

Both sources discuss _____. This piece of writing will summarize how the points that the writer discusses ~~are challenged by the speaker.~~ *are addressed by the speaker*

The writer first claims that _____. The speaker states that _____. He/She goes on to state that _____. This is one way that the lecture challenges the reading.

The writer next says that _____. The speaker argues that _____. He/She continues by arguing that _____. This is another way that the lecture casts doubt on the reading.

The writer then asserts that _____. The speaker makes the point that _____. He/She then points out that _____. This is the final way that the lecture contradicts the reading.

1. Cross out a phrase in each paragraph that is suitable for Challenge questions but not for Problem-Solution questions.
2. Replace the crossed out phrase with one of these phrases. (It does not matter which answer replaces which phrase.)
    *   addresses issues from the reading
    *   answers questions in the reading
    *   takes up points in the reading

F2 Complete sentences 1, 3, and 5 in this unfinished response by paraphrasing information from the passage or notes in exercise D1. Then complete sentences 2, 4, and 6 by summarizing the notes in exercise E2. Work with a partner.

Both sources discuss the environmental impact of the urban heat island effect. This piece of writing will summarize how the points that the writer makes are addressed by the speaker.

The writer first claims that 1. _____. The speaker states that planting trees in cities can reduce the urban heat island effect. She goes on to state that 2. _____. This is one way that the lecture addresses issues from the reading.

The writer next says that 3. _____. The speaker argues that using special construction materials can cool water before it reaches rivers. She continues by arguing that 4. _____. This is another way that the lecture answers questions in the reading.

The writer then asserts that 5. _____. The speaker says that 6. _____. She then says that many cities have locations where residents can stay cool, which reduces the effect on mortality. This is the final way that the lecture takes up points in the reading.

F3 Complete this response to a Writing Task 1 Problem-Solution question using either the notes below or your own notes from exercise **D2** (reading) and exercise **E3** (lecture).

Reading Notes	Lecture Notes
MV lion popul decreasing (LPD) → may go extinct	MV Lions (L) go extinct is pessimistic view / simple actions can remove threat
P1 LPD cause = hunting by wealthy foreigners for trophies	P1 make L endangered species in hunter's countries also ban trophy imports → likely to reduce hunting of L
P2 also habitat loss (HL) due to human popul growth also	P2 national parks (NP) in Africa = L + other animals protected
P3 also popul bottleneck (PB) caused by low popul + isolation	HL continue outside NP, but with NP, HL not too bad
	P3 Conservationists can move female L to new regions Reduces PB and lets L survive not go extinct

Summarize the points made in the lecture, being sure to explain how they address the problems discussed in the reading.

Both sources discuss _____.
This piece of writing will summarize how the points that the writer makes are addressed by the speaker.

The writer first claims that _____
_____.

The speaker states that _____
_____.

She goes on to state that _____
_____.

This is one way that the lecture addresses issues from the reading.

The writer next says that _____
_____.

The speaker argues that _____
_____.

She continues by arguing that _____
_____.

This is another way that the lecture answers questions in the reading.

The writer then asserts that _____
_____.

The speaker says that _____
_____.

She then says that _____
_____.

This is the final way that the lecture takes up points in the reading.

TEST TACTIC

If you often run out of time when typing your response, write body paragraphs with only three sentences. one to summarize the passage, one to summarize the talk, and one to explain how the two are related. This shorter response is quicker to write, but is still likely to get a good score.

G Mastering Writing Task 1 – Avoiding Common Problems

Correctly and clearly summarizing the ideas that the speaker discusses in the lecture is an essential skill for Writing Task 1. As a result, summarizing the lecture incorrectly or incompletely is likely to reduce your score.

🔊 Tracks 392–394   **G1** **Listen to excerpts (short parts) from three lectures and complete tasks 1–3. When you have finished, compare answers with a partner. Then listen again to confirm your answers.**

1. Listen to excerpt 1 and take notes. Then use your notes and memory to correct any mistakes in this summary of the two solutions to the problem of rising sea levels that the speaker discusses.

   The speaker states that climate change is the main cause of rising sea levels so stopping climate change might reduce sea level rise. He goes on to state that another way to deal with rising oceans would be to build a small system of earthworks, similar to the ones in Holland, to hold back the sea.

2. Listen to excerpt 2 and take notes. Then use your notes and memory to correct any mistakes in this summary of the two ways of reducing pollution caused by incineration that the speaker discusses.

   The speaker argues that the amount of pollution from incineration can be reduced by filtering the waste gases after they are released into the atmosphere. She continues by arguing that another way to reduce pollution levels in waste gases is to force them through a liquid called a scrubber before they are released.

3. Listen to excerpt 3 and take notes. Then use your notes and memory to correct any mistakes in this summary of the two ways that consumers can avoid paying high prices for organic produce that the speaker discusses.

   The speaker says that organic food that is in season in the local area typically costs more than fruits and vegetables that are grown using conventional methods. He then says that consumers can also buy organic food from grocery stores because prices there are generally cheaper than at farmer's markets.

H Test Challenge

H1 **Practice writing a Problem-Solution question by completing the Writing Task 1 question on page 251. First spend three minutes reading the passage. Then listen to the lecture. Finally, take exactly 20 minutes to write or type your response. Use the checklist of skills you studied in this unit as a guide.**

TEST TACTIC

To save time when typing your response, first type the model phrases for the first body paragraph. Use your mouse to highlight the paragraph. Then click the Cut button once and the Paste button three times. Finally, change the second and third body paragraphs so they match the model phrases.

Before you begin writing

☑ Scan the passage and make a note of the main view and the three points, ideas, or theories that the writer gives.

☑ Listen to the lecture and take notes; focus especially on points that are related to the three points from the reading.

While you are writing

☑ Write an introduction that summarizes the topic of the reading and lecture and the relationship between the sources.

☑ Write three body paragraphs that describe in detail how points discussed in the lecture relate to ideas in the reading.

Different nations and institutions have a different definition of what constitutes food waste, but regardless of how it is defined, food waste is a serious and growing global problem. A study conducted by the International Congress in 2011 estimates that approximately one-third of all food produced for human consumption gets lost or wasted and that this happens at every stage of the food supply chain. Let's look at three specific problems common in developed nations.

One issue that results in food waste is overproduction. Agricultural producers contractually agree on quantities of food to deliver to retailers. They may produce more than necessary to be sure they can fulfil their contract despite bad weather or other adverse factors. In many cases where farmers have produced too much, the excess is left to rot in the ground.

So-called appearance quality standards are another cause of food waste. Supermarkets in developed countries have strict standards about the shape, color, size, weight, and appearance of crops. Items not meeting those standards may be sold as animal feed, but are often simply discarded. For some crops, the waste may be up to 30 percent of the harvest.

In industrialized countries, food is often processed before being sold during which loss and wastage can occur. The processing includes cutting, cleaning, and packaging so that the processed food has the right look and size. Food that is damaged or not up to quality is often thrown out even though it would be safe to eat, as disposal is cheaper than the alternatives.

Track 395 Now listen to a lecture on the topic you just read about.

Summarize the points made in the lecture you just heard, being sure to specifically explain how they address issues raised in the reading passage.

Next Steps

You may have questions and topics related to the environment in every section of the TOEFL Test. As a result, learning more vocabulary about this topic, as well as practicing key skills for Writing Task 1 questions, may raise your overall test score.

To learn and practice more vocabulary related to the environment:

1. Do an Internet search for "news stories about the environment."
2. Read one of the stories and make a list of words in the story that are related to the environment.
3. Study the new words carefully and learn their meanings and how they are used.
4. Repeat steps 1–3, but this time do an Internet search for "news stories about <word>", replacing <word> with one of the words related to the environment that you learned in steps 2 and 3.

To practice a key skill for Writing Task 1 questions:

1. Find some sources of academic lectures that have a script of the speaker's words. You can find these in textbooks on academic English or academic listening such as the *Lecture Ready* series by Oxford University Press, or on the Internet.
2. Choose a lecture that sounds interesting. Then do some basic research on the topic of the lecture before you listen to it.
3. Listen to the lecture and take detailed notes. After listening for 2–3 minutes, pause the lecture.
4. Compare your notes to the script of the lecture. For each word in the script that you accurately noted, give yourself one point. (You should give yourself one point even if you used an abbreviation when you noted the word.)
5. Repeat steps 1–4 with a different lecture (or the next 2–3 minutes of the same lecture). Challenge yourself to get a higher points total each time.

Unit Focus

In the writing section of the TOEFL Test you will have two tasks. Task 1 is called the integrated writing task. There are three types of Task 1 questions that all require a slightly different response. For Support questions, you will need to explain how information from a lecture supports or adds to information mentioned in a reading passage. In this unit you will learn key skills and a model answer that will help you write effective responses to Support questions, including:

- taking notes about the main points when you first see the reading passage.
- taking detailed notes about ideas in the lecture that are related to ideas in the reading.
- learning natural model phrases to write an effective introduction and three body paragraphs.
- avoiding common problems like making too many basic grammar, vocabulary, and spelling mistakes.

The vocabulary focus is on academic words and phrases related to:

- technology.

A Warm-up

A1 Choose two phrases from the box or think of your own ideas to complete the first part of sentences 1–4. Then think of and add an example to support each statement.

1. In my opinion, technology has _____. For example, _____.
2. In my view, technology has _____. For instance, _____.
3. I think that technology has _____. To give an example, _____.
4. It is my belief that technology has _____. To illustrate, _____.

changed	had an effect on	affected	influenced
how I learn	my health	my social life	my hobbies

B Academic Vocabulary

B1 Choose the best words from A–H to complete these paragraphs about technology. One answer has been done for you.

A 1. ___device___ is a tool or machine that has been designed to perform a particular function. For example, a computer hard disk is a device designed for the 2. _____ of data. In the modern world, many devices are 3. _____, meaning they contain computer chips that give them specific capabilities. A rice cooker with numerous programmable settings, for instance, is an electronic device.

A computer system typically comprises equipment like a central processing unit, screen, disk storage, and so on, that are collectively known as 4. _____. For computer hardware to be useful, it must run 5. _____. This is the code, or 6. _____, that allows a computer user to perform functions as diverse as accessing data from a 7. _____, playing a game, browsing the Internet, or writing a report. When hardware is out of date, it must be replaced with a more advanced device; when software is out of date, however, a user can often 8. _____ it to the latest version, usually by downloading a file from the Internet.

A database	C electronic	E program	G storage
B device	D hardware	F software	H upgrade

C Analyzing Writing Task 1 — Support Questions

For Writing Task 1, you will first see a reading passage on the screen. The passage will be between 230 and 300 words long and will present three ideas, arguments, theories, or examples related to an academic topic. You will have three minutes to read the passage and take notes.

After three minutes, the passage will disappear from the screen and an announcer will tell you to listen to a lecture on the same topic. The lecture will last two to three minutes, and you will only have one chance to listen to it, so you should take notes as you listen. In rare cases, the speaker might discuss information that supports or adds to the ideas, arguments, theories, or examples from the reading passage. In these cases you will have a Support question like one of the examples below.

After listening, the writing task will appear on the screen and the announcer will read it aloud. You will then have exactly 20 minutes to prepare and type your response. During this time you will be able to see the passage again.

Support questions typically include a word like "support" or "strengthen," as in these examples:

> Summarize the points made in the lecture, being sure to explain how they support the points in the reading passage.

> Summarize the points made in the lecture, being sure to explain how they strengthen specific arguments made in the reading passage.

To answer Writing Task 1 Support questions effectively and get a good score, it is important to:

- paraphrase, summarize, or quote the ideas and supporting details from the lecture.
- give a detailed explanation of how each point from the lecture supports or adds to a point in the reading passage.
- use model paragraphs with natural phrases so your response is well-organized and has few mistakes.

One common problem that can reduce your score when answering all types of Writing Task 1 questions is:

- making too many grammar, vocabulary, or spelling errors by being careless or using language that is too hard for you.

TEST TACTIC

Remember that your task when responding to any type of Writing Task 1 question is to explain how the lecture relates to the reading. If you express your own opinion about the topic, you may not have enough time to write an effective response, which will reduce your score.

C1 **Choose the best answer from A–C to fill in blanks 1–3 in the questions below.**

Support Questions

- Summarize the points in the lecture, being sure to explain how they confirm the points in the reading.
- Summarize the points made in the lecture you just heard, being sure to specifically explain how they 1. _____ for the points made in the reading passage.

Challenge Questions (see Writing Unit 21)

- Summarize the points in the lecture, taking care to explain how they contradict points made in the reading.
- Summarize the points made in the lecture you just heard, being sure to state how they 2. _____ specific points made in the reading passage.

Problem-Solution Questions (see Writing Unit 22)

- Summarize the points made in the lecture, being sure to explain how they address the questions raised in the passage.
- Summarize the points made in the lecture, making sure you explain how they 3. _____ mentioned in the reading.

A cast doubt on   B give supporting evidence   C solve the problems

D Mastering Writing Task 1 – Reading the Passage

A key skill is to recognize information in the passage that will help you understand the lecture. You will see the passage again after the lecture, so you do not need to understand every word when you first see it. However, you *do* need to make a note of the writer's main view about the topic (usually given in paragraph 1) as well as the three main points that he or she makes (usually given in the final three paragraphs). When you take notes, use abbreviations to save time.

D1 Underline the writer's main view and three main points in this reading passage from a Writing Task 1 question. When you have finished, compare ideas with a partner. One answer has been done for you.

> The Internet has only been a global phenomenon for around 20 years, but many could not imagine life without it. We use the Internet for so many things – education, work, friendship, entertainment – that it has become a vital part of everyday life for many. People are now starting to realize, however, that the Internet has negative effects, too.
>
> One issue that is often mentioned is how the Internet is eroding people's ability to communicate well in writing. In many forms of written communication on the Internet, correct spelling, grammar, and use of punctuation are not expected. So, many young people develop bad writing habits that can lead to problems when they attend college or begin work.
>
> The Internet has also had an impact on people's physical health. Browsing sites, playing games, chatting with friends, watching videos, and all the other activities that people typically engage in while using the Internet are all sedentary activities, meaning that they can be done without any physical exertion. People who spend many hours each day not moving are at risk for weight gain and all the many health problems associated with obesity.
>
> Another problem relates to what could be called intellectual laziness. Several books have been written describing how the Internet affects not just people's willingness to read lengthy texts, but also, over time, their ability to do so. An abbreviation sometimes seen in user-posted comments on the Internet is "tldr," standing for "too long, didn't read."

D2 Look at these notes about the reading in exercise **D1**. Which set of notes is better: A or B? Why? Discuss with a partner.

A Notes	
MV	internet (IN) phenomenon for 20 years + used for many things
	vital part of everyday life for many people but sometimes negative
P1	people bad at spelling etc. because not attend college or get a job
P2	IN is fun (games, chat, videos) but people should exercise more
P3	Intellectual laziness is caused by IN

B Notes	
MV	internet (IN) used for many good things BUT has bad effects
P1	IN = bad spell/grammar/punc → prob at univ/job because poor writing
P2	IN activities = no movement → gain weight + health prob
P3	people not willing / able read long articles on IN → intellectual laziness

D3 Read this passage and take notes. Use the better set of notes in exercise **D2** as a guide. Complete the task in three minutes.

> The use of cloud computing has become a major trend in computing over the past decade because of the advantages it offers to businesses. Cloud computing is the use of a network, usually the Internet, to access computing resources that are stored remotely. In other words, a user in one location can access computer hardware or software in a different location via the network.

Cost efficiency is one of the major advantages of cloud computing. Using the cloud, businesses can typically get access to business applications like word processing, spreadsheets, and databases, far cheaper than if they had to purchase individual licenses for these programs for every employee. Paying for data storage on the cloud is also typically much cheaper than purchasing physical storage devices.

Another huge advantage of cloud computing for many businesses and their employees is continuous access to data. Provided they have access to a network, users can access their work data from anywhere, anytime, and on almost any device. This gives employees the option to work from home – a practice often known as telecommuting. It also allows employees to work together on shared documents easily.

One more benefit of cloud computing is data safety. Backing up data to and restoring or recovering it from physical backup drives is typically an expensive and time-consuming process. Cloud service providers, however, typically offer data backup, data restoration, and data recovery services. This gives businesses the peace of mind to know that should anything go wrong, they will easily be able to access or restore backup data and even recover lost data.

E Mastering Writing Task 1 – Listening to the Lecture

While you listen to the lecture, take detailed notes about the speaker's points. You will not have time to note every word the speaker says, so focus on ideas that relate to the three main points in the passage. Use abbreviations to save time.

Tracks 396–399 **E1** Listen to some excerpts (short parts) from academic lectures and take notes. Then use your notes to write responses to tasks 1–3. One response has been written for you.

1. Summarize the examples of tool use among animals that the speaker mentions.
   The speaker mentions that several species of animals use tools to find food and for other basic needs.

2. Summarize the information about Luddites that the speaker gives.
   _____

3. Summarize the details about ENIAC that the speaker discusses.
   _____

Track 400 **E2** Look at these partial notes from a lecture about the negative effects of the Internet. Then listen to the lecture and take notes about the other two points the speaker discusses.

> MV   agree IN great but causes prob
> P1   IN also affect spoken communic as IN communic usu written
>   people not good + uncomfortable at face-face conversations

Track 401 **E3** Listen to a lecture about cloud computing. Take notes as you listen. Use the partial notes in exercise **E2** as a guide.

E4 Check (✓) Yes or No in response to statements 1–5 about listening to the lecture and taking notes.

1. I am generally able to recognize and note the speaker's main view.   ☐ Yes   ☐ No
2. In most cases I can recognize and note the speaker's three main points.   ☐ Yes   ☐ No
3. I am confident that the notes I take are clear and have enough detail.   ☐ Yes   ☐ No
4. In general, I find it easy to use abbreviations when I am taking notes.   ☐ Yes   ☐ No
5. I never lose concentration in the middle of the lecture when taking notes. ☐ Yes   ☐ No

TEST TACTIC

Before you begin Writing Task 1, fold your note paper into eight sections: use the four left sections to note the main idea and three main points from the passage, and the four right sections for the main idea and points from the talk. This will help you easily find related points when typing your response.

E5 Complete tasks 1–3 about your responses to exercise **E4**.

1. Find one or two partners who have roughly the same number of "No" responses as you.
2. For each "No" response, discuss how to improve that aspect of listening or note-taking.
3. Share your ideas from task 2 with other students in the class. Then listen to their ideas.

F Mastering Writing Task 1 – Writing an Effective Response

Your response should begin with an introduction and then have three body paragraphs, one for each matching point in the passage and lecture. You do not need a conclusion. Support questions are similar to the other question types, so you can use the standard paragraphs you learned for Challenge and Problem-Support questions as long as you change the last sentence of each paragraph.

F1 Complete blanks 1–10 in this response about the passage in exercise **D1** and the lecture in **E2** by copying answers from A–J. One answer has been done for you.

Both sources discuss 1. __how the Internet can negatively affect people__ . This piece of writing will summarize how the points that 2. _____
_____ .

The writer first claims that the Internet has affected people's ability to write well. The speaker states that 3. _____
_____ .

She goes on to state that many people find it difficult and uncomfortable to have a conversation with someone. 4. _____
_____ .

The writer next says that 5. _____
_____ .

The speaker argues that the Internet can also make people's eyes become tired and stressed. She continues by arguing that 6. _____
_____ .

7. _____
_____ .

The writer then asserts that 8. _____
_____ .

The speaker makes the point that 9. _____
_____ .

She then points out that 10. _____
_____ .

This is the final way that the lecture endorses the reading.

A   using the Internet can affect people's health because they do not move.
B   the Internet has also affected people's ability to talk to each other.
C   many people accept opinions without thinking about problems with a writer's ideas.
D   the writer makes are supported by the speaker.
E   a study shows that more people than 30 years ago cannot see distant things clearly.
F   the Internet makes people intellectually lazy because they dislike reading long articles.
G   people are also intellectually lazy about thinking about what they read.
H   This is one way that the lecture supports the reading.
I   how the Internet can negatively affect people.
J   This is another way that the lecture confirms ideas in the reading.

F2 Complete this unfinished response to a Writing Task 1 Support question using either the notes below or your own notes from exercise **D3** (reading) and exercise **E3** (lecture).

Reading Notes	Lecture Notes
MV cloud computing (CC) = trend → advans for businesses (B)	MV CC has many advans for B like writer said
P1 cost efficiency = cheaper access to B software (SW) + data	P1 low cost is advan = small business upgrade SW for employees is $2000 CC license for SW just $100 / year
P2 data access = users can access data from anywhere and share files	P2 data access is benefit = people want quality of life + balance of work/life employees want work from home → CC lets B attract good workers
P3 data safety = CC makes easy to back up/restore/recover data	P3 most people know should back up data but never do it CC → data backup is automatic so huge benefit to B

Summarize the points made in the lecture, being sure to explain how they support the points mentioned in the reading.

Both sources discuss _____ .

This piece of writing will summarize how the points that the writer makes are supported by the speaker.

The writer first claims that _____ .
The speaker states that _____ .
He goes on to state that _____ .
This is one way that the lecture challenges the reading.

The writer next says that _____ .
The speaker argues that _____ .
He continues by arguing that _____ .
This is another way that the lecture casts doubt on the reading.

The writer then asserts that _____ .
The speaker makes the point that _____ .
He then points out that _____ .
This is the final way that the lecture contradicts the reading.

F3 Challenge questions (see Writing Unit 21) are more common in the TOEFL Test than Support questions. Complete tasks 1 and 2 to get some extra practice at writing Challenge questions.

Track 402   1.   Listen to a new lecture about cloud computing. Take notes as you listen.
      2.   Use your reading notes from exercise **D3** (or the reading notes from exercise **F2**) and your lecture notes from task 1 to write or type a response to the Writing Task 1 Challenge question below. Complete the task in 20 minutes.

Summarize the points made in the lecture you just heard, being sure to specifically explain how they cast doubt on points made in the reading passage.

TEST TACTIC

Even though the question will ask you to "Summarize the points made in the lecture," it is fine to paraphrase or even quote phrases from the speaker instead of summarizing his or her ideas. Quoting means to copy the exact words that the speaker uses.

G Mastering Writing Task 1 – Avoiding Common Problems

Using standard paragraphs can help you get a good score for Writing Task 1. Avoiding basic grammar, vocabulary, and spelling errors will also help. Making a few basic mistakes may not affect your score, but if there are too many errors, your score is likely to be reduced.

G1 A teacher has circled and noted the errors in this response to a Writing Task 1 Challenge question. Work with a partner to decide how to correct each mistake. Then write out a corrected copy of the response in your notebook.

Both sources discuss the cloud computing trend. This piece of writing will summarize how the points that the writer discusses are challenged by the speaker.

The writer first claims that cloud computing helped [TENSE] businesses due to [CONJ] it gives them cost efficiency. The speaker states that cloud computing may help big corporations which have offices in many locations and numerous workers. He goes on to state that smaller companies with less [WW] employees may not save the money [ART] by using cloud computing. This is one way that the lecture challenges the reading.

The writer next says that cloud computing is convenient because users can access to [PREP] their data any time they want, using any device they want. The speaker argues that cloud computing is only convenience [WF] when there are no network problem. [PL] He continues by arguing that every cloud service provider has had network issues which make it impossible for employee [PL] to access data. This is another way that the lecture casts doubt on the reading.

The writer then asserts that cloud computing is safe because data can be backed up and restored easy. [WF] The speaker makes the point that data stored in the cloud is not safe and can easily be lost, stolen, deleted, or copyed. [SP] He then points out that we hear often [WO] news stories about businesses that lost customer data stored [PREP] the cloud. This is the final way that the lecture contradicts the reading.

Error Codes   ART – missing or incorrect article / CONJ – missing or incorrect conjunction / PL – this word should or should not be plural
PREP – missing or incorrect preposition / SP – incorrect spelling / TENSE – incorrect tense
WF – incorrect word form (e.g., noun instead of adjective) / WO – incorrect word order / WW – wrong word

TEST TACTIC

If you do not have good notes about one of the three main points from the reading or lecture, try writing a body paragraph with only three sentences about that point: one sentence to summarize the passage, one to summarize the talk, and one to explain how they are related.

H Test Challenge

H1 Practice writing a Support question by completing the Writing Task 1 question on page 259. First spend three minutes reading the passage. Then listen to the lecture. Finally, take exactly 20 minutes to write or type your response. Use the checklist of skills you studied in this unit as a guide.

Before you begin writing

☑ Scan the passage and make a note of the main view and the three points, ideas, or theories that the writer gives.

☑ Listen to the lecture and take notes; focus especially on points that are related to the three points from the reading.

While you are writing

☑ Write an introduction that summarizes the topic of the reading and lecture and the relationship between the sources.

☑ Write three body paragraphs that describe in detail how points discussed in the lecture relate to ideas in the reading.

For a number of years, people have been debating the merits of electronic voting systems. There are many arguments against such systems, but as electronic voting technology matures, the strength of those arguments weakens.

One criticism of electronic voting is that it might lead to fewer votes because some people would choose not to vote from fear of technology. In fact, electronic voting would likely lead to higher voter turnout. In surveys, most voters 18 to 30 – an age group with historically low voting rates – say they would be more likely to vote if they could vote online. And only a small proportion of those over 30 say they would be less likely to vote if electronic voting were introduced.

A related issue is concern that voters might make mistakes when voting, such as accidentally voting for a candidate they do not endorse, or voting for too many candidates, because they are unfamiliar with computer technology. In practice, however, electronic voting systems can be designed so that these kinds of errors become either impossible or extremely unlikely.

Another aspect of electronic voting that is commonly criticized is whether the results can be trusted. The worry is that an error in the computer program that counts the votes for each candidate could lead to incorrect results. Again, it is likely that electronic voting will lead to more accurate results, not less trustworthy ones. The vote counting software can be tested an unlimited number of times on sample data to ensure it works correctly under all circumstances.

Track 403 Now listen to a lecture on the topic you just read about.

Summarize the points made in the lecture you just heard, being sure to explain how they support the points in the reading.

Next Steps

You may have questions and topics related to technology in every section of the TOEFL Test. As a consequence, learning more vocabulary about this topic, as well as practicing key skills for Writing Task 1 questions, may raise your overall test score.

To learn and practice more vocabulary related to technology:

1. Make a list of the ten most important examples of technology that you use regularly. For example, your list might include "the Internet" and "smartphone."
2. Read articles or listen to lectures about the "history of" or the "development of" the first item on your list. For example, if the first item on your list is "television," you would learn about the "history of television." You can find articles or lectures about most topics on the Internet.
3. As you read or listen, make a note of new vocabulary related to technology. Then study these words and try using them.
4. Repeat steps 2 and 3 with the other nine items on the list you made in step 1.

To practice a key skill for Writing Task 1 questions:

1. Write ten sentences every day. Focus on writing perfect sentences with no grammar, vocabulary, or spelling mistakes.
2. Show your sentences to a teacher or native speaker of English and ask that person to underline any mistakes. Ask that person not to correct or explain the mistakes.
3. Look at all of the underlined mistakes in your sentences, and find out what your mistake is and why it is a mistake.
4. Rewrite each sentence with mistakes ten times correctly. By writing the corrected form of each mistake ten times, you will fix the correct grammar, vocabulary, or spelling in your memory. This will help you avoid the same mistake in the future.

Unit Focus

In the writing section of the TOEFL Test you will have two tasks. Task 2 is called the independent writing task. There are three types of Task 2 questions. For Single Opinion questions, which are the most common type, you will have to express one opinion about a familiar topic and support that opinion with two different reasons. In this unit you will learn key skills and a model answer that will help you write effective responses to Single Opinion questions, including:

- thinking of relevant ideas and planning an effective response.
- learning natural model phrases to write an introduction, two body paragraphs with examples, and a conclusion.
- avoiding common problems like making too many basic grammar, vocabulary, and spelling mistakes.

The vocabulary focus is on practical words and phrases related to:

- having a job or working.

A Warm-up

A1 Work with a partner to complete tasks 1–4.

1. Write a list of characteristics of good and bad jobs. For example, you might write "good pay" or "too much stress."
2. Share your ideas with other students. Then listen to their ideas and add new points to your lists.
3. What is one job that you would love to have in the future? Why? Support your answer.
4. What is one job that you would never like to do? Why? Give detailed reasons.

B Practical Vocabulary

B1 Answer questions 1–8 by looking at headlines A–D about work. Check your answers with a partner when you have finished. One answer has been done for you.

A
Many workers socialize with colleagues, but not supervisors

B
Survey: Perfect position has high salary, plenty of time off

C
Retail workers want less overtime, opportunities for promotion

D
Report says employees average 9.3 hours per day at workplace

1. Which word in headline A is a synonym for *bosses*? _____ supervisors _____
2. Which word in headline A means the same as *coworkers*? _____
3. Which word in headline B means *money paid for doing work*? _____
4. Which word in headline B has basically the same meaning as *job*? _____
5. Which word in headline C means *extra time spent working after normal hours?* _____
6. Which word in headline C means *a move up to a more senior position at a job?* _____
7. Which word in headline D is a synonym for *staff* or *workers*? _____
8. Which word in headline D means *the place, such as an office, where a person works?* _____

C Analyzing Writing Task 2 – Single Opinion Questions

In Writing Task 2, you will have 30 minutes to prepare and type a response to a question. You will not have a choice of questions. There are three different question types, with Single Opinion questions being the most common. To answer these questions you need to give one opinion about a familiar topic and support your opinion with two different reasons and examples.

Some Single Opinion questions describe two opinions about a topic and ask which of the two opinions you have, as in this example:

> Some people think _____ is good. Others feel that _____ is better. Which do you prefer? Support your answer with detailed reasons.

Other Single Opinion questions ask whether you agree or disagree with a statement, as in this example:

> Do you agree or disagree with the following statement? It is beneficial to _____. Give reasons and examples to support your point of view.

The final kind of Single Opinion questions ask whether you would like to do something or not, as in this example:

> Would you like to _____? Why or why not? Support your answer.

Notice how all three examples ask you to express an opinion about one of two options: in the first example, either the option that "Some people think" or the one that "Others feel," in the second example, either agreeing or disagreeing with the statement, and in the third example, either explaining why or why not.

To answer Single Opinion questions effectively and get a good score, it is important to:

- plan your response by thinking of at least two ideas with examples that support your opinion and reasons.
- use model paragraphs with natural phrases so your response is well organized and has few mistakes.
- write clear sentences that express ideas which are directly related to the question.

One common problem that can reduce your score when answering all types of Writing Task 2 questions is:

- making too many grammar, vocabulary, or spelling errors by being careless or using language that is too hard for you.

TEST TACTIC

It is possible to answer a Single Opinion question by discussing both sides of the topic. However, doing this is more difficult than focusing on just one side of the topic, so you will probably make more mistakes. The reader may also find it harder to understand your response.

C1 Summarize the two options you could express an opinion about from questions 1–4. One answer has been done for you.

1. Would you like to get a job in another country or would you prefer to work in your country? Why?

   Option 1 ___*get a job in another country*___   Option 2 ___*get a job in my country*___

2. Do you think it is a good idea for students to work part time while they attend university? Why or why not?

   Option 1 _____   Option 2 _____

3. Do you agree or disagree that workers need good computer skills in order to get a job? Why? Support your answer.

   Option 1 _____   Option 2 _____

4. Some people are happy to work overtime in order to make extra money. Others prefer not to work overtime because they want to enjoy their free time. What is your preference? Why?

   Option 1 _____   Option 2 _____

D Mastering Writing Task 2 – Planning an Effective Response

For all types of Writing Task 2 questions, learning how to plan your response effectively is a key skill for the TOEFL Test.

🔊 Track 404 **D1** **Listen to an experienced teacher discuss preparing for a Writing Task 2 essay. Which ideas does the teacher express? One answer has been done for you.**

1. As there are only 30 minutes to answer Writing Task 2 questions, planning a response is not necessary. ☐ Yes ☑ No

2. Planned answers are generally better organized, have less repetition, and achieve a better score. ☐ Yes ☐ No

3. In general, if you decide to plan your response, you should finish your planning in two minutes or less. ☐ Yes ☐ No

4. Learning how to plan a response quickly and effectively is a key skill for doing well on the TOEFL Test. ☐ Yes ☐ No

5. The ideas and examples you come up with when you plan your response do not have to be true. ☐ Yes ☐ No

🔊 Track 405 **D2** **Listen to the teacher explain how to plan a Writing Task 2 essay. As you listen, underline the words in steps 1–3 that the teacher does NOT say. What words does she say instead of these words? Two answers have been done for you.**

Step 1	Read the question carefully and <u>notice</u> [recognize] the two <u>choices</u> [options] from the question that you could write about.
Step 2	Make a note of two reasons with detailed examples why you might choose each option from the question.
Step 3	Look at the reasons and examples you noted and decide which of the two options is easier to write about.

D3 **Look at these planning notes for a Writing Task 2 question. Then do tasks 1–4. The first task has been done for you.**

Would you like to get a job in another country or would you prefer to work in your country? Why?

1 get job overseas
more money → salaries in my country low
new experiences → new country / new people / new ideas

2 get job in my country
less stress → not have to learn new language / new culture
easy to get job → lots of jobs in my country now

1. Circle the two options in the notes that summarize the two options from the question.
2. Circle the first reason and supporting example for the first option.
3. Circle the second reason and supporting example for the second option.
4. Which of the two options would you find easier to write about? Why? Discuss with a partner.

D4 **Plan a response to Writing Task 2 questions 1–3. Follow the steps listed in D2.**

1. Do you agree or disagree that workers need good computer skills in order to get a job? Why?
2. Some people feel work is the most important part of their life. Others think friends and family are more important than work. What do you think? Why?
3. Do you agree or disagree with the following statement? Success only comes through hard work. Support your opinion with reasons and examples.

E Mastering Writing Task 2 – Writing an Effective Introduction

After planning your response, you need to type it. Every response should begin with an introduction in which you state your opinion about the question. You do not have to express your real opinion. Using a model introduction paragraph that is suitable for all Single Opinion questions is an effective way to write your introduction quickly and without errors.

E1 Choose the best description, A–D, for each sentence of this example introduction. One of the descriptions does NOT match any of the sentences.

Would you like to get a job in another country or would you prefer to work in your country? Why?

I can see why some might feel that finding work in a foreign country has advantages.
On the whole, however, it is my opinion that getting a job in my country is preferable.
This piece of writing will explain my views on this topic in more detail.

The first sentence of the introduction _____

The second sentence _____

The third sentence _____

A   Contrasts the first opinion with your view about the topic
B   Introduces a detailed reason with a supporting example
C   Gives an opinion about the topic that is not your opinion
D   Gives a general description of the rest of your essay

E2 Complete these introductions by copying phrases from the example introduction in exercise **E1**. Note that the missing phrases are the same for both introductions. One answer has been done for you.

Do you think it is a good idea for students to work part time while they attend university? Why or why not?

_____*I can see why some might feel that*_____ university students should not work part time.
_____ students benefit when they work part time. _____
_____.

Do you agree or disagree that workers need good computer skills in order to get a job? Why? Support your answer.

_____ good computer skills are useful but not necessary to find work.
_____ without such skills, finding a job is very hard _____
_____.

E3 Write introductions to Writing Task 2 questions 1 and 2. Use this checklist as a guide.

☑   Use a phrase from the example introduction you studied in exercise **E1** to begin each sentence of your introduction.

☑   Use ideas from the notes that you made when you did exercise **D5** to complete each sentence of your introduction.

1. Some people feel work is the most important part of their life. Other people think other aspects of life are more important. What do you think? Why?
2. Do you agree or disagree with the following statement? Success only comes through hard work. Support your opinion.

F Mastering Writing Task 2 – Writing Effective Body Paragraphs

After your introduction, you need two body paragraphs. Each paragraph should give a clear, direct reason for your opinion, and support that reason with a detailed example. Your reason, details, and examples do not have to be true. Using model body paragraphs that are suitable for all Single Opinion questions is an effective way to write quickly and with few errors.

F1 **Read this example response to a Writing Task 2 question. Then complete the description of how to organize body paragraphs 1 and 2 by matching the three steps to statements A, B, and C. One answer has been done for you.**

Would you like to get a job in another country or would you prefer to work in your country? Why?

INTRODUCTION

I can see why some might feel that working overseas has advantages. On the whole, however, it is my opinion that getting a job in my country is preferable. This piece of writing will explain my views on this topic in more detail.

BODY PARAGRAPH 1

First of all, I am reasonably sure that working in my country would be less stressful than working overseas. Recently, I read an interesting article about this subject. According to what I read, living and working in another country causes most people to feel stress, which can lead to health problems like heart disease. The article also mentioned that there are three main reasons for this stress: difficulty communicating in a foreign language, difficulty dealing with different customs, and not being able to see friends and family.

BODY PARAGRAPH 2

In addition, I am completely confident that I could find a job in my country more easily and more quickly than a position in another country. In my experience, these days many companies in my country are hiring new workers, but companies in other countries are not hiring so many employees. To give an example, my sister and her friends recently graduated from college and all of them found a job within a few weeks, but my friend who lives in another country says it is not very likely that he will find a job soon.

Step 1	_Give a reason for your point of view that is clear, simple, and direct._
Step 2	_____
Step 3	_____

A   Mention supporting information from your experience or an article you read.
B   Give a reason for your point of view that is clear, simple, and direct.
C   Add one or more additional supporting details from your experience or from the article.

F2 **Rewrite the response from exercise F1 to express the opposite point of view. Use the notes in exercise D3 to help you, if necessary. Some parts of the response have been written for you.**

I can see why some might feel that _____
On the whole, however, it is my opinion that _____
This piece of writing will explain my views on this topic in more detail.

First of all, _____
Recently, I read an interesting article about this subject. According to what I read, _____
_____
The article also mentioned that _____

In addition, _____
In my experience, _____
To give an example, _____

TEST TACTIC

Academic essays written for college courses generally need three body paragraphs. However, 30 minutes is not enough time to write three well-organized body paragraphs. For TOEFL, you can still get a perfect score with two well-written body paragraphs.

F3 Plan a response to Writing Task 2 questions 1 and 2 below. (Review section **D**, if necessary.) Then use your plans to write an introduction and two body paragraphs in response to each question. Use the model phrases from exercise **F2**.

1. Do you agree or disagree with the following statement? Education is the key to success at work. Support your opinion.
2. Some people want a job that has a high salary. Other people want a job that gives them plenty of time off. Which type of job would you prefer? Why? Give reasons and details to support your answer.

G Mastering Writing Task 2 – Writing an Effective Conclusion

The last paragraph of your response should be a short conclusion. The conclusion should paraphrase your opinion about the topic and then express a hope, plan, or possibility related to your opinion and the topic. As with the introduction and body paragraphs, it is a good idea to use a model conclusion paragraph that is suitable for all Single Opinion questions.

G1 Choose the answer, A–C, that best describes the two sentences in this example conclusion. One of the answers does NOT describe either sentence.

Would you like to get a job in another country or would you prefer to work in your country? Why?

In conclusion, for the reasons given, my preference would be to find work in my country.

In the future, my plan is to apply for jobs in my country rather than positions overseas.

The first sentence of the conclusion _____

The second sentence _____

A   gives a further reason for your point of view
B   expresses a future possibility, hope, or plan
C   paraphrases your opinion about the topic

G2 Put phrases A–F in order to make conclusions for Writing Task 2 questions 1 and 2. You should use some phrases twice. Use the example conclusion from exercise **G1** as a guide.

1. Do you think it is a good idea for students to work part time while they attend university? Why or why not?
2. Do you agree or disagree that workers need good computer skills in order to get a job? Why? Support your answer.

A   I feel that it is better for students to work part time
B   improve my computer skills before I apply for a job
C   In conclusion, for the reasons given,
D   good computer skills make finding a job easier
E   In the future, my plan is to
F   get a part-time job when I attend college

H Mastering Writing Task 2 – Using Natural Expressions

Planning your response well and using model paragraphs can help you get a good score for Writing Task 2. Using natural expressions to give your view about whether something is likely or unlikely may also help you write an effective response.

H1 Do the highlighted phrases in sentences 1–4 suggest that something is likely or not likely to happen? Check the box (✓) to mark your answer. One answer has been done for you.

1. In the future, I think there is a slim chance that my boss will give me a promotion.
   ☐ Likely to happen ☑ Not likely to happen
2. I am reasonably sure that in the future I will apply for a job working with technology.
   ☐ Likely to happen ☐ Not likely to happen
3. Because I dislike selling, I am completely confident that I will never work in a store.
   ☐ Likely to happen ☐ Not likely to happen
4. It is doubtful that I will apply for any jobs abroad because I would be homesick.
   ☐ Likely to happen ☐ Not likely to happen

H2 Write some sentences using the highlighted phrases from exercise **H1** to describe some things that you are likely or unlikely to do. Then show your sentences to a partner and give each other useful feedback.

I Mastering Writing Task 2 – Avoiding Common Problems

Avoiding basic grammar, vocabulary, and spelling errors will help you get a good score in Writing Task 2. Making a few basic mistakes may not affect your score, but if there are too many errors, your score is likely to be reduced.

I1 A teacher has circled and noted the errors in this response to a Single Opinion question. Work with a partner to decide how to correct each mistake. Then write out the corrected response in your notebook.

Would you like a career as a teacher? Explain why or why not and give details and examples to support your answer.

I can see why some might feel that being a teacher would not be (enjoy). [WF] On the whole, however, it is my opinion that getting a job as a teacher would have many (advantage). [PL] This piece of writing will explain my views on this topic in more detail.

First of all, as a teacher I would be able to make a lot of money because teachers in my country (earned) [TENSE] a high salary. Recently, I read an interesting article about this subject. According to what I read, even inexperienced teachers who have just graduated from (the college) [ART] get above-average salaries. The article also mentioned that teachers get a pay increase every (years). [PL] These days, buying food, clothes, and renting or buying a place to live is expensive in my city, so I want to earn as much money (than) [WW] possible when I get a job.

In addition, as a teacher I would get plenty of paid vacation time each year. In my experience, teachers in my country get more than 12 weeks of time off each year. To give an example, my uncle is a teacher and he gets six weeks of vacation time (on) [PREP] the summer and two weeks in spring, fall, and winter. (Because of) [CONJ] he has a high salary he can afford to (travel) [PREP] new places each year. I love traveling, and it would be great to have so (many) [WW] time off so that I can travel to many new places.

In conclusion, for the reasons given, I would (be definitely) [WO] interested in training as a teacher. In the future, there is a chance that I will (majer) [SP] in education at university and become a teacher.

Error Codes ART – missing or incorrect article / CONJ – missing or incorrect conjunction / PL – this word should or should not be plural
PREP – missing or incorrect preposition / SP – incorrect spelling / TENSE – incorrect tense
WF – incorrect word form (e.g., noun instead of adjective) / WO – incorrect word order / WW – wrong word

---

J   Test Challenge

TEST TACTIC

To get the most realistic practice for the TOEFL Test, type your response on a computer. Before you begin, turn off spelling check and grammar check if your software has them.

J1   **Practice Writing Task 2 by answering either question 1 or 2. Plan and write or type your response in exactly 30 minutes in order to get realistic practice for the TOEFL Test. Use this checklist of skills that you studied in this unit as a guide.**

Before you begin writing

Remember that in the TOEFL Test you will not get a choice of Writing Task 2 questions. You will have just one question, and the first step in planning your response should be to recognize what type of question it is: Single Opinion, Double Opinion (see Writing Unit 25), or Contrast Opinion (see Writing Unit 26).

- ☑   For Single Opinion questions, first read the question and recognize the two options that you could write about.
- ☑   Think and make a note of reasons with supporting examples why you might choose each option.
- ☑   Look at your reasons and examples and decide which of the two options is easier for you to write about.

While you are writing

- ☑   Write an introduction, two body paragraphs, and a conclusion using the model phrases you learned in this unit.
- ☑   Use natural phrases to make additional points or express contrasting ideas.
- ☑   Take care to avoid basic grammar, vocabulary, and spelling mistakes.

1. Do you agree or disagree with the following statement? A good supervisor should be friendly, but not a friend. Support your answer.
2. Some people want a workplace where they can wear casual clothes. Others are happy to work at a company where they have to wear professional clothes. Which kind of workplace do you like? Why? Support your answer.

Next Steps

You may see questions and topics related to working and having a job in all sections of the TOEFL Test. As a result, learning more vocabulary related to working, as well as practicing key skills for Writing Task 2 Single Opinion questions, may raise your overall test score.

To learn and practice more vocabulary related to working or having a job:

1. Search online job advertisements and find an advertisement for a position that looks interesting.
2. Read the advertisement carefully and make a list of words in the advertisement you do not know.
3. Learn the meanings of these words as well as how to use them in a sentence.
4. Write a cover letter as if you were applying for the position in the ad. Use the words you learned in your letter. (If you are not confident about how to write a cover letter, search the Internet for "sample cover letters".)

To practice key skills for Writing Task 2 Single Opinion questions:

1. Look again at the job advertisement you found from step 1 above. Do some research about the job, such as learning what kinds of duties and responsibilities it requires or what salary is typical. Then decide if you would like to do the job or not.
2. Write an essay that states whether or not you would like to do the job, gives two reasons for your opinion, and supports each reason with a detailed example. Use the model phrases that you learned in this unit in your essay.

UNIT 25
WRITING • Independent Writing Task 2 — Double Opinion Questions

Unit Focus

In the writing section of the TOEFL Test you will have two tasks. Task 2 is called the independent writing task. There are three types of Task 2 questions. For Double Opinion questions, you will have to express two related opinions about a familiar topic and support each opinion with a different reason. In this unit you will learn key skills and a model answer that will help you write effective responses to Double Opinion questions, including:

- thinking of relevant ideas and planning an effective response.
- learning natural model phrases to write an introduction, two body paragraphs with examples, and a conclusion.
- avoiding common problems like writing too many simple sentences.

The vocabulary focus is on practical words and phrases related to:

- health.

A Warm-up

A1 Answer questions 1–3. For each question, write at least three different answers.

1. What are some good things to do in order to stay healthy?
2. What are some of the most common effects of catching a cold?
3. What are some things that people should *not* do when they are sick?

A2 Complete tasks 1–4.

1. Share your answers to question 1 from exercise **A1** with a partner.
2. Listen to your partner's answers to question 1 from **A1**. Add your partner's ideas to your list.
3. Look at your list of answers to question 1 in **A1**. Decide which two answers would be easiest for you to write about if you had to write an essay on that topic.
4. Repeat tasks 1–3 for the other questions in **A1**. For each question, work with a different partner.

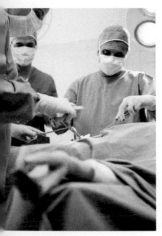

B Practical Vocabulary

B1 Answer questions 1–7 by looking at statements A–C about healthcare. Check your answers with a partner when you have finished. One answer has been done for you.

1. Which word in statement A means *people who see a doctor because of a medical problem*?
   _____patients_____
2. Which word in statement A is a synonym for *doctors*? _____
3. Which word in statement A means *actions or medicines that help a sick person get better*?

   _____
4. Which *two* words in statement B describe kinds of medical problems? _____
5. Which word in statement B is a more formal word for *drugs*? _____
6. Which word in statement C means *an unexpected event that must be dealt with urgently*? _____
7. Which word in statement C is a synonym for the word *operations*? _____

A According to a national survey, almost seven out of ten patients say their physicians prescribe effective treatments.
B Compared with twenty years ago, roughly twice as many conditions and diseases can be treated with medicines.
C Nearly 40 percent of surgeries performed in some hospitals are emergency procedures; the rest are planned operations.

TEST TACTIC

Using statistics – such as *seven out of ten*, *twice as many*, and *40 percent of* – in your written and spoken responses is an effective way to make them more natural and detailed. Your statistics do not have to be true.

C Analyzing Writing Task 2 — Double Opinion Questions

In Writing Task 2, you will have 30 minutes to prepare and type a response to a question. You will not have a choice of questions. Some questions are Double Opinion questions. Unlike Single Opinion questions (see Writing Unit 24), to answer Double Opinion questions effectively you need to express two opinions about the topic, and support each opinion with a different reason and example.

Most Double Opinion questions include a plural noun like *causes, effects, factors, qualities, reasons*, or *ways*, as in the examples below. This plural noun makes it clear that you need to write about more than one cause, effect, factor, quality, reason, or way:

> These days, people have more _____ than they did in the past. What are the causes of this phenomenon? Support your opinion with reasons and details.

> In your opinion, what are the qualities of a good _____? Support your opinion with reasons and detailed examples.

> In what ways has _____ had an effect on _____? Give reasons and examples to support your response.

Some Double Opinion questions ask about current situations or about what people could do. These questions may include a plural noun that is specific to the question, such as *problems* or *advantages*, but often will not have a plural noun:

> _____ is a problem in some countries. What similar problems exist in your country? Support your opinion.

> What can people do to make _____ better? Give details and examples that support your answer.

To answer Double Opinion questions effectively and get a good score, it is important to:

- plan your response by thinking of at least two opinions with supporting examples that answer the question.
- use model paragraphs with natural phrases so your response is well organized and has few mistakes.
- write clear sentences that express ideas which are directly related to the question.

One common problem that can reduce your score when answering all types of Writing Task 2 questions is:

- using too many simple sentences instead of a variety of simple, compound, and complex sentences.

C1 Summarize what you would need to do to answer Double Opinion questions A–D. One answer has been done for you.

1. To answer question A, I would need to discuss two *factors that have led to people living longer lives than in the past* .
2. To answer question B, I would need to discuss two _____
3. To answer question C, I would need to discuss two _____
4. To answer question D, I would need to discuss two _____

A These days, many people live longer lives than they did in the past. What factors are responsible for this situation?

B People visit a doctor when they are sick. In your view, what are the qualities of a good physician? Support your opinion.

C In what ways has technology affected people's health? Give reasons and examples to support your response.

D Obesity (being overweight) is a problem in some countries. What health problems are common in your country?

D Mastering Writing Task 2 – Planning an Effective Response

For all types of Writing Task 2 questions, responses that are planned are generally more effective and get a higher score than ones that are unplanned. As a result, learning how to plan your response effectively is a key skill for the TOEFL Test. However, it is important to remember that the ideas and examples you think of while planning do not have to be true.

D1 Copy answers A–C into the correct space to complete the descriptions of the three steps in planning an effective response to Double Opinion questions.

Step 1	First, decide _____
Step 2	For Double Opinion questions, think _____
Step 3	Finally, look _____

A of and make a note of at least three ideas (each with an example) that answer the question.
B if the question is Single Opinion (see Writing Unit 24), Double Opinion (this unit), or Contrast Opinion (Writing Unit 26).
C at your ideas and examples from the second step and choose the two easiest ideas to write about.

D2 Read this advice about how to think of ideas for Double Opinion Writing Task 2 questions. Then answer questions 1–6. When you answer, try to paraphrase the passage rather than copy it. One answer has been done for you.

In general, good ideas that match Writing Task 2 questions need three characteristics. First, they should be familiar ideas. This means ideas you have spoken or written about before in English. The reason is that when you write about familiar ideas, you will usually write more quickly and make fewer mistakes.

Second, good ideas for Writing Task 2 questions need to be simple ideas, not complex ones. The reason is that simple ideas are easy for you to explain – so you can write them more quickly – and easy for the reader to understand – so he or she is not likely to get confused. A good way to recognize whether an idea is simple is to think whether a child could easily understand the idea.

And third, good ideas for Writing Task 2 questions should be directly related to the topic. As with the other two characteristics, this is because ideas that are directly related to the topic are easier to write about. For example, if a Writing Task 2 question asks you about the best ways to stay healthy, you might have two ideas – exercise regularly and listen to music. The first idea is directly related to the topic – everyone knows that exercise is good for health – so it would be easy to write about. The second idea, however, is not directly related to the topic. You could explain that stress causes many health issues and listening to music can reduce stress so it is good for health, but this is more difficult, so it will take longer to write about it, and there is a greater chance that you will make mistakes and confuse the reader.

1. What is the first characteristic of a good idea for Writing Task 2 questions?
   A good idea that matches a Writing Task 2 question should be a familiar idea.

2. How can you recognize whether an idea is familiar or not?
   A familiar idea is one that you _____

3. What are two advantages of thinking of familiar ideas?
   Two advantages are _____

4. What is the second characteristic that good ideas need and why is it important?
   Second, good ideas should _____
   The reason is that _____

5. How can you judge whether one of your ideas has this characteristic?
 You can ask yourself if _____

6. What is the final characteristic of good ideas for Writing Task 2 questions? Why?
 Finally, good ideas should because _____

D3 Look at these planning notes for a Double Opinion Writing Task 2 question. Then complete tasks 1–4.

> People do many different things to maintain their health. In your view, what are the best ways to stay healthy? Why?

(exercise regularly)	e.g., running or walking → cheap way to lose weight
get different job	e.g., most stress from job → if different job, maybe less stress
visit doctor often	e.g., doctor does tests → tests show problems → doctor gives medicine
eat more vegetables	e.g., vegetables have vitamins → good for body

1. Read and circle the four ideas in the notes that match the question. The first idea has already been circled.
2. Put a check (✓) next to each idea if it is a familiar idea for you, or an *X* if it is unfamiliar for you.
3. Put a second check next to each idea if it is simple and direct, or an *X* if it is complex and indirect.
4. Tell a partner which two of the ideas you would choose to write about and why.

D4 Look at these partial planning notes for a Double Opinion Writing Task 2 question. Then complete tasks 1–4.

> What are the most important qualities of a nurse? Use details and examples to explain why these qualities are important.

friendly	e.g., hospitals are stressful places → feel less stress if people friendly
good at communicating	_____
careful	_____

1. Only one of the ideas has a supporting example. Think of and add supporting examples for the other two ideas.
2. There are only three ideas that match the question. Think of and add at least one more idea with a supporting example.
3. Decide which of the ideas are most familiar to you. Also decide which of the ideas are the most simple and direct.
4. Tell a partner which two of the four ideas you would choose to write about and why.

D5 Plan responses to Writing Task 2 questions 1–4. Follow the steps to planning listed in exercise D1. Focus on coming up with ideas that are familiar, simple, and direct.

1. In general, people's health is better than it was in the past. What are some reasons for this situation?
2. Becoming a doctor, nurse, or other medical professional typically requires years of training. Why do you think some people choose to become a medical professional? Give details and examples that support your answer.
3. In many countries, the number of elderly people in the population is rising. What are some causes of this phenomenon?
4. Nowadays food is easier to prepare than it was in the past. How has this change improved people's quality of life? Support your ideas.

TEST TACTIC

To save time, use one of the ideas that you thought about while planning, but did not choose as your opinion, as the idea that you write about in the first sentence of your introduction.

E Mastering Writing Task 2 – Writing an Effective Response

After planning your response, you need to type it. Every response needs an introduction, two body paragraphs, and a conclusion. To produce an effective response with few errors, it is a good idea to use model paragraphs. The model paragraphs that you learned for Single Opinion questions in Writing Unit 24 are also suitable for Double Opinion questions.

E1 **Read this response to a Double Opinion Writing Task 2 question. Then complete the table below by copying the answer, A–K, that best describes each part of the response. Two answers have been done for you.**

> People do many different things to maintain their health. In your view, what are the best ways to stay healthy? Why?

I can see why some might feel that making regular appointments to see a doctor is a good way to stay healthy. **On the whole, however, it is my opinion that** there are more effective ways to maintain my health. **This piece of writing will discuss my views on this topic in more detail.**

First of all, I feel that eating healthy food, especially fruits and vegetables, is a great way to become healthy and stay healthy. **Recently I read an interesting article about this subject. According to what I read,** fresh fruits and vegetables like apples, bananas, and carrots contain vitamins and other things that are good for my body. **The article also mentioned that** people who regularly eat fresh fruits and vegetables are sick 47% less often than people who rarely eat these things.

In addition, I think that exercising regularly is one of the best, easiest, and cheapest ways to stay in good health. **In my experience,** there are many places where people can work out and many activities that people can easily do without spending a lot of money. **To give an example,** there is a park near my home where I can easily run, play tennis with my friends, or just walk. These activities do not cost any money, which is good for me because I do not have a job these days.

In conclusion, for the reasons given, I think doing regular exercise and eating foods that are good for me are the best ways to stay healthy. **In the future,** I will exercise every day and eat more fruits and vegetables for lunch and dinner.

Introduction	Part 1	
	Part 2	
	Part 3	
Body paragraph 1	Part 1	Give a simple, familiar, and direct first opinion and reason
	Part 2	
	Part 3	
Body paragraph 2	Part 1	
	Part 2	
	Part 3	Add a supporting example to your personal experience
Conclusion	Part 1	
	Part 2	

A   Give a simple, familiar, and direct first opinion and reason
B   Add a supporting example to your personal experience
C   Give an opinion about the topic that some people have
D   Introduce a personal experience that supports your view
E   Give a simple, familiar, and direct second opinion and reason

F   Contrast the first opinion with your views about the topic
G   Introduce information from an article you recently saw
H   Express a hope, idea, plan, or possibility for the future
I   Give a general description of the rest of your essay
J   Paraphrase (or summarize) your views about the topic
K   Describe additional supporting details from the article

E2 **Compare the response to a Double Opinion question in exercise E1 with the response to a Single Opinion question in exercise I1 in Writing Unit 24 (page 266). Which statement, A, B, or C, accurately describes how the two responses differ?**

A   The two body paragraphs in the Single Opinion response use different model phrases than the two body paragraphs in the Double Opinion response.
B   The introduction and conclusion in the Single Opinion response have a different organization than the introduction and conclusion in the Double Opinion response.
C   In the Single Opinion response, body paragraphs 1 and 2 discuss the same opinion, but in the Double Opinion response, body paragraphs 1 and 2 discuss different opinions.

E3 **Look at this unfinished response to a Double Opinion Writing Task 2 question. Finish the second body paragraph and write a conclusion based on the notes below. Use the model response in exercise E1 as a guide.**

friendly	e.g., hospitals are stressful places → feel less stress if people are friendly
good at communicating	e.g., can explain things to patients and doctors well → good communication avoids mistakes
careful	e.g., patients get better when nurse careful / medical mistakes caused by careless nurses

What are the most important qualities of a nurse? Use details and examples to explain why these qualities are important.

I can see why some might feel that nurses should be good communicators. On the whole, however, it is my opinion that there are two more important qualities that nurses should have. **This piece of writing will explain my views on this topic in more detail.**

First of all, it is my belief that being careful is a very important quality that nurses need. **Recently I read an interesting article about this subject. According to what I read,** patients get better quickly when they have nurses who are careful to make sure that their patients get the right medicine and the right treatment. **The article also mentioned that** roughly one third of all medical mistakes are caused by a medical professional, like a doctor or nurse, making a careless mistake.

In addition, from my point of view another key quality for nurses is being friendly. _____

_____

_____

_____

_____

_____

_____

_____

_____

F Mastering Writing Task 2 – Using Natural Expressions

Planning your response well and using model paragraphs can help you get a good score for Writing Task 2. It is also a good idea to use multi-word expressions when you write about your ideas and express your opinions. This will not only make your writing seem more natural, but it will increase the word count of your response as well.

F1 Put the words in order to make five natural expressions for giving your opinion. One answer has been done for you.

1. of view, / my / from / point _____ *From my point of view,* _____
2. of the / that / I am / opinion _____
3. belief / it is / my / that _____
4. seems / that / to me / it _____
5. thinking, / to my / of / way _____

F2 Write a sentence in response to questions 1–5. Begin each sentence with one of the expressions from exercise **F1**.

1. Do you think doctors and nurses should be paid more money?
2. What do you think about the quality of hospitals in your country?
3. Do you believe that children or the elderly need more medical care?
4. Should your government spend more on healthcare, on education, or on sports?
5. Do you think it is more important for physicians to be friendly or good at communicating?

G Mastering Writing Task 2 – Avoiding Common Problems

Planning your response well and using model paragraphs can help you get a good score for Writing Task 2. It is also a good idea to avoid common problems like writing a response with too many simple sentences. To get a good score for Writing Task 2, your response should include a variety of simple, compound, and complex sentences.

G1 Practice writing some complex sentences. Combine each pair of sentences, 1–4, using the given relative pronoun (*which* or *who*). One answer has been done for you.

1. Obesity is definitely a problem in my country. It can have several serious effects on people's health. *(which)*
   <u>Obesity, which can have several serious effects on people's health, is definitely a problem in my country.</u>

2. Stress is another health problem that many people in my country have. Stress can lead to problems like heart disease. *(which)*
   _____
   _____

3. Medical research is one factor that has helped people live longer lives. The research includes finding better treatments for dangerous diseases. *(which)*
   _____
   _____

4. Another factor that has helped people live longer in my country is improved medical training for physicians. They must now study for six years before they get a medical license. *(who)*
   _____
   _____

TEST TACTIC

ETS, the organization that develops TOEFL, says effective Writing Task 2 responses typically have 300 words. However, shorter responses that are well organized and answer the question directly can still get the maximum score. The sample response in section E of in this unit is a good example of a high-scoring short response.

H Test Challenge

H1 Practice Writing Task 2 by answering either question 1 or 2. Plan and write or type your response in exactly 30 minutes in order to get realistic practice for the TOEFL Test. Use this checklist of skills that you studied in this unit as a guide.

Before you begin writing

Remember that in the TOEFL Test you will not get a choice of Writing Task 2 questions. You will have just one question, and the first step in planning your response should be to recognize what type of question it is: Single Opinion (see Writing Unit 24), Double Opinion, or Contrast Opinion (Writing Unit 26).

☑ For Double Opinion questions, think and make a note of at least three ideas with supporting examples that answer the question.

☑ Look at your ideas and choose the two ideas that are the easiest for you to write about.

While you are writing

☑ Write an introduction, two body paragraphs, and conclusion that use the model phrases you learned in this unit.

☑ Use natural phrases to express your opinion clearly and directly.

☑ Try to write a variety of sentences, including complex sentences that use relative pronouns.

1. In what ways does exercise affect people's health? Use reasons and specific examples to support your answer.
2. Why do you think some people have habits that are bad for their health? Support your opinion.

Next Steps

You may have questions and topics related to health and medicine in all sections of the TOEFL Test. As a result, learning more vocabulary about this topic, as well as practicing key skills for responding to Writing Task 2 Double Opinion questions, may raise your overall test score.

To learn and practice more vocabulary related to health and medicine:

1. Make a list of illnesses and medical problems that you or someone you know has had. If necessary, use a dictionary or the Internet to find the English name for each medical condition.
2. For the first medical condition on your list, do an Internet search for "history of [condition]". For example, you might search for "history of the flu". Read some of the articles that you find, and make a list of useful vocabulary in the articles.
3. Repeat step 2, but this time do a search for "cures for [condition]". (For example, search for "cures for the flu".)
4. Review your list of useful vocabulary from steps 2 and 3 and study the words carefully. Then repeat steps 2 and 3 for the other conditions on your list from step 1.

Do the following steps each day to practice key skills for Writing Task 2 Double Opinion questions:

1. Come up with your own Double Opinion questions by replacing the underlined phrase in questions A and B below with a different phrase. For example, instead of *dentist* in question A, you could put *nurse, friend*, and so on.
2. Plan and type a response to your Double Opinion question. Use the strategies and expressions you learned in this unit.
3. Wait a few days and then review your essay. Fix all the mistakes you can find, including sentences that are too simple.

A   What are the qualities of a good dentist? Why are these qualities important? Support your answer.
B   What are the best ways to become healthy? Give detailed reasons and examples to support your view.

Unit Focus

In the writing section of the TOEFL Test you will have two tasks. Task 2 is called the independent writing task. There are three types of Task 2 questions. For Contrast Opinion questions, you will have to express two contrasting opinions about a familiar topic and support each opinion with a different reason. In this unit you will learn key skills and a model answer that will help you to write effective responses to Contrast Opinion questions, including:

- thinking of relevant ideas and planning an effective response.
- learning natural model phrases to write an introduction, two body paragraphs with examples, and a conclusion.
- avoiding common problems like writing a response that is too short.

The vocabulary focus is on practical words and phrases related to:

- transportation and travel.

A Warm-up

A1 Complete tasks 1 and 2.

1. Make a list of many different ways of traveling. For example, you might list vehicles like trains or cars, or traveling alone or with friends.
2. Share your list with a partner. Work together to write comparison sentences about every way of traveling on your lists. Use the example as a guide.

Example   *To my way of thinking, cars and trains are equally good when you need to travel a long distance.*

B Practical Vocabulary

B1 Choose the best answer from A–H to complete definitions 1–8 of expressions related to transportation and travel. One answer has been done for you.

1. _____Distance_____ is the number of miles or kilometers (or other system for measuring length) between two places.
2. Taking a _____ involves traveling between two places, especially two places that are located some distance apart.
3. _____ are machines, often with wheels, that can be used to transport people or goods from one place to another.
4. Many cities have a _____ system of buses, trains, and subways that residents use to travel around.
5. The way a bus or other public transportation vehicle travels between its starting and end points is called its _____ .
6. The last station or stop on the route of a train, bus, streetcar, or airplane is known as the final _____ .
7. The people who travel on public transportation (or on other forms of mass transit like airplanes) are called _____ .
8. When there is bad weather, airplanes may experience a _____ and passengers may arrive at their destination late.

A delay	C distance	E public transportation	G route
B destination	D journey	F passengers	H vehicles

TEST TACTIC

The example responses in this book do not use contractions (e.g., *don't*). Using contractions in your TOEFL responses is not wrong, but contractions are not common in formal writing. As a result, writing without contractions will mean your responses look natural.

C Analyzing Writing Task 2 – Contrast Opinion Questions

In Writing Task 2, you will have 30 minutes to prepare and type a response to a question on the computer screen. You will not have a choice of questions. There are three different question types, including Contrast Opinion questions. To answer Contrast Opinion questions effectively you need to give two contrasting opinions about a familiar topic and support each opinion with a different reason and example. You may also need to say which of the two opinions you prefer.

Most Contrast Opinion questions include phrases like "compare and contrast," "like and dislike," or "advantages and disadvantages," as in these examples:

Compare and contrast _____ with _____. Which do you think is better? Why?

What do you like and dislike about _____? Why? Give details and reasons to support your opinions.

Other Contrast Opinion questions mention two methods of doing something or two ways of thinking about a situation and then ask you to compare or discuss the two methods or ways, as in these examples:

Some people like _____. Other people prefer _____. Compare the advantages of _____ and _____. Which do you prefer? Why?

Some think _____ are good. Others feel _____ are better. Discuss these views.

To answer Contrast Opinion Writing Task 2 questions effectively and get a good score, it is important to:

- plan your response by thinking of ideas with supporting examples for both aspects of the question.
- use model paragraphs with natural phrases so your response is well organized and has few mistakes.
- write clear sentences that express ideas which are directly related to the question.

One common problem that can reduce your score when answering all types of Writing Task 2 questions is:

- writing a response that is too short.

C1 Are Writing Task 2 questions 1–4 examples of Single Opinion, Double Opinion, or Contrast Opinion questions? (If necessary, review page 261 of Writing Unit 24 and page 269 of Writing Unit 25.) One answer has been done for you.

1. What are the best ways for visitors to travel around your hometown? Why?
   ☐ Single Opinion   ☑ Double Opinion   ☐ Contrast Opinion
2. Would you like to work as an airline pilot or flight attendant? Why or why not?
   ☐ Single Opinion   ☐ Double Opinion   ☐ Contrast Opinion
3. What do you like and dislike about visiting a foreign country? Support your views.
   ☐ Single Opinion   ☐ Double Opinion   ☐ Contrast Opinion
4. What are some of the benefits and problems of driving to work each day?
   ☐ Single Opinion   ☐ Double Opinion   ☐ Contrast Opinion

C2 Add your own travel-related words to the blanks to complete Contrast Opinion questions 1–4. Work with a partner. When you have finished, share your ideas with other students. One answer has been done for you.

1. Compare _taking a train_ with _taking a bus_. Which way of traveling do you prefer? Why?
2. What are the advantages and disadvantages of _____? Support your opinion with details and examples.
3. What do you like and dislike about _____? Why? Give reasons in support of your view.
4. Some people feel _____. Other people think _____. Compare these views. Then explain your view.

D Mastering Writing Task 2 – Planning an Effective Response

For all types of Writing Task 2 questions, responses that are planned are generally more effective and get a higher score than ones that are unplanned. As a result, learning how to plan your response effectively is a key skill for the TOEFL Test. However, it is important to remember that the ideas and examples you think of while planning do not have to be true.

D1 Read the information about planning a response to Contrast Opinion questions. Then decide which statement, A–C, paraphrases which step, 1–3, in the information. One answer has been done for you.

Step 1	First, decide if the Task 2 question is Single Opinion (see Writing Unit 24), Double Opinion (Writing Unit 25), or Contrast Opinion (this unit).
Step 2	For Contrast Opinion questions, think of several ideas for each aspect of the question.
Step 3	Choose the ideas you will mention for each aspect of the question, and the order you will write about them.

A   Decide which ideas to write about and how to organize them.
   This answer paraphrases   ☐ Step 1   ☐ Step 2   ☐ Step 3
B   Recognize the type of question that you need to answer.
   This answer paraphrases   ☐ Step 1   ☐ Step 2   ☐ Step 3
C   Come up with ideas that match each part of the question.
   This answer paraphrases   ☐ Step 1   ☐ Step 2   ☐ Step 3

D2 Choose the best title, A–C, for these two strategies for planning effective responses to Writing Task 2 questions. One title does NOT match either of the strategies.

1. _____

   • Stock reasons are familiar reasons that match many Writing Task 2 topics.
   • Examples of stock reasons include money, time, health, work, relationships, and education.
   • Using stock reasons regularly can help you to save time and avoid mistakes.

2. _____

   • Detailed supporting examples are a good way to improve your Writing Task 2 responses.
   • One effective way to add details to your examples is to answer unspoken questions.
   • Some unspoken questions you could answer are *when*, *where*, *who*, and *how much*.

A   Method for improving the quality of your supporting examples
B   Technique for coming up with effective reasons for your ideas
C   Strategy for developing more effective academic arguments

D3 Look at these planning notes for Contrast Opinion Writing Task 2 questions 1 and 2. Match each circled reason to one of the stock reasons listed in exercise **D2**.

1. Compare and contrast traveling around your country by bus and by airplane. Which way of traveling around your country do you think is better? Why?

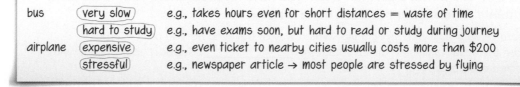

bus	very slow	e.g., takes hours even for short distances = waste of time
	hard to study	e.g., have exams soon, but hard to read or study during journey
airplane	expensive	e.g., even ticket to nearby cities usually costs more than $200
	stressful	e.g., newspaper article → most people are stressed by flying

2. Some people like traveling to different cities when they have free time. Other people prefer to stay home. Compare the advantages of these different ways of spending free time. Which view do you support? Why?

different cities (learn new things)   e.g., can visit local museums to learn about local history
               (make new friends)   e.g., traveled to new city last year and made very good friends
stay home   (can work if needed)   e.g., job is busy now, so boss often asks me to do extra hours
               (less stress)   e.g., newspaper article → travel to new places is very stressful

D4 Look again at the planning notes in exercise **D3** and answer questions 1–5. One answer has been done for you.

1. Which example answers the unspoken question "How much?" ___First example about airplanes in___ ___question 1___

2. Which example answers the unspoken question "How long?" _____

3. Which three examples answer the unspoken question "When?" _____

4. Which two examples answer the unspoken question "Where?" _____

5. Which two examples answer the unspoken question "Why?" _____

E Mastering Writing Task 2 — Writing an Effective Introduction

After planning your response, you need to type it. Every response should begin with an introduction. For Contrast Opinion questions, you will have to learn a slightly different final sentence from the model introduction paragraph you learned for Single Opinion and Double Opinion questions (see Writing Units 24 and 25).

E1 Choose the best answers from A–D to complete the introduction paragraphs for Writing Task 2 questions 1 and 2. One answer has been done for you.

1. What do you like and what do you dislike about traveling by airplane? Explain your opinions.

I can see why some might feel that 1. _____there is nothing to dislike about traveling by plane_____ .

On the whole, however, it is my opinion that 2. _____

This piece of writing will explain my views on both aspects of this topic in more detail.

2. Some believe bicycles are the best vehicle for traveling short distances. Others think cars are better. Discuss these views.

I can see why some might feel that 3. _____

On the whole, however, it is my opinion that 4. _____

This piece of writing will explain my views on both aspects of this topic in more detail.

A bicycles are definitely the better choice for short journeys.
B there is nothing to dislike about traveling by plane.
C airplane travel actually has both good points and bad points.
D both automobiles and bicycles have good points for short journeys.

E2 Now write an introduction for this Contrast Opinion Writing Task 2 question. Use the bold model phrases in the example introductions in exercise **E1** in your response.

Discuss the advantages and disadvantages of using public transportation to travel around a city that you know. Support your views.

TEST TACTIC

Re-using many of the same model phrases for the introduction, body paragraphs, and conclusion for Single Opinion, Double Opinion, and Contrast Opinion questions has several advantages. Your memory of the model phrases will be better if you use them more often, so you will make fewer mistakes and save time.

F Mastering Writing Task 2 – Writing Effective Body Paragraphs

After writing your introduction, you need to type two body paragraphs. For Contrast Opinion questions, each body paragraph should discuss one part of the question. For this reason, you will have to learn different first sentences for the two model body paragraphs you learned for Single Opinion and Double Opinion questions (see Writing Units 24 and 25).

F1 Read these two body paragraphs in response to a Contrast Opinion question. Then answer questions 1 and 2.

What do you like and what do you dislike about traveling by airplane? Explain your opinions.

Thinking about the first aspect of this topic, one thing I like about air travel is that it is a quick, convenient, and safe way to visit foreign destinations. Recently I read an interesting article about this subject. According to what I read, traveling by airplane is much safer than traveling by another method such as by automobile or train. The article also mentioned that air travel is both faster and more convenient than traveling to another country by road, rail, or ship.

In contrast, one thing I dislike about air travel is how expensive it is. In my experience, traveling by plane usually costs at least twice as much as traveling by car, train, or bus. For example, even though I can fly from my home in France to Spain, Portugal, the UK, or other places in less than 90 minutes, the cost of an airline ticket is usually several hundred dollars. Taking a train to these destinations would be slower, but the price would be less than $100, which is more affordable.

1. Which answer, A or B, best describes the organization of both body paragraphs in the response?
    A Each paragraph mentions one or two points that answer the question.
    B Both paragraphs discuss positive ideas that are related to the question.

2. Complete this table by matching model phrases A–H to the correct question type and paragraph. (If necessary, review section **F** in Writing Unit 24 and Writing Unit 25.) Use some answers twice. One answer has been done for you.

Single Opinion and Double Opinion Questions	Contrast Opinion Questions
Body Paragraph 1 • First of all, … • •	**Body Paragraph 1** • • •
Body Paragraph 2 • • •	**Body Paragraph 2** • • •

A First of all, …
B In addition, …
C In contrast, …
D In my experience, …

E Recently I read an interesting article about this subject. According to what I read, …
F The article also mentioned that …
G Thinking about the first aspect of this topic, …
H To give an example, …

F2 Work with a partner to write two body paragraphs for this Contrast Opinion question by putting sentences A–F on the next page in the correct order.

Some believe cars are the best vehicles for traveling short distances. Others think bicycles are better. Discuss these views.

A   Thinking about the first aspect of this topic, in most cases cars are a very fast and convenient way to carry out daily activities like going to a shopping mall or visiting a friend who lives nearby.

B   In contrast, bicycles are a great choice for short journeys for people who want to become healthy.

C   In my experience, riding a bicycle helps me stay fit and healthy but driving a car makes me gain weight because I am not doing any exercise.

D   Recently I read an interesting article about this subject. According to what I read, journeys by car take less than 17 minutes on average, but journeys by other vehicles like bicycles or buses take much longer.

E   The article also mentioned that people prefer cars for many short trips because they offer protection from the weather.

F   To give an example, in the winter I rarely ride my bicycle because it is cold and I usually feel unhealthy and overweight, but in the summer I ride my bicycle as often as I can when I am traveling somewhere close, so I feel healthy and strong.

F3 **Now write body paragraphs for this Contrast Opinion Writing Task 2 question. Use the model phrases from exercise F1 in your response.**

Discuss the advantages and disadvantages of using public transportation to travel around a city that you know. Support your views.

G   Mastering Writing Task 2 – Writing an Effective Conclusion

The last paragraph of your response should be a conclusion. For Contrast Opinion questions, you can use the model conclusion you learned for Single Opinion and Double Opinion questions with a different final sentence that expresses your preference for one of the two aspects of the topic.

G1   **Copy the best answers from A–E to complete the conclusion paragraphs for Writing Task 2 questions 1 and 2. One of the answers does NOT belong in either conclusion.**

1.   What do you like and what do you dislike about traveling by airplane? Explain your opinions.

   In conclusion, for the reasons given, _____

   Overall, however, _____

2.   Some believe bicycles are the best vehicle for traveling short distances. Others think cars are better. Discuss these views.

   In conclusion, for the reasons given, _____

   Overall, however, _____

A   I think the advantages of air travel outweigh the disadvantages.

B   my feeling is that the situation will definitely change in the future.

C   I feel that both bicycles and cars have some advantages, depending on the situation.

D   I think the advantages of traveling by bicycle outweigh the advantages of going by car.

E   I believe there are both good points and bad points about air travel.

G2   **Write a conclusion for this Contrast Opinion question. Use the model phrases from exercise G1 in your response.**

Discuss the advantages and disadvantages of using public transportation to travel around a city that you know. Support your views.

H Mastering Writing Task 2 – Using Natural Expressions

Planning your response well and using model paragraphs can help you get a good score for Writing Task 2. It is also a good idea to use multi-word expressions to support your examples with specific, detailed statistics. This will not only make your writing seem more natural, but it will increase the word count of your response as well.

H1 Match each expression, A–F, to one of the three categories. One answer has been done for you.

Expressions between 0% and 33%	Expressions between 34% and 66%	Expressions between 67% and 100%
•	•	• about seven in every ten
•	•	•

A about seven in every ten   C nearly 20 percent of   E almost two thirds of
B just under one quarter of   D something like half of all   F around 90 out of 100

H2 Write a sentence in response to questions 1–4. If you do not know the answer, make one up. Begin each sentence with one of the expressions from exercise **H1**. When you have finished, compare sentences with a partner.

1. What proportion of the journeys that people make in your country are by train?
2. How many people in your country take vacations overseas every year?
3. What percentage of the people you know prefer traveling with friends?
4. How many employees who work in your country's capital city take public transportation each day?

I Mastering Writing Task 2 – Avoiding Common Problems

It is possible to get a perfect score for a Writing Task 2 response that has fewer than 300 words if the response is well organized and answers the question directly. However, in general longer responses tend to be better than shorter ones.

I1 Complete tasks 1 and 2. Work with a partner on task 1.

1. Rewrite each sentence, 1–8, so that it has the same meaning but uses more words. Use the examples as a guide.
2. When you have finished, share your answers with other students. Make a note of the longest, clearest answers.

Examples   I dislike walking.
　　　　　　→ In general, I do not enjoy walking very much.

　　　　　　Bus journeys in my city are slow.
　　　　　　→ Using a bus to travel around my city usually takes a long time.

　　　　　　Many people buy insurance before traveling.
　　　　　　→ A lot of people choose to buy travel insurance before they take a trip.

1. Traveling by train is expensive.   5. Ticket prices have increased.
2. I recently traveled by boat.   6. I dislike waiting at airports.
3. Many people dislike flying.   7. Visiting another country can be fun.
4. Bicycles are good for short journeys.   8. Some vehicles cause pollution.

J Test Challenge

TEST TACTIC

TOEFL does not give you tools such as bold text, spell check, or a built-in dictionary. If you are used to tools like these, you may find it hard to type your response in the test. To overcome this problem, turn off all tools like these when you practice typing at home.

J1 Practice Writing Task 2 by answering either question 1 or 2. Plan and write or type your response in exactly 30 minutes in order to get realistic practice for the TOEFL Test. Use this checklist of skills that you studied in this unit as a guide.

Before you begin writing

In the TOEFL Test you will not get a choice of Writing Task 2 questions. You will have just one question, and the first step in planning your response should be to recognize what type of question it is: Single Opinion (see Writing Unit 24), Double Opinion (Unit 25), or Contrast Opinion.

☑ For Contrast Opinion questions, think of several reasons for each aspect of the question. Thinking of stock reasons – money, time, health, work, relationships, and education – is usually a good idea.

☑ Look at your reasons and decide which ones you will write about and in which order you will write about them.

While you are writing

☑ Write an introduction, two body paragraphs, and conclusion that use the model phrases you learned in this unit.

☑ Give detailed supporting examples by answering unspoken questions and by using natural phrases to add statistics.

☑ Try to write clear, direct sentences which match the topic and which are neither too short nor too long.

1. Compare and contrast traveling long distances by train with traveling long distances by airplane. Give details to support your points.
2. Discuss the advantages and disadvantages of traveling somewhere with friends and traveling somewhere alone. Which method of traveling do you prefer? Why?

Next Steps

You may have questions and topics related to transportation and travel in every section of the TOEFL Test. As a result, learning more vocabulary related to traveling, as well as practicing key skills for Writing Task 2 Contrast Opinion questions, may raise your overall test score.

To learn and practice more vocabulary related to transportation and travel:

1. Make a list of all the vehicles that you know. Start with the word "trains."
2. Write "Things I Did Not Know about Trains" at the top of a blank sheet of paper.
3. Do some research about trains. When you find something you did not know about trains, paraphrase it on your sheet of paper. Continue researching until you have paraphrased at least ten new pieces of information about trains.
4. Review the information you did not know about trains to find and learn useful vocabulary related to transportation or travel.
5. Repeat steps 2–4 for the other vehicles on your list from step 1.

To practice key skills for Writing Task 2 Contrast Opinion questions, practice either of these tasks every day:

1. Think of a person, place, object, activity, or event. Then spend two minutes making a list of several advantages or things you like about it and another two minutes making a list of disadvantages or things you dislike. Repeat the task five times.
2. Write two contrasting opinions about a topic, such as "Computers are convenient tools" and "Computers are too expensive." Then take 30 minutes to write an essay that compares these two viewpoints and expresses your own view.

Directions

This writing review test is intended to help you find out your strengths and weaknesses in writing. You will complete two writing tasks in 50 minutes. The total time required for the test is approximately 56 minutes. The tasks are designed to be at the same level as the ones you will see on the TOEFL Test. For the first task you will listen to a lecture. For the most realistic practice, cover the question when you listen. You may take notes while you listen. If possible, type your answers. When you have finished, ask a teacher to evaluate both responses from 0–5 or do it yourself. Then use the conversion chart on page 285 to convert your raw scores to your likely score on the TOEFL Test.

Test

TASK 1 – WRITING BASED ON READING AND LISTENING

For this task, you will read a passage about an academic topic. You will have three minutes to read. You may take notes on the passage while you read. You will then listen to a lecture about the same topic. While you listen you may also take notes. You may use your notes to help you answer the question.

You will then write a response to a question that asks you about the relationship between the lecture you heard and the reading passage. Try to answer the question as completely as possible using information from the reading passage and the lecture. The question does not ask you to express your personal opinion. Your response will be judged on the quality of your writing and on the completeness and accuracy of the content. Typically, an effective response will be 150 to 225 words.

Now read this passage. You have three minutes to read.

Coral reefs are among the most biodiverse ecosystems in the ocean, with up to one quarter of all marine species living in or near a reef environment. Sadly, many of these beautiful, fragile structures are dying out. Climate change is a major threat to reefs, but direct human activities have a serious impact, too.

Water pollution caused by humans adversely affects coral reefs. Pollutants can affect reefs in two ways. Certain substances that can contaminate ocean water, such as oil and pesticides, are poisonous to coral and other forms of marine life. Other pollutants, such as animal waste and fertilizer, cause an overgrowth of simple plant-like organisms called algae. These algae block sunlight from reaching the coral, causing it to die.

Three exploitive methods of fishing can cause damage and degradation to coral reefs. First, overfishing of some species can lead to a lack of biodiversity that affects the overall health of the reef. Blast fishing – the use of explosives to stun and kill fish so they are easier to catch – often kills coral polyps and destroys sections of the reef. And the use of cyanide, a poison, to stun large, economically-important fish species often kills both coral and smaller species of fish.

Even tourism has been implicated in the destruction of coral reefs. Many reefs are popular spots for diving, and although many tourists are careful, coral is easily damaged when it is touched. Even stirring up sand and small particles from the sea floor can lead to the degradation of reefs. And waste and pollution from tourists' boats, ocean-front hotels, and even tourists themselves are also a factor.

Track 406 Now listen to a lecture on the topic you just read about.

You now have 20 minutes to plan and write your response. You may see the reading passage again while you write.

Summarize the points made in the lecture you just heard, being sure to specifically explain how they support points made in the reading passage.

TASK 2 – WRITING BASED ON KNOWLEDGE AND EXPERIENCE

In this task you will demonstrate your ability to write an essay in response to a question that asks you to express and support your opinion about a topic or issue. Your essay will be scored on the quality of your writing. This includes the development of your ideas, the organization of your essay, and the quality and accuracy of the language you use to express your ideas. Typically, an effective essay will contain a minimum of 300 words.

Read the question below. You have 30 minutes to plan, write, and revise your essay.

In the last 20 years, technology has become both more advanced and more available. In what ways has greater access to advanced technology affected the way people work? Use specific reasons and details to support your answer.

Score Conversion

Ask a teacher or native speaker to evaluate both responses from 0–5. (If necessary, you can evaluate your responses yourself. See pages 230–233 of the Writing Reference unit for criteria for scoring.) Then add up the score for each response to find your raw score and use this conversion chart to find out your approximate writing score range on the TOEFL Test.

Raw Score (out of 10)	Probable Level	Approximate Score Range
10		30
9	Good	27
8		24
7		21
6	Fair	18
5		15
4		12
3	Limited	8
2		6
1		3

PHOTO CREDITS

VOCABULARY INDEX

Practice Test A

General Information

This practice test measures your ability to understand and use English in an academic context. There are four sections. Before each section, you will see specific directions that explain how to answer the questions in that section.

In the **Reading** section, you will read and answer questions about three passages. The passages will be similar to excerpts from introductory college-level textbooks. The passages will cover a variety of different subjects. You do not need existing knowledge because all the information needed to answer the questions will be in the passage.

In the **Listening** section, you will hear two conversations and four lectures. The conversations will be about typical topics that affect students at university in North America. After each conversation, you must answer five questions. The lectures will be about academic topics that students in their first year at college are likely to study. The lectures will cover a variety of different subjects. You do not need existing knowledge because all the information needed to answer the questions will be mentioned by the speaker or speakers. After each lecture, you must answer six questions.

In the **Speaking** section, you will see six questions. The first two questions ask you to respond based on your experience and opinions. The third and fourth questions ask you to speak about information that you have read and heard. The final two questions ask you to speak about information you have heard. For each question, you will have a specific amount of time to prepare and deliver your response.

In the **Writing** section, you will answer two questions. In the first question, you will have to write about the relationship between the information in a passage that you have read and the information in a lecture that you have heard. In the second question, you will have to write a response based on your experience and opinions.

You may now begin the test by looking at the next page. Alternatively, you can take Practice Test A online at www.oxfordenglishtesting.com.

Reading Section Directions

The Reading section measures your ability to understand academic passages in English. You will have 60 minutes to read three passages and answer 40 questions about what you have read.

Most questions are worth 1 point but the last question in each set is worth more than 1 point. The directions for these questions indicate how many points you may receive.

For most questions, you should choose one answer. For some questions, however, you may need to choose from two to five answers. These questions have special directions that explain how many answers you should choose.

You may now begin the Reading section.

Cloud Seeding

Weather modification, or weather control as it is sometimes known, is any scientific manipulation of the environment intended to change weather patterns. The goal of weather modification is typically either to produce desirable weather, generally rain or snow, or to prevent adverse weather events, such as hail or severe storms. It is distinct from well-intentioned but unscientific attempts to influence the weather used by various cultures since prehistoric times. For example, the Zuni people from the southwestern United States tried to coax water from the sky by performing ritual dances. And there are reports from a few hundred years ago of farmers in Switzerland, Austria, and Italy ringing bells and firing guns in an effort to prevent hailstorms from damaging their crops.

Cloud seeding is the most common form of weather modification. The first attempt at cloud seeding took place in 1946 when scientist Vincent Schaefer dropped six pounds of dry ice (frozen carbon dioxide) from an airplane into a cloud and produced snow. The experiment was only modestly successful, but it spawned optimism among farmers everywhere. It seemed to them that science had finally triumphed over nature. Unfortunately, that was not the case. Although there were extensive cloud-seeding operations during the late 1940s and early 1950s, there was no compelling evidence to indicate that they had any significant effect on precipitation. Clearly, cloud seeding was more complicated than had been believed. It was not until the 1970s that scientists better understood the processes involved. New experiments indicated that only certain kinds of clouds are amenable to seeding. One of the most responsive is the winter orographic cloud, formed when winter air currents encounter a mountain slope and rise. If the temperature in such a cloud is right, seeding may increase precipitation by five to 15 percent. However, to judge the success of cloud seeding accurately, scientists must determine how much precipitation would have fallen without seeding, and this is always difficult to gauge.

One form of cloud seeding, static seeding, was developed by Bernard Vonnegut, brother of the famous novelist Kurt Vonnegut. Silver iodide, which has a crystalline structure similar to that of ice, is heated on the ground in a generator fueled by propane gas. The heat and smoke carry particles of silver iodide up to the clouds where they act as nuclei for the formation of ice crystals, which then fall as rain or snow. The system first used by Schaefer, the glaciogenic method, employs airplanes – or sometimes rockets – to deliver dry ice pellets. Aircraft seeding is typically more effective than ground-based seeding because accurate delivery of the seeding agent is possible. However, it is considerably more expensive. A third method, hygroscopic seeding, has been in use only for a few years and requires more research. This method involves using planes to carry salt crystals to the lower portions of clouds.

Cloud seeding in the United States has mostly taken place in western states. The population of the West has expanded rapidly over recent decades, and this area relies more heavily on snowfall than other regions of the United States. About 75 percent of the water in western rivers comes from melted snow. Indeed, without consistent and heavy snowfall in the Rocky Mountains and the Sierra Nevada range, the West would experience droughts. The most intensive effort to produce precipitation, mainly conducted by the federal government, took place during the West's snow drought in the winter of 1976–77. Although it is difficult to judge the effectiveness of cloud seeding based on one crash program, most experts doubted that large-scale cloud seeding led to a significant increase in the amount of snow that fell during that period. Because the program was not a clear-cut success, the US federal government discontinued cloud-seeding operations in the late 1970s, but some individual states continue to seed clouds as do nongovernmental organizations, including ski resorts and agricultural cooperatives. Cloud seeding is also practiced in other countries, particularly those with regions prone to drought, such as Australia, India, and China. In fact, China probably has the most extensive weather-modification programs of any nation in the world.

1. The word "adverse" in paragraph 1 most likely means
   - (A) advanced
   - (B) discovered
   - (C) impossible
   - (D) undesirable

2. Why does the author mention farmers from Switzerland, Austria, and Italy in paragraph 1?
   - (A) To compare their goals with those of the Zuni people of the US Southwest
   - (B) To give an example of a nonscientific attempt to control weather patterns
   - (C) To point out that they were successful at producing the weather they wanted
   - (D) To emphasize how important it was for them to protect their crops from hail

3. The word "spawned" in paragraph 2 is closest in meaning to
   - (A) came up with
   - (B) gave rise to
   - (C) grew out of
   - (D) went in for

4. What can be inferred about the feelings of farmers after the cloud-seeding operations of the late 1940s and early 1950s?
   - (A) They were pleased that these extensive operations were producing significant evidence.
   - (B) They were optimistic that future cloud-seeding operations would be even more successful.
   - (C) They were upset that scientists were trying to modify the weather without consulting with them.
   - (D) They were disappointed because these operations were less successful than the first experiment.

5. According to paragraph 2, what had scientists learned about cloud seeding by the 1970s?
   - (A) Not all types of clouds can be successfully seeded.
   - (B) It is difficult to seed clouds in mountainous areas.
   - (C) Seeding is more successful when the weather is cold.
   - (D) Seeding always leads to higher levels of precipitation.

6. The word "gauge" in paragraph 2 is closest in meaning to
   - Ⓐ define
   - Ⓑ prevent
   - Ⓒ measure
   - Ⓓ observe

7. According to the author, in what way are the glaciogenic and hygroscopic methods of cloud seeding similar?
   - Ⓐ They were developed at about the same time.
   - Ⓑ They use chemicals with similar structures.
   - Ⓒ They employ the same delivery method.
   - Ⓓ They were developed by the same scientist.

8. The word "it" in paragraph 3 refers to
   - Ⓐ the seeding agent
   - Ⓑ accurate delivery
   - Ⓒ ground-based seeding
   - Ⓓ aircraft seeding

9. In paragraph 3, the author states that clouds are seeded with all of the following substances EXCEPT
   - Ⓐ silver iodide
   - Ⓑ propane gas
   - Ⓒ dry ice pellets
   - Ⓓ salt crystals

10. Which of the following best expresses the essential information in the highlighted sentence in paragraph 4? Incorrect choices change the meaning in important ways or leave out essential information.
    - Ⓐ Although a large amount of snow fell during the period, experts were unsure how to judge cloud seeding.
    - Ⓑ Most experts felt that, on balance, the program did not contribute to increased snowfall during the period.
    - Ⓒ Experts asked to judge if cloud seeding was effective felt there was insufficient time to make an assessment.
    - Ⓓ So much snow fell during the period that it was difficult to judge whether clouds had been seeded or not.

11. What point does the author make in paragraph 4?
    - Ⓐ Although the US government no longer has a weather modification program, other nations and organizations do.
    - Ⓑ Because the US government has stopped cloud-seeding operations, other countries have increased their efforts.
    - Ⓒ Few regions of the US are prone to drought, so the US government made the decision to discontinue cloud seeding.
    - Ⓓ Countries like Australia, India, and China have used data from the US government to develop extensive programs.

12. Look at the four squares (■) that indicate where the following sentence could be added to the passage.

Unlike silver iodide, dry ice works not by providing ice-forming nuclei, but by lowering the temperature near the water droplets in the clouds, causing them to freeze instantly.

Where would the sentence best fit? Choose position **A**, **B**, **C**, or **D**.

One form of cloud seeding, static seeding, was developed by Bernard Vonnegut, brother of the famous novelist Kurt Vonnegut. Silver iodide, which has a crystalline structure similar to that of ice, is heated on the ground in a generator fueled by propane gas. The heat and smoke carry particles of silver iodide up to the clouds where they act as nuclei for the formation of ice crystals, which then fall as rain or snow. **A** The system first used by Schaefer, the glaciogenic method, employs airplanes – or sometimes rockets – to deliver dry ice pellets. **B** Aircraft seeding is typically more effective than ground-based seeding because accurate delivery of the seeding agent is possible. **C** However, it is considerably more expensive. **D** A third method, hygroscopic seeding, has been in use only for a few years and requires more research. This method involves using planes to carry salt crystals to the lower portions of clouds.

13. **Directions:** An introductory sentence for a brief summary of the passage is provided below. Complete the summary by selecting the THREE answer choices that express the most important ideas in the passage. Some sentences do not belong in the summary because they express ideas that are not presented in the passage or are minor ideas in the passage. **This question is worth 2 points.**

> **Weather modification involves using scientific methods to change the weather in ways that benefit humans.**
>
> -
> -
> -

- Ⓐ Hygroscopic seeding is a common method of cloud seeding, although scientists are still researching its effectiveness.
- Ⓑ One scientist involved in cloud-seeding experiments is famous because of his sibling, who is a well-known writer.
- Ⓒ The most common form of weather modification involves seeding clouds with chemicals to induce precipitation.
- Ⓓ Scientists' knowledge of the processes involved in cloud seeding improved as they conducted more experiments.
- Ⓔ A snow drought during the winter of 1976–77 led to a variety of efforts to modify the weather in mountainous areas.
- Ⓕ An early experiment in cloud seeding was successful, but later experiments did not have such impressive results.

North American Colonial Furniture

Britain's North American colonies covered a vast area, far larger than most European nations, and during the Colonial Period from roughly 1620 to 1776, no single metropolis emerged as a cultural center equivalent to London or Paris. There was, therefore, no single "American" style of furniture-making during that period. A transplanted British style of furniture-making predominated throughout most of the Colonies, but artisans of British ancestry in different locations adjusted their products to suit local differences in materials, climate, and taste. Cities as close geographically as Boston, in the Massachusetts colony, and Hartford, in the colony of Connecticut, produced strikingly different styles of furniture even though both were derived from the same British sources. Although the British influence was strong, many artisans in the Colonies continued to work in the idiom of their respective mother countries. Colonists of Dutch ancestry in the Hudson Valley of the New York colony, for instance, produced wardrobes and other pieces in the style of the Netherlands. In the colonies of Pennsylvania and North Carolina, furniture-makers of German ancestry maintained furniture traditions from their homeland, as did Swedish artisans in Delaware.

In the early Colonial Period (pre-1720), few colonists could afford to furnish their homes with more than strictly essential and utilitarian pieces: stools, benches, chests, straight chairs, tables, and beds. Most furniture of this period was of a style known as Jacobean, though Colonial Jacobean furniture is far plainer than British Jacobean furniture. Few pieces had the kinds of decorative, elaborately carved features seen on European furniture at that time. Jacobean pieces were simple in design and heavy-looking, and frequently served multiple purposes. Houses of the time often consisted of only one small room with a low ceiling. The table-chair, a chair that could tilt forward to form a table, was typical of the space-saving furniture popular at the time. Only a few simple tools were required to build these pieces, and they were made of readily available native woods such as pine, maple, oak, and walnut. Many pieces were literally homemade and used construction techniques that would have been considered outmoded in Europe.

However, around 1720, the Colonies became more affluent, and wealthy merchants demanded grander furniture. For the next three and a half decades, the Queen Anne furniture style was the rage. Unlike the boxy, bulky furniture of the early Colonial Period, Queen Anne pieces were more graceful and curved. The most distinctive feature of Queen Anne pieces was the *cyma*, or S-shaped curve, and carved ornaments such as seashells were common. Simple, multi-purpose pieces such as the bench gave way to more specialized pieces like the tea table. Colonial homes, especially in cities, grew larger and contained more rooms: several bedrooms, a dining room, a central hall, and a parlor, each requiring specific items of furniture.

Although published in London in 1754, British craftsman Thomas Chippendale's book of furniture patterns, *The Gentleman and Cabinet-Maker's Director*, did not become available in the Colonies until the 1760s. When it did arrive, it had such a profound influence on furniture-makers that Chippendale furniture is the name given to Colonial furniture of this period. Chippendale furniture has a refined and graceful form, with curving lines and elaborate carvings. Some Chippendale pieces clearly show the influence of Chinese furnishings. Many were made not of native woods but of tropical woods, especially mahogany, which were imported from Caribbean islands under British rule. Sofas and chairs of this period were upholstered in expensive fabrics such as velvet. The father and son team of John and Thomas Goddard, whose workshop was in Newport, in the Rhode Island colony, produced splendid Chippendale cabinets, desks, and bookshelves. William Savery of Philadelphia, the largest city in the Colonies, also produced high-quality Chippendale furniture, and his pieces were as popular in the Colonies as Thomas Chippendale's were in England.

Around 1900, a style of furniture called Colonial Revival (or Early American), which mimicked Colonial styles, became popular in part because of the efforts of a historian and furniture-maker named Wallace Nutting. Mass-produced reproductions of Colonial pieces were common sights in suburban homes across the United States during the mid-twentieth century. Pieces of Colonial Revival furniture can still be seen in thrift shops and secondhand furniture stores.

14. Which of the following best expresses the essential information in the highlighted sentence in paragraph 1? Incorrect choices change the meaning in important ways or leave out essential information.
- Ⓐ Furniture made in Boston was different from that made in Hartford even though the two cities were in the same colony.
- Ⓑ Although Boston and Hartford are close to each other, the styles of furniture produced in those cities were dissimilar.
- Ⓒ People in Boston and Hartford produced furniture that was different from furniture made in nearby Colonial cities.
- Ⓓ Furniture-makers in Boston and Hartford wanted to produce furniture that was different from furniture made in Britain.

15. The word "idiom" in paragraph 1 is closest in meaning to
- Ⓐ language
- Ⓑ style
- Ⓒ materials
- Ⓓ effect

16. Which of the following can be inferred from paragraph 1?
- Ⓐ There was high demand for furniture made by colonists originally from the Netherlands.
- Ⓑ People in Delaware liked traditional furniture more than people in the New York colony.
- Ⓒ British furniture styles had little influence on furniture made by people from other countries.
- Ⓓ Many people of German ancestry lived in Pennsylvania or North Carolina after emigrating.

17. The word "utilitarian" in paragraph 2 is closest in meaning to
- Ⓐ practical
- Ⓑ precious
- Ⓒ primitive
- Ⓓ profitable

18. Why does the author mention the "table-chair" in paragraph 2?
- Ⓐ To suggest that not every piece of furniture could be made with simple tools
- Ⓑ To show that furniture-makers in the colonies produced some clever designs
- Ⓒ To give an example of a piece of furniture that had more than one purpose
- Ⓓ To contrast Colonial Jacobean furniture with Jacobean furniture from Britain

19. The word "outmoded" in paragraph 2 is closest in meaning to
- Ⓐ rarely seen
- Ⓑ old-fashioned
- Ⓒ overpriced
- Ⓓ little-known

20. How does the author organize the information in paragraph 3?
- Ⓐ By contrasting Queen Anne furniture with pieces made in earlier times
- Ⓑ By discussing one piece of ornamental Queen Anne furniture in detail
- Ⓒ By explaining why the design of Queen Anne furniture was so attractive
- Ⓓ By giving examples of Queen Anne furniture designed for specific rooms

21. The word "Many" in paragraph 4 refers to
- Ⓐ curving lines
- Ⓑ elaborate carvings
- Ⓒ Chippendale pieces
- Ⓓ Chinese furnishings

22. In paragraph 4, the author mentions all of the following about Chippendale furniture EXCEPT:
- Ⓐ Some pieces were influenced by Chinese designs.
- Ⓑ Chairs and sofas were the most popular pieces.
- Ⓒ Pieces were often made using costly materials.
- Ⓓ It was popular both in the Colonies and Britain.

23. What can be inferred from paragraph 4?
- Ⓐ During the 1760s, Britain had other colonies in addition to North America.
- Ⓑ Native woods were not strong enough to use in making Chippendale furniture.
- Ⓒ Thomas Goddard learned how to make Chippendale furniture from his father.
- Ⓓ At first, Thomas Chippendale's book was not successful in North America.

24. The word "mimicked" in paragraph 5 is closest in meaning to
- Ⓐ illustrated
- Ⓑ designed
- Ⓒ copied
- Ⓓ produced

25. What does the author imply about Colonial Revival furniture in paragraph 5?
- Ⓐ It became popular because of the success of Wallace Nutting's furniture designs.
- Ⓑ Like Colonial furniture, it was mostly handmade by individual furniture-makers.
- Ⓒ Homeowners liked to have it in their homes because their neighbors also had it.
- Ⓓ It was more popular during the middle of the twentieth century than it is now.

26. Look at the four squares (■) that indicate where the following sentence could be added to the passage.

Although the Colonial Period ended in 1776, furniture from that period had an influence on later styles.

Where would the sentence best fit? Choose position **A**, **B**, **C**, or **D**.

A Around 1900, a style of furniture called Colonial Revival (or Early American), which mimicked Colonial styles, became popular in part because of the efforts of a historian and furniture-maker named Wallace Nutting. **B** Mass-produced reproductions of Colonial pieces were common sights in suburban homes across the United States during the mid-twentieth century. **C** Pieces of Colonial Revival furniture can still be seen in thrift shops and secondhand furniture stores. **D**

27. **Directions:** Select the phrases that correctly describe features associated with each type of furniture. One of the answer choices will NOT be used. **This question is worth 3 points.**

Jacobean

- •

- •

Queen Anne

- •

Chippendale

- •

- •

- Ⓐ Designed to be easy to construct
- Ⓑ Featured curves and carved marine motifs
- Ⓒ Had relatively few decorative elements
- Ⓓ Influenced by a book of design patterns
- Ⓔ Made from imported types of wood
- Ⓕ Produced by Dutch and Swedish artisans

Urban Zoning

Zoning regulations are laws that control land use in towns and cities. Their primary purpose is to segregate areas of land that are considered incompatible. They divide a municipality into geographic areas (zones) where, for example, only residences or only factories may be built. Exceptions to zoning laws, known as variances, are sometimes allowed with the permission of the government involved when the laws would cause hardships for property owners. In the United States, most zoning regulations are passed by local governments – cities, towns, and counties – but a few states, including Vermont and Hawaii, have retained considerable power to administer land use through zoning.

Until the late nineteenth century, few cities and towns had land-use regulations of any kind, and no tough laws governing urban land use were passed at all. A few cities did enact some legislation, including San Francisco, which in 1883 restricted the location of laundries, and Boston, which in 1891 became the first of several cities to limit the height of buildings. A few years later, Washington, DC, followed the "City Beautiful" movement and planned redevelopment in the center. This movement was inspired by the model communities built for the 1893 Chicago World's Fair and provided momentum for reform. The first zoning law that provided a city with sweeping powers over land use was the New York City law of 1916. This law was passed in reaction to the construction of the Equitable Building. This skyscraper towered over other buildings in its neighborhood. It blocked both sunlight and the views from the windows of nearby buildings. The law gave the New York City government control over the construction of new buildings, and served as a blueprint for zoning regulations in other large cities.

There are various types of zoning laws in use today. One system of zoning laws is called Euclidian zoning, named for Euclid, Ohio, the small city where it was first used. This is by far the most common zoning system in the United States, and it is used in both big cities and small towns. It creates zones and strictly limits the kind of development that can take place inside each zone. The most common types of zones are agricultural, one-family residential, multi-family residential, commercial, light industrial, and industrial. There may also be mixed zones, such as commercial/industrial.

Another type of zoning regulation is design-based zoning. A relatively new type of zoning, design-based laws are more flexible than Euclidian zoning and provide local zoning committees with a wide range of powers. As a result, critics say they are more difficult to understand and enforce. Design-based zoning regulations focus more on the type of building than on the use of the land and they allow some mixed use. For example, businesses might be allowed to operate in buildings that were formerly used as residences. On the other hand, a modern-looking twenty-first-century ten-story apartment building would not be permitted in a neighborhood of two-story nineteenth-century houses.

Supporters say that zoning keeps local taxes low, preserves the quality of neighborhoods, and protects the environment. However, there has been much criticism of various aspects of zoning, some of it well deserved. Critics say that zoning interferes with the building of low-cost homes and slows the growth of business and industry. They also say zoning laws, such as those that require houses to be on very large lots, keep less wealthy families out of desirable neighborhoods. More recently, zoning laws have been criticized by some urban planners and scholars, such as Jane Jacobs. They say, with some justification, that zoning laws have helped create unsightly urban sprawl or the spread of buildings into open areas around a city, and made US cities less distinctive. They also say that zoning has promoted the American "car culture," since people must drive to the places where they work and shop if residential zones are separate from commercial and industrial zones. Critics associated with the New Urbanism school of urban planning want a return to the 1920s, when residences, shops, and offices could all be found on the same block and even in the same building.

28. The word "segregate" in paragraph 1 is closest in meaning to
   - (A) deviate
   - (B) eliminate
   - (C) separate
   - (D) validate

29. Based on the information in paragraph 1, which of these people might be given a variance?
   - (A) A factory owner who wanted to build a new residence near her factory
   - (B) A store owner whose shop would have to close because of zoning laws
   - (C) A home owner who accidentally violated zoning regulations in the past
   - (D) A city resident who lived in one zone but traveled to work in another zone

30. Why does the author mention Vermont and Hawaii in paragraph 1?
   - (A) To contrast land-use laws in these states with those in other states
   - (B) To emphasize that zoning regulations give states a great deal of power
   - (C) To give an example of states that have an atypical approach to zoning
   - (D) To suggest that zoning regulations are more relaxed in these states

31. The phrase "sweeping powers" in paragraph 2 is closest in meaning to
   - (A) clear knowledge
   - (B) broad control
   - (C) careful analysis
   - (D) typical behavior

32. Which of the following best expresses the essential information in the highlighted sentence in paragraph 2? Incorrect choices change the meaning in important ways or leave out essential information.
   - (A) The governments of New York City and other large urban areas were able to construct new buildings in various zones.
   - (B) A law passed in New York City gave the city government control over zoning; it was also used as a model by other cities.
   - (C) The law that passed in New York City served as a blueprint for the successful construction of buildings in zoned areas.
   - (D) Other cities that instituted zoning regulations wanted the same degree of control that New York City government had.

33. It can be inferred from paragraph 2 that early land-use legislation
   - (A) did not affect rural communities
   - (B) was inspired by global reforms
   - (C) did not apply to tall buildings
   - (D) was intended to make cities safer

34. What point does the author NOT make about Euclidean zoning in paragraph 3?
   - (A) It sets strict limits on land use within each zone.
   - (B) It is the most widespread zoning system in the US.
   - (C) There are a variety of different types of single-use zones.
   - (D) It is predominantly used as a zoning system in small cities.

35. How does design-based zoning differ from Euclidean zoning? *Choose two answers.*
   - [A] It restricts buildings based on their appearance rather than their use.
   - [B] It provides a varied mix of zones within different neighborhoods in a city.
   - [C] It divides cities into zones where some types of land use are not allowed.
   - [D] It permits the use of a building in a particular zone to change over time.

36. The word "it" in paragraph 5 refers to
   - (A) zoning
   - (B) criticism
   - (C) environment
   - (D) quality

37. The word "lots" in paragraph 5 is closest in meaning to
- Ⓐ plots of land
- Ⓑ types of zone
- Ⓒ periods of time
- Ⓓ amounts of money

38. What does the author imply in paragraph 5?
- Ⓐ Zoning regulations have ensured that cities in the US remain attractive.
- Ⓑ More relaxed zoning laws would mean fewer people would need cars.
- Ⓒ New Urbanism did not work in the 1920s but might be successful today.
- Ⓓ Jane Jacobs and other critics of zoning laws do not make valid arguments.

39. Look at the four squares (■) that indicate where the following sentence could be added to the passage.

For instance, they give the zoning authority control over many aspects of a building, from its architectural style to its height, from the amount of space it may occupy to its location on a lot, and even how much parking it must provide.

Where would the sentence best fit? Choose position Ⓐ, Ⓑ, Ⓒ, or Ⓓ.

Ⓐ Another type of zoning regulation is design-based zoning. Ⓑ A relatively new type of zoning, design-based laws are more flexible than Euclidian zoning and provide local zoning committees with a wide range of powers. Ⓒ As a result, critics say they are more difficult to understand and enforce. Ⓓ Design-based zoning regulations focus more on the type of building than on the use of the land and they allow some mixed use. For example, businesses might be allowed to operate in buildings that were formerly used as residences. On the other hand, a modern-looking twenty-first-century ten-story apartment building would not be permitted in a neighborhood of two-story nineteenth-century houses.

40. **Directions:** An introductory sentence for a brief summary of the passage is provided below. Complete the summary by selecting the THREE answer choices that express the most important ideas in the passage. Some sentences do not belong in the summary because they express ideas that are not presented in the passage or are minor ideas in the passage. **This question is worth 2 points.**

> **Zoning laws divide municipal areas into zones and regulate how the land in each zone can be used.**
>
> -
> -
> -

- Ⓐ Some zones in large cities are mixed zones that allow for both commercial and industrial use.
- Ⓑ Zoning has been criticized by some people who feel that it can lead to urban problems.
- Ⓒ Two main systems of zoning used in the United States are Euclidian zoning and design-based zoning.
- Ⓓ The "City Beautiful" movement inspired by the Chicago World's Fair created interest in land use.
- Ⓔ According to its critics, design-based zoning is neither flexible nor easy to understand or implement.
- Ⓕ Some cities had early land-use regulations, but the first tough zoning law was only enacted in 1916.

Listening Section Directions

The Listening section measures your ability to understand conversations and lectures in English. The Listening section will take about 60 minutes. This includes time to listen to the two conversations and four lectures, and 30 minutes to answer 34 questions about what you have heard. You will hear each conversation and lecture just **once**.

After each conversation or lecture, you will see some questions. Each question is worth 1 point. The questions typically ask about the main idea of the talk or about details that the speakers mention. Some questions ask about a speaker's attitude or reason for saying something. You should answer the questions based on what is stated or implied by the speakers.

You should take notes while you listen to the conversations and lectures. You can use your notes to help you answer the questions. Your notes will **not** be scored.

For some questions you will hear part of the conversation or lecture again. These questions are clearly marked.

You may now begin the Listening section by looking at the next page.

Tracks
408–413   Listen to a conversation between a student and a professor.

Now get ready to answer the questions. You may use your notes to help you answer.

1. What do the professor and student mainly discuss?
   - Ⓐ The reason why the student joined the professor's class late
   - Ⓑ An experiment that the student will perform next semester
   - Ⓒ The grade that the student received for her final project
   - Ⓓ The steps involved in undertaking a psychology experiment

2. How does the professor clarify his explanation of a "hypothesis"?
   - Ⓐ He asks the student for an example she knows from her own experience.
   - Ⓑ He reminds the student of an experiment he already described in class.
   - Ⓒ He gives an example of an experiment conducted by his former students.
   - Ⓓ He describes a common experiment that could be done in a few minutes.

3. What does the professor say about the control group and the experimental group in the experiment he describes?
   - Ⓐ Those in the control group had better memories than those in the experimental group.
   - Ⓑ The experimental group saw names on colored cards; the control group saw white cards.
   - Ⓒ The control group did not display any meaningful difference from the experimental group.
   - Ⓓ The experimental group did not understand the hypothesis, but the control group did.

4. Listen again to part of the conversation. Then answer the question. Why does the professor say this?
   - Ⓐ To confirm that the student understood an earlier explanation
   - Ⓑ To check that the student knows the meaning of an important term
   - Ⓒ To demonstrate that the student knows more than she thinks
   - Ⓓ To ask the student to summarize the information he has just said

5. Listen again to part of the conversation. Then answer the question. What can be inferred about the student when she says this?
   - Ⓐ She is concerned that her lack of knowledge will be a problem.
   - Ⓑ She wants the professor to spend time explaining statistics.
   - Ⓒ She is surprised that statistics is so important in a psychology class.
   - Ⓓ She feels that she has misunderstood some of the professor's ideas.

Track 414–420 Listen to a discussion in an anthropology class.

teepee | lodgepole pine

Now get ready to answer the questions. You may use your notes to help you answer.

6. What does the professor mainly discuss?
   - Ⓐ The ways in which Native American shelters changed over time
   - Ⓑ The various types of shelters Plains Indians used during the year
   - Ⓒ The origin and construction of a well-known kind of shelter
   - Ⓓ How teepees influenced the actions of Native American groups

 7. Listen again to part of the lecture. Then answer the question. Why does the professor say this?
   - Ⓐ To argue that scholars have good evidence for how teepees looked
   - Ⓑ To suggest that the culture of the Plains Indians changed rapidly
   - Ⓒ To point out that many aspects of life on the Plains were surprising
   - Ⓓ To correct a misconception about teepees that students might have

8. According to the professor, why were buffalo important to the Plains Indians? *Choose two answers.*
   - Ⓐ They allowed Plains Indians to follow horse herds.
   - Ⓑ They taught the Plains Indians to move quickly.
   - Ⓒ They were an important source of food.
   - Ⓓ Their skins were used for clothes and shelter.

9. The professor discusses how the daily life of Plains Indians changed over time. Put the events in the order in which they occurred.

First	
Second	
Third	
Fourth	

   - Ⓐ Their shelters became much taller than before.
   - Ⓑ They copied cone-shaped tents from Arctic Indians.
   - Ⓒ They got hold of horses and began hunting buffalo.
   - Ⓓ They used dogs to move teepees from place to place.

10. Why did the Plains Indians use lodgepole pine trees as poles for their teepees?
   - Ⓐ Their wood was durable and straight.
   - Ⓑ Their wood was light and easy to move.
   - Ⓒ They were easy to find and cut down.
   - Ⓓ They had very flexible wooden trunks.

11. Listen again to part of the lecture. Then answer the question. What does the professor imply when he says this?
   - Ⓐ Plains Indians often moved from one place to another.
   - Ⓑ The behavior of Plains Indians was affected by the weather.
   - Ⓒ Plains Indians valued wooden teepee poles highly.
   - Ⓓ The lifestyle of the Plains Indians is easy to understand.

Tracks
421–427   Listen to a lecture in a world history class.

Now get ready to answer the questions. You may use your notes to help you answer.

12. What is the main purpose of this lecture?
- Ⓐ   To explain why people in the Middle Ages ate certain types of food
- Ⓑ   To compare the lives of wealthy people with those of poor people
- Ⓒ   To describe what certain aspects of daily life were like in the past
- Ⓓ   To contrast the typical modern diet with the typical medieval one

13. What is the professor's attitude to the American history class she took when she was a student?
- Ⓐ   She found it very influential.
- Ⓑ   She thought it was kind of boring.
- Ⓒ   She disliked learning about presidents.
- Ⓓ   She enjoyed hearing her teacher's theories.

14. Indicate which foods were typically eaten by poor people in the Middle Ages. *Place a check (✓) in the correct box.*

	Yes	No
Bread made from wheat		
Vegetables, such as carrots and onions		
Meat, including deer and rabbits		
Food flavored with honey or vinegar		
Soups, stews, and porridge-like dishes		

15. What does the professor say about the diet of wealthy people in medieval times?
- Ⓐ   They only ate food that they had hunted themselves.
- Ⓑ   They ate a wide variety of different kinds of meat.
- Ⓒ   They often ate bread dipped in sauce or soup.
- Ⓓ   They typically ate vegetables preserved with salt and spices.

16. Listen again to part of the lecture. What does the professor imply when she says this?
- Ⓐ   Trade was not the reason that Europeans originally made contact with people from other nations.
- Ⓑ   Many people in Europe became wealthy by importing spices from countries like India and China.
- Ⓒ   Because spice routes were very long, only the very wealthy could afford to eat spices regularly.
- Ⓓ   Although only rich people ate spiced foods, many poor people knew about spice trade routes.

17. According to the professor, what were the main uses of spices in medieval cooking? *Choose two answers.*
- Ⓐ   To preserve fish and meat
- Ⓑ   To give food additional flavor
- Ⓒ   To cover unpleasant tastes
- Ⓓ   To make foods easier to cook

 Tracks 428–433 Listen to a conversation between a student and his professor.

Now get ready to answer the questions. You may use your notes to help you answer.

18. What do the student and professor mainly discuss?
   - (A) Why the student transferred from Upper State University
   - (B) Why the student had not taken any statistics classes previously
   - (C) Why the student lacked knowledge of some important concepts
   - (D) Why the student should spend additional time in the library

19. What does the student say about the class he took at Upper State University?
   - (A) He learned things that have not been discussed in his current class.
   - (B) He felt that there were too many other students in the class.
   - (C) He found the teaching assistant for the class to be very helpful.
   - (D) He found some of the concepts difficult to understand.

20. Listen again to part of the conversation. What does the professor mean when she says this?
   - (A) She feels that there are already too many students taking her class.
   - (B) She will not be able to provide more help to the student during class.
   - (C) She is concerned that the student has a disadvantage to overcome.
   - (D) She believes it would not take long to explain concepts to the student.

21. Listen again to part of the conversation. Then answer the question. Why does the professor say this?
   - (A) To suggest that the student is speaking too quickly
   - (B) To imply that the student has misunderstood her idea
   - (C) To emphasize that the student should talk to James Park first
   - (D) To indicate that she wants to say something else to the student

22. What does the professor suggest that the student should do? *Choose two answers.*
   - [A] Ask other students in the professor's class for help
   - [B] Do some extra reading to increase his knowledge
   - [C] Drop the professor's class and take a different one
   - [D] Talk to the teaching assistant from a different class

Tracks 434–440   Listen to a discussion in a marketing class.

   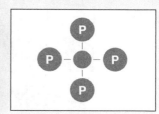

Now get ready to answer the questions. You may use your notes to help you answer.

23. How is the discussion mainly organized?
- Ⓐ The professor discusses each element of the marketing mix in turn.
- Ⓑ The professor asks students to give their ideas before giving his views.
- Ⓒ The professor contrasts the four Ps with other ideas about marketing.
- Ⓓ The professor explains how marketing theories have changed over time.

24. What does the professor say about Neil Borden's original concept of the marketing mix?
- Ⓐ It was a variable theory that some marketers misunderstood.
- Ⓑ It described more than 12 categories of marketing elements.
- Ⓒ It could be adjusted to help marketers understand their targets.
- Ⓓ It was widely used by managers but not by other marketers.

25. In the professor's view, which is the most important of the four Ps?
- Ⓐ Placement
- Ⓑ Pricing
- Ⓒ Product
- Ⓓ Promotion

🎧 26. Listen again to part of the lecture. What does the professor mean when he says this?
- Ⓐ Placement and distribution are different names for similar concepts.
- Ⓑ Regardless of which name is used, placement is a vital part of marketing.
- Ⓒ Consumers do not mind which name is used for distributing products.
- Ⓓ The name "placement" was chosen more for its spelling than its meaning.

27. What does the professor say about advertising? *Choose two answers.*
- Ⓐ Its purpose is to make consumers aware that a product is for sale.
- Ⓑ Some people find it confusing even though it is a simple concept.
- Ⓒ It is not the same as marketing despite what some people believe.
- Ⓓ It is a key part of the marketing mix when consumers are aware of it.

28. What is the professor's opinion of the four Ps model?
- Ⓐ He feels that it is still valid although it was developed a long time ago.
- Ⓑ He thinks that it would benefit from having one or two elements added.
- Ⓒ He finds it a useful concept even though it has a few fundamental issues.
- Ⓓ He believes it needs to be updated to account for Internet marketing.

Tracks 441–447 Listen to a lecture in a film studies class.

Now get ready to answer the questions. You may use your notes to help you answer.

29. What does the professor mainly discuss?
  Ⓐ The rise and fall in popularity of animated movies
  Ⓑ The history and development of animated movies
  Ⓒ Films from the "golden age" of animated movies
  Ⓓ Techniques used in creating animated movies

30. Indicate whether each of the following describes the work of Winsor McCay. *Place a check (✓) in the correct box.*

	Yes	No
He made the films by drawing funny faces on a blackboard.		
His characters seemed to move naturally and have personalities.		
One of his characters was the most popular one of the 1920s.		
His films were more sophisticated than earlier animations.		

31. What can be inferred about animated films before Walt Disney's *Steamboat Willie*?
  Ⓐ They lacked star characters.
  Ⓑ They used primitive techniques.
  Ⓒ They were not very popular.
  Ⓓ They did not have sound.

32. What does the professor say about the animated films of Walt Disney? *Choose two answers.*
  Ⓐ They were based on classic children's stories.
  Ⓑ They were longer than earlier animated films.
  Ⓒ They were popular with people of all ages.
  Ⓓ They were created using two kinds of animation.

33. Listen again to part of the lecture. Then answer the question. Why does the professor say this?
  Ⓐ To emphasize the amount of work involved in making a Disney movie
  Ⓑ To suggest that the movie *Bambi* was extremely expensive to produce
  Ⓒ To point out that artists needed a variety of skills to make Disney movies
  Ⓓ To illustrate a technique required to make realistic animated movies

34. What does the professor say about the "silver age" of animated movies?
  Ⓐ The Disney studio produced a number of quality movies during this period.
  Ⓑ The movies produced during this period were not as popular as earlier movies.
  Ⓒ Some of the movies made during this period were produced using computers.
  Ⓓ Each animated film released during this period took about one year to make.

Speaking Section Directions

The Speaking test measures your ability to speak about a variety of topics. You will have about 20 minutes to deliver spoken responses to six questions. This includes time for reading and listening to information that you will speak about, preparing your responses, and delivering your responses. When you respond, you should answer each of the questions as completely as possible.

In Tasks 1 and 2, you will be asked to speak about familiar topics. For each question, you will have 15 seconds to prepare and 45 seconds to speak. Your response will be scored from 0–4 based on your ability to speak clearly and coherently about the topics.

In Tasks 3 and 4, you will read a short passage and then listen to a conversation or lecture on the same topic. You will then be asked to talk about what you have read and heard. For each question, you will have 30 seconds to prepare and 60 seconds to speak. Your response will be scored from 0–4 based on your ability to speak clearly and coherently and on your ability to give an accurate summary or paraphrase of what you have read and heard.

In Tasks 5 and 6, you will listen to a conversation or a lecture. You will then be asked to talk about what you have heard. For each question, you will have 20 seconds to prepare and 60 seconds to speak. Your response will be scored from 0–4 based on your ability to speak clearly and coherently and on your ability to give an accurate summary or paraphrase of what you have read and heard.

You may now begin the Speaking section by looking at the next page.

Tracks 448–449 **Task 1**

Describe the best advice that you have ever received. Explain why you think it was good advice. Include specific details and examples to support your explanation.

Preparation time: 15 seconds

Response time: 45 seconds

Tracks 450–451 **Task 2**

Some people prefer to communicate with friends in writing using email or text messages. Others prefer to communicate with their friends using a telephone. Which method of staying in touch with friends do you prefer? Explain and support your choice.

Preparation time: 15 seconds

Response time: 45 seconds

Tracks 452–455 **Task 3**

You will now read a short passage and then listen to a conversation on the same topic. You will then be asked a question about them. After you hear the question, you will have 30 seconds to prepare your response and 60 seconds to speak.

A university official wrote a notice to all students. Read the notice. You have 45 seconds to read the letter. Begin reading now.

Food and Beverage Policy for All Campus Events

This notice serves to remind all students of the university's food and beverage policy. In order to ensure that students receive high-quality and great-value food and drink, Astoria University has an exclusive contract with NorthCo Food Services to provide food and beverage services for all events and meetings. This means that students may not bring their own food or drinks to any on-campus event. Exemptions to this policy will be made only in exceptional cases. Anybody wishing to apply for an exemption must contact Yolanda Lopez, the Director of University Dining Services, for written approval.

Now listen to two students as they discuss the notice.

The woman expresses her opinion of the policy. State her opinion and explain the reasons she gives for holding that opinion.

Preparation time: 30 seconds

Response time: 60 seconds

Tracks 456–459 Task 4

You will now read a short passage and then listen to a discussion on the same academic subject. You will then be asked a question about what you have read and heard. After you hear the question, you will have 30 seconds to prepare your response and 60 seconds to speak.

Now read the passage about metallic elements. You have 45 seconds to read the passage. Begin reading now.

Metallic Elements

There are over 80 known metallic elements. A few of these have been known for thousands of years, but most have been discovered since about 1700. The metals actually have very little in common. People think of them as being dense and heavy, and that's true of some metals, such as iron and lead, but others, like sodium, are very lightweight. People think of metals as being strong, and some are, but many pure metals are soft or brittle. Some metals, such as gold and platinum, are known as the precious metals because their rarity makes them valuable and expensive. Other metals, such as aluminum and iron, are very common.

Now listen to part of a lecture on this topic in a chemistry class.

Using details and examples from the talk, explain how titanium relates to metallic elements in general and why it is a useful element.

Preparation time: 30 seconds

Response time: 60 seconds

Tracks 460–462 Task 5

You will now listen to a conversation. You will then be asked a question about it. After you hear the question, you will have 20 seconds to prepare your response and 60 seconds to speak.

Listen to a conversation between two students.

The woman discusses two possible solutions to the man's problem. Describe the problem. Then state which of the two solutions you prefer and explain why.

Preparation time: 20 seconds

Response time: 60 seconds

Tracks 463–465 **Task 6**

You will now listen to part of a lecture. You will then be asked a question about it. After you hear the question, you will have 20 seconds to prepare your response and 60 seconds to speak.

Listen to a lecture in an economics class.

Using examples and points from the lecture, explain the concept of opportunity cost.

Preparation time: 20 seconds

Response time: 60 seconds

Writing Section Directions

The Writing section measures your ability to use writing to communicate in an academic environment. The Writing section will take just under one hour. This includes time for reading and listening to information that you will write about, as well as for writing your responses.

In Task 1, you will read a passage and then listen to a lecture on the same topic. You may take notes while you read and listen. You will then have 20 minutes to write your response. Your response will be scored from 0–5 based on the quality of your writing, and on how accurately and completely you summarize or paraphrase the relationship between the passage and the lecture. Typically, an effective response will have between 150 and 225 words and should **not** describe your personal opinion about the topic.

In Task 2, you will be asked a question about a topic of general interest. You will have 30 minutes to write a response based on your experience and opinions. Your response will be scored from 0–5 based on the quality of your writing and on how well you have developed and organized your ideas. Typically, an effective response will have at least 300 words.

You may now begin the Writing section by looking at the next page.

◀)) Tracks 466–468 **Task 1**

Now look at the passage below. You have three minutes to read the passage.

Biofuels are energy sources that are made from living plants, such as corn, sugar cane, palm trees, or other organic matter. Examples of biofuels include ethanol, biodiesel, green diesel, and biogas. Unlike fossil fuels, which come from plants that died millions of years ago, biofuels are renewable. Someday, our supply of coal and oil will be used up, but biofuels are a renewable resource.

One major benefit of using biofuels is that countries that currently must import petroleum will become independent. They will no longer need to rely on foreign sources of energy because they can meet their energy needs by growing large quantities of biofuels.

Growing biofuels provides an economic benefit for individuals, too. Using land to grow biofuels helps farmers because they can usually sell biofuels for more money than they can sell food crops. So farmers make more money, and non-farmers save money because when energy is plentiful, their fuel costs go down.

We know energy based on biofuels is a workable model from the example of Brazil, where a lot of ethanol is produced by growing sugar cane. In fact, much of Brazil's energy needs are met by biofuels, and if it works in Brazil, there is no reason to think it could not work in other countries.

Now listen to a lecture on the topic you just read about.

Now answer the question. You have 20 minutes to complete your response.

Summarize the points made in the lecture, explaining how they challenge the points made in the reading passage.

◀)) Track 469 **Task 2**

Answer the question. You have 30 minutes to complete your response.

Do you agree or disagree with the following statement?

The most important things that people learn in their lives are not learned in school.

Use specific reasons and examples to support your opinion.

Practice Test B

General Information

This practice test measures your ability to understand and use English in an academic context. There are four sections. Before each section, you will see specific directions that explain how to answer the questions in that section.

In the **Reading** section, you will read and answer questions about three passages. The passages will be similar to excerpts from introductory college-level textbooks. The passages will cover a variety of different subjects. You do not need existing knowledge because all the information needed to answer the questions will be in the passage.

In the **Listening** section, you will hear two conversations and four lectures. The conversations will be about typical topics that affect students at university in North America. After each conversation, you must answer five questions. The lectures will be about academic topics that students in their first year at college are likely to study. The lectures will cover a variety of different subjects. You do not need existing knowledge because all the information needed to answer the questions will be mentioned by the speaker or speakers. After each lecture, you must answer six questions.

In the **Speaking** section, you will see six questions. The first two questions ask you to respond based on your experience and opinions. The third and fourth questions ask you to speak about information that you have read and heard. The final two questions ask you to speak about information you have heard. For each question, you will have a specific amount of time to prepare and deliver your response.

In the **Writing** section, you will answer two questions. In the first question, you will have to write about the relationship between the information in a passage that you have read and the information in a lecture that you have heard. In the second question, you will have to write a response based on your experience and opinions.

You may now begin the test by looking at the next page. Alternatively, you can take Practice Test B online at www.oxfordenglishtesting.com.

Reading Section Directions

The Reading section measures your ability to understand academic passages in English. You will have 60 minutes to read three passages and answer 40 questions about what you have read.

Most questions are worth 1 point but the last question in each set is worth more than 1 point. The directions for these questions indicate how many points you may receive.

For most questions, you should choose one answer. For some questions, however, you may need to choose from two to five answers. These questions have special directions that explain how many answers you should choose.

You may now begin the Reading section by looking at the next page.

Hydrothermal Vents

Scientists have long known that creatures, such as viperfish and anglerfish, live in the ocean deeps. Even though sunlight cannot penetrate deeper than 200 meters (656 feet) and these fish live in conditions of near total darkness, they ultimately rely on sunlight for food. Small deep-ocean creatures feed on particles of organic matter that fall from the sunlit upper ocean, and predatory creatures like the viperfish in turn eat these smaller organisms. Scientists had assumed light was essential for all marine life, so it was a shock when, in 1973, researchers on the exploratory submarine DSV *Alvin* discovered colonies of creatures that, unlike other deep-ocean life forms, did not need sunlight to survive. It was almost as startling as if they had discovered living organisms not based on the element carbon.

What these marine scientists found in 1973 were entire ecosystems living around hydrothermal vents – openings in the ocean floor similar to geysers on land. They are typically found in geologically active underwater mountain ranges such as the Mid-Atlantic Ridge or the East Pacific Rise. Like geysers, vents tend to be found in groups, called vent fields, many of which have been given colorful names: Lost City, Rose Garden, and Clam Acres, for example. Vents form when water seeps deep into the oceanic crust where it is heated by subsurface magma. The superheated water dissolves minerals such as sulfides as it rises before exiting the seabed through a cylindrical structure known as a black smoker. As it exits, the water may be as much as 400 degrees Celsius (752 Fahrenheit) hotter than the near-freezing ambient water temperature, and this difference causes the dissolved minerals to precipitate out, adding to the height of the structure. One smoker off the coast of Oregon with the rather unscientific nickname of Godzilla reached 40 meters (131 feet) before it fell over, but is now growing again. There are also white smokers, which emit plumes of superheated water rich in boron, calcium, and other elements.

Although the discovery of life around the vents was a shock, the discovery of thermal vents themselves was not unanticipated. Scientists knew that there were greater amounts of certain minerals such as manganese present in seawater than could be accounted for by runoff from rivers. It is the chemical soup and the warmth provided by the black smokers that permit life to exist there. Bacteria convert hydrogen sulfide from the vents into usable nutrients, a process called chemosynthesis. To animals other than those in vent communities, these chemicals would be highly toxic, but in vent communities, hydrogen sulfide–eating bacteria form the lower link of the food chain. Small organisms can safely eat these bacteria and, in turn, act as a food source for larger organisms.

It is remarkable how concentrated life is in small areas around these vents, far more so than in other regions of the deep oceans. There are mats of bacteria several inches thick, enormous beds of clams and mussels, millions of eyeless shrimp, swarms of crabs, and clumps of giant tubeworms called tubeworm bushes. For unknown reasons, tubeworms and many other vent-community creatures display gigantism. That is, they are much larger than similar species found in shallow waters. These tubeworms are among the most extraordinary members of the vent community. Their bodies consist of a tube up to 3 meters (10 feet) long – one end anchored to the seabed, the other waving in the currents. They have no digestive system, depending instead on bacteria that line the inside of their tubes for their nutritional needs. The bacteria convert chemicals from the vent into food that they share with the tubeworms. In turn, the tubeworms supply the bacteria with hemoglobin, a chemical found in blood, which carries oxygen that the bacteria need in order to break down the minerals in the water.

Studying these phenomena deep beneath the ocean may seem of little value, but in fact hydrothermal vents may provide a source of valuable mineral resources. They may also provide insights into how life on Earth originated. Some scientists believe that early life evolved under conditions similar to those found at deep-ocean vents. Furthermore, astronomers believe phenomena similar to hydrothermal vents may exist on other worlds, such as Europa, an icy moon of Jupiter. If so, hydrothermal vents may also provide clues about possible extraterrestrial life.

1. The word "ultimately" in paragraph 1 is closest in meaning to
   - (A) to the maximum extent
   - (B) for the longest time
   - (C) at the most basic level
   - (D) for the most part

2. How does the author explain the surprise felt by scientists when they first discovered vent communities in 1973?
   - (A) By comparing it to an even more unlikely finding
   - (B) By providing comments made by the scientists
   - (C) By contrasting it with the reaction of other scholars
   - (D) By giving examples of additional exciting discoveries

3. Which of the following can be inferred from paragraph 2 about the East Pacific Rise?
   - (A) It is less geologically active than the Mid-Atlantic Range.
   - (B) Magma is found under the surface of the seabed there.
   - (C) It contains all the hydrothermal vent fields with colorful names.
   - (D) More vent fields are found there than in other parts of the ocean.

4. The word "ambient" in paragraph 2 is closest in meaning to
   - (A) average
   - (B) surface
   - (C) surrounding
   - (D) estimated

5. The author's description of Godzilla in paragraph 2 mentions which of the following?
   - (A) It has been both taller and shorter than it is at present.
   - (B) It is the name both of a black smoker and a vent field.
   - (C) It was the highest black smoker in the world before it fell over.
   - (D) Scientists have not studied it as much as other black smokers.

6. According to paragraph 2, what is one way in which black smokers differ from white smokers?
   - (A) The water emitted from black smokers is not as hot as that from white smokers.
   - (B) Black smokers build up quickly, whereas white smokers tend to grow slowly.
   - (C) Black smokers and white smokers contain different types of chemicals.
   - (D) There are vent communities around black smokers but not around white smokers.

7. Why does the author mention the mineral "manganese" in paragraph 3?
   - (A) To suggest that it alerted scientists to the possibility of finding communities of live organisms around vents
   - (B) To describe a substance that posed a possible threat to the future safety of vent-community organisms
   - (C) To point out that rivers were depositing more manganese into the ocean than had been previously thought
   - (D) To indicate that its presence in large amounts in seawater signaled the existence of undersea vents

8. The word "clumps" in paragraph 4 is closest in meaning to
   - (A) masses
   - (B) extensions
   - (C) remnants
   - (D) images

9. The word "they" in paragraph 4 refers to
   - (A) chemicals
   - (B) bacteria
   - (C) needs
   - (D) tubes

10. According to paragraph 4, which of the following best describes the relationship between giant tubeworms and the bacteria found inside their tubes?
- Ⓐ The bacteria harm the tubeworms by removing hemoglobin from their blood.
- Ⓑ The tubeworms and the bacteria both benefit from their relationship.
- Ⓒ The tubeworms receive useful nutrients, but the bacteria do not benefit.
- Ⓓ The bacteria are harmed by chemicals that the tubeworms use for digestion.

11. According to paragraph 5, which of the following is NOT a reason to study hydrothermal vents?
- Ⓐ To understand the origins of life on Earth
- Ⓑ To exploit minerals found around vent sites
- Ⓒ To develop useful techniques for astronomy
- Ⓓ To learn how life on other planets may develop

12. Look at the four squares (■) that indicate where the following sentence could be added to the passage.

At the apex of this chain are several species of predatory octopuses.

Where would the sentence best fit? Choose position Ⓐ, Ⓑ, Ⓒ, or Ⓓ.

Although the discovery of life around the vents was a shock, the discovery of thermal vents themselves was not unanticipated. Scientists knew that there were greater amounts of certain minerals such as manganese present in seawater than could be accounted for by runoff from rivers. It is the chemical soup and the warmth provided by the black smokers that permit life to exist there. Ⓐ Bacteria convert hydrogen sulfide from the vents into usable nutrients, a process called chemosynthesis. Ⓑ To animals other than those in vent communities, these chemicals would be highly toxic, but in vent communities, hydrogen sulfide–eating bacteria form the lower link of the food chain. Ⓒ Small organisms can safely eat these bacteria and, in turn, act as a food source for larger organisms. Ⓓ

13. **Directions:** An introductory sentence for a brief summary of the passage is provided below. Complete the summary by selecting the THREE answer choices that express the most important ideas in the passage. Some sentences do not belong in the summary because they express ideas that are not presented in the passage or are minor ideas in the passage. **This question is worth 2 points.**

> **The discovery of creatures living around hydrothermal vents was a surprise to scientists.**
>
> - •
> - •
> - •

- Ⓐ Tubeworms consist of a long tube filled with bacteria plus a digestive tract and anchor.
- Ⓑ The study of hydrothermal vents may provide the answer to several scientific questions.
- Ⓒ DSV *Alvin* was the submarine that made the initial exploration of deep-sea vents.
- Ⓓ Numerous organisms cluster around hydrothermal vents to form concentrated communities.
- Ⓔ Chemicals and heat released by black and white smokers allow life to exist at vents.
- Ⓕ Vent fields often have interesting names like Rose Garden, Clam Acres, or Godzilla.

The Stages of Sleep

We all think we know what sleep is and how sleep and wakefulness differ. However, according to scientists, any definition of sleep must involve at least four components. One component is reduced movement. Most voluntary muscle functions cease during sleep. If a person is writing an email, dancing, or playing soccer, the odds are good that he or she is not asleep. Another is reduced response to stimuli. There is very little awareness of the external environment during sleep, and sleepers are unaware of low-level noises or visual cues that are easily detected when awake. The third component is a characteristic posture. In humans, this usually, though not always, involves lying down. The final component is reversibility: unlike people in a coma or animals in a state of hibernation, sleepers can be woken fairly easily.

Sleep can be divided into two broad categories: rapid eye movement (REM) sleep and non-rapid eye movement (NREM) sleep. Each category has a set of associated physical and psychological features. The discovery that different kinds of sleep exist was first made by psychologists in 1937. They used an electroencephalogram (EEG), a device that can track rhythmic brain activity, usually called brain waves, by measuring the electrical impulses of neurons inside people's brains. Originally, they divided sleep into five stages, A through E, from wakefulness through deep sleep. Then, in 1953, REM sleep was identified as a distinct stage of sleep. Fifteen years later, the older model was superseded and scientific definitions of the stages of sleep were standardized as REM sleep and NREM sleep, with the latter being divided into four stages: N1, N2, N3, and N4. In 2007, the N3 and N4 stages were combined.

Stage N1, sometimes called "drowsy sleep," is the transition from wakefulness to sleep. During N1, which typically lasts only about ten minutes, sleepers lose most awareness of the external environment and their muscles relax, though they may experience involuntary twitches. During N2, muscular activity further decreases, and awareness of the environment disappears. This stage generally represents 45 to 50 percent of a subject's sleep, the most of any stage. N3, the deepest stage of sleep, is also known as delta sleep because slow-moving delta waves appear in EEG readings. Breathing is regular during NREM sleep, and not many motor events occur; however, body repositioning and, in some people, sleepwalking can occur, especially during N3.

REM sleep, which accounts on average for about 25 percent of total sleep, is marked by the rapid movement of a sleeper's eyeballs. As a sleeper's brain is more active during this stage than NREM sleep, but his or her muscles are most relaxed, it is also known as paradoxical sleep. The EEG pattern during REM sleep is nearly the same as it is when a person is awake, and almost all dreaming occurs during this phase. Psychologists believe that the body is relaxed during this stage to prevent dreamers from acting out scenes from the vivid dreams that often occur. Psychologists also believe that the eye movement represents a visual scanning of the images seen in dreams.

Sleep is something of a roller coaster. From a study of EEG patterns, scientists know that subjects first enter N1 sleep, then N2, and then slip into deep N3 sleep. Sleepers next return to N2 sleep and then enter the REM sleep state. In a typical night, a sleeper might go through the cycle of N2-N3-N2-REM sleep from five to eight times. As the night progresses, the periods of time spent in REM sleep increase, and late-night REM episodes may last as long as an hour, with more bursts of eye movements and more dreams than during those that occur earlier in the night.

The amount of REM sleep that a person needs varies according to age. For example, infants sleep about sixteen hours per day and spend about 50 percent of that time in REM sleep. Adults typically sleep six to eight hours per day and spend 20 to 30 percent of that time in REM sleep. And assuming that people dream whenever they are in REM sleep, in an average lifetime, a person may have around 150,000 dreams. Although the amount of REM sleep may vary with age, it remains a vital part of the sleep cycle: studies have shown that a lack of REM sleep can negatively affect the brain's ability to learn and remember.

14. According to the passage, which of the following is NOT an essential part of the scientific definition of sleep?

   Ⓐ   The sleeper must be able to wake up relatively easily.

   Ⓑ   The sleeper must have reduced environmental awareness.

   Ⓒ   The sleeper must be lying down in a comfortable position.

   Ⓓ   The sleeper must make few, if any, voluntary movements.

15. In stating that "the odds are good" in paragraph 1, the author means

   Ⓐ   it is beneficial

   Ⓑ   it is relevant

   Ⓒ   it is certain

   Ⓓ   it is unusual

16. Why does the author mention "hibernation" in paragraph 1?

   Ⓐ   To compare the characteristics of being in a coma with those of hibernation

   Ⓑ   To point out a mistaken belief some people have about animals that hibernate

   Ⓒ   To explain why it is both difficult and dangerous to wake some sleepers up

   Ⓓ   To contrast one component of sleep with the same aspect of hibernation

17. Which of the following can be inferred from paragraph 2?

   Ⓐ   Electroencephalograms were not available for use in research until the 1930s.

   Ⓑ   Psychologists modified their classification of sleep as new data was identified.

   Ⓒ   REM sleep is such a distinct stage that it should have been classified sooner.

   Ⓓ   The electrical impulses of neurons cannot be measured when people are awake.

18. The word "they" in paragraph 2 refers to

   Ⓐ   sleepers' brains

   Ⓑ   electrical impulses

   Ⓒ   brain waves

   Ⓓ   psychologists

19. What does the author say about the N3 stage of sleep?

   Ⓐ   It was originally considered a less important stage than N4 sleep.

   Ⓑ   It is the stage of NREM sleep when people are most likely to move.

   Ⓒ   It accounts for about half of most people's total amount of sleep.

   Ⓓ   Scientists cannot easily take EEG readings during this stage.

20. The word "twitches" in paragraph 3 is closest in meaning to

   Ⓐ   sudden movements

   Ⓑ   environmental changes

   Ⓒ   mild sensations

   Ⓓ   dreamlike feelings

21. Why is REM sleep also known as "paradoxical sleep"?

   Ⓐ   The eyes move quickly during this stage, but the rest of the body is relaxed.

   Ⓑ   It is the longest stage of sleep but provides the least amount of rest for the body.

   Ⓒ   This stage is marked both by high levels of mental activity and physical relaxation.

   Ⓓ   It is the deepest form of sleep and the stage when the most vivid dreams occur.

22. According to paragraph 5, which stage of sleep comes immediately after REM sleep?

   Ⓐ   N1 sleep

   Ⓑ   N2 sleep

   Ⓒ   N3 sleep

   Ⓓ   Deeper REM sleep

23. Why does the author describe sleep as "something of a roller coaster" in paragraph 5?
  Ⓐ   Some sleepers occasionally dream about activities that scare them.
  Ⓑ   Sleepers move from deep sleep to lighter sleep and back again.
  Ⓒ   The night seems to pass very quickly for many sleepers.
  Ⓓ   Discoveries made by sleep scientists have been very exciting.

24. Which of the following best expresses the essential information in the highlighted sentence in paragraph 5? Incorrect choices change the meaning in important ways or leave out essential information.
  Ⓐ   A person who goes to sleep early will have more REM episodes and more dreams than someone who goes to sleep late.
  Ⓑ   The number of dreams that a sleeper has depends on the length of the REM episodes that he or she experiences.
  Ⓒ   REM sleep episodes grow longer as the night goes on and sleepers experience more eye movements and dreams.
  Ⓓ   Bursts of rapid eye movements and dreams that occur in REM sleep late at night may be an hour or more in length.

25. Look at the four squares (■) that indicate where the following sentence could be added to the passage.

Toddlers and school-age children generally spend about ten to thirteen hours asleep, one-third of which is REM sleep, while adolescents sleep nine to ten hours a day and spend about one-quarter of their total sleep time in the REM stage.

Where would the sentence best fit? Choose position **A**, **B**, **C**, or **D**.

The amount of REM sleep that a person needs varies according to age. For example, infants sleep about sixteen hours per day and spend about 50 percent of that time in REM sleep. **A** Adults typically sleep six to eight hours per day and spend 20 to 30 percent of that time in REM sleep. **B** And assuming that people dream whenever they are in REM sleep, in an average lifetime, a person may have around 150,000 dreams. **C** Although the amount of REM sleep may vary with age, it remains a vital part of the sleep cycle: studies have shown that a lack of REM sleep can negatively affect the brain's ability to learn and remember. **D**

26. **Directions:** Select the phrases that correctly describe features associated with each type of sleep. TWO of the answer choices will NOT be used. **This question is worth 3 points.**

| **NREM Sleep** |
| • |
| • |
| • |

| **REM Sleep** |
| • |
| • |

  Ⓐ   Involves regular breathing but few motor movements
  Ⓑ   Shows brain waves similar to a state of wakefulness
  Ⓒ   Is divided into a number of named stages
  Ⓓ   Cannot be observed through EEG readings
  Ⓔ   Is not experienced by infants or children
  Ⓕ   Is related to learning and memory
  Ⓖ   Includes the deepest form of sleep

The Story of the Piano

The piano is such an integral part of many types of music. It was for the piano that Mozart wrote 27 concertos and Beethoven wrote his famous sonatas. Chopin, Schubert, and Liszt composed music for the piano in the nineteenth century that opened up new worlds of sound. In the twentieth century, some of the most memorable jazz was produced by bands centered on pianists such as Duke Ellington and Oscar Peterson, and popular music standards were composed on the pianos of George Gershwin, Irving Berlin, and Cole Porter. Rock music has also had its share of outstanding pianists, including Elton John, Stevie Wonder, and Billy Joel. Despite all of this, the piano is only about 300 years old.

The ultimate ancestor of the piano – and of all stringed instruments, including the lute, guitar, and violin – is the harp. The clavichord and the harpsichord, which are the piano's immediate predecessors, were influenced by the harp, too. As instruments for public performances, however, both the clavichord and the harpsichord had drawbacks. The clavichord produces sound when a metal blade, the tangent, strikes a string inside the body of the instrument. The tangent remains in contact with the string while the note is played, which dampens the vibrations and lowers the volume. The harpsichord works on a different principle. When a key is pressed, a plectrum plucks the corresponding string. Since the plectrum does not remain in contact with the string, the volume of the note is not reduced, but there is no way to change how hard or for how long the plectrum strikes the string, and thus no way to vary the volume or sustain the note.

Around the beginning of the eighteenth century, Italian instrument maker Bartolomeo Cristofori di Francesco was credited with developing an instrument with a completely novel method of striking the strings. When a key was pressed, a metal hammer struck a metal string and rebounded, allowing the string to vibrate. This vibration was carried through a bridge to a sounding board – technology that Cristofori borrowed from the harpsichord – which released the acoustic energy into the air as sound. The volume of the sound depended on the musician's touch: the harder a key was struck, the more forcefully the hammer hit the string, and the louder the note. At first, Cristofori's invention was called "gravicembalo col piano e forte," which can be loosely translated as "soft and loud keyboard instrument." This rather clumsy name was soon changed to *pianoforte* and eventually *piano*.

Despite its advantages, the piano was not an immediate success. It was not until an Italian writer, Francesco Scipione, wrote a glowing review of the new instrument that it became popular. During the eighteenth and early nineteenth centuries, the piano underwent many changes. Foot pedals were added to give more control over volume and the ability to sustain a note. Stronger, heavier piano wire was used for the strings, giving the piano greater volume. The hammers, originally covered with leather, were covered with cloth, producing a more consistent tone. And the tonal range of a standard piano increased from five octaves to seven and one-third octaves or even more.

The piano's golden age arguably lasted from the mid-nineteenth century to the mid-twentieth. Pianos appeared in the parlors and living rooms of private homes of both the working class and the wealthy, suggesting they were valued not just as a musical instrument, but also as a piece of furniture and a status symbol. The piano's popularity provided employment for piano teachers, piano tuners, and piano movers. Music publishers churned out millions of pages of sheet music for the popular songs of the day, though tastes have changed and few are played or even remembered today. Concert pianists were as popular as musical superstars of today, and their social lives were written up in newspapers and discussed at social gatherings.

Even today, the piano remains popular. Technological developments have continued, with electric pianos using an amplifier to boost the sound, and digital pianos employing computer technology in place of piano strings. These latter instruments not only are far more portable than standard pianos, but also are capable of producing sounds that no acoustic piano could make.

27. Which of the following is true of the people mentioned in paragraph 1?
    - (A) All of them are well-known composers of piano music.
    - (B) They were all well-known pianists from the 1900s.
    - (C) They were pioneers in the development of the piano.
    - (D) They are famous figures in the history of piano music.

28. The word "immediate" in paragraph 2 is closest in meaning to
    - (A) oldest
    - (B) fastest
    - (C) closest
    - (D) loudest

29. Which of the following statements is supported by paragraph 2?
    - (A) Stringed instruments like the lute and violin are ancestors of the piano.
    - (B) The action of a tangent both produces notes and reduces their volume.
    - (C) The techniques used when playing a harp have an influence on its sound.
    - (D) Harpsichords are more suited for public performances than clavichords.

30. The word "sustain" in paragraph 2 is closest in meaning to
    - (A) prolong
    - (B) increase
    - (C) repeat
    - (D) soften

31. According to the passage, what was Bartolomeo Cristofori's primary accomplishment?
    - (A) Inventing a new arrangement of the keys on a piano keyboard
    - (B) Utilizing hammers to strike the strings when keys are touched
    - (C) Inventing a bridge to carry sound from the strings to the sounding board
    - (D) Using a plectrum to construct a new style of piano with a louder sound

32. Which of the following can be inferred about the original Italian name for the piano?
    - (A) It could not easily be translated into other languages.
    - (B) It did not describe the features of the piano accurately.
    - (C) It was both too long and inconvenient for everyday use.
    - (D) It was first used by Scipione to describe Cristofori's invention.

33. The phrase "glowing review" in paragraph 4 is closest in meaning to
    - (A) positive assessment
    - (B) famous remembrance
    - (C) careful analysis
    - (D) fictional account

34. According to paragraph 4, all of the following changes occurred in the eighteenth or nineteenth century EXCEPT:
    - (A) The piano became louder because new types of strings were developed.
    - (B) The piano's hammers were covered with a different type of material.
    - (C) The piano's keyboard was expanded to include a greater number of keys.
    - (D) Foot pedals were added to give the piano a more consistent tone.

35. Which of the following best expresses the essential information in the highlighted sentence in paragraph 5? Incorrect choices change the meaning in important ways or leave out essential information.
    - (A) All kinds of people enjoyed listening to the music that pianos could produce.
    - (B) People from all social groups appreciated pianos for a number of reasons.
    - (C) Like other items of furniture, pianos were considered to be a status symbol.
    - (D) Pianos commonly appeared in private homes because they were valuable.

36. The word "few" in paragraph 5 refers to
    (A) piano teachers
    (B) music publishers
    (C) millions of pages
    (D) popular songs

37. Why does the author mention musical superstars of today in paragraph 5?
    (A) To show how they were influenced by pianists from the golden age
    (B) To explain why piano music continues to be popular in modern times
    (C) To illustrate how well known concert pianists of the golden age were
    (D) To contrast the musical ability of golden age pianists and modern ones

38. In the discussion of technological developments in paragraph 6, which of the following points does the author make?
    (A) Computers have replaced strings in electric pianos.
    (B) Digital pianos are more easily moved than other pianos.
    (C) Amplifiers allow acoustic pianos to produce more volume.
    (D) Digital and electric pianos are replacing traditional pianos.

39. Look at the four squares (■) that indicate where the following sentence could be added to the passage.

This required a larger keyboard, and the standard piano eventually settled at 36 black keys and 52 white ones.

Where would the sentence best fit? Choose position **A**, **B**, **C**, or **D**.

Despite its advantages, the piano was not an immediate success. It was not until an Italian writer, Francesco Scipione , wrote a glowing review of the new instrument that it became popular. During the eighteenth and early nineteenth centuries, the piano underwent many changes. **A** Foot pedals were added to give more control over volume and the ability to sustain a note. Stronger, heavier piano wire was used for the strings, giving the piano greater volume. **B** The hammers, originally covered with leather, were covered with cloth, producing a more consistent tone **C** And the tonal range of a standard piano increased from five octaves to seven and one-third octaves or even more. **D**

40. **Directions:** An introductory sentence for a brief summary of the passage is provided below. Complete the summary by selecting the THREE answer choices that express the most important ideas in the passage. Some sentences do not belong in the summary because they express ideas that are not presented in the passage or are minor ideas in the passage. **This question is worth 2 points.**

> **Though only about 300 years old, the piano has played a major role in many forms of music.**
>
> -
> -
> -

    (A) The piano became famous after Francesco Scipione wrote about it and gave it a shorter name.
    (B) During the eighteenth century, many people found jobs teaching, tuning, and moving pianos.
    (C) All stringed instruments – including keyboard instruments – originally evolved from the harp.
    (D) The piano was at the height of its popularity from the mid-nineteenth to mid-twentieth centuries.
    (E) Digital pianos use computer technology to produce sounds that people have never heard before.
    (F) Cristofori's piano gave musicians more control over volume than previous keyboard instruments.

Listening Section Directions

The Listening section measures your ability to understand conversations and lectures in English. The Listening section will take about 60 minutes. This includes time to listen to the two conversations and four lectures, and 30 minutes to answer 34 questions about what you have heard. You will hear each conversation and lecture just **once**.

After each conversation or lecture, you will see some questions. Each question is worth 1 point. The questions typically ask about the main idea of the talk or about details that the speakers mention. Some questions ask about a speaker's attitude or reason for saying something. You should answer the questions based on what is stated or implied by the speakers.

You should take notes while you listen to the conversations and lectures. You can use your notes to help you answer the questions. Your notes will **not** be scored.

For some questions you will hear part of the conversation or lecture again. These questions are clearly marked.

You may now begin the Listening section by looking at the next page.

Conversation 1

 Tracks 471–476   Listen to a conversation between a professor of American literature and a student.

Now get ready to answer the questions. You may use your notes to help you answer.

1. Why does the student go to see the professor?
   - Ⓐ To ask him to change a grade
   - Ⓑ To discuss the symbolist poets
   - Ⓒ To ask for his opinion about her paper
   - Ⓓ To ask him to speak to Professor Bryant

2. What problems with the student's essay did Professor Bryant mention? *Choose two answers.*
   - Ⓐ The paper was not long enough.
   - Ⓑ She cited too few research sources.
   - Ⓒ She turned it in after the specified due date.
   - Ⓓ The essay did not include enough examples.

3. Listen again to part of the conversation. Then answer the question. What does the student mean when she says this?
   - Ⓐ She is unsure what grade she will receive.
   - Ⓑ She believes she will receive a poor grade.
   - Ⓒ She thinks Professor Bryant is a great teacher.
   - Ⓓ She thinks it is too late to drop the class now.

4. What can be inferred about the student's friend?
   - Ⓐ He is currently a student in Professor White's poetry class.
   - Ⓑ He received a good grade when he took Professor Bryant's class.
   - Ⓒ He agrees with Professor White's opinion of Professor Bryant.
   - Ⓓ He thinks the student should drop Professor Bryant's class.

5. Indicate which suggestions the professor gives the student. *Place a check (✓) in the correct box.*

	Yes	No
Rewrite her paper so it includes more specific examples		
Transfer out of Professor Bryant's class into another class		
Discuss her academic concerns with Professor Bryant		
Talk about her paper with the dean of academic affairs		

Lecture 1

 Tracks 477–483 Listen to a lecture in an art history class.

Now get ready to answer the questions. You may use your notes to help you answer.

6. What does the professor mainly discuss?
   - Ⓐ Famous artists and performers from the 1960s
   - Ⓑ A history and comparison of Op art and Pop art
   - Ⓒ The ways in which Op art influenced Pop art
   - Ⓓ An analysis of how art trends follow fashion

7. According to the professor, what mistaken idea do many people have about Op art and Pop art?
   - Ⓐ That they both appeared about the same time
   - Ⓑ That they were both equally popular with critics
   - Ⓒ That they were similar in a number of important ways
   - Ⓓ That they were both dominated by the same artists

8. Why does the lecturer mention the bands The Beatles and The Who?
   - Ⓐ To illustrate an aspect of British culture that was popular in the 1960s
   - Ⓑ To imply that musicians were more popular in the 1960s than visual artists
   - Ⓒ To point out that musicians influenced the styles of clothing people wore
   - Ⓓ To remind students of the influence these musicians had on the visual arts

9. What difference between Bridget Riley and Victor Vasarely does the professor discuss?
   - Ⓐ The critics appreciated Vasarely's work, but did not like Riley's.
   - Ⓑ Riley's works were exhibited in New York in 1965 but Vasarely's were not.
   - Ⓒ Vasarely worked in color, but Riley worked only in black and white.
   - Ⓓ Unlike Riley, Vasarely didn't object to his designs being used in fashion.

10. Indicate whether each of the following is a characteristic of Op art, Pop art, or both Op art and Pop art. *Place a check (✓) in the correct box.*

	Op art	Pop art	Both Op art and Pop art
Mostly black and white rather than color			
Popular with critics and ordinary people			
Used in fashion designs			
Nonrepresentational			

11. What is the professor's opinion of Andy Warhol?
   - Ⓐ He could have been successful if he had worked harder.
   - Ⓑ He took too many of his ideas from other Pop artists.
   - Ⓒ He is among the best known of all American artists.
   - Ⓓ He made some unusual choices of objects to paint.

Lecture 2

 Tracks 484–490 Listen to part of a discussion in an astronomy class.

   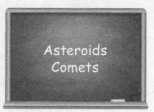

Meteors
Meteoroids
Meteorites

Micro-meteoroids

Asteroids
Comets

Now get ready to answer the questions. You may use your notes to help you answer.

12. What is the main purpose of this discussion?
  - Ⓐ To discuss impact damage caused by meteorites
  - Ⓑ To contrast meteoroids and micro-meteoroids
  - Ⓒ To introduce meteors, meteoroids, and meteorites
  - Ⓓ To review evidence for life on other planets

 13. Listen again to part of the discussion. Then answer the question. What does the professor imply about micro-meteoroids?
  - Ⓐ Some of them are the size of small boulders.
  - Ⓑ They are smaller than a small pebble.
  - Ⓒ They are the most commonly seen meteor.
  - Ⓓ They sometimes affect the weather on Earth.

14. What does the professor say about the fireball of 1972? *Choose two answers.*
  - Ⓐ It entered the Earth's atmosphere and then returned to space.
  - Ⓑ It caused only a small amount of damage when it struck Earth.
  - Ⓒ It could be seen from Earth despite appearing in the afternoon.
  - Ⓓ It could be observed from everywhere in North America.

15. What does the professor say about asteroids and comets?
  - Ⓐ Both comets and asteroids are sources of meteoroids.
  - Ⓑ Comets are made from different materials than asteroids.
  - Ⓒ Scientists do not know exactly what they are made of.
  - Ⓓ They usually appear in the sky at the same time each year.

16. What does the professor indicate about meteors that appear during meteor showers?
  - Ⓐ They are usually much brighter than other meteors.
  - Ⓑ They are fragments of stony or stony-metal meteoroids.
  - Ⓒ They appear when Earth passes through the tails of comets.
  - Ⓓ They can have an effect on the orbits of comets or asteroids.

17. What does the professor imply about Mars?
  - Ⓐ It has always had conditions too harsh for life.
  - Ⓑ There is no evidence for any kind of life there.
  - Ⓒ Intelligent life exists there, but it is very rare.
  - Ⓓ It is possible that life exists or has existed there.

Conversation 2

 Tracks 491–496 Listen to a conversation between a student and a department administrator.

Now get ready to answer the questions. You may use your notes to help you answer.

18. Why does the student visit the department?
    - Ⓐ To make an appointment with a professor
    - Ⓑ To arrange to make a payment for a class
    - Ⓒ To get information about an unusual class
    - Ⓓ To ask when spring break will take place

19. How did the student first learn about the Ecology of Tropical Reefs course?
    - Ⓐ From the university website
    - Ⓑ From Professor Garrison
    - Ⓒ From a poster on campus
    - Ⓓ From talking to a friend

20. According to the administrator, which two components of the Ecology of Tropical Reefs class take place before the field trip? *Choose two answers.*
    - Ⓐ Getting diving certification
    - Ⓑ Giving an oral progress report
    - Ⓒ Attending evening lectures
    - Ⓓ Collecting data and observations

21. What can be inferred about the Ecology of Tropical Reefs course?
    - Ⓐ Most participants already have diving certification.
    - Ⓑ It usually involves a field trip to a tropical destination.
    - Ⓒ It is not popular among students because of its cost.
    - Ⓓ Participants will stay in luxurious accommodation.

22. Indicate whether each of the following is a step that the student will probably take before registering for Professor Garrison's class. *Place a check (✔) in the correct box.*

	Yes	No
Attend an organizational meeting		
Discuss the situation with his parents		
Have a talk with Professor Garrison		
Learn more about the course online		
Pay travel and accommodation fees		

Lecture 3

 Tracks 497–503   Listen to a lecture in a political science class.

First Party System
Federalists
Democrat-Republicans

Era of Good Feelings
Republicans

Second Party System
Whigs
Democrats

Now get ready to answer the questions. You may use your notes to help you answer.

23. What is the main topic of this lecture?
- (A) Name changes among political parties in the US.
- (B) Well-known leaders of the main US political parties
- (C) The development of the US political party system
- (D) Factors that led to the success of some political parties

24. According to the professor, what were two policies of the Federalist party? *Choose two answers.*
- [A] They supported a strong central government.
- [B] They wanted Britain, not France, as their main ally.
- [c] They favored agriculture over business.
- [D] They opposed the creation of a central bank.

25. Listen again to part of the conversation. Then answer the question. Why does the professor say this?
- (A) To emphasize that history has many hard-to-answer questions
- (B) To express surprise that no one is able to answer his question
- (C) To point out that there is actually no answer to his question
- (D) To imply that the students should read the US Constitution

26. Which of these politicians acted as official leader of the Republican party?
- (A) Alexander Hamilton
- (B) George Washington
- (C) James Madison
- (D) Thomas Jefferson

27. What point does the professor make about the Whigs?
- (A) They were led by Andrew Jackson.
- (B) They were not formed until 1854.
- (C) They used to be called Federalists.
- (D) They favored progressive policies.

28. Indicate whether each statement is related to the First Party System, the Era of Good Feelings, or the Second Party System. *Place a check (✓) in the correct box.*

	First Party System	Era of Good Feelings	Second Party System
The nation had one rather weak political party.			
Andrew Jackson and Henry Clay were leaders.			
First one party was dominant and then another.			
Lack of competition led to parties being formed.			

Lecture 4

🔊 Tracks 504–510 Listen a lecture in an archaeology class.

Now get ready to answer the questions. You may use your notes to help you answer.

29. What does the professor mainly discuss?
   - Ⓐ How Folsom points were made
   - Ⓑ Where Clovis people were from
   - Ⓒ How people lived at Monte Verde
   - Ⓓ Who first arrived in the Americas

30. According to the lecture, what is fluting?
   - Ⓐ A way to make Folsom points easier to produce
   - Ⓑ A wooden shaft attached to a Folsom point
   - Ⓒ A groove carved into the face of a Folsom point
   - Ⓓ A tool used in the manufacture of Folsom points

🎧 31. Listen again to part of the lecture. Then answer the question. Why does the professor say this?
   - Ⓐ To argue that special tools were needed to make Folsom points
   - Ⓑ To point out that making Folsom points required little training
   - Ⓒ To suggest that she lacks the skill to manufacture useful objects
   - Ⓓ To emphasize the skill required to make Folsom points

32. The professor discusses the discovery of Paleo-Indian artifacts. Put the events in the order in which they occurred.

First	
Second	
Third	
Fourth	

   - Ⓐ An amateur scientist found the bones of an extinct giant bison.
   - Ⓑ Archaeologists discovered stone tools and the remains of houses.
   - Ⓒ Archaeologists found points in the bones of a type of extinct elephant.
   - Ⓓ Museum scientists learned about and looked into the discovery.

🎧 33. Listen again to part of the lecture. What does the professor imply when she says this?
   - Ⓐ The hunting sites in North America were temporary sites.
   - Ⓑ The people who lived at Monte Verde rarely hunted.
   - Ⓒ Archaeologists studied the Monte Verde site in more detail than other sites.
   - Ⓓ The North American hunting sites were not as interesting as Monte Verde.

34. How does the professor organize the information about Paleo-Indians in her lecture?
   - Ⓐ In chronological order from the earliest known culture to the most recent
   - Ⓑ According to the relative importance of the artifacts that were discovered
   - Ⓒ In the order in which archaeologists discovered and identified each culture
   - Ⓓ According to the amount of information that is known about each culture

Speaking Section Directions

The Speaking test measures your ability to speak about a variety of topics. You will have about 20 minutes to deliver spoken responses to six questions. This includes time for reading and listening to information that you will speak about, preparing your responses, and delivering your responses. When you respond, you should answer each of the questions as completely as possible.

In Tasks 1 and 2, you will be asked to speak about familiar topics. For each question, you will have 15 seconds to prepare and 45 seconds to speak. Your response will be scored from 0–4 based on your ability to speak clearly and coherently about the topics.

In Tasks 3 and 4, you will read a short passage and then listen to a conversation or lecture on the same topic. You will then be asked to talk about what you have read and heard. For each question, you will have 30 seconds to prepare and 60 seconds to speak. Your response will be scored from 0–4 based on your ability to speak clearly and coherently and on your ability to give an accurate summary or paraphrase of what you have read and heard.

In Tasks 5 and 6, you will listen to a conversation or a lecture. You will then be asked to talk about what you have heard. For each question, you will have 20 seconds to prepare and 60 seconds to speak. Your response will be scored from 0–4 based on your ability to speak clearly and coherently and on your ability to give an accurate summary or paraphrase of what you have read and heard.

You may now begin the Speaking section by looking at the next page.

Tracks 511–512 **Task 1**

What is the most enjoyable vacation that you have ever taken? Explain why you liked this vacation. Include specific details and examples to support your explanation.

Preparation time: 15 seconds

Response time: 45 seconds

Tracks 513–514 **Task 2**

When they want to relax, some people enjoy reading books. Other people prefer watching television. Which of these two options do you prefer? Explain your choice. Support your opinion with specific details and examples.

Preparation time: 15 seconds

Response time: 45 seconds

Tracks 515–518 **Task 3**

You will now read a short passage and then listen to a conversation on the same topic. You will then be asked a question about them. After you hear the question, you will have 30 seconds to prepare your response and 60 seconds to speak.

A university official wrote a letter to campus tour guides. Read the letter. You have 45 seconds to read the letter. Begin reading now.

Letter to Campus Tour Guides

I'd like to begin by thanking all the students who have interrupted their summer activities to serve as guides for incoming first-year students and their families. Since it was instituted five years ago, the Summer Campus Tours have become a valuable and popular program. However, I'm sorry to inform you that the university can no longer provide guides with payment for their services. This is partially due to budget cuts, but also because the new president is trying to encourage a spirit of community service and volunteerism among students. We'll continue to provide guides from out of town with dormitory rooms and with meals at the cafeteria.

Now listen to two students as they discuss the letter.

The man expresses his opinion of the letter. State his opinion and explain the reasons he gives for having that opinion.

Preparation time: 30 seconds

Response time: 60 seconds

Tracks
519–522 **Task 4**

You will now read a short passage and then listen to a discussion on the same academic subject. You will then be asked a question about what you have read and heard. After you hear the question, you will have 30 seconds to prepare your response and 60 seconds to speak.

Now read the passage about the Law of Unintended Consequences. You have 45 seconds to read the passage. Begin reading now.

The Law of Unintended Consequences

The Law of Unintended Consequences is an idea dating at least as far back as the eighteenth-century economist Adam Smith. However, American sociologist Robert Merton invented the term and popularized the concept in the 1930s. The law indicates that when a simple solution is applied to a complex problem, it often causes unexpected results. Merton lists three types of unintended consequences. One is the unexpected positive result of an action. The second is a negative result that occurs in addition to the positive result. The third is called a "perverse effect," which occurs when the result of some action is the opposite of what was intended.

Now listen to part of a lecture on this topic in an ecology class.

Using details from the talk, explain how the importation of rabbits into Australia relates to the Law of Unintended Consequences.

Preparation time: 30 seconds

Response time: 60 seconds

 Tracks
523–525 **Task 5**

You will now listen to a conversation. You will then be asked a question about it. After you hear the question, you will have 20 seconds to prepare your response and 60 seconds to speak.

Now listen to a conversation between a man and a woman.

The speakers discuss two possible solutions to a problem. Describe the problem. Then state which of the two solutions you prefer and why.

Preparation time: 20 seconds

Response time: 60 seconds

Task 6

You will now listen to part of a lecture. You will then be asked a question about it. After you hear the question, you will have 20 seconds to prepare your response and 60 seconds to speak.

Now listen to part of a lecture in a finance class.

Using points and examples from the talk, say what an income statement is and what information it includes.

Preparation time: 20 seconds

Response time: 60 seconds

Writing Section Directions

The Writing section measures your ability to use writing to communicate in an academic environment. The Writing section will take just under one hour. This includes time for reading and listening to information that you will write about, as well as for writing your responses.

In Task 1, you will read a passage and then listen to a lecture on the same topic. You may take notes while you read and listen. You will then have 20 minutes to write your response. Your response will be scored from 0–5 based on the quality of your writing, and on how accurately and completely you summarize or paraphrase the relationship between the passage and the lecture. Typically, an effective response will have between 150 and 225 words and should **not** describe your personal opinion about the topic.

In Task 2, you will be asked a question about a topic of general interest. You will have 30 minutes to write a response based on your experience and opinions. Your response will be scored from 0–5 based on the quality of your writing and on how well you have developed and organized your ideas. Typically, an effective response will have at least 300 words.

You may now begin the Writing section by looking at the next page.

🔊 Tracks 529–531   **Task 1**

Now look at the passage below. You have three minutes to read the passage.

In recent years, more and more students have been taking online courses. According to a recent report, which has tracked online learning at the university level since 2002, the rate of students in the US taking at least one online course has continued to grow at a much faster rate than regular university enrollment. In 2002, for example, 1.6 million students were taking at least one online course; but recent statistics that I've seen indicate that 5 million are studying online. That translates to a 21 percent rate of growth in online education. In contrast, total enrollment in university has grown at a rate of only 2.2 percent.

What has spurred this remarkable growth? There are a number of factors, but probably the most important is financial. The cost of tuition and fees has grown drastically, at a much higher rate than general inflation. For example, face-to-face instruction at one four-year private college averages about $24,000 a year. This same university offers a mostly online degree program for about $15,000. Taking an online course also removes the cost of room and board and other assorted fees associated with attending school.

Another important factor is flexibility. Students can take classes whenever they want and wherever they want. If they like, they can take classes while wearing their pajamas! And if they have a job, they can arrange their class schedule around their working hours, and get a top-quality education while continuing to earn a salary.

Now listen to a lecture on the topic you just read about.

Now answer the question. You have 20 minutes to complete your response.

Summarize the points made in the lecture, explaining how they challenge the points made in the reading passage.

🔊 Track 532   **Task 2**

Answer the question. You have 30 minutes to complete your response.

Many people say that they would like to travel back in time to experience what life in the past was like and to witness great events. Others would like to travel into the future if they could. If it were possible to travel back or forward in time, which would you prefer to do? Why? Use specific reasons and details to explain your decision.